Finite Difference Methods
in Financial Engineering

For other titles in the Wiley Finance Series
please see www.wiley.com/finance

Finite Difference Methods
in Financial Engineering

A Partial Differential Equation Approach

Daniel J. Duffy

John Wiley & Sons, Ltd

Copyright © 2006 Daniel J. Duffy

Published by   John Wiley & Sons Ltd, The Atrium, Southern Gate, Chichester,
                            West Sussex PO19 8SQ, England

                            Telephone   (+44) 1243 779777

Email (for orders and customer service enquiries): cs-books@wiley.co.uk
Visit our Home Page on www.wiley.com

Reprinted October 2006

Other Wiley Editorial Offices

John Wiley & Sons Inc., 111 River Street, Hoboken, NJ 07030, USA

Jossey-Bass, 989 Market Street, San Francisco, CA 94103-1741, USA

Wiley-VCH Verlag GmbH, Boschstr. 12, D-69469 Weinheim, Germany

John Wiley & Sons Australia Ltd, 42 McDougall Street, Milton, Queensland 4064, Australia

John Wiley & Sons (Asia) Pte Ltd, 2 Clementi Loop #02-01, Jin Xing Distripark, Singapore 129809

John Wiley & Sons Canada Ltd, 22 Worcester Road, Etobicoke, Ontario, Canada M9W 1L1

Wiley also publishes its books in a variety of electronic formats. Some content that appears
in print may not be available in electronic books.

Library of Congress Cataloguing-in-Publication Data

Duffy, Daniel J.
Finite difference methods in financial engineering : a partial differential equation approach / Daniel J. Duffy.
     p.   cm.
  ISBN-13: 978-0-470-85882-0
  ISBN-10: 0-470-85882-6
  1. Financial engineering—Mathematics.   2. Derivative securities—Prices—Mathematical models.
  3. Finite differences.   4. Differential equations, Partial—Numerical solutions.   I. Title.
    HG176.7.D84   2006
    332.01′51562—dc22   2006001397

British Library Cataloguing in Publication Data

A catalogue record for this book is available from the British Library

ISBN 13 978-0-470-85882-0 (HB)
ISBN 10 0-470-85882-6 (HB)

Typeset in 10/12pt Times by TechBooks, New Delhi, India
Printed and bound in Great Britain by Antony Rowe Ltd, Chippenham, Wiltshire
This book is printed on acid-free paper responsibly manufactured from sustainable forestry
in which at least two trees are planted for each one used for paper production.

Contents

0

Goals of this Book and Global Overview

0.1 WHAT IS THIS BOOK?

The goal of this book is to develop robust, accurate and efficient numerical methods to price a number of derivative products in quantitative finance. We focus on one-factor and multi-factor models for a wide range of derivative products such as options, fixed income products, interest rate products and 'real' options. Due to the complexity of these products it is very difficult to find exact or closed solutions for the pricing functions. Even if a closed solution can be found it may be very difficult to compute. For this and other reasons we need to resort to approximate methods. Our interest in this book lies in the application of the finite difference method (FDM) to these problems.

This book is a thorough introduction to FDM and how to use it to approximate the various kinds of partial differential equations for contingent claims such as:

- One-factor European and American options
- One-factor and two-factor barrier options with continuous and discrete monitoring
- Multi-asset options
- Asian options, continuous and discrete monitoring
- One-factor and two-factor bond options
- Interest rate models
- The Heston model and stochastic volatility
- Merton jump models and extensions to the Black–Scholes model.

Finite difference theory has a long history and has been applied for more than 200 years to approximate the solutions of partial differential equations in the physical sciences and engineering.

What is the relationship between FDM and financial engineering? To answer this question we note that the behaviour of a stock (or some other underlying) can be described by a stochastic differential equation. Then, a contingent claim that depends on the underlying is modelled by a partial differential equation in combination with some initial and boundary conditions. Solving this problem means that we have found the value for the contingent claim.

Furthermore, we discuss finite difference and variational schemes that model free and moving boundaries. This is the style for exercising American options, and we employ a number of new modelling techniques to locate the position of the free boundary.

Finally, we introduce and elaborate the theory of partial integro-differential equations (PIDEs), their applications to financial engineering and their approximations by FDM. In particular, we show how the basic Black–Scholes partial differential equation is augmented by an integral term in order to model jumps (the Merton model). Finally, we provide worked-out C++ code on the CD that accompanies this book.

0.2   WHY HAS THIS BOOK BEEN WRITTEN?

There are a number of reasons why this book has been written. First, the author wanted to produce a text that showed how to apply numerical methods (in this case, finite difference schemes) to quantitative finance. Furthermore, it is important to justify the applicability of the schemes rather than just rely on numerical recipes that are sometimes difficult to apply to real problems. The second desire was to construct robust finite difference schemes for use in financial engineering, creating algorithms that describe how to solve the discrete set of equations that result from such schemes and then to map them to C++ code.

0.3   FOR WHOM IS THIS BOOK INTENDED?

This book is for quantitative analysts, financial engineers and others who are involved in defining and implementing models for various kinds of derivatives products. No previous knowledge of partial differential equations (PDEs) or of finite difference theory is assumed. It is, however, assumed that you have some knowledge of financial engineering basics, such as stochastic differential equations, Ito calculus, the Black–Scholes equation and derivative pricing in general. This book will be of value to those financial engineers who use the binomial and trinomial methods to price options, as these two methods are special cases of explicit finite difference schemes. This book will also hopefully be employed by those engineers who use simulation methods (for example, the Monte Carlo method) to price derivatives, and it is hoped that the book will help to bridge the gap between the stochastics and PDE approaches.

Finally, this book could be interesting for mathematicians, physicists and engineers who wish to see how a well-known branch of numerical analysis is applied to financial engineering. The information in the book may even improve your job prospects!

0.4   WHY SHOULD I READ THIS BOOK?

In the author's opinion, this is one of the first self-contained introductions to the finite difference method and its applications to derivatives pricing. The book introduces the theory of PDE and FDM and their applications to quantitative finance, and can be used as a self-contained guide to learning and discovering the most important finite difference schemes for derivative pricing problems.

Some of the advantages of the approach and the resulting added value of the book are:

- A defined process starting from the financial models through PDEs, FDM and algorithms
- An application of robust, accurate and efficient finite difference schemes for derivatives pricing applications.

This book is more than just a cookbook: it motivates why a method does or does not work and you can learn from this knowledge in a meaningful way. This book is also a good companion to my other book, *Financial Instrument Pricing in C++* (Duffy, 2004). The algorithms in the present book can be mapped to C++, the de-facto object-oriented language for financial engineering applications

In short, it is hoped that this book will help you to master all the details needed for a good understanding of FDM in your daily work.

0.5   THE STRUCTURE OF THIS BOOK

The book has been partitioned into seven parts, each of which deals with one specific topic in detail. Furthermore, each part contains material that is required by its successor. In general, we interleave the parts by first discussing the theory (for example, basic finite difference schemes) in a given part and then applying this theory to a problem in financial engineering. This 'separation of concerns' approach promotes understandability of the material, and the parts in the book discuss the following topics:

    I.   The Continuous Theory of Partial Differential Equations
    II.   Finite Difference Methods: the Fundamentals
    III. Applying FDM to One-Factor Instrument Pricing
    IV. FDM for Multidimensional Problems
    V.   Applying FDM to Multi-Factor Instrument Pricing
    VI. Free and Moving Boundary Value Problems
    VII. Design and Implementation in C++

Part I presents an introduction to partial differential equations (PDE). This theory may be new for some readers and for this reason these equations are discussed in some detail. The relevance of PDE to instrument pricing is that a contingent claim or derivative can be modelled as an initial boundary value problem for a second-order parabolic partial differential equation. The partial differential equation has one time variable and one or more space variables. The focus in Part I is to develop enough mathematical theory to provide a basis for work on finite differences.

Part II is an introduction to the finite difference method for a number of partial differential equations that appear in instrument pricing problems. We learn FDM in the following way: (1) We introduce the model PDEs for the heat, convection and convection–diffusion equations and propose several important finite difference schemes to approximate them. In particular, we discuss a number of schemes that are used in the financial engineering literature and we also introduce some special schemes that work under a range of parameter values. In this part, focus is on the practical application of FDM to parabolic partial differential equations in one space variable.

Part III examines the partial differential equations that describe one-factor instrument models and their approximation by the finite difference schemes. In particular, we concentrate on European options, barrier options and options with jumps, and propose several finite difference schemes for such options. An important class of problems discussed in this part is the class of barrier options with continuous or discrete monitoring and robust methods are proposed for each case. Finally, we model the partial integro-differential equations (PIDEs) that describe options with jumps, and we show how to approximate them by finite difference schemes.

Part IV discusses how to define and use finite difference schemes for initial boundary value problems in several space variables. First, we discuss 'direct' scheme where we discretise the time and space dimensions simultaneously. This approach works well with problems in two space dimensions but for problems in higher dimensions we may need to solve the problem as a series of simpler problems. There are two main contenders: first, alternating direction implicit (ADI) methods are popular in the financial engineering literature; second, we discuss operator splitting methods (or the method of fractional steps) that have their origins in the former Soviet Union. Finally, we discuss some modern developments in this area.

Part V applies the results and schemes from Part IV to approximating some multi-factor problems. In particular, we examine the Heston PDE with stochastic volatility, Asian options, rainbow options and two-factor bond models and how to apply ADI and operator splitting methods to them.

Part VI deals with instrument pricing problems with the so-called early exercise feature. Mathematically, these problems fall under the umbrella of free and moving boundary value problems. We concentrate on the theory of such problems and the application to one-factor American options. We also discuss ADI method in conjunction with free boundaries.

Part VII contains a number of chapters that support the work in the previous parts of the book. Here we address issues that are relevant to the design and implementation of the FDM algorithms in the book. We provide hints, guidelines and C++ sources to help the reader to make the transition to production code.

0.6 WHAT THIS BOOK DOES NOT COVER

This book is concerned with the application of the finite difference method to instrument pricing. This viewpoint implies that we concentrate on a number of issues while neglecting others. Thus, this book is not:

- an introduction to numerical analysis
- a guide to the theoretical foundations of the theory of finite differences
- an introduction to instrument pricing
- a full 'production' C++ course.

These problems are considered in detail in other books and will be discussed elsewhere.

0.7 CONTACT, FEEDBACK AND MORE INFORMATION

The author welcomes your feedback, comments and suggestions for improvement. As far as I am aware, all typos and errors have been removed from the text, but some may have slipped past unnoticed. Nevertheless, all errors are my responsibility.

I am a trainer and developer and my main professional interests are in quantitative finance, computational finance and object-oriented programming. In my free time I enjoy judo and studying foreign (natural) languages.

If you have any questions on this book, please do not hesitate to contact me at dduffy@datasim.nl.

Part I
The Continuous Theory of Partial Differential Equations

1
An Introduction to Ordinary
Differential Equations

1.1 INTRODUCTION AND OBJECTIVES

Part I of this book is devoted to an overview of ordinary and partial differential equations. We discuss the mathematical theory of these equations and their relevance to quantitative finance. After having read the chapters in Part I you will have gained an appreciation of one-factor and multi-factor partial differential equations.

In this chapter we introduce a class of *second-order ordinary differential equations* as they contain derivatives up to order 2 in one independent variable. Furthermore, the (unknown) function appearing in the differential equation is a function of a single variable. A simple example is the *linear* equation

$$Lu \equiv a(x)u'' + b(x)u' + c(x)u = f(x) \tag{1.1}$$

In general we seek a solution u of (1.1) in conjunction with some auxiliary conditions. The coefficients a, b, c and f are known functions of the variable x. Equation (1.1) is called linear because all coefficients are independent of the unknown variable u. Furthermore, we have used the following shorthand for the first- and second-order derivatives with respect to x:

$$u' = \frac{du}{dx} \quad \text{and} \quad u'' = \frac{d^2u}{dx^2} \tag{1.2}$$

We examine (1.1) in some detail in this chapter because it is part of the Black–Scholes equation

$$\frac{\partial C}{\partial t} + \frac{1}{2}\sigma^2 S^2 \frac{\partial^2 C}{\partial S^2} + rS\frac{\partial C}{\partial S} - rC = 0 \tag{1.3}$$

where the asset price S plays the role of the independent variable x and t plays the role of time. We replace the unknown function u by C (the option price). Furthermore, in this case, the coefficients in (1.1) have the special form

$$\begin{aligned} a(S) &= \tfrac{1}{2}\sigma^2 S^2 \\ b(S) &= rS \\ c(S) &= -r \\ f(S) &= 0 \end{aligned} \tag{1.4}$$

In the following chapters our intention is to solve problems of the form (1.1) and we then apply our results to the specialised equations in quantitative finance.

1.2 TWO-POINT BOUNDARY VALUE PROBLEM

Let us examine a general second-order ordinary differential equation given in the form

$$u'' = f(x; u, u') \tag{1.5}$$

where the function f depends on three variables. The reader may like to check that (1.1) is a special case of (1.5). In general, there will be many solutions of (1.5) but our interest is in defining extra conditions to ensure that it will have a unique solution. Intuitively, we might correctly expect that two conditions are sufficient, considering the fact that you could integrate (1.5) twice and this will deliver two constants of integration. To this end, we determine these extra conditions by examining (1.5) on a *bounded* interval (a, b). In general, we discuss linear combinations of the unknown solution u and its first derivative at these end-points:

$$\begin{aligned} a_0 u(a) - a_1 u'(a) &= \alpha , \quad |a_0| + |a_1| \neq 0 \\ b_0 u(b) + b_1 u'(b) &= \beta , \quad |b_0| + |b_1| \neq 0 \end{aligned} \tag{1.6}$$

We wish to know the conditions under which problem (1.5), (1.6) has a unique solution. The full treatment is given in Keller (1992), but we discuss the main results in this section. First, we need to place some restrictions on the function f that appears on the right-hand side of equation (1.5).

Definition 1.1. The function $f(x, u, v)$ is called uniformly Lipschitz continuous if

$$|f(x; u,v) - f(x; w, z)| \leq K \max(|u - w|, |v - z|) \tag{1.7}$$

where K is some constant, and x, ut, and v are real numbers.

We now state the main result (taken from Keller, 1992).

Theorem 1.1. *Consider the function $f(x; u, v)$ in (1.5) and suppose that it is uniformly Lipschitz continuous in the region R, defined by:*

$$R : a \leq x \leq b, \ u^2 + v^2 < \infty \tag{1.8}$$

Suppose, furthermore, that f has continuous derivatives in R satisfying, for some constant M,

$$\frac{\partial f}{\partial u} > 0, \qquad \left| \frac{\partial f}{\partial v} \right| \leq M \tag{1.9}$$

and, that

$$a_0 a_1 \geq 0, \qquad b_0 b_1 \geq 0, \qquad |a_0| + |b_0| \neq 0 \tag{1.10}$$

Then the boundary-value problem (1.5), (1.6) has a unique solution.

This is a general result and we can use it in new problems to assure us that they have a unique solution.

1.2.1 Special kinds of boundary condition

The linear boundary conditions in (1.6) are quite general and they subsume a number of special cases. In particular, we shall encounter these cases when we discuss boundary conditions for the Black–Scholes equation. The main categories are:

- Robin boundary conditions
- Dirichlet boundary conditions
- Neumann boundary conditions.

The most general of those is the Robin condition, which is, in fact, (1.6). Special cases of (1.6) at the boundaries $x = a$ or $x = b$ are formed by setting some of the coefficients to zero. For example, the boundary conditions at the end-point $x = a$:

$$u(a) = \alpha$$
$$u'(a) = \beta \tag{1.11}$$

are called Dirichlet and Neumann boundary conditions at $x = a$ and at $x = b$, respectively.

Thus, in the first case the value of the unknown function u is known at $x = a$ while, in the second case, its derivative is known at $x = b$ (but not u itself). We shall encounter the above three types of boundary condition in this book, not only in a one-dimensional setting but also in multiple dimensions. Furthermore, we shall discuss other kinds of boundary condition that are needed in financial engineering applications.

1.3 LINEAR BOUNDARY VALUE PROBLEMS

We now consider a special case of (1.5), namely (1.1). This is called a **linear equation** and is important in many kinds of applications. A special case of Theorem 1.1 occurs when the function $f(x; u, v)$ is linear in both u and v. For convenience, we write (1.1) in the canonical form

$$-u'' + p(x)u' + q(x)u = r(x) \tag{1.12}$$

and the result is:

Theorem 1.2. *Let the functions $p(x)$, $q(x)$ and $r(x)$ be continuous in the closed interval $[a, b]$ with*

$$
\begin{aligned}
q(x) &> 0, & a \leq x \leq b, \\
a_0 a_1 &\geq 0, & |a_0| + |a_1| \neq 0, \\
b_0 b_1 &\geq 0, & |b_0| + |b_1| \neq 0,
\end{aligned}
\tag{1.13}
$$

Assume that

$$|a_0| + |b_0| \neq 0$$

then the two-point boundary value problem (BVP)

$$
\begin{aligned}
Lu &\equiv -u'' + p(x)u' + q(x)u = r(x), & a < x < b \\
a_0 u(a) - a_1 u'(a) &= \alpha, & b_0 u(b) + b_1 u'(b) = \beta
\end{aligned}
\tag{1.14}
$$

has a unique solution.

Remark. The condition $|a_0| + |b_0| \neq 0$ excludes boundary value problems with Neumann boundary conditions at both ends.

1.4   INITIAL VALUE PROBLEMS

In the previous section we examined a differential equation on a bounded interval. In this case we assumed that the solution was defined in this interval and that certain boundary conditions were defined at the interval's end-points. We now consider a different problem where we wish to find the solution on a semi-infinite interval, let's say (a, ∞). In this case we define the initial value problem (IVP)

$$u'' = f(x; u, u')$$
$$a_0 u(a) - a_1 u'(a) = \alpha \tag{1.15}$$
$$b_0 u(a) - b_1 u'(a) = \beta$$

where we assume that the two conditions at $x = a$ are independent, that is

$$a_1 b_0 - a_0 b_1 \neq 0 \tag{1.16}$$

It is possible to write (1.15) as a first-order system by a change of variables:

$$u' = v, \qquad v' = f(x; u, v)$$
$$a_0 u(a) - a_1 v(a) = \alpha \tag{1.17}$$
$$b_0 u(a) - b_1 v(a) = \beta$$

This is now a first-order system containing no explicit derivatives at $x = a$. System (1.17) is in a form that can be solved numerically by standard schemes (Keller, 1992). In fact, we can apply the same transformation technique to the boundary value problem (1.14) to get

$$-v' + p(x)v + q(x)u = r(x)$$
$$u' = v$$
$$a_0 u(a) - a_1 v(a) = \alpha, \tag{1.18}$$
$$b_0 u(b) + b_1 v(b) = \beta$$

This approach has a number of advantages when we apply finite difference schemes to approximate the solution of problem (1.18). First, we do not need to worry about approximating derivatives at the boundaries and, second, we are able to approximate v with the same accuracy as u itself. This is important in financial engineering applications because the first derivative represents an option's delta function.

1.5   SOME SPECIAL CASES

There are a number of common specialisations of equation (1.5), and each has its own special name, depending on its form:

$$
\begin{array}{lll}
\text{Reaction–diffusion:} & u'' = q(x)u & \\
\text{Convection–diffusion:} & u'' = p(x)u' & \quad (1.19) \\
\text{Diffusion:} & u'' = 0 &
\end{array}
$$

Each of these equations is a model for more complex equations in multiple dimensions, and, we shall discuss the time-dependent versions of the equations in (1.19). For example, the convection–diffusion equation has been studied extensively in science and engineering and has applications to fluid dynamics, semiconductor modelling and groundwater flow, to name just a few (Morton, 1996). It is also an essential part of the Black–Scholes equation (1.3).

We can transform equation (1.1) into a more convenient form (the so-called *normal form*) by a change of variables under the constraint that the coefficient of the second derivative $a(x)$ is always positive. For convenience we assume that the right-hand side term f is zero. To this end, define

$$
p(x) = \exp \int \frac{b(x)}{a(x)} \, dx
$$
$$
q(x) = \frac{c(x)p(x)}{a(x)}
$$

(1.20)

If we multiply equation (1.1) (note $f = 0$) by $p(x)/a(x)$ we then get:

$$
\frac{d}{dx} p(x) \frac{du}{dx} + q(x)u = 0
$$

(1.21)

This is sometimes known as the *self-adjoint form*. A further change of variables

$$
\zeta = \int \frac{dx}{p(x)}
$$

(1.22)

allows us to write (1.21) to an even simpler form

$$
\frac{d^2 u}{d\zeta^2} + p(x)q(x)u = 0
$$

(1.23)

Equation (1.23) is simpler to solve than equation (1.1).

1.6   SUMMARY AND CONCLUSIONS

We have given an introduction to second-order ordinary differential equations and the associated two-point boundary value problems. We have discussed various kinds of boundary conditions and a number of sufficient conditions for uniqueness of the solutions of these problems. Finally, we have introduced a number of topics that will be required in later chapters.

2
An Introduction to Partial Differential Equations

2.1 INTRODUCTION AND OBJECTIVES

In this chapter we give a gentle introduction to partial differential equations (PDEs). It can be considered to be a panoramic view and is meant to introduce some notation and examples. A PDE is an equation that depends on several independent variables. A well-known example is the Laplace equation:

$$\frac{\partial^2 u}{\partial x^2} + \frac{\partial^2 u}{\partial y^2} = 0 \tag{2.1}$$

In this case the dependent variable u satisfies (2.1) in some bounded, infinite or semi-infinite space in two dimensions.

In this book we examine PDEs in one or more space dimensions and a single time dimension. An example of a PDE with a derivative in the time direction is the heat equation in two spatial dimensions:

$$\frac{\partial u}{\partial t} = \frac{\partial^2 u}{\partial x^2} + \frac{\partial^2 u}{\partial y^2} \tag{2.2}$$

We classify PDEs into three categories of equation, namely *parabolic, hyperbolic* and *elliptic*. Parabolic equations are important for financial engineering applications because the Black–Scholes equation is a specific instance of such a category. Furthermore, generalisations and extensions to the Black–Scholes model may have hyperbolic equations as components. Finally, elliptic equations are useful because they form the time-independent part of the Black–Scholes equations.

2.2 PARTIAL DIFFERENTIAL EQUATIONS

We have attempted to categorise partial differential equations as shown in Figure 2.1. At the highest level we have the three major categories already mentioned. At the second level we have classes of equation based on the orders of the derivatives appearing in the PDE, while at level three we have given examples that serve as model problems for more complex equations. The hierarchy is incomplete and somewhat arbitrary (as all taxonomies are). It is not our intention to discuss all PDEs that are in existence but rather to give the reader an overview of some different types. This may be useful for readers who may not have had exposure to such equations in the past.

What makes a PDE parabolic, hyperbolic or elliptic? To answer this question let us examine the *linear* partial differential equation in two independent variables (Carrier and Pearson, 1976; Petrovsky, 1991)

$$Au_{xx} + 2Bu_{xy} + Cu_{yy} + Du_x + Eu_y + Fu + G = 0 \tag{2.3}$$

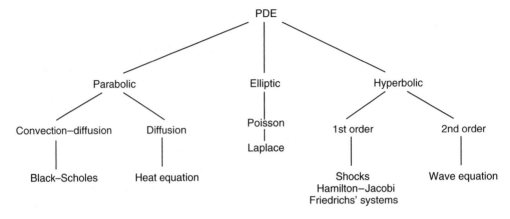

Figure 2.1 PDE classification

where we have used the (common) shorthand notation

$$u_x = \frac{\partial u}{\partial x}, \qquad u_y = \frac{\partial u}{\partial y}$$

$$u_{xx} = \frac{\partial^2 u}{\partial x^2}, \qquad u_{yy} = \frac{\partial^2 u}{\partial y^2} \qquad (2.4)$$

$$u_{xy} = \frac{\partial^2 u}{\partial x \partial y}$$

and the coefficients A, B, C, D, E, F and G are functions of x and y in general. Equation (2.3) is linear because these functions do not have a dependency on the unknown function $u = u(x, y)$. We assume that equation (2.3) is specified in some region of (x, y) space. Note the presence of the cross (mixed) derivatives in (2.3). We shall encounter these terms again in later chapters.

Equation (2.3) subsumes well-known equations in mathematical physics as special cases. For example, the Laplace equation (2.1) is a special case, having the following values:

$$\begin{aligned} A = C &= 1 \\ B = D = E = F = G &= 0 \end{aligned} \qquad (2.5)$$

A detailed discussion of (2.3), and the conditions that determine whether it is elliptic, hyperbolic or parabolic, is given in Carrier and Pearson (1976). We give the main results in this section. The discussion in Carrier and Pearson (1976) examines the quadratic equation:

$$A\xi_x^2 + 2B\xi_x\xi_y + C\xi_y^2 = 0 \qquad (2.6)$$

where $\xi(x, y)$ is some family of curves in (x, y) space (see Figure 2.2). In particular, we wish to find the solutions of the quadratic form by defining the variables:

$$\theta = \frac{\xi_x}{\xi_y} \qquad (2.7)$$

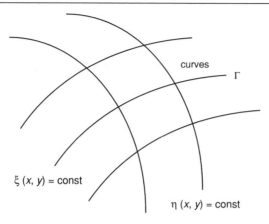

curves
Γ

ξ (x, y) = const

η (x, y) = const

Figure 2.2   (ξ, η) Coordinate system

Then we get the roots

$$A\theta^2 + 2B\theta + C = 0$$

$$\theta = \frac{-2B \pm 2\sqrt{B^2 - AC}}{2A} = \frac{-B \pm \sqrt{B^2 - AC}}{A} \qquad (2.8)$$

Thus, we distinguish between the following cases:

$$
\begin{aligned}
\text{elliptic:} \quad & B^2 - AC < 0 \\
\text{parabolic:} \quad & B^2 - AC = 0 \qquad (2.9)\\
\text{hyperbolic:} \quad & B^2 - AC > 0
\end{aligned}
$$

We note that the variables x and y appearing in (2.3) are generic and in some cases we may wish to replace them by other more specific variables – for example, replacing y by a time variable t as in the well-known one-dimensional wave equation

$$\frac{\partial^2 u}{\partial t^2} - \frac{\partial^2 u}{\partial x^2} = 0 \qquad (2.10)$$

It is easy to check that in this case the coefficients are: $A = 1$, $C = -1$, $B = D = E = F = G = 0$ and hence the equation is hyperbolic.

2.3   SPECIALISATIONS

We now discuss a number of special cases of elliptic, parabolic and hyperbolic equations that occur in many areas of application. These equations have been discovered and investigated by the greatest mathematicians of the last three centuries and there is an enormous literature on the theory of these equations and their applications to the world around us.

2.3.1   Elliptic equations

These time-independent equations occur in many kinds of application:

- Steady-state heat conduction (Kreider *et al.*, 1966)
- Semiconductor device simulation (Fraser, 1986; Bank and Fichtner, 1983)

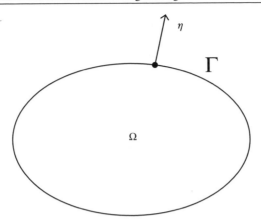

Figure 2.3   Two-dimensional bounded region

- Harmonic functions (Du Plessis, 1970; Rudin, 1970)
- Mapping functions between two-dimensional regions (George, 1991).

In general, we must specify boundary conditions for elliptic equations if we wish to have a unique solution. To this end, let us consider a two-dimensional region Ω with smooth boundary Γ as shown in Figure 2.3, and let η be the positive outward normal vector on Γ. A famous example of an elliptic equation is the Poisson equation defined by:

$$\Delta u \equiv \frac{\partial^2 u}{\partial x^2} + \frac{\partial^2 u}{\partial y^2} = f(x, y) \text{ in } \Omega \tag{2.11}$$

where Δ is the Laplace operator.

Equation (2.11) has a unique solution if we define boundary conditions. There are various options, the most general of which is the Robin condition:

$$\alpha \frac{\partial u}{\partial \eta} + \beta u = g \tag{2.12}$$

where α, β and g are given functions defined on the boundary Γ. A special case is when $\alpha = 0$, in which case (2.12) reduces to Dirichlet boundary conditions.

A special case of the Poisson equation (2.11) is when $f = 0$. This is then called the Laplace equation (2.1).

In general, we must resort to numerical methods if we wish to find a solution of problem (2.11), (2.12). For general domains, the finite element method (FEM) and other so-called variational techniques have been applied with success (see, for example, Strang *et al.*, 1973; Hughes, 2000). In this book we are mainly interested in square and rectangular regions because many financial engineering applications are defined in such regions. In this case the finite difference method (FDM) is our method of choice (see Richtmyer and Morton, 1967).

In some cases we can find an exact solution to the problem (2.11), (2.12) when the domain Ω is a rectangle. In this case we can then use the *separation of variables* principle, for example. Furthermore, if the domain is defined in a spherical or cylindrical region we can transform (2.11) to a simpler form. For a discussion of these topics, see Kreider *et al.* (1966).

2.3.2 Free boundary value problems

In the previous section we assumed that the boundary Γ of the domain of interest is known. In many applications, however, we not only need to find the solution of a PDE in some region but we define auxiliary constraints on some *unknown* boundary. This boundary may be internal or external to the domain. For time-independent problems we speak of free boundaries while for time-dependent problems we use the term 'moving' boundaries. These boundaries occur in numerous applications, some of which are:

- Flow in dams (Baiocchi, 1972; Friedman, 1979)
- Stefan problem: standard model for the melting of ice (Crank, 1984)
- Flow in porous media (Huyakorn and Pinder, 1983)
- Early exercise and American style option (Nielson *et al.*, 2002).

The following is a good example of a free boundary problem. Imagine immersing a block of ice in luke-warm water at time $t = 0$. Of course, the ice block eventually disappears because of its state change to water. The interesting question is: What is the profile of the block at any time after $t = 0$? This is a typical moving boundary value problem.

Another example that is easy to understand is the following. Consider a rectangular dam $D = \{(x, y) : 0 < x < a, \quad 0 < y < H\}$ and suppose that the walls $x = 0$ and $x = a$ border reservoirs of water maintained at given levels $g(t)$ and $f(t)$, respectively (see Figure 2.4). The so-called piezometric head is given by $u = u(x, y, t) = y + p(x, y, t)$, where p is the pressure in the dam. The velocity components are given by:

$$\text{velocity of water} = -(u_x, u_y) \tag{2.13}$$

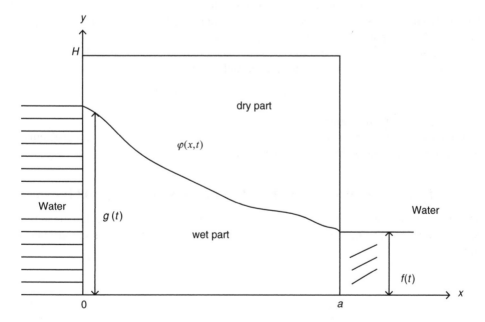

Figure 2.4 Dam with wet and dry parts

Furthermore, we distinguish between the dry part and the wet part of the dam as defined by the function $\varphi(x, t)$. The defining equations are (Friedman, 1979; Magenes, 1972):

$$
\begin{aligned}
&\frac{\partial^2 u}{\partial x^2} + \frac{\partial^2 u}{\partial y^2} = 0 \quad \text{if } 0 < x < a, \quad 0 < y < \varphi(x, t), \quad t > 0 \\
&u(0, y, t) = g(t), \quad 0 < y < g(t) \\
&u(0, y, t) = y, \quad g(t) < y < \varphi(0, t) \\
&u(a, y, t) = f(t), \quad 0 < y < f(t) \\
&u(a, y, t) = y, \quad f(t) < y < \varphi(a, t) \\
&u_y(x, 0, t) = 0, \quad 0 < x < a, \, t > 0
\end{aligned}
\tag{2.14}
$$

The function $\varphi(x, t)$ is called the free boundary and it separates the wet part from the dry part of the dam.

Furthermore, on the free boundary $y = \varphi(x, t)$ we have the following conditions:

$$
\begin{aligned}
u &= y \\
u_t &= u_x^2 + u_y^2 - u_y
\end{aligned}
\tag{2.15}
$$

Finally, we have the initial conditions:

$$
\begin{aligned}
&\varphi(x, 0) = \varphi_0(x), \quad 0 \leq x \leq a \\
&\varphi_0(x) > 0, \quad \varphi_0(0) \geq g(0), \quad \varphi_0(a) \geq f(0)
\end{aligned}
\tag{2.16}
$$

We thus see that the problem is the solution of the Laplace equation in the wet region of the dam while, on the free boundary, the equation is a first-order nonlinear hyperbolic equation. Thus, the free boundary is part of the problem and it must be evaluated.

A discussion of analytic and numerical methods for free and moving boundary value problems is given in Crank (1984). Free and moving boundary problems are extremely important in financial engineering, as we shall see in later chapters.

A special case of (2.14) is the so-called stationary dam problem (Baiocchi, 1972). In this case the levels of the reservoirs do not change and we then have the special cases

$$
g(t) \equiv g(0) \qquad f(t) \equiv f(0)
$$

and $y = \varphi_0(x)$ is the free boundary.

There may be similarities between the above problem and the free boundary problems that we encounter when modelling options with early excercise features.

2.4 PARABOLIC PARTIAL DIFFERENTIAL EQUATIONS

This is the most important PDE category in this book because of its relationship to the Black–Scholes equation. The most general linear parabolic PDE in n dimensions in this context is given by

$$
\begin{aligned}
&\frac{\partial u}{\partial t} = Lu \\
&Lu \equiv \sum_{i,j=1}^{n} a_{i,j}(x, t) \frac{\partial^2 u}{\partial x_i \partial x_j} + \sum_{j=1}^{n} b_j(x, t) \frac{\partial u}{\partial x_j} + cu
\end{aligned}
\tag{2.17}
$$

where x is a point in n-dimensional real space and t is the time variable, where t is increasing from $t = 0$. We assume that the operator L is *uniformly elliptical*, that is, there exist positive constants α and β such that

$$\alpha|\xi|^2 \le \sum_{i,j=1}^{n} a_{i,j}(x,t)\xi_i\xi_j \le \beta|\xi|^2$$

$$|\xi|^2 \equiv \xi_1^2 + \cdots + \xi_n^2$$

(2.18)

for x in some region of n-dimensional space and $t \ge 0$. Another way of expressing (2.18) is by saying that matrix A, defined by

$$A = (a_{i,j})_{i,j=1}^{n}$$

(2.19)

is positive-definite.

A special case of (2.17) is the famous multivariate Black–Scholes equation

$$\frac{\partial C}{\partial \tau} + \frac{1}{2}\sum_{i,j=1}^{n} \rho_{i,j}\sigma_i\sigma_j S_i S_j \frac{\partial^2 C}{\partial S_i \partial S_j} + \sum_{j=1}^{n}(r - d_j)S_j\frac{\partial C}{\partial S_j} - rC = 0$$

(2.20)

where τ is the time left to the expiry T and C is the value of the option on n underlying assets. The other parameters and coefficients are:

$$\begin{aligned}
\sigma_j &= \text{volatility of asset } j \\
\rho_{ij} &= \text{correlation between asset } i \text{ and asset } j \\
r &= \text{risk-free intererst rate} \\
d_j &= \text{dividend yield of the } j\text{th asset}
\end{aligned}$$

(2.21)

Equation (2.20) can be derived from the following stochastic differential equation (SDE):

$$dS_j = (\mu_j - d_j)S_j dt + \sigma_j S_j dz_j$$

(2.22)

where

$$\begin{aligned}
S_j &= j\text{th asset} \\
\mu_j &= \text{expected growth rate of } j\text{th asset} \\
dz_j &= \text{the } j\text{th Wiener process}
\end{aligned}$$

(2.23)

and using the generalised Ito's lemma (see, for example, Bhansali, 1998).

In general, we need to define a unique solution to (2.17) by augmenting the equation with initial conditions and boundary conditions. We shall deal with these in later chapters but for the moment we give one example of a parabolic initial boundary value problem (IBVP) on a bounded domain Ω with boundary Γ. This is defined as the PDE augmented with the following extra boundary and initial conditions

$$\alpha\frac{\partial u}{\partial \eta} + \beta u = g \quad \text{on} \quad \Gamma \times (0, T)$$

$$u(x, 0) = u_0(x), \quad x \in \overline{\Omega}$$

(2.24)

where $\overline{\Omega}$ is the closure of Ω.

We shall discuss parabolic equations in detail in this book by examining them from several viewpoints. First, we discuss the properties of the continuous problem (2.17), (2.24); second, we introduce finite difference schemes for these problems; and finally we examine their relevance to financial engineering.

2.4.1 Special cases

The second-order terms in (2.17) are called *diffusion terms* while the first-order terms are called *convection* (or *advection*) terms. If the convection terms are zero we then arrive at a diffusion equation, and if the diffusion terms are zero we then arrive at a first-order (hyperbolic) convection equation.

An even more special case of a diffusion equation is when all the diffusion coefficients are equal to 1. We then arrive at the heat equation in non-dimensional form. For example, in three space dimensions this equation has the form

$$\frac{\partial u}{\partial t} = \frac{\partial^2 u}{\partial x^2} + \frac{\partial^2 u}{\partial y^2} + \frac{\partial^2 u}{\partial z^2} \tag{2.25}$$

A special class of equations is called *convection–diffusion*. A prototypical example in one space dimension is

$$\frac{\partial u}{\partial t} = \sigma(x, t)\frac{\partial^2 u}{\partial x^2} + \mu(x, t)\frac{\partial u}{\partial x} + b(x, t)u \tag{2.26}$$

Convection–diffusion equations will receive much attention in this book because they model the behaviour of one-factor option pricing problems.

2.5 HYPERBOLIC EQUATIONS

Whereas parabolic equations model fluid and heat flow phenomena, hyperbolic equations model wave phenomena, and there are many application areas where hyperbolic wave equations play an important role:

- Shock waves (Lax, 1973)
- Acoustics (Kinsler *et al.*, 1982)
- Neutron transport phenomena (Richtmyer and Morton, 1967)
- Deterministic models in quantitative finance (for example, deterministic interest rates).

We are interested in two sub-categories, namely second-order and first-order hyperbolic equations.

2.5.1 Second-order equations

In this case we have a PDE containing a second-order derivative in time. A typical example is the equation (written in self-adjoint form)

$$\frac{\partial^2 u}{\partial t^2} = Lu = \sum_{i,j=1}^{n} \frac{\partial}{\partial x_i}\left(a_{i,j}(x, t)\frac{\partial u}{\partial x_j}\right) - q(x)u \tag{2.27}$$

In order to define a unique solution to (2.27) we define boundary conditions in space in the usual way. However, since we have a second derivative in time, we shall need to give two initial conditions.

We now take a specific example. Consider an infinite stretched rod of negligible mass. The equations for the displacement of the string given a certain displacement are given by:

$$\frac{\partial^2 u}{\partial t^2} = c^2 \frac{\partial^2 u}{\partial x^2}, \quad x \in (-\infty, \infty), \quad t \geq 0$$

$$u(x, 0) = \varphi(x), \qquad \frac{\partial u}{\partial t}(x, 0) = \psi(x), \quad x \in (-\infty, \infty) \tag{2.28}$$

A common procedure when viewing (2.28) both analytically and numerically is to define new variables v and w:

$$v = \frac{\partial u}{\partial x} \quad \text{and} \quad w = \frac{\partial u}{\partial t} \tag{2.29}$$

We can write equations (2.28) as a first-order system:

$$A\frac{\partial U}{\partial t} + B\frac{\partial U}{\partial x} + CU = 0 \tag{2.30}$$

where we define the vectors

$$U = \begin{pmatrix} u \\ v \\ w \end{pmatrix} \tag{2.31}$$

and

$$A = \begin{pmatrix} 1 & 0 & 0 \\ 0 & 1 & 0 \\ 0 & 0 & 1 \end{pmatrix}, \quad B = \begin{pmatrix} 0 & 0 & 0 \\ 0 & -1 & 0 \\ 0 & -c^2 & 0 \end{pmatrix}, \quad C = \begin{pmatrix} 0 & 0 & -1 \\ 0 & 0 & 0 \\ 0 & 0 & 0 \end{pmatrix} \tag{2.32}$$

It can be advantageous from both an analytical and numerical viewpoint to transform higher-order equations to a first-order system.

2.5.2   First-order equations

First-order hyperbolic equations occur in many applications, especially in the theory of gas flow and in shock waves. The prototypical scalar initial value problem is

$$\frac{\partial u}{\partial t} + a(x, t)\frac{\partial u}{\partial x} = 0 \quad \text{in } (-\infty, \infty) \times (0, T)$$

$$u(x, 0) = u_0(x), \quad x \in (-\infty, \infty) \tag{2.33}$$

Furthermore, the smoothness of the solution of (2.33) is determined by its discontinuities (determined by the continuity of the initial condition) and these will be propagated indefinitely. This is different from parabolic PDEs where discontinuities in the initial condition become smeared out as time goes on.

Closely associated with first-order equations is the Method of Characteristics (MOC) (see Courant and Hilbert, 1968). We shall discuss MOC later as a method for solving first-order equations numerically.

2.6 SYSTEMS OF EQUATIONS

In some applications we may wish to solve a PDE for vector-valued functions, that is systems of equations. We shall also come across some examples of such systems in the financial engineering applications in this book. Typical cases are chooser options and compound options.

2.6.1 Parabolic systems

Let us consider the two-dimensional problem

$$\frac{\partial U}{\partial t} = A\frac{\partial^2 U}{\partial x^2} + B\frac{\partial^2 U}{\partial y^2} + C\frac{\partial U}{\partial x} + D\frac{\partial U}{\partial y} + EU \tag{2.34}$$

where U is a vector of unknowns and A, B, C, D and E are matrices. We say that the system (2.34) is parabolic if for each vector $\mathbf{w} \in \mathbb{R}^2$

$$\mathbf{w} = {}^t(w_1, w_2) \text{ the eigenvalues } K_j(\mathbf{w}), \quad j = 1, \ldots, n \text{ of } -w_1^2 A - w_2^2 B \tag{2.35}$$

satisfy $\operatorname{Re} K_j(w) \le \delta|w|^2$, $\quad j = 1, \ldots, n$ for some $\delta > 0$ independent of $\mathbf{w}$ (Thomas, 1998).

2.6.2 First-order hyperbolic systems

This is an important and common class of partial differential equations. In particular, the Friedrichs systems constitute an important sub-category (Friedrichs, 1958). Let us take an example (Duffy, 1977). Let $I = (0, 1)$, the open unit interval, and let T be a number such that $0 < T < \infty$. Define the domain $Q = I \times (0, T)$. Let U be a vector of length n and define partitions of U as follows

$$\begin{aligned} U^{\mathrm{I}} &= {}^t(u_1, \ldots, u_l), \quad l < n \\ U^{\mathrm{II}} &= {}^t(u_{l+1}, \ldots, u_n) \end{aligned} \tag{2.36}$$

We now consider the initial boundary value problem.
  Find $U : Q \to \mathbb{R}^n$ such that

$$\frac{\partial U}{\partial t} + A\frac{\partial U}{\partial x} = F \text{ in } Q \tag{2.37}$$

that is augmented with boundary conditions

$$\begin{aligned} U^{\mathrm{I}}(0, t) &= \alpha U^{\mathrm{II}}(0, t) + g_0(t), \quad t \in (0, T) \\ U^{\mathrm{II}}(1, t) &= \beta U^{\mathrm{I}}(1, t) + g_1(t), \quad t \in (0, T) \end{aligned} \tag{2.38}$$

where $g_0 \in \mathbb{R}^l$, $g_1 \in \mathbb{R}^{n-l}$ and α and β are matrices of size $l \times (n - l)$ and $(n - l) \times l$, respectively (existence and uniqueness proofs are given in Friedrichs, 1958), and initial condition

$$u(x, 0) = u_0(x), \quad x \in I \tag{2.39}$$

Many problems of interest can be cast into the form (2.36) to (2.39).

2.7 EQUATIONS CONTAINING INTEGRALS

Equations that involve integrals occur in many kinds of applications:

- Applications that model the past behaviour of a process
- The effect of temperature feedback in a nuclear reactor model (Pao, 1992)
- Problems in epidemics and combustion (Pao, 1992)
- Instrument pricing applications (Tavella *et al.*, 2000).

In general, we solve a problem by finding the solution of an integral equation. To begin with, we consider a function of one variable only. The two main categories are

- Fredholm integral equations
- Volterra integral equations.

Let $f(t)$ be the unknown function and suppose that $g(t)$ and $K(s, t)$ are known functions. Then Fredholm equations of the first kind are:

$$g(t) = \int_a^b K(t, s) f(s) \, ds \qquad (2.40)$$

and Fredholm equations of the second kind are:

$$f(t) = \lambda \int_a^b K(t, s) f(s) \, ds + g(t) \qquad (2.41)$$

In both cases we are interested in finding the solution $f(t)$ in the interval (a, b). This interval may be bounded, infinite or semi-infinite. Volterra integral equations are slightly different. The interval of integration is variable. Volterra integral equations of the first kind are:

$$g(t) = \int_a^t K(t, s) f(s) \, ds \qquad (2.42)$$

while Volterra integral equations of the second kind are:

$$f(t) = \lambda \int_a^t K(t, s) f(s) \, ds + g(t) \qquad (2.43)$$

The main difference between Volterra and Fredholm equations is in the limits of integration in the integral terms.

We can combine PDEs and integral equations to form an integro-parabolic equation (also known as partial integro-differential equations, PIDEs). An example is the Fredholm type PIDE defined by

$$\frac{\partial u}{\partial t} - Lu = f(x, t, u) + \int_\Omega g(x, t, \xi, u(x, t), u(\xi, t)) \, d\xi \qquad (2.44)$$

where the operator L is the same as in equation (2.17). An example of a Volterra type PIDE that models the effect of temperature feedback is

$$\frac{\partial u}{\partial t} - D \Delta u = au - bu \int_0^t u(s, x) \, ds \qquad (2.45)$$

In this equation the constants a and b associated with the various physical parameters are both positive or both negative, depending on whether the temperature feedback is negative or positive.

A more general PIDE of Volterra type is

$$\frac{\partial u}{\partial t} - Lu = f(x, t, u) + \int_0^t g(x, t, s, u(x, t), u(x, s)) \, \mathrm{d}s \qquad (2.46)$$

For an introductory discussion of numerical methods for solving integral equations, see Press *et al.* (2002), and for a more detailed discussion, see Kress (1989). We shall examine integral equations when we model option problems containing jumps.

2.8 SUMMARY AND CONCLUSIONS

We have given an overview of some categories of partial differential equations as well as their specialisations. We distinguished between parabolic, elliptic and hyperbolic equations. Our main interest in this book is in parabolic equations because of their relationship with the Black–Scholes model.

We have given a short introduction to systems of first-order hyperbolic equations and partial integro differential equations (PIDE). We shall encounter applications of these special equations to financial engineering in later chapters.

3

Second-Order Parabolic
Differential Equations

3.1 INTRODUCTION AND OBJECTIVES

In this chapter we introduce second-order parabolic partial differential equations in some detail as well as their relevance to the Black–Scholes model. In particular, we study essential properties of the solutions of initial boundary value problems:

- How positive initial and boundary values lead to positive values of the solution
- How the solution of a parabolic initial boundary value problem is bounded by its input data
- Constructing the solution of a parabolic initial boundary value problem by using the Green's function.

The results in this chapter are interesting in their own right because they are applicable to a whole range of PDEs that occur in many kinds of application (see Morton, 1996, for a discussion), and not just the Black–Scholes model.

In later chapters we shall develop similar results to those in this chapter for the discrete approximations of parabolic PDEs and the associated initial boundary value problems. We give the main results that we need later without becoming too involved in mathematical detail. For a rigorous discussion, see Il'in *et al.* (1962) and Pao (1992).

For readers who are new to this theory, we recommend the works of Kreider *et al.* (1966), Petrovsky (1991) and Carrier and Pearson (1976) as good introductory text books.

3.2 LINEAR PARABOLIC EQUATIONS

Many of the topics in this chapter are based on some of the fundamental results that were developed in Il'in *et al.* (1962).

Let us define the elliptic differential operator L_E by

$$L_E u \equiv \sum_{i,j=1}^{n} a_{ij}(x,t) \frac{\partial^2 u}{\partial x_i \, \partial x_j} + \sum_{j=1}^{n} b_j(x,t) \frac{\partial u}{\partial x_j} + c(x,t) u \tag{3.1}$$

where

The functions a_{ij}, b_j and c are real and take finite values $\tag{3.2a}$

$$a_{ij} = a_{ji} \quad \text{and} \quad \sum_{i,j=1}^{n} a_{ij}(x,t)\alpha_i \alpha_j > 0 \quad \text{if} \quad \sum_{j=1}^{n} \alpha_j^2 > 0 \tag{3.2b}$$

$x = {}^t(x_1, \ldots, x_n)$ is an n-dimensional point in real space $\tag{3.2c}$

Let t represent a time variable. We examine the second-order linear parabolic equation

$$Lu \equiv -\frac{\partial u}{\partial t} + L_E u = f(x,t) \tag{3.3}$$

at the point (x, t) where u is continuous and has continuous derivatives

$$\frac{\partial u}{\partial x_j}, \frac{\partial u}{\partial t}, \frac{\partial^2 u}{\partial x_i \partial x_j} \quad (i, j = 1, \ldots, n) \tag{3.4}$$

Furthermore, $f = f(x, t)$ is some given function.

In general there will be many solutions of (3.3) and in order to define a unique solution we must define some *auxiliary conditions*. We shall now discuss some specific scenarios.

We denote by $\mathbb{R}^n$ the n-dimensional Euclidean space of points with coordinates

$$(x_1, \ldots, x_n)$$

Furthermore, the notation (x, t) will denote an arbitrary point in the $(n + 1)$-dimensional space

$$\mathbb{R}^{n+1} = \mathbb{R}^n \times (-\infty, \infty)$$

We distinguish between space and time coordinates because we shall use different discretisations for them.

3.3   THE CONTINUOUS PROBLEM

We introduce the basic set of equations that model the behaviour of a class of derivative products. In particular, we model derivatives that are described by so-called initial boundary value problems of parabolic type (see Il'in *et al.*, 1962). To this end, consider the general parabolic equation (3.1) again.

The variable x is a point in n-dimensional space and t is considered to be a positive time variable. Equation (3.1) is the general equation that describes the behaviour of many derivative types. For example, in the one-dimensional case $(n = 1)$ it reduces to the famous Black–Scholes equation (see Black and Scholes, 1973)

$$\frac{\partial V}{\partial t^\star} + \frac{1}{2}\sigma^2 S^2 \frac{\partial^2 V}{\partial S^2} + (r - D)S \frac{\partial V}{\partial S} - rV = 0 \tag{3.5}$$

where V is the derivative type, S is the underlying asset (or stock), σ is the constant volatility, r is the interest rate and D is a dividend. Equation (3.5) can be generalised to the multivariate case

$$\frac{\partial V}{\partial t^\star} + \sum_{j=1}^{n}(r - D_j)S_j \frac{\partial V}{\partial S_j} + \frac{1}{2}\sum_{i,j=1}^{n} \rho_{ij}\sigma_i\sigma_j S_i S_j \frac{\partial^2 V}{\partial S_i \partial S_j} - rV = 0 \tag{3.6}$$

(see Bhansali, 1998). This equation models a multi-asset environment. In this case σ_i is the volatility of the ith asset and ρ_{ij} is the correlation between assets i and j. We see that the local change in time (namely the factor $\partial V/\partial t^\star$) is written as the sum of three terms:

- Interest earned on cash position: $r\left(V - \sum_{j=1}^{n} S_j \frac{\partial V}{\partial S_j}\right)$

- Gain from dividend yield: $\sum_{j=1}^{n} D_j S_j \frac{\partial V}{\partial S_j}$

- Hedging costs or slippage: $-\frac{1}{2}\sum_{i,j=1}^{n} \rho_{ij}\sigma_i\sigma_j \frac{\partial^2 V}{\partial S_i \partial S_j}$

Returning to equation (3.1) we note that it has an infinite number of solutions in general. In order to reduce this number to 1, we need to define some extra constraints. To this end, we define so-called initial condition and boundary conditions for (3.1). We achieve this by defining the space in which this equation is assumed to be valid. Since the equation has a second-order derivative in x and a first-order derivative in t, we should expect that a unique solution can be found by defining two boundary conditions and one initial condition.

In general, we note that there are three types of boundary condition associated with equation (3.1) (see Il'in *et al.*, 1962). These are:

- First boundary value problem (Dirichlet problem)
- Second boundary value problem (Neumann/Robins problems)
- Cauchy problem

The first boundary value problem is concerned with the solution of (3.1) in a domain $D = \Omega \times (0, T)$ where Ω is a bounded subset of $\mathbb{R}^n$ and T is a positive number. In this case we seek to find a solution of (3.1) satisfying the conditions

$$u|_{t=0} = \varphi(x) \quad \text{(initial condition)}$$
$$u|_\Gamma = \psi(x, t) \quad \text{(boundary condition)} \tag{3.7}$$

where Γ is the boundary of Ω and ψ is a given function. The boundary conditions in (3.7) are called Dirichlet boundary conditions. These conditions arise when we model single and double barrier options in the one-factor case, for example. They also occur when we model European options.

The second boundary value problem is similar to (3.7) except that instead of giving the value of u on the boundary Γ, the directional derivatives are included, as seen in the following specification:

$$\left[\frac{\partial u}{\partial \eta} + a(x, t)u \right]_\Gamma = \psi(x, t) \quad x \in \Gamma \tag{3.8}$$

In this case $a(x, t)$ and $\psi(x, t)$ are known functions of x and t, and $\partial u / \partial \eta$ denotes the derivative of u with respect to the outward normal η at Γ. A special case of (3.8) arises when $a(x, t) \equiv 0$; there are the so-called Neumann boundary conditions. That occur when modelling certain kinds of put options.

Finally, the solution of the Cauchy problem for (3.1) in the strip $\mathbb{R}^n \times (0, T)$ is given by the initial condition

$$u|_{t=0} = \varphi(x) \tag{3.9}$$

where, first, $\varphi(x)$ is a given continuous function, and, second, $u(x, t)$ is a function that satisfies (3.1) in $\mathbb{R}^n \times (0, T)$. A special case of the Cauchy problem can be seen in the modelling of one-factor European and American options (see Wilmott, 1993) where x plays the role of the underlying asset S. Boundary conditions are given by values at $S = 0$ and $S = \infty$. For European options these conditions are:

$$C(0, t) = 0$$
$$C(S, t) \to S \quad \text{as} \quad S \to \infty \tag{3.10}$$

Here C (the role played by u in equation (3.1)) is the variable representing the price of the call option. For European put options, on the other hand, the boundary conditions are:

$$P(0, t) = K\, e^{-r(T-t^*)}$$
$$P(S, t) \to 0 \quad \text{as} \quad S \to \infty \tag{3.11}$$

Here P (the role played by u in equation (3.1)) is the variable representing the price of the put option, K is the strike price, r is the risk-free interest rate, T is the time to expiry and t is the current time.

In practice, it is common to solve European options problems numerically by assuming a finite domain – that is, one in which the right-hand boundary conditions in (3.10) or (3.11) are defined at large but finite values of S.

3.4   THE MAXIMUM PRINCIPLE FOR PARABOLIC EQUATIONS

The results in this section are very important because they tell us things about the solutions of parabolic PDEs. In particular, the results have a physical and financial interpretation. In general terms, we say that positive input to a problem gives us a positive solution. For example, the value of an option is always non-negative.

Theorem 3.1. *Assume that the function $u(x, t)$ is continuous in D and assume that the coefficients in (3.1) are continuous. Suppose that $Lu \leq 0$ in $\bar{D}\backslash\Gamma$, where $b(x, t) < M$ (M is some constant) and suppose furthermore that $u(x, t) \geq 0$ on Γ. Then*

$$u(x, t) \geq 0 \quad in\ \bar{D},$$

where $D = (0, 1) \times (0, T)$.

This theorem states that positive initial and boundary conditions lead to a positive solution in the interior of the domain D. This has far-reaching consequences. For example, we can use this theorem to prove that the solution of the Black–Scholes PDE is positive. Furthermore, the finite difference schemes that approximate the Black–Scholes equation should have similar properties.

Theorem 3.2. *Suppose that $u(x, t)$ is continuous and satisfies (3.1) in $\bar{D}\backslash\Gamma$, where $f(x, t)$ is a bounded function ($|f| \leq N$) and $b(x, t) \leq 0$. If $|u(x, t)|_\Gamma \leq m$, then*

$$|u(x, t)| \leq Nt + m \quad in\ \bar{D} \tag{3.12}$$

We can sharpen the results of Theorem 3.2 in the case where $b(x, t) \leq b_0 < 0$. In this case estimate (3.12) is replaced by

$$|u(x, t)| \leq \max\left(\frac{-N}{b_0}, m\right) \tag{3.13}$$

Proof. Define the so-called 'barrier' function $w^\pm(x, t) = N_1 \pm u(x, t)$, where $N_1 = \max(-N/b_0, m)$. Then $w^\pm \geq 0$ and $Lw^\pm \leq 0$. By Theorem 3.1 we deduce that $w^\pm \geq 0$ in $\bar{D}$. The desired result follows.

The inequality (3.13) states that the growth of u is bounded by its initial and boundary values. It is interesting to note that in the special cases $b \equiv 0$ and $f \equiv 0$ we can deduce the following maximum and minimum principles for the heat equation and its variants.

Corollary 3.1. *Assume that the conditions of Theorem 3.2 are satisfied and that $b \equiv 0$ and $f \equiv 0$. Then the function $u(x, t)$ takes its least and greatest values on Γ, that is*

$$m_1 = \min u(x, t) \leq u(x, t) \leq \max u(x, t) \equiv m_2$$

The results from Theorems 3.1 and 3.2 and Corollary 3.1 are very appealing: you cannot get negative values of the solution u from positive input. It would be nice if the corresponding finite difference scheme for this problem gave similar estimates. Generalisation of these results can be found in Pao (1992).

3.5   A SPECIAL CASE: ONE-FACTOR GENERALISED BLACK–SCHOLES MODELS

We now focus on a specific problem, namely the one-factor generalised Black–Scholes equation with initial condition and Dirichlet boundary conditions. We formulate the problem in a general setting; the specification can be used in various kinds of pricing applications by a specialisation process.

Define $\Omega = (A, B)$, where A and B are two real finite numbers. Further, let $D = \Omega \times (0, T)$. The formal statement of the problem is: Find a function $u : D \to \mathbb{R}^1$ such that

$$Lu \equiv -\frac{\partial u}{\partial t} + \sigma(x, t)\frac{\partial^2 u}{\partial x^2} + \mu(x, t)\frac{\partial u}{\partial x} + b(x, t)u = f(x, t) \quad \text{in } D \qquad (3.14)$$

$$u(x, 0) = \varphi(x), \quad x \in \Omega \qquad (3.15)$$

$$u(A, t) = g_0(t), \qquad u(B, t) = g_1(t), \quad t \in (0, T) \qquad (3.16)$$

The initial boundary value problem (3.14)–(3.16) is very general and it subsumes many specific cases (in particular it is a generalisation of the original Black–Scholes equation).

In general, the coefficients $\sigma(x, t)$ and $\mu(x, t)$ represent volatility (diffusivity) and drift (convection), respectively. Equation (3.14) is called the convection–diffusion and has been the subject of much study. It serves as a model for many kinds of physical phenomena. Much research has been carried out in this area, both on the continuous problem and its discrete formulations (for example, using finite difference and finite element methods). In particular, research has shown that standard centred-difference schemes fail to approximate (3.14)–(3.16) properly in certain cases (see Duffy, 1980). The problems are well known in the scientific and engineering worlds.

We now investigate some special limiting cases in the system (3.14)–(3.16). One particular case is when the function $\sigma(x, t)$ tends to zero. The Black–Scholes equation assumes that volatility is constant, but this is not always true in practice. For example, the volatility may be time-dependent (see Wilmott *et al.*, 1993). In general, the volatility may be a function of both time and the underlying variable. If the volatility is a function of time only, then an explicit solution can be found but an explicit solution cannot be found in more complicated cases. For example we note that the so-called exponentially declining volatility functions (see Van Deventer and Imai, 1997) – as given by the formula

$$\sigma(t) = \sigma_0 \, e^{-\alpha(T-t)} \qquad (3.17)$$

where σ_0 and α are given constants – can be used in this model.

Having described situations in which the coefficient σ is small or tends to zero, we now discuss the mathematical implications. This is very important in general because finite difference schemes must be robust enough to approximate the exact solution in these extreme cases as well as in 'normal' regimes. Setting σ to zero in (3.14) leads to a formally first-order hyperbolic equation

$$L_1 u \equiv -\frac{\partial u}{\partial t} + \mu(x, t)\frac{\partial u}{\partial x} + b(x, t)u = f(x, t) \qquad (3.18)$$

Since the second derivative in x is not present in (3.18) we conclude that only one boundary condition and one initial condition are needed in order to specify a unique solution (see Friedrichs, 1958; Duffy, 1977). But the question is: Which boundary condition in (3.16) should we choose? In order to answer this question we must define the so-called characteristic lines associated with equation (3.18) (see Godounov, 1973; Godounov *et al.*, 1979). These are defined as lines that satisfy the ordinary differential equation

$$\frac{dx}{dt} = -\mu \qquad (3.19)$$

The lines have positive or negative slope depending on whether μ has negative or positive values. In general, it can be shown (see Friedrichs, 1958, for a definitive report) how to discover the 'correct' boundary condition for (3.18), namely:

$$
\begin{aligned}
u(A, t) &= g_0(t) \quad \text{if } \mu < 0 \\
u(B, t) &= g_1(t) \quad \text{if } \mu > 0
\end{aligned}
\qquad (3.20)
$$

We see that one of the boundary conditions in (3.16) is superfluous.

3.6 FUNDAMENTAL SOLUTION AND THE GREEN'S FUNCTION

When studying linear parabolic partial differential equations such as (3.3), the so-called *fundamental solution* plays an important role. In general the fundamental solution has a singularity of a certain type – for example, a Dirac delta function $\delta(x)$. This function is defined on the real line $(-\infty, \infty)$ and is zero there, except at $x = 0$. Furthermore, $\int_{-\infty}^{\infty} \delta(x) = 1$.

We now construct the fundamental solution for parabolic equations. In general, a function

$$\Gamma(x, t; \xi, \tau)$$

is called a fundamental solution of the parabolic operator

$$L \equiv -\frac{\partial}{\partial t} + L_E \quad \text{in } \mathbb{R}^n \times [0, T]$$

if for any fixed

$$(\xi, \tau) \in \mathbb{R}^n \times [0, T]$$

it satisfies the equation

$$L\Gamma \equiv -\frac{\partial \Gamma}{\partial t} + L_E \Gamma = \delta(x - \xi)\,\delta(t - \tau)$$

where δ is the Dirac δ-function. For the operator L, the function Γ is a positive function in $\mathbb{R}^n \times (0, T]$ except at the singular point (ξ, τ).

We now discuss the Green's function and its relationship with the fundamental solution, the parabolic operator L defined by equation (3.3) and the boundary operator

$$Bu \equiv \alpha \frac{\partial u}{\partial \eta} + \beta u \qquad (3.21)$$

Then the Green's function is expressed as

$$G(x, t; \xi, \tau) = \Gamma(x, t; \xi, \tau) + W(x, t; \xi, \tau) \quad \text{with } (x, t) \neq (\xi, \tau) \qquad (3.22)$$

It can be shown (Il'in *et al.*, 1962; Pao, 1992) that W is smooth. The function W is the solution of the PDE

$$LW = 0, \quad (x, t) \in \Omega \times (\tau, T]$$

$$BW = -B\Gamma, \quad (x, t) \in \partial\Omega \times (\tau, T] \qquad (3.23)$$

$$W(x, t; \xi, \tau) = 0, \quad t \leq \tau, \ x \in \Omega$$

where $\partial\Omega$ is the boundary of Ω. We shall need the above results in the next section.

3.7 INTEGRAL REPRESENTATION OF THE SOLUTION OF PARABOLIC PDEs

This discussion until now has implicitly assumed that a parabolic PDE has a solution. We must now prove that a parabolic initial boundary value problem has a solution having certain smoothness properties and, if possible, we would like to describe the solution analytically. To this end, we focus on the initial boundary value problem

$$-\frac{\partial u}{\partial t} + L_E u = f(x, t) \quad \text{in } D \equiv \Omega \times (0, T) \qquad (3.24a)$$

$$\alpha(x, t) \frac{\partial u}{\partial \eta} + \beta(x, t)u = h(x, t) \quad \text{on } \partial\Omega \times (0, T) \qquad (3.24b)$$

$$u(x, 0) = u_0(x), \quad x \in \Omega \qquad (3.24c)$$

This problem subsumes Dirichlet, Neumann and Robin boundary conditions as special cases and hence a number of cases in quantitative finance.

We define the following functions based on the fundamental solution, the Green's function and a new function that we define shortly.

Let Γ and G be defined as before.

Define the functions:

$$J^{(0)}(x, t) \equiv \int_\Omega \Gamma(x, t; \xi, 0)u_0(\xi)\, d\xi \qquad (3.25a)$$

$$J^{(1)}(x, t) \equiv \int_\Omega G(x, t; \xi, 0)u_0(\xi)\, d\xi \qquad (3.25b)$$

$$J^{(2)}(x, t) \equiv \int_\Omega Q(x, t; \xi, 0)u_0(\xi)\, d\xi \qquad (3.25c)$$

where the function Q is defined by

$$Q(x, t; \xi, \tau) \equiv \frac{\partial \Gamma}{\partial \eta_x}(x, t; \xi, \tau) + \beta(x, t)\Gamma(x, t; \xi, \tau) \tag{3.26}$$

where η_x = normal direction to Γ at the point x.

Finally, we define the function $H(x, t)$ as:

$$H(x, t) = J^{(2)}(x, t) + h(x, t) + \int_0^t d\tau \int_\Omega Q(x, t; \xi, \tau) f(\xi, \tau) d\xi \tag{3.27}$$

We are now ready to give integral expressions for the solution u of system (3.24). We distinguish two cases as far as boundary conditions are concerned:

- $\alpha = 0$ (Dirichlet boundary conditions)
- α is non-zero (Robin/Neumann boundary conditions).

We give the main results in both these cases (for the mathematical niceties, see Pao, 1992, chapter 2)

Theorem 3.3. *(First boundary value problem.) Let u be the solution of system (3.24) with $\alpha = 0$ and assume the compatibility conditions*

$$\beta(x, 0)u_0(x) = h(x, 0) \quad \text{on } \partial\Omega$$

Then

$$u(x, t) = J^{(1)}(x, t) + \int_0^t d\tau \int_\Omega G(x, t; \xi, \tau) f(\xi, \tau) d\xi$$

$$+ \int_0^t d\tau \int_{\partial\Omega} \frac{\partial \Gamma}{\partial \eta_\xi}(x, t; \xi, \tau) \psi(\xi, \tau) d\xi \tag{3.28}$$

where ψ is the so-called density function defined as the solution of the integral equation

$$\psi(x, t) = 2 \int_0^t d\tau \int_{\partial\Omega} \frac{\partial \Gamma}{\partial \eta_\xi}(x, t; \xi, \tau) \psi(\xi, \tau) d\xi - 2h(x, t)/\beta(x, t) \tag{3.29}$$

Theorem 3.4. *(Robin/Neumann boundary condition.) The solution of system (3.24) with $\alpha = 1$ has the integral representation*

$$u(x, t) = J^{(0)}(x, t) + \int_0^t d\tau \int_\Omega \Gamma(x, t; \xi, \tau) f(\xi, \tau) d\xi$$

$$+ \int_0^t d\tau \int_{\partial\Omega} \Gamma(x, t; \xi, \tau) \psi(\xi, \tau) d\xi \tag{3.30}$$

where ψ is again a density function (see Pao, 1992, for details).

Remark. The solutions in Theorems 3.3 and 3.4 must have continuous partial derivatives

$$\frac{\partial u}{\partial t}, \quad \frac{\partial u}{\partial x_j}, \quad \frac{\partial^2 u}{\partial x_i \partial x_j}, \quad i, j = 1, \dots, n$$

and must satisfy (3.24a) for every (x, t) in D. Furthermore, the boundary and initial conditions in system (3.24) are also satisfied in the pointwise sense. Then the solution has continuous first derivatives in the time variable t and continuous second derivatives in the space variable x.

We now consider the problem (3.24) in an infinite domain. This is called the Cauchy problem:

$$-\frac{\partial u}{\partial t} + L_E u = f(x, t) \quad \text{in } \mathbb{R}^n \times (0, T)$$

$$u(x, 0) = u_0(x), \quad x \in \mathbb{R}^n$$

(3.31)

where we assume the following growth conditions on the initial condition and the right-hand forcing function:

$$|f(x, t)| \leq A e^{b|x|^2} \quad \text{and} \quad |u_0(x)| \leq C e^{b|x|^2} \quad \text{as } x \to \infty$$

(3.32)

where $|x|^2 = \sum_{j=1}^{n} x_j^2$.

Theorem 3.5. *(Cauchy problem.) Let $u = u(x, t)$ be the solution of (3.31) given the conditions (3.32). Then the dependent variable u can be expressed in integral equation form:*

$$u(x, t) = J^{(0)}(x, t) + \int_0^t d\tau \int_{\mathbb{R}^n} \Gamma(x, t; \xi, \tau) f(\xi, \tau) \, d\xi$$

(3.33)

where

$$J^{(0)}(x, t) = \int_{\mathbb{R}^n} \Gamma(x, t; \xi, 0) u_0(\xi) \, d\xi$$

(3.34)

Furthermore, the solution is bounded as follows:

$$|u(x, t)| \leq C e^{b'|x|^2} \quad \text{as } x \to \infty$$

(3.35)

3.8 PARABOLIC EQUATIONS IN ONE SPACE DIMENSION

In this section we look at a second-order parabolic partial differential equation in one space dimension. In other words, this is a specialisation of the equations in previous sections for the case $n = 1$. To this end, we examine the equation

$$-\frac{\partial u}{\partial t} + \sigma(x, t)\frac{\partial^2 u}{\partial x^2} + \mu(x, t)\frac{\partial u}{\partial x} + b(x, t)u = f(x, t)$$

(3.36)

in the domain D defined by

$$D = \{(x, t) : 0 \leq t \leq T, \quad s_1(t) < x < s_2(t)\}$$

(3.37)

subject to the conditions

$$s_1(0) = 0, \quad s_2(0) = 1$$

$$s_1(t) < s_2(t), \quad 0 \leq t \leq T$$

(3.38)

Furthermore, we augment (3.36) with boundary conditions

$$\left. \begin{array}{l} u(s_1(t), t) = \psi_1(t) \\ u(s_2(t), t) = \psi_2(t) \end{array} \right\} \quad 0 \leq t \leq T$$

(3.39)

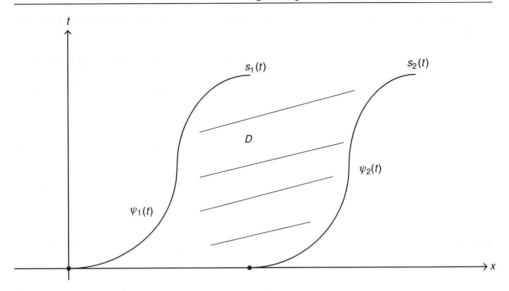

Figure 3.1   Region of integration D

and initial conditions

$$u(x, 0) = \varphi(x), \quad s_1(t) < x < s_2(t) \tag{3.40}$$

(see Figure 3.1). Here, ψ_1, ψ_2 and φ are given functions.

Finally, we assume the so-called compatibility conditions

$$\psi_1(0) = \varphi(0)$$
$$\psi_2(0) = \varphi(1) \tag{3.41}$$

The domain D is somewhat irregular because it is a function of time. We can map D onto the unit square by a change of variables

$$z = \frac{x - s_1(t)}{s_2(t) - s_1(t)}, \quad s_1(t) \neq s_2(t) \tag{3.42}$$

In this case the point (x, t) is mapped to the point (z, t) (see Bobisud, 1967).

The above problem is a model for many one-factor Black–Scholes equations (Wilmott, 1998; Tavella *et al.*, 2000). For example, standard European options can be formulated as a system (3.36), (3.39), (3.40) having constant boundaries while barrier options also fit into this model because in practice the boundaries (see Figure 3.1 again) are time-dependent. For example, a down-and-out/up-and-out call barrier option is described by the following model (Tavella *et al.*, 2000, p. 183):

$$\frac{\partial V}{\partial t} + \frac{1}{2}\sigma^2 S^2 \frac{\partial^2 V}{\partial S^2} + (r - D_0)S \frac{\partial V}{\partial S} - rV = 0$$
$$V[S \leq L(t), \ t] = 0$$
$$V[S \geq U(t), \ t] = 0 \tag{3.43}$$
$$V(S, T) = \max(S - K, 0)$$

In general, the barrier functions $L(t)$ and $U(t)$ can be analytic functions but they could also be the solution of ordinary differential equations or even the solution of other PDEs (for example, $U(t)$ could be a forward swap rate). We shall have more to say about this problem in later chapters.

3.9   SUMMARY AND CONCLUSIONS

We have given an introduction to second-order parabolic partial differential equations. We focused on expressing the solution of a parabolic initial boundary value problem in terms of its input data and we discussed several positivity and maximum principle theorems. We have also paid some attention to proving the existence of the solution to parabolic initial boundary value problems.

4
An Introduction to the Heat Equation
in One Dimension

4.1 INTRODUCTION AND OBJECTIVES

In this chapter we examine one of the most important differential equations in mathematical physics. This is the heat equation and it models many *diffusion phenomena* in real and artificial worlds. It is a special case of the second-order parabolic differential equations that we discussed in Chapter 3. In general terms diffusion describes the movement of one species, entity or material through some medium due to the presence of some concentration gradient. There are numerous examples of diffusion processes:

- Flow of heat in a one-dimensional bar (Tolstov, 1962)
- Animal and plant diffusion to new regions (Lotka, 1956)
- Movement of doping atoms into crystals (Fraser, 1986)
- VLSI device simulation (SIAM, 1983)
- Flow of water in a porous media (Bear, 1979)
- Diffusion models of neuron activity using Wiener and Ornstein–Uhlenbeck models (Arbib, 1998)
- Numerical reservoir engineering (Peaceman, 1977)
- Diffusion that can be attributed to Markov processes (Karatzas and Shreve, 1991).

Many of the diffusion processes originate in the physical sciences and we shall attempt to apply some of the results in this book. In particular, we need to show the role of the heat equation in the context of the Black–Scholes equation. In fact, the original Black-Scholes equation with constant volatility and risk-free interest rate can be reduced to the heat equation by a suitable change of variables (Wilmott, 1998).

Other reasons for studying the heat equation are:

- It is an essential component in more general convection–diffusion equations. These equations are models for the one-factor Black–Scholes equation and its generalisation to multiple dimensions.
- A number of the techniques in this chapter (for example, Fourier and Laplace transforms) are widely used in financial engineering and we discuss how they are applied in a simple but illustrative context.
- We produce an exact solution to *initial boundary value problems* for the heat equation. We can then compare this solution with discrete solutions from the Finite Difference Method.

In general, understanding the heat equation and its corresponding initial boundary value problems will help in our understanding of more general problems. A number of books on financial engineering discuss the heat equation while this chapter complements such treatments by examining it from a partial differential equation viewpoint. Eventually we shall show how to approximate the heat equation using several finite difference schemes.

4.2 MOTIVATION AND BACKGROUND

The one-dimensional heat equation describes the temperature distribution $u(x, t)$ at some point x in space and at some moment in time t. To be more specific, we shall be interested in the following regions:

- A bounded interval (both ends are finite) (a, b), $-\infty < a, b < \infty$
- A semi-infinite interval (this is usually the positive semi-infinite interval), $(0, \infty)$
- An infinite interval $(-\infty, \infty)$.

We introduce some key properties. In this chapter the interval represents a rod of some kind of material (for example, copper or steel). First, let K be the *thermal conductivity* of the rod material, c its *heat capacity* and ρ its *density*. It can be shown (Tolstov, 1962) that the temperature $u(x, t)$ satisfies the differential equation:

$$\frac{\partial u}{\partial t} = a^2 \frac{\partial^2 u}{\partial x^2} \quad (a^2 = K/c\rho) \tag{4.1}$$

In general, the coefficient a is a function of x and t and can even be nonlinear, for example, $a = a(x, t, u)$. Furthermore, it may be discontinuous or even degenerate (that is, it is zero at certain points). These cases occur in real applications but for the purposes of this chapter we shall assume that a is a constant.

If sources are present in the rod, then (4.1) is replaced by the *non-homogeneous* equation:

$$\frac{\partial u}{\partial t} = a^2 \frac{\partial^2 u}{\partial x^2} + q(x, t) \tag{4.2}$$

where the source term q is a function of x and t. As before, q may be nonlinear and even discontinuous at certain points.

For the moment we assume that the rod has finite length; it extends from $x = 0$ to $x = L$. Examining equation (4.1) we suspect that we need three auxiliary conditions in order to produce a unique solution. This intuition is well founded and to this end we define the following constraints:

- *Initial condition*: Equation (4.1) is first order in time, so we need one condition:

$$u(x, 0) = f(x), \quad 0 \le x \le L \tag{4.3}$$

- *Boundary conditions*: Equation (4.1) is second order with respect to the space variable x and thus we need two conditions. There are various possibilities:

  (a) Dirichlet conditions: The temperature is given at the end-point(s), for example,

$$u(0, t) = g(t), \quad t > 0 \tag{4.4}$$

  where $g(t)$ is a given function
  (b) Neumann conditions: The derivative of u is given at the end-point(s), for example,

$$\frac{\partial u}{\partial x}(0, t) = g(t), \quad t > 0 \tag{4.5}$$

  A special case is when $g(t) = 0$; in this case the rod is insulated, which means that the heat flux is zero on the boundary

(c) Robin condition: This is a combination of Dirichlet and Neumann boundary conditions

$$K\frac{\partial u}{\partial x}(0, t) = H[u(0, t) - F(t)], \quad t > 0$$

$$-K\frac{\partial u}{\partial x}(L, t) = H[u(L, t) - F(t)], \quad t > 0$$
(4.6)

Physically, the end-points are in contact with another medium and in this case we have applied Newton's law of cooling, which states that the heat flux at an end-point is proportional to the difference between the temperature of the rod and the (known) temperature $F(t)$ of the external medium. The parameter $H > 0$ is called *heat transfer coefficient*.

In general, we speak of an *initial boundary value problem* (IBVP) consisting of the partial differential equation (4.1) and its associated initial condition (4.3) and boundary conditions (of Dirichlet, Neumann or Robin type). In general, mathematicians are interested in determining necessary and sufficient conditions under which an IBVP will have a unique solution. Furthermore, they may also be interested in finding conditions under which the solution is sufficiently smooth.

We conclude this section defining the boundary conditions for semi-infinite and infinite intervals. For the semi-infinite case we formulate the problem as follows:

$$\frac{\partial u}{\partial t} = a^2\frac{\partial^2 u}{\partial x^2}, \quad 0 < x < \infty, \quad t > 0$$

$$u(x, 0) = f(x), \quad 0 \leq x < \infty$$
(4.7)

$$u(x, t) \text{ is bounded as } x \to \infty$$

whereas for a rod of infinite length we can formulate the problem (the so-called *Cauchy problem*) as follows:

$$\frac{\partial u}{\partial t} = a^2\frac{\partial^2 u}{\partial x^2}, \quad -\infty < x < \infty, \quad t > 0$$

$$u(x, 0) = f(x), \quad -\infty < x < \infty$$
(4.8)

$$u(x, t), \quad \frac{\partial u}{\partial x}(x, t) \to 0 \text{ as } x \to \pm\infty, \quad t > 0$$

In practical applications (for example, using finite differences) we must approximate infinity by some large number. Another tactic is to transform the original problem to one on a bounded interval by a change of variables, for example. We are then left with the problem of determining what the boundary condition should be at this new boundary point. We discuss this issue in detail in later chapters.

4.3   THE HEAT EQUATION AND FINANCIAL ENGINEERING

The heat equation is fundamental to financial engineering for a number of reasons. First, it is a component in the Black–Scholes equation and an understanding of it helps in our appreciation of Black–Scholes. Second, the Black–Scholes equation can be transformed to the heat equation by a change of variables, thus allowing us to produce closed form solutions. Finally, the boundary conditions for the heat equation can also be applied to the Black–Scholes equation, and it is possible to transform the Black–Scholes equation to the heat equation by a change of variables (Wilmott, 1998). To this end, consider the Black–Scholes equation

$$\frac{\partial V}{\partial t} + \frac{1}{2}\sigma^2 S^2 \frac{\partial^2 V}{\partial S^2} + rS\frac{\partial V}{\partial S} - rV = 0 \tag{4.9}$$

and let us define the new variable V by

$$V(S, t) = e^{\alpha x + \beta \tau} u(x, t) \tag{4.10}$$

where $\alpha = -\frac{1}{2}(2r/\sigma^2 - 1)$

$\beta = -\frac{1}{4}(2r/\sigma^2 + 1)^2$

$S = e^x, \quad t = T - 2\tau/\sigma^2$

We can then show that the function u satisfies the basic heat equation

$$\frac{\partial u}{\partial \tau} = \frac{\partial^2 u}{\partial x^2} \tag{4.11}$$

Specifying boundary conditions for the Black–Scholes equation is somewhat of a black art. It is possible to define Dirichlet, Neumann and Robin conditions but there are other alternatives.

Let us consider the semi-infinite case. This corresponds to the problem in which we model the underlying asset price as lying between zero and infinity. For a European call option $C(S, t)$ the boundary conditions are:

$$C(0, t) = 0$$
$$C(S, t) = S \quad \text{as } S \rightarrow \infty \tag{4.12}$$

The motivation in this case is that if the value of the asset is zero then the call option is worthless, and for very large S the value of the option will be the asset price. For a European put option $P(S, t)$ the boundary condition is

$$P(0, t) = Ke^{-r(T-t)}$$
$$P(S, t) = 0 \quad \text{as } S \rightarrow \infty \tag{4.13}$$

Here K is the option strike price, T is the expiry date and r is the risk-free interest rate. The first condition states that the value of the put option at $S = 0$ is the present value of the amount K received at time T. More generally, in the case of time-dependent (deterministic) interest rates we have

$$P(0, t) = K \exp\left(-\int_t^T r(s)\, ds\right) \tag{4.14}$$

The second condition in equation (4.13) states that we are unlikely to exercise, thus the value is zero when S is large.

4.4   THE SEPARATION OF VARIABLES TECHNIQUE

In this and the following sections we give an introduction to a technique that allows us to find the solution (in closed form) to certain kinds of partial differential equations. This is called the method of separation of variables (Kreider *et al.*, 1966; Tolstov, 1962; Constanda, 2002).

To this end, we motivate the method by applying it to the heat equation with zero Dirichlet boundary conditions. We examine the following initial boundary value problem for the heat equation:

$$\frac{\partial u}{\partial t} = a^2 \frac{\partial^2 u}{\partial x^2}, \quad 0 < x < L, \quad t > 0$$

$$u(x, 0) = f(x), \quad 0 \le x \le L \tag{4.15}$$

$$u(0, t) = u(L, t) = 0, \quad t > 0$$

We seek a solution of this problem in the form

$$u(x, t) = X(x)T(t)$$

Substituting this representation into the partial differential equation gives

$$\frac{X''(x)}{X(x)} = \frac{T'(t)}{a^2 T(t)} = -\lambda^2 \tag{4.16}$$

The left-hand side of (4.16) is a function of x only and the right-hand side is a function of t only. We then deduce that this is possible only when each side is equal to a so-called separation constant. Rearranging terms in (4.16) gives us the following ordinary differential equations:

$$X''(x) + \lambda^2 X(x) = 0, \quad 0 < x < L$$

$$T'(t) + \lambda^2 a^2 T(t) = 0, \quad t > 0 \tag{4.17}$$

Investigating the boundary conditions in (4.15) in relation to the representation $u = XT$ allows us to conclude that

$$X(0) = X(L) = 0$$

In general, the function X is the solution of a *Sturm–Liouville problem* whose eigenvalues and eigenvectors are given by

$$\lambda_n = \frac{n\pi}{L}, \quad X_n(x) = \sin\frac{n\pi x}{L}, \quad n = 1, 2, \ldots \tag{4.18}$$

respectively (Constanda, 2002). Furthermore, from (4.17) we see that the solution of the time component is given by

$$T_n(t) = A_n e^{-a^2 \lambda_n^2 t} = A_n e^{\frac{-a^2 n^2 \pi^2}{L^2} t}, \quad A_n \text{ constant} \tag{4.19}$$

The complete solution is then given by

$$u(x, t) = \sum_{n=1}^{\infty} u_n(x, t) \tag{4.20a}$$

where

$$u_n(x, t) = A_n \sin\frac{n\pi x}{L} \exp\left(-\frac{a^2 n^2 \pi^2}{L^2} t\right) \tag{4.20b}$$

It only remains now to determine the constant A_n in (4.20b). We achieve this end by using the initial condition in (4.15) and the orthogonal property of the trigonometric sin function. Thus

$$A_n = \frac{2}{L} \int_0^L f(x) \frac{\sin n\pi x}{L} dx, \quad n = 1, 2, \ldots \tag{4.21}$$

Summarising, we have produced a solution of the initial boundary value problem by the method of separation of variables. For more information, we refer the reader to Tolstov (1962).

We can calculate (4.20a) and (4.21) numerically for each value of x and t by summing the series. We can use the value as a benchmark against the solution from a finite difference scheme.

4.4.1   Heat flow in a rod with ends held at constant temperature

Consider the problem (Tolstov, 1962)

$$\frac{\partial u}{\partial t} = a^2 \frac{\partial^2 u}{\partial x^2}, \quad 0 < x < L, \quad t > 0$$

$$u(x, 0) = f(x), \quad 0 \le x \le L \tag{4.22}$$

$$u(0, t) = A, \quad u(L, t) = B, \quad (A, B \text{ constant}), \quad t > 0$$

The solution to this problem is given by

$$u(x, t) = \sum_{n=1}^{\infty} T_n(t) \sin \frac{n\pi x}{L} \tag{4.23}$$

where

$$T_n(t) = A_n \exp\left(-\frac{a^2 n^2 \pi^2}{L^2}\right) t + 2 \left[\frac{A - (-1)^n B}{\pi n}\right]$$

and

$$A_n = \frac{2}{L} \int_0^L f(x) \frac{\sin n\pi x}{L} dx - 2 \left[\frac{A - (-1)^n B}{\pi n}\right]$$

4.4.2   Heat flow in a rod whose ends are at a specified variable temperature

Consider the problem where the boundary conditions are time-dependent:

$$\frac{\partial u}{\partial t} = a^2 \frac{\partial^2 u}{\partial x^2}, \quad 0 < x < L, \quad t > 0$$

$$u(x, 0) = f(x), \quad 0 \le x \le L \tag{4.24}$$

$$u(0, t) = \varphi(t), \quad u(L, t) = \psi(t), \quad t > 0$$

The solution to this problem is given by

$$T_n = A_n \exp\left(-\frac{a^2 n^2 \pi^2}{L^2} t\right) + \frac{2a^2 \pi n}{L^2} \exp\left(-\frac{a^2 \pi^2 n^2}{L^2}\right) t$$

$$\times \int_0^L \exp\left(\frac{a^2 \pi^2 n^2 s}{L^2}\right) [\varphi(s) - (-1)^n \psi(s)] ds \tag{4.25}$$

where

$$A_n = \frac{2}{L} \int_0^L f(x) \frac{\sin \pi n x}{L} \, dx$$

4.4.3 Heat flow in an infinite rod

We now consider the important case of a rod that extends to infinity in both directions:

$$\frac{\partial u}{\partial t} = a^2 \frac{\partial^2 u}{\partial x^2}, \quad -\infty < x < \infty, \quad t > 0$$

$$u(x, 0) = f(x), \quad -\infty < x < \infty$$

(4.26)

In this case there are no boundary conditions but we do place some restrictions on the solution, for example, that u and its derivative with respect to the variable x should tend to zero at plus and minus infinity. Again we can apply the separation of variables technique but in contrast to a finite rod (where the eigenvalues are discrete), the eigenvalues vary continuously in this case. After a lengthy analysis (Tolstov, 1962) we produce a solution to problem (4.26):

$$u(x, t) = \frac{1}{2a\sqrt{\pi t}} \int_{-\infty}^{\infty} f(s) \exp\left(-\frac{(x - s)^2}{4a^2 t}\right) ds$$

(4.27)

From this equation we can see that the temperature approaches zero for very large x (the heat 'spreads' out). We can also see how the initial temperature $f(x)$ influences the subsequent evolution of the temperature in the rod. Incidentally, the function

$$G(x, t; \xi, 0) \equiv \frac{1}{2a\sqrt{\pi t}} \exp\left(-\frac{(x - \xi)^2}{4a^2 t}\right)$$

(4.28)

is called the *Gauss–Weierstrass kernel* or *influence* function and it is important in stochastic calculus and Brownian motion applications (see Karatzas and Shreve, 1991). Furthermore, this function has the following properties (Varadhan, 1980):

$$\int G(x, t; 0, 0) \, dx = 1 \quad \forall t > 0$$

$$\lim_{t \to 0+} \int G(x, t; 0, 0) f(x) \, dx = f(0)$$

(4.29)

4.4.4 Eigenfunction expansions

In this section we discuss the non-homogeneous heat equation:

$$\frac{\partial u}{\partial t} = a^2 \frac{\partial^2 u}{\partial x^2} + q(x, t), \quad 0 < x < L, \quad t > 0$$

$$u(x, 0) = f(x), \quad 0 \leq x \leq L$$

$$u(0, t) = u(L, t) = 0, \quad t > 0$$

(4.30)

The separation of variables technique does not work in this case because of the term $q(x, t)$. Instead, we consider the solution of (4.30) in the form

$$u(x, t) = \sum_{n=1}^{\infty} c_n(t) X_n(x)$$

(4.31)

where

$$X_n(x) = \frac{\sin n\pi x}{L}, \qquad \lambda_n = \frac{n\pi}{L}, \quad n = 1, 2, \ldots$$

In this case we wish to determine the time-dependent coefficients appearing in (4.31). To this end, differentiating the series term by term and noting that

$$X_n'' + \lambda_n^2 X_n = 0$$

we get

$$\sum_{n=1}^{\infty} [c_n'(t) + a^2 \lambda_n^2 c_n(t)] X_n(x) = q(x, t) \tag{4.32}$$

Multiplying this equation by the nth eigenfunction and integrating between 0 and L gives us

$$c_n'(t) + a^2 \lambda_n^2 c_n(t) = \frac{\displaystyle\int_0^L q(x, t) X_n(x)}{\displaystyle\int_0^L X_n^2(x)\, dx}, \quad t > 0, \quad n = 1, 2 \ldots \tag{4.33}$$

It is also easy to show that the initial condition for the time-dependent terms is given by:

$$c_n(0) = \frac{\displaystyle\int_0^L f(x) X_n(x)\, dx}{\displaystyle\int_0^L X_n^2(x)\, dx} \tag{4.34}$$

Thus, (4.33) and (4.34) constitute an initial-value problem whose solution can be found, either analytically or numerically.

The discussion in this subsection is very important because many approximate methods use a finite-dimensional variant of the series representation (4.31). For example, the finite element method (FEM), collocation, spectral and Meshless methods are based on the assumption that the approximate solution is represented as a series solution of some kind.

4.5 TRANSFORMATION TECHNIQUES FOR THE HEAT EQUATION

We now discuss some more techniques for finding the solution of the heat equation. This equation is a function of two independent variables. The essence of an integral transformation method is to reduce the original problem to some kind of ordinary differential equation, finding the solution of this problem and then applying the inverse transform to recover the solution of the original problem. We discuss the Laplace and Fourier transforms as applied to the heat equations. These are popular techniques in the financial engineering literature (Carr and Madan, 1999; Fu et al., 1998; Craddock et al., 2000).

4.5.1   Laplace transform

Consider the following initial boundary value problem equation on a bounded interval:

$$\frac{\partial u}{\partial t} = a^2 \frac{\partial^2 u}{\partial x^2}, \quad 0 < x < L, \quad t > 0$$

$$u(x, 0) = f(x), \quad 0 < x < L \tag{4.35}$$

$$u(0, t) = u(L, t) = 0, \quad t > 0$$

The Laplace transform of a function f is given by

$$\mathcal{L}[f](s) = F(s) = \int_0^\infty f(t) e^{-st} \, dt$$

Applying this transform to the initial boundary value problem (4.35) gives us the two-point boundary value problem:

$$a^2 U''(x, s) - sU(x, s) + f(x) = 0, \quad 0 < x < \infty$$

$$U(0, s) = U(L, S) = 0 \tag{4.36}$$

$$U(x, s) \text{ bounded as } x \to \infty$$

where $\mathcal{L}[u](x, s) = U(x, s)$.

We can now apply well-known techniques to find the solution $U(x, s)$ of (4.36). Having done that we can then use Laplace transform tables to find the original solution of problem (4.23) (Hochstadt, 1964).

4.5.2   Fourier transform for the heat equation

Consider the Cauchy problem on an infinite interval:

$$\frac{\partial u}{\partial t} = a^2 \frac{\partial^2 u}{\partial x^2}, \quad -\infty < x < \infty, \quad t > 0$$

$$u(x, 0) = f(x), \quad -\infty < x < \infty \tag{4.37}$$

$$u(x, t), \quad \frac{\partial u}{\partial x}(x, t) \to 0 \text{ as } x \to \pm\infty, \quad t > 0$$

The Fourier transform is defined by

$$\mathcal{F}[f](\omega) = \frac{1}{2\pi} \int_{-\infty}^\infty f(x) e^{i\omega x} \, dx \tag{4.38}$$

We now apply the Fourier transform the initial value problem (4.37) to an initial value problem for an ordinary differential equation in the *transform domain*.

$$U'(\omega, t) + a^2 \omega^2 U(\omega, t) = 0, \quad t > 0$$

$$U(\omega, 0) = F(\omega) \tag{4.39}$$

where

$$\mathcal{F}[u](\omega, t) = U(\omega, t) \quad \text{and} \quad \mathcal{F}[f](\omega) = F(\omega)$$

In order to recover the original solution we apply the inverse Fourier transform defined by

$$\mathcal{F}^{-1}[F](x) = f(x) = \int_{-\infty}^{\infty} F(\omega) e^{-i\omega x} \, dw$$

to (4.39). After some calculations we find (Constanda 2002) that the solution of (4.39) is given by

$$U(\omega, t) = F(\omega) e^{-a^2 \omega^2 t} \tag{4.40}$$

and then

$$u(x, t) = \frac{1}{2a\sqrt{\pi t}} \int_{-\infty}^{\infty} f(\xi) \exp\left(-\frac{(x - \xi)^2}{4a^2 t}\right) d\xi \tag{4.41}$$

which is the same as the result we obtained by using the method of separation of variables (see equation (4.27)).

4.6   SUMMARY AND CONCLUSIONS

In this chapter we have examined the one-dimensional heat equation. This is a prototype example of a diffusion equation and an understanding of it will be of benefit when we discuss more general equations. The focus in this chapter is on giving an overview of a number of analytical methods that allow us to produce an exact solution to the heat equation. The techniques are:

- Separation of variables
- Eigenfunction expansions
- Laplace transform
- Fourier transform.

These techniques are of interest in their own right and they have many applications in numerical analysis and financial engineering. As good references we recommend Kreider *et al.* (1966), Tolstov (1962) and Constanda (2002).

5
An Introduction to the Method
of Characteristics

5.1 INTRODUCTION AND OBJECTIVES

In this chapter we introduce the Method of Characteristics (MOC). This method is used in the analysis of fluid flow applications; it is simple to use and to code in a programming language and it has been used in financial engineering applications, for example, Asian options and certain kinds of real options. The reader can skip this chapter on a first reading without loss of continuity.

This chapter discusses the following topics. In section 2 we motivate MOC by applying it to a first-order scalar hyperbolic equation. It is useful to understand this problem because it is an essential component when studying certain classes of two-factor models in financial engineering. In particular, convection terms are of this type. Section 3 is an extension of MOC to second-order hyperbolic equations and we discuss how to solve these equations numerically. We then move to a discussion of hyperbolic equations for financial engineering applications in section 5.4, with special applications to real options (in this case the harvesting of wood). In section 5.5 we show how to apply MOC to systems of equations and how to transform such equations to systems of ordinary differential equations. Finally, section 5.6 deals with the nasty world of discontinuous initial conditions and other problems (such as reflections at downstream computational boundaries) and why discontinuous initial conditions always lead to discontinuous solutions along the characteristic lines.

It can be proved that the solutions of parabolic equations are smooth even if the initial conditions or boundary conditions are not smooth. Hyperbolic equations are different because discontinuities in the initial conditions are propagated as discontinuities into the solution domain.

The MOC is used in combination with convection–diffusion equations and for this reason we consider it to be important to pay some attention to it.

5.2 FIRST-ORDER HYPERBOLIC EQUATIONS

In order to motivate how MOC works we consider the first-order scalar, quasilinear hyperbolic equation

$$b\frac{\partial u}{\partial t} + a\frac{\partial u}{\partial x} = c \tag{5.1}$$

where any of the coefficients a, b or c is a function of x, t and u (this latter dependence on the unknown solution u makes equation (5.1) quasilinear). If b is not zero we can write (5.1) in the form

$$\frac{\partial u}{\partial t} + \frac{a}{b}\frac{\partial u}{\partial x} - \frac{c}{b} = 0 \tag{5.2}$$

Now, from the chain rule for differentiation we see that

$$\frac{du}{dt} = \frac{\partial u}{\partial t} + \frac{dx}{dt}\frac{\partial u}{\partial x}$$

or

$$\frac{dx}{dt}\frac{\partial u}{\partial x} + \frac{\partial u}{\partial t} - \frac{du}{dt} = 0 \tag{5.3}$$

By subtracting (5.3) from (5.2) and using a little bit of arithmetic we get

$$\left(\frac{a}{b} - \frac{dx}{dt}\right)\frac{\partial u}{\partial x} - \left(\frac{c}{b} - \frac{du}{dt}\right) = 0 \tag{5.4}$$

This equation holds at arbitrary points in (x, t) space. We now define special points where equation (5.4) reduces to an ordinary differential equation. To this end, if we define the so-called characteristic curves

$$\frac{dx}{dt} = \frac{a}{b} \tag{5.5}$$

then (5.4) reduces to the ordinary differential equation

$$\frac{du}{dt} = \frac{c}{b} \tag{5.6}$$

Equation (5.6) can now be integrated by analytical methods or numerical methods (see Dahlquist, 1974). For example, we can use an Euler scheme or some kind of predictor–corrector to integrate (5.6) along the *characteristic curves* (5.5). Finally, we can write equations (5.5) and (5.6) in the combined forms

$$\frac{dx}{a} = \frac{dt}{b} = \frac{du}{c} \tag{5.7}$$

A discussion of ordinary differential equations, their numerical approximation and implementation in C++ is given in Duffy (2004).

5.2.1   An example

We give an example of how to use MOC (the example is taken from Huyakorn and Pinder, 1983). The equation is

$$u\frac{\partial u}{\partial t} + \sqrt{x}\frac{\partial u}{\partial x} + u^2 = 0 \tag{5.8}$$

with initial condition

$$u(x, 0) = 1, \quad 0 < x < \infty \tag{5.9}$$

In this case equation (5.7) takes the form

$$\frac{dx}{\sqrt{x}} = \frac{dt}{u} = \frac{du}{-u^2} \tag{5.10}$$

We now consider a point on the characteristic curve with $x = A$ and $t = 0$. We wish to integrate the first equation in (5.10) from this point to another arbitrary point (x, t) as follows

$$\int_A^x \frac{dy}{\sqrt{y}} = \int_0^t \frac{dt}{u}$$

or

$$2\left(\sqrt{x} - \sqrt{A}\right) = \int_0^t \frac{dt}{u} \tag{5.11}$$

We now use the second equation in (5.10) to evaluate the integral on the right-hand side of (5.11); again, this equation is:

$$\frac{dt}{u} = \frac{du}{-u^2} \quad \text{or} \quad dt = -\frac{du}{u}$$

Thus

$$\int_0^t dt = -\int_{u_0}^u \frac{du}{u}$$

Integrating this equation and using the initial condition (5.9) we get

$$t = \ln\left(\frac{1}{u}\right)$$

from which we deduce that

$$\frac{1}{u} = e^t$$

Substituting this equation into equation (5.11) and integrating in $(0, t)$ we get

$$t = \ln\left(2\sqrt{x} + 1 - 2\sqrt{A}\right)$$

or

$$e^t - 1 = 2(\sqrt{x} - \sqrt{A})$$

Finally, along this characteristic direction the solution of equation (5.8) is given by

$$u = e^{-t} = \frac{1}{2\sqrt{x} + 1 - 2\sqrt{A}}$$

This example shows how to find the exact solution of a first-order quasilinear hyperbolic differential equation using an analytical approach. To summarise the main steps, we first found the characteristic direction and then found the solution of the equation along this direction. We can use this technique in a number of quantitative finance applications relating to stochastic volatility and bond models. In general, it can be difficult to find an analytical solution and for this reason we resort to numerical methods.

5.3   SECOND-ORDER HYPERBOLIC EQUATIONS

We now extend MOC to the study of the second-order hyperbolic equation

$$a\frac{\partial^2 u}{\partial x^2} + b\frac{\partial^2 u}{\partial x \partial t} + c\frac{\partial^2 u}{\partial t^2} + e = 0 \tag{5.12}$$

where the coefficients a, b, c and e are functions of x, t, u and the first derivatives of u. Define p and q as follows

$$p = \frac{\partial u}{\partial x}, \qquad q = \frac{\partial u}{\partial t}$$

Then using the chain rule we get

$$\begin{cases} \dfrac{dp}{dx} = \dfrac{\partial^2 u}{\partial x^2} + \dfrac{\partial^2 u}{\partial t \partial x}\dfrac{dt}{dx} \\[4mm] \dfrac{dq}{dt} = \dfrac{\partial^2 u}{\partial t^2} + \dfrac{\partial^2 u}{\partial x \partial t}\dfrac{dx}{dt} \end{cases} \tag{5.13}$$

Solving for the 'pure' second derivative terms in equation (5.13) in x and t, and inserting the result into equation (5.12), shows that

$$\frac{\partial^2 u}{\partial x \partial t}\left(-a\frac{dt}{dx} + b - c\frac{dx}{dt}\right) + a\frac{dp}{dx} + c\frac{dq}{dt} + e = 0 \tag{5.14}$$

Multiplying (5.14) by $-dt/dx$ gives

$$\frac{\partial^2 u}{\partial x \partial t}\left[a\left(\frac{dt}{dx}\right)^2 - b\frac{dt}{dx} + c\right] - \left(a\frac{dp}{dx} + c\frac{dq}{dt} + e\right)\frac{dt}{dx} = 0 \tag{5.15}$$

We now define the so-called *characteristic curves* so that the term in the square brackets in (5.15) is zero. Since this term is a quadratic equation in dt/dx we get the following expression for dt/dx:

$$\left(\frac{dt}{dx}\right)_{\pm} = \frac{b \pm \sqrt{b^2 - 4ac}}{2a} \tag{5.16}$$

Since (5.12) is hyperbolic we know that the square root term in (5.16) is positive and hence the characteristic curves exist in real space (that is, they are not complex-valued).

5.3.1   Numerical integration along the characteristic lines

We now describe how to solve equation (5.12) by numerical integration along the two characteristic lines (5.16). For convenience, we define the roots of equation (5.16) as follows

$$\left(\frac{dt}{dx}\right)_{+} = f, \qquad \left(\frac{dt}{dx}\right)_{-} = g$$

We focus on an initial boundary-value problem and to this end we examine the situation as shown in Figure 5.1. In particular, we give boundary conditions at $x = 0$ and at $x = L$ as well as the initial conditions at $t = 0$. To commence, let us assume that we are given the values of u at the points P and Q because they are on the initial line $t = 0$. By moving along the

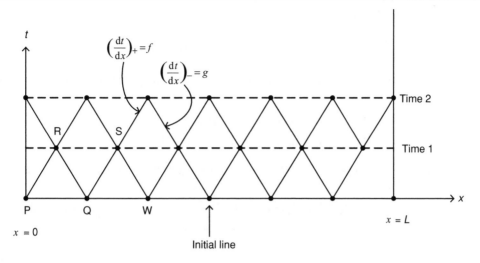

Figure 5.1   Grid points for MOC

characteristic lines passing through these points, the point R can be located as shown in the figure. In other words, we determine complete information about point R by the following two-stage procedure:

1. Find the coordinates of R by solving equation (5.16) by an application of the explicit Euler method. We take the positive characteristic as an example. We can then rewrite the equation as follows:

$$dt = dxf$$

or

$$\int_P^R dt = \int_P^R dxf \approx f_P \int_P^R dx = f_P(x_R - x_P)$$

or

$$t_R - t_P = f_P(x_R - x_P)$$

A similar equation for the negative characteristic gives

$$t_R - t_Q = g_Q(x_R - x_Q)$$

Solving for the coordinates of R in these last two equations (two equations in two unknowns x_R and t_R) gives:

$$x_R = \frac{f_P x_P - g_Q x_Q + t_Q - t_P}{f_P - g_Q}$$
$$t_R = t_P + f_P(x_R - x_P)$$

2. We find the first-order derivatives in x and t of u at the point R. To this end, we now write the non-bracketed part of equation (5.15) along the charateristic curve in the following form

by multiplying it by dx:

$$a\left(\frac{dt}{dx}\right)dp + c\,dq + e\,dt = 0 \tag{5.17}$$

in finite difference form (using the explicit Euler scheme) along the line $(dt/dx)_+ = f$ and $(dt/dx)_- = g$, respectively:

$$\begin{cases} a_p f_p (p_R - p_P) + c_p(q_R - q_P) + e_P (t_R - t_P) = 0 \\ a_Q g_Q(p_R - p_Q) + c_Q(q_R - q_Q) + e_Q (t_R - t_Q) = 0 \end{cases}$$

Some tedious but simple arithmetic gives the following needed information by solving the above equation:

$$p_R = \frac{a_p f_P p_P/c_p - a_Q f_Q p_Q/C_Q + q_p - q_Q + (e_p c_p - e_Q/c_Q)t_R + e_p t_p/c_p - e_Q t_Q/c_Q}{a_p f_p/c_p - a_Q f_Q/c_Q}$$

$$q_R = e_p(t_P - t_Q)/c_p + a_p f_p(p_P - p_R)/c_p + q_P$$

3. Having found the derivatives p and q at the point R we find the value u by using the formula

$$du = p\,dx + q\,dt$$

We now integrate this equation using the midpoint scheme in order to achieve second-order accurary. The formula that we use in going from P to R is

$$\int_P^R du = \int_P^R p\,dx + \int_P^R q\,dt$$

or

$$u_R - u_P \approx \tfrac{1}{2}(p_P + p_R)(x_R - x_P) + \tfrac{1}{2}(q_P + q_R)(t_R - t_P)$$

Similarly, in going from Q to R we get

$$u_R - u_Q \approx \tfrac{1}{2}(p_Q + p_R)(x_R - x_Q) + \tfrac{1}{2}(q_Q + q_R)(t_R - t_Q)$$

Adding these last two equations we then get the final representation for the value of u at the point R

$$\begin{aligned} u_R = \tfrac{1}{2}\big[&u_p + \tfrac{1}{2}(p_R + p_P)(x_R - x_P) + \tfrac{1}{2}(q_R + q_p)(t_R - t_P) \\ &+ u_Q + \tfrac{1}{2}(p_R + p_Q)(x_R - x_Q) + \tfrac{1}{2}(q_R + q_Q)(t_R - t_Q)\big] \end{aligned} \tag{5.18}$$

In general this is a quasilinear equation and we must use some kind of iteration to solve it at R. To this end, improved values are obtained by solving

$$t_R - t_P = \tfrac{1}{2}(f_P + f_R)(x_R - x_P)$$

$$t_R - t_Q = \tfrac{1}{2}(f_P + f_Q)(x_R - x_Q)$$

Improved values for p_R and q_R are obtained by solving

$$\bar{a}_p \bar{f}_P(p_R - p_P) + \bar{c}_p(q_R - q_P) + \bar{e}_P(t_R - t_P) = 0$$

$$\bar{a}_Q \bar{g}_Q(p_R - p_Q) + \bar{c}_Q(q_R - q_Q) + \bar{e}_Q(t_R - t_Q) = 0$$

where

$$\bar{a}_p = \tfrac{1}{2}(a_P + a_R), \qquad \bar{c}_p = \tfrac{1}{2}(c_P + c_R), \qquad \bar{e}_p = \tfrac{1}{2}(e_P + e_R)$$

$$\bar{a}_Q = \tfrac{1}{2}(c_Q + a_R), \qquad \bar{c}_Q = \tfrac{1}{2}(c_Q + c_R), \qquad \bar{e}_Q = \tfrac{1}{2}(e_Q + e_R)$$

If Q is close to P the number of iterations should be small.

4. Having found the solution at R, we can then apply steps (1) to (3) to the point S (see Figure 5.1). This point is the intersection of the characteristic lines through Q and another initial point W. Notice that at the vertical boundaries $x = 0$ and $x = L$ either the value u or its derivative p are given.

A special case is when the hyperbolic equation (5.12) is linear; then the terms on the right-hand side of (5.18) are known or can be calculated.

5.4 APPLICATIONS TO FINANCIAL ENGINEERING

Although hyperbolic equations are not as common as parabolic equations in financial engineering applications, there are opportunities for the application of MOC to certain classes of PDE that model two-factor equations. In general, we can employ MOC in cases where one of the underlying quantities has no diffusion term and is in fact modelled as a deterministic process.

A prototypical PDE is:

$$\frac{\partial V}{\partial t} + \sigma_1 \frac{\partial^2 V}{\partial x^2} + \mu_1 \frac{\partial V}{\partial x} + \mu_2 \frac{\partial V}{\partial y} + bV = f \tag{5.19}$$

In this case V is a derivative quantity based on the two state variables x and y. The PDE is second-order parabolic in x and first-order hyperbolic in y. The PDE in y is a wave equation and thus is deterministic. Some examples where this kind of equation is necessary up are:

1. Asian options (Ingersoll, 1987; Wilmott *et al.*, 1993); in this case the variable x plays the role of the underlying asset price S and y plays the role of some average (for example, denoted by I or A) of the underlying:

$$I = \int_0^t S(\tau)\,d\tau \tag{5.20}$$

2. Pricing Bermudan swaptions (Cheyette, 1992, Andreason, 2001); the Cheyette model is the specification of the volatility structure of the continuously compounded forward rates in the HJM (Heath–Jarrow–Morton) model. We do not go into the details of how the Cheyette PDE is set up, but the basic PDE is given by

$$\frac{\partial V}{\partial t} + \tfrac{1}{2}\eta^2 \frac{\partial^2 V}{\partial x^2} + (-Kx + y)\frac{\partial V}{\partial x} + (\eta^2 - 2Ky)\frac{\partial V}{\partial y} - rV = 0 \tag{5.21}$$

Equations of the form (5.21) can be used to model zero-coupon bonds, for example. Again, we see that this equation has the same form as equation (5.19). As noted in Andreasen (2001), standard ADI difference schemes are prone to spurious oscillations because of the absence of a second-order derivative in the y direction. Using centred difference schemes in the y direction will also cause problems because these schemes are only weakly stable (Peaceman, 1977). Some alternatives to these schemes are:

- Use one-sided difference schemes in the y direction (*upwinding*)
- Use ADI or splitting methods, using centred difference schemes in the x direction and the method of characteristics in the y direction (since this is a first-order hyperbolic equation)
- Modern schemes, such as Implicit Explicit (IMEX) splitting schemes (Hundsdorfer and Verwer, 2003).

We shall discuss each of these methods in later chapters.

3. Real options and forest harvesting decisions (Insley and Rollins, 2002). This is a two-factor real options model of the harvesting decisions over infinite rotations with mean reverting stochastic prices. The authors view the opportunity to harvest a stand of trees as a real option similar to an American option that can be exercised at any time. The exercise price is the cost of harvesting the trees and transporting them to the point of sale. Embedded in the tree-harvesting opportunity is the option to choose the optimal harvest time based on wood volume and price. There is also an option to abandon the investment if wood prices are too low.

The mean reverting price process is given by

$$dP = \eta(P_{avg} - P)\,dt + \sigma P\,dz \tag{5.22}$$

where
P = the price of saw logs

η = mean reversion parameter

σ = the constant variance rate

dz = increment of a Wiener process.

In general, this model tells us that the price reverts to a long run average of P_{avg}. We assume the wood volume Q is deterministic and depends on the time since the last harvest

$$dQ = \varphi(Q)\,dt$$

for some function φ.

The basic PDE model for this problem is (Dixit and Pindyck, 1994; Insley and Rollins, 2002)

$$\frac{\partial V}{\partial \tau} - \varphi\frac{\partial V}{\partial Q} = \tfrac{1}{2}\sigma^2 P^2\frac{\partial^2 V}{\partial P^2} + \eta(P_{avg} - P)\frac{\partial V}{\partial P} - \rho V + A + \Pi(V) \tag{5.23}$$

where
V = value of the opportunity to harvest

τ = time to expiry of the option ($\tau = T - t$)

Q = current volume of timber

$\varphi = dQ/dt$

P = price of saw logs

A = the per-period amenity value of standing forest less any management costs

P = annual discount rate.

Furthermore, the term $\Pi(V)$ is a so-called *penalty term* that prevents the value of the option V from ever falling below the payout from harvesting immediately. We shall encounter more examples of penalty terms in the chapters on options with early exercise features.

We must now specify the boundary conditions for problem (5.23). The region of integration is a two-dimensional semi-infinite region in (P, Q) space and we specify boundary conditions as follows:

$$
\begin{cases}
\text{(a) As } P \to 0, \quad \mathrm{d}P \to \eta \overline{P} \\[6pt]
\text{(b) As } P \to \infty, \text{ chose } \frac{\partial^2 V}{\partial P^2} = 0 \text{ (linearity boundary condition)} \\[6pt]
\text{(c) As } Q \to 0, \text{ since } \varphi(Q) \geq 0 \text{ when } Q \geq 0, \text{ no boundary condition is needed} \\[2pt]
\quad \text{and in this case we have a first-order hyperbolic equation in the } Q \text{ direction.} \\[6pt]
\qquad\qquad \dfrac{\partial V}{\partial \tau} - \varphi \dfrac{\partial V}{\partial Q} = 0 \\[6pt]
\quad \text{We see that the outgoing characteristics are in the negative } Q \text{ direction.} \\[6pt]
\text{(d) As } Q \to \infty, \text{ we assume } \varphi(Q) \to 0, \text{ no boundary condition is needed.}
\end{cases}
\tag{5.24}
$$

The initial/terminal condition is given by

$$
V(P, Q, T) = 0 \quad (t = T) \tag{5.25a}
$$

or equivalently

$$
V(P, Q, 0) = 0 \quad (\tau = 0) \tag{5.25b}
$$

We then assume that $V = 0$ when T is large, and thus we make T large enough that this assumption has a negligible effect on the current V.

5.4.1   Generalisations

The details of the numerical approximation of this problem are given in Insley and Rollins (2000). In short, they use central difference schems in the P direction and MOC in the Q direction.

We return to the general equation (5.19). In financial terms, we reason that its solution depends on the state variable x (which is stochastic) and hence we see a specific convective term and volatility term σ. This reflects the stochastic differential equation for the state variable x. However, the variable y is deterministic and has no volatility terms. Hence we expect its derivative quantity to have a more 'wave-like' property, and this is seen in the hyperbolic component in equation (5.19).

5.5   SYSTEMS OF EQUATIONS

It is possible to apply the Method of Characteristics to system of equations. To this end, let us consider the quasilinear system of first-order equations

$$
\sum_{j=1}^{n} a_{ij} \frac{\partial u_i}{\partial x} + \sum_{j=1}^{n} b_{ij} \frac{\partial u_i}{\partial t} = F_i, \quad i = 1, \dots, n \tag{5.26}
$$

in the two independent variables x and t. The coefficients appearing in (5.26) are functions of x, t and u but they do not depend on the derivatives of u. Let us define the matrices and the vectors

$$\left. \begin{array}{l} A = (a_{ij}) \\ B = (b_{ij}) \end{array} \right\} \quad i, j = 1, \ldots, n \tag{5.27a}$$

$$\left. \begin{array}{l} U = {}^t(u_1, \ldots, u_n) \\ F = {}^t(F_1, \ldots, F_n) \end{array} \right\} \quad i = 1, \ldots, n \tag{5.27b}$$

We can then write (5.26) in vector form

$$A \frac{\partial U}{\partial x} + B \frac{\partial U}{\partial t} = F \tag{5.28}$$

Definition 1. The system (5.28) is said to be *hyperbolic* if the eigenvalue problem

$$\det(A - \lambda B) = 0 \tag{5.29}$$

has n real roots corresponding n real directions in the (x, t) plane (we assume that these roots are distinct).

We now find the characteristic lines for system (5.28) by a generalisation of the process for the scalar case. As before, the total derivative of U is given by

$$dU = \frac{\partial U}{\partial t} dt + \frac{\partial U}{\partial x} dx \tag{5.30}$$

We then see that equations (5.28) and (5.30) constitute a system of $2n$ equations in the $2n$ unknowns

$$\frac{\partial u_j}{\partial t}, \quad \frac{\partial u_j}{\partial x}, \quad j = 1, \ldots, n \tag{5.31}$$

Formally, the system of equations is

$$\begin{aligned} A \frac{\partial U}{\partial x} + B \frac{\partial U}{\partial t} &= F \\ I \, dt \frac{\partial U}{\partial x} + I \, dx \frac{\partial U}{\partial x} &= dU \end{aligned} \tag{5.32}$$

where I is the unit diagonal matrix of size n.
Define the matrix D by

$$D = \begin{pmatrix} A & B \\ Idt & Idx \end{pmatrix} \tag{5.33}$$

Then the system (5.32) has a solution if

$$\det(D) = 0 \tag{5.34}$$

Thus, condition (5.34) allows us to find the characteristic directions for the system (5.26).

5.5.1   An example

Let us consider the 2×2 system

$$\left.\begin{array}{l} \dfrac{\partial u}{\partial t} + a_1 \dfrac{\partial v}{\partial x} = 0 \\[2mm] \dfrac{\partial v}{\partial t} + a_2 \dfrac{\partial u}{\partial x} = 0 \end{array}\right\} \quad a_1, a_2 > 0 \text{ constant} \qquad (5.35)$$

By calculating the determinant, the condition (5.34) reduces to

$$\left(\frac{dx}{dt}\right)^2 = a_1 a_2 \qquad \text{or} \qquad \frac{dx}{dt} = \pm\sqrt{a_1 a_2} \qquad (5.36)$$

A special case of (5.35) occurs with acoustic waves in a homogeneous medium

$$\begin{array}{l} \dfrac{\partial u}{\partial t} + \dfrac{1}{\rho} \dfrac{\partial p}{\partial x} = 0 \\[3mm] \dfrac{\partial p}{\partial t} + \rho c^2 \dfrac{\partial u}{\partial x} = 0 \end{array} \qquad (5.37)$$

where u is the sound and p is the pressure. The variable ρ is the density and c is the local speed of sound in the medium. In this case the local ordinary differential equations and characteristic directions are

$$\begin{array}{l} \dfrac{du}{dt} = 0 \text{ on } C^+ = \left\{(x,t): \dfrac{dx}{dt} = +c\right\} \\[4mm] \dfrac{du}{dt} = 0 \text{ on } C^- = \left\{(x,t): \dfrac{dx}{dt} = -c\right\} \end{array} \qquad (5.38)$$

5.6   PROPAGATION OF DISCONTINUITIES

A property of hyperbolic equations is that discontinuities in initial conditions lead to discontinuous solutions at later times. We shall give an example that has a discontinuous initial value. Consider the initial value problem

$$\frac{\partial u}{\partial x} + \frac{\partial u}{\partial y} = 1, \quad y \geq 0, \quad -\infty < x < \infty \qquad (5.39)$$

where u is known at point $A(x_a, 0)$ on the x-axis (see Figure 5.2). The characteristic direction is given by $dx = dy$ and u satisfies $du = dy$ on this line. Hence the characteristic through A is $y = x - x_a$ and the solution is $u = u(A) + y$. Now consider the initial condition

$$\begin{array}{l} u(x,0) = f_1(x), \quad -\infty < x < x_b \\[2mm] u(x,0) = f_2(x), \quad x_b < x < \infty \end{array} \qquad (5.40)$$

To the left of the characteristic $y = x - x_b$ the solution is

$$u_{(L)} = f_1(x_a) + y \text{ along } y = x - x_b$$

To the right of the characteristic $y = x - x_b$ the solution is

$$u_{(R)} = f_2(x_c) + y \text{ along } y = x - x_c$$

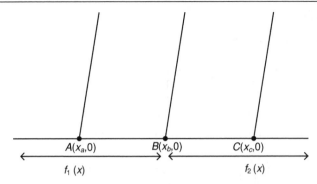

Figure 5.2   Discontinuous initial condition

The jump in the solution to the left and right of B is

$$u_{(L)} - u_{(R)} = f_1(x_a) - f_2(x_c)$$

Letting both A and C converge to B we see that the solution is discontinuous because we have assumed that the initial condition (5.40) is not continuous, i.e. $f_1(x_b) \neq f_2(x_b)$.

Hence we conclude that when the initial condition is discontinuous at a particular point B, then the solution is discontinuous along the characteristic curve Γ emanating from B. The effect of this initial discontinuity does not diminish as we move away from B along Γ. The situation with parabolic equations is quite different: initial discontinuities tend to be localised and diminish rapidly with distance from the point of discontinuity.

5.6.1   Other problems

It is possible to analyse first-order hyperbolic problems in an infinite interval using Fourier transforms, but this technique is not suitable for initial boundary value problems with discontinuities at the boundaries or when we need to perform mesh refinement (Vichnevetsky and Bowles, 1982). Let us consider the model hyperbolic problem

$$\frac{\partial u}{\partial t} + a \frac{\partial u}{\partial x} = 0, \quad a > 0, \quad x \in (0, L)$$

and its semi-discretisation

$$\frac{du_j}{dt} + a \left(\frac{u_{j+1} - u_{j-1}}{2h} \right) = 0, \quad j = 1, \ldots, J - 1$$

The boundary conditions are: at $x = 0$,

$$u(0, t) = g(t)$$

and at $x = L$,

$$\frac{du_J}{dt} + a \left(\frac{u_J - u_{J-1}}{h} \right) = 0$$

We thus impose the 'real' boundary condition at $x = 0$, while at $x = L$ we approximate the differential equation itself by a one-sided difference scheme. As discussed in Vichnevetsky and Bowles (1982), this approach leads to spurious reflections.

5.7 SUMMARY AND CONCLUSIONS

We have given an introduction to the Method of Characteristics (MOC), which is used mainly for hyperbolic equations. Its added value is that a partial differential equation can be reduced to an ordinary differential equation along so-called *characteristic curves*.

We discussed the application of MOC to financial engineering applications and it can be seen as an alternative to the finite difference method in such situations.

First-order hyperbolic equations need to be studied in certain financial engineering applications, for example in two-factor models where one underlying has a deterministic behaviour. Asian and Real options are typical examples. Then the derivative quantity will be modelled by a partial differential equation, one of whose components has no diffusion term.

Part II
Finite Difference Methods: the Fundamentals

6

An Introduction to the Finite
Difference Method

6.1 INTRODUCTION AND OBJECTIVES

Part II introduces the finite difference method (FDM). The chapters in this part focus on producing accurate and robust schemes for second-order parabolic and first-order hyperbolic partial differential equations in two independent variables, usually called x and t. The first variable x plays the role of a space coordinate and the second variable t plays the role of time. We model the partial differential equations by approximating the derivatives using divided differences. These latter quantities are defined at so-called discrete mesh points. Having motivated FDM in a generic setting we then apply the resulting finite difference schemes to the one-factor Black–Scholes model in Part III.

In this chapter we investigate the application of FDM to ordinary differential equations (ODEs). An ODE has one independent variable and hence it is conceptually easier to understand and to approximate than equations in two or more variables. In particular, we examine a special kind of problem in this chapter. This is called first-order initial value problems (IVP). They are useful objects of study in their own right and our objective is to approximate them using FDM in order to pave the way for more complex applications later in the book. In particular, the added value is:

- Initial value problems provide the motivation for finite difference schemes that will be used to approximate the time dimension in the Black–Scholes partial differential equation.
- In this chapter we introduce notation that will be used throughout the book. We aim to be as consistent as possible in our use of notation.

We shall also introduce the concept of divided differences and how we use them to approximate the first- and second-order derivatives of real-valued functions of one variable. The chapter should be read and understood before embarking on the other chapters. It is fundamental.

6.2 FUNDAMENTALS OF NUMERICAL DIFFERENTIATION

In this section let us look at a real-valued function of a real variable, as follows:

$$y = f(x) \tag{6.1}$$

In general we are interested in finding approximations to the first and second derivatives of the function f. This is needed because, in general, the form of the function f is unknown and it is thus impossible to calculate its derivatives analytically. To this end, we must resort to numerical approximations. Suppose that we wish to approximate the first derivative of y at some point a (see Figure 6.1) and assume that h is a (small) positive number. The first

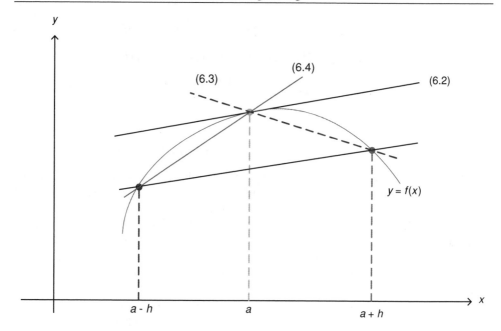

Figure 6.1   Motivating divided differences

approximation (called the *centred difference formula*) is given by

$$f'(a) \approx \frac{f(a+h) - f(a-h)}{2h} \tag{6.2}$$

Another approximation is called the *forward difference formula* given by

$$f'(a) \approx \frac{f(a+h) - f(a)}{h} \tag{6.3}$$

Finally, the *backward difference formula* is given by

$$f'(a) \approx \frac{f(a) - f(a-h)}{h} \tag{6.4}$$

For future work, we use the following notation:

$$D_0 f(a) \equiv \frac{f(a+h) - f(a-h)}{2h} \tag{6.5a}$$

$$D_+ f(a) \equiv \frac{f(a+h) - f(a)}{h} \tag{6.5b}$$

$$D_- f(a) \equiv \frac{f(a) - f(a-h)}{h} \tag{6.5c}$$

The next question is: How good are these approximations to the derivative of f at a and which one should we use? The answer to the second question will be addressed in later sections. To answer the first question, let us examine the centred difference case. We use Taylor's expansion

(Davis, 1975) to show that

$$f(a \pm h) = f(a) \pm h f'(a) + \frac{h^2}{2!} f''(a) \pm \frac{h^3}{3!} f'''(\eta_\pm)$$

(6.6)

$$\eta_- \in (a - h, a), \quad \eta_+ \in (a, a + h)$$

from which we conclude that in this particular case

$$D_0 f(a) = f'(a) + \frac{h^2}{6} \left(\frac{f'''(\eta_+) + f'''(\eta_-)}{2} \right)$$

(6.7)

We thus see that centred differences give a second-order approximation to the first derivative if h is small enough and if f has continuous derivatives up to order 3. Similarly, some arithmetic shows that forward and backward differencing give first-order approximation to the first derivative of f at the point a:

$$D_+ f(a) = f'(a) + \frac{h}{2} f''(\eta_+), \quad \eta_+ \in (a, a + h)$$

(6.8)

$$D_- f(a) = f'(a) - \frac{h}{2} f''(\eta_-), \quad \eta_- \in (a - h, a)$$

We see that these one-sided schemes are first-order accurate. On the other hand, they place low continuity constraints on the function f, namely we only need to assume that its second derivative is continuous.

We now discuss divided differences for the second derivative of f at some point a. To this end, we propose the following popular and much used three-point formula (see Conte, 1980):

$$D_+ D_- f(a) \equiv \frac{f(a - h) - 2f(a) + f(a + h)}{h^2}$$

(6.9)

Thus, this divided difference is a second-order approximation to the second derivative of f at the point a and we assume that this function has continuous derivatives up to and including order 4. The discretisation error is given by

$$D_+ D_- f(a) = f''(a) + \frac{h^4}{4!} \left(f^{(iv)}(\eta_+) + f^{(iv)}(\eta_-) \right)$$

(6.10)

In later chapters we shall apply the divided differences as defined in equations (6.5) to PDEs whose solutions may not have the necessary degree of continuity. In general, you cannot get a high-order approximation to a problem whose solution is discontinuous at certain points. For example, trying to find the derivatives in the classical sense of a Heaviside function or Dirac function is pointless.

6.3   CAVEAT: ACCURACY AND ROUND-OFF ERRORS

From the previous section we can deduce that it is possible (at least in theory) to approximate the derivatives of a smooth function to any degree of accuracy by choosing the mesh distance h to be as small as desired. In practice, however, the fact that computers have limited word length and that loss of significant digits occurs when nearly equal quantities are subtracted combine to make high accuracy difficult to obtain (Conte and de Boor, 1980; Dahlquist, 1974). In particular, if the computer cannot handle numbers with more than s digits, then the exact

Table 6.1 Approximating first derivatives

h	Single precision (float)	Double
1	1.752	1.1752
10^{-1}	1.00167	1.00167
10^{-2}	1.00002	1.00002
10^{-3}	1.00001	1
10^{-4}	1.00006	1
10^{-5}	1.00068	1
10^{-6}	0.976837	1
10^{-7}	1.09605	1

Table 6.2 Approximating second derivatives

h	Single precision (float)	Double
10^{-3}	1	1
10^{-4}	1	1
10^{-5}	1	0.999999
10^{-6}	1.00004	0.999962
10^{-7}	1.0107	0.994338

product of two s-digit numbers cannot be used in subsequent calculations, and in this case the product must be rounded off. The effect of such rounding off can be noticeable in calculations. The conclusion is that there is a critical size of h below which the results of calculations cannot be trusted. Some authors resort to interval analysis techniques (see Moore, 1966, 1979) to resolve this problem. The solution to a problem is no longer a single point estimate but is situated in a range or interval.

Let us take an example (taken from Conte and de Boor, 1980). We discuss the application of the divided differences in formulae (6.5) (the centred difference option) and (6.9) to approximating the derivatives of the exponential function at $x = 0$. Of course, all derivatives have the value 1 at $x = 0$ and we investigate how well the divided differences approximate these values as the mesh size h becomes progressively smaller. Furthermore, we investigate the effect of round-off error when using single-precision float data type and double-precision double data type. We first discuss approximating the first derivative and the results are shown in Table 6.1. In the case of single-precision numbers we see that the approximation gets better until the mesh size h becomes 0.0001, after which time the approximation becomes worse. No appreciable degradation occurs in the double precision case. The results are shown in Table 6.2. On the other hand, when applying the somewhat more complex formula (6.9) we see that the accuracy becomes worse for values of h smaller than 0.0001 for both single-precision and double-precision cases. It is possible to calculate the critical value of h below which the round-off errors start to play a role. See Conte and de Boor (1980) for the example in this section. This optimum value of h is the value for which the sum of the magnitude of the round-off error and of the discretisation error is minimised. In Conte and de Boor (1980) the authors determine this value as $h = 0.0033$.

We shall develop finite difference schemes in later chapters and in these cases we may need to choose very small mesh sizes in order to improve accuracy. We must also be careful that we do not introduce round-off errors, thus destroying accuracy rather than improving it!

6.4   WHERE ARE DIVIDED DIFFERENCES USED IN INSTRUMENT PRICING?

This book is about approximating the solution of partial differential equations (PDEs) that describe the behaviour of financial derivatives. In general, the PDE is multidimensional. It has a time dimension and one or more space (or underlying) dimensions. The order of the derivatives in the PDE are:

- First order in time
- First order and second order in space.

Since it is not possible or even desirable to search for an exact solution to the initial boundary value problem for the PDE, we have to seek refuge in some kind of approximate method. In this book we examine the applicability of the finite difference method (FDM) to such problems. If we had to summarise FDM we would say that it is a method that approximates the derivatives in a PDE (defined on a continuous region) by so-called divided differences defined on a discrete mesh.

6.5   INITIAL VALUE PROBLEMS

In this section we consider a class of first-order linear systems of ordinary differential equations in the independent variable t (this is usually a time dimension):

$$\frac{dV(t)}{dt} + A(t)V(t) = F(t), \quad 0 < t \le T \tag{6.11}$$

where $V(t) = {}^t(u_1(t), \dots, u_n(t))$

$F(t) = {}^t(f_1(t), \dots, f_n(t))$

$A(t) = (a_{ij}(t))_{1 \le i, j \le n}$

(see Varga, 1962; Crouzeix, 1975; Le Roux, 1979). In this case the vector $F(t)$ and matrix function $A(t)$ are known quantities and the vector $V(t)$ is unknown. The system (6.11) will have a unique solution if we give an initial condition for $V(t)$ when $t = 0$:

$$V(0) = U_0, U_0 = {}^t(u_{01}, \dots, u_{0n}) \tag{6.12}$$

where U_0 is a given constant vector.

The initial value problem (IVP) is highly relevant to the material in this book and in particular its applications to finite difference methods for parabolic initial boundary problems. For the moment, we concentrate on two aspects of the problem:

- Analytical properties of IVP (6.11), (6.12)
- Finite difference approximations to IVP (6.11), (6.12).

We now discuss these two approaches.

6.5.1 Padé matrix approximations

Let us assume for the moment that the matrix A in equation (6.11) is independent of t. We define (formally) the exponential of a matrix as follows:

$$\exp(A) \equiv I + A + \frac{A^2}{2!} + \cdots \equiv \sum_{j=0}^{\infty} \frac{A^n}{n!} \tag{6.13}$$

where I is the identity matrix. This is the $n \times n$ matrix with the value 1 on the main diagonal and zero everywhere else. Based on this definition, the solution of (6.11), (6.12) is given by:

$$V(t) = \exp(-At)U_0 + \exp(-At)\int_0^t \exp(A\lambda)F(\lambda)\,d\lambda, \quad t \geq 0 \tag{6.14}$$

(see Varga, 1962). In general, it is difficult or undesirable to attempt to use (6.14) directly in calculations. Furthermore, the matrix A can be a function of time, in which case formula (6.14) needs to be modified. Thus, we resort to numerical techniques to approximate the IVP (6.11), (6.12). Some examples are:

- One-step and multi-step finite difference method (FDM)
- Runge–Kutta methods (Stoer and Bulirsch, 1980)
- Predictor–corrector methods.

In this chapter we concentrate on one-step methods. To this end, we partition the interval $[0, T]$ into sub-intervals

$$\begin{aligned} 0 = t_0 < t_1 < t_2 < \cdots < t_N = T \\ k_n = t_{n+1} - t_n, \; n = 0, \ldots, N-1 \end{aligned} \tag{6.15}$$

The sub-intervals do not necessarily have to be of the same size but for convenience we partition $[0, T]$ into N equal sub-intervals as follows:

$$\begin{aligned} k = T/N \\ k = t_{n+1} - t_n, \quad n = 0, \ldots, N-1 \end{aligned} \tag{6.16}$$

Having done this, we must approximate the solution of IVP (6.11), (6.12). The case $n = 1$ (the so-called scalar IVP) has been discussed in detail in Duffy (2004) and we extend some of the results to the general case here.

The challenge is to approximate the derivative appearing in (6.11). To this end, some popular schemes are:

Implicit Euler scheme

$$\frac{U^{n+1} - U^n}{k} + A^{n+1}U^{n+1} = F^{n+1}, \quad n = 0, \ldots, N-1$$

$$U^0 = U_0 \tag{6.17}$$

$$A^{n+1} \equiv A(t_{n+1}), \qquad F^{n+1} \equiv F(t_{n+1})$$

Explicit Euler scheme

$$\frac{U^{n+1} - U^n}{k} + A^n U^n = F^n, \quad n = 0, \ldots, N - 1$$

$$U^0 = U_0 \tag{6.18}$$

$$A^n \equiv A(t_n), \qquad F^n \equiv F(t_n)$$

Crank–Nicolson scheme

$$\frac{U^{n+1} - U^n}{k} + A^{n+\frac{1}{2}} \frac{U^{n+1} + U^n}{2} = F^{n+\frac{1}{2}}, \quad n = 0, \ldots, N - 1$$

$$U^0 = U_0 \tag{6.19}$$

$$t_{n+\frac{1}{2}} \equiv \frac{t_{n+1} + t_n}{2}, \qquad A^{n+\frac{1}{2}} \equiv A(t_{n+\frac{1}{2}}), \qquad F^{n+\frac{1}{2}} \equiv F(t_{n+\frac{1}{2}})$$

Noting from these schemes that data is known at time level n we can then calculate new values at time level $n + 1$. Formally, the new values are:

Implicit Euler scheme

$$(I + kA^{n+1})U^{n+1} = U^n + kF^{n+1} \tag{6.20}$$

Explicit Euler scheme

$$U^{n+1} = (I - kA^n)U^n + kF^n \tag{6.21}$$

Crank–Nicolson scheme

$$\left(I + \frac{kA^{n+\frac{1}{2}}}{2}\right) U^{n+1} = \left(I - \frac{kA^{n+\frac{1}{2}}}{2}\right) U^n + kF^{n+\frac{1}{2}} \tag{6.22}$$

where I is the identity matrix.

The solution at time level $n + 1$ in equation (6.21) can be found directly while we must solve a matrix system for the equations (6.20) and (6.22). We note that the implicit Euler scheme is also called the backward-difference method and the explicit Euler method is called the forward-difference method.

Let us now take the case of $F(t) = 0$ and where the matrix A is independent of time. We can then write equations (6.20), (6.21) and (6.22) in the equivalent forms (at least formally)

$$U^{n+1} = (I + kA)^{-1}U^n \tag{6.23a}$$

$$U^{n+1} = (I - kA)U^n \tag{6.23b}$$

$$U^{n+1} = \left(I + \frac{k}{2}A\right)^{-1} \left(I - \frac{k}{2}A\right) U^n \tag{6.23c}$$

If we compare these solutions with the exact solution, namely (see equation (6.14))

$$W(t) = \exp(-tA)U_0 \tag{6.24}$$

we realise that the solutions in system (6.23) are essentially approximations to the exponential matrix term in (6.24). We can show how well the approximate solutions agree with the series in equation (6.13). To make this statement more clear, we look at the Crank–Nicolson scheme because of its popularity in financial engineering applications (by the way, it does not always live up to its name, as we shall see in later chapters). Let us assume that the time-step k is sufficiently small. Then we can formally expand the expression for the approximate solution as follows (with A replaced by $-A$):

$$\left(I + \frac{k}{2}A\right)^{-1}\left(I - \frac{k}{2}A\right) = I - kA + \frac{(kA)^2}{2} - \frac{(kA)^3}{4} + \cdots \qquad (6.25)$$

and we thus see that this series agrees with that in (6.13) to second order. Similarly it can be shown that the other numerical solutions in equations (6.23) approximate the exponential term to first order in k. However, the scheme for the explicit Euler scheme is only *conditionally stable*, which means that k must be chosen to be less than some critical value. The implicit Euler and Crank–Nicolson schemes are *unconditionally stable* for any value of k. This means that

$$\|U^n\| \leq M\|U_0\| \quad n = 0, 1, \ldots \qquad (6.26)$$

in some norm. Here the constant M is independent of the step size k.

Theorem 6.1. *(Stability of the explicit Euler scheme.) Let A be an $n \times n$ matrix whose eigenvalues λ_j satisfy $0 < \infty \leq \Re \lambda_j \leq \beta$, $1 \leq j \leq n$ (here $\Re \lambda_j$ denotes the real part of the complex number λ_j)*

Then, the explicit Euler scheme approximant $I - kA$ is stable for

$$0 \leq k \leq \min_{1 \leq j \leq n}\left(\frac{2\Re \lambda_j}{|\lambda_j|^2}\right)$$

Looking at equations (6.23) again, we might ask ourselves how the approximations to the exponential are generated. In fact, the approximations in (6.23) are special cases of Padé rational approximations (Varga, 1962; de Bruin and Van Rossum, 1980). A rational function is a quotient of two polynomials and we use such functions to approximate the exponential function as follows:

$$\exp(-z) = \frac{n_{p,q}(z)}{d_{p,q}(z)} \qquad (6.27)$$

where n (the numerator) and d (the denominator) are polynomials of degrees q and p in z, respectively. In general, we select for each pair of non-negative integers p and q those polynomials n and d such that the Taylor's series expansion of n/d agrees with as many leading terms of Taylor expansion of $\exp(-z)$. We can thus create a so-called Padé table for $\exp(-z)$. Some of the first few terms in the table are shown in Table 6.3.

Table 6.3   Padé table for $\exp(-z)$

	$q = 0$	$q = 1$	$q = 2$
$p = 0$	1	$1 - z$	$1 - z + z^2/2$
$p = 1$	$\dfrac{1}{1 + z}$	$\dfrac{2 - z}{2 + z}$	$\dfrac{6 - 4z + z^2}{6 + 2z}$
$p = 2$	$\dfrac{1}{1 + z + z^2/2}$	$\dfrac{6 - 2z}{6 + 4z + z^2}$	$\dfrac{12 - 6z + z^2}{12 + 6z + z^2}$

The reader can verify that the entries in Table 6.3 are correct. An important result concerning Padé approximations and stability of difference schemes for IVP (6.11), (6.12) is that if the eigenvalues of a matrix A are positive real numbers, then the Padé matrix approximation is unconditionally stable if and only if $p \geq q$. The Padé matrix approximation technique can be applied to other functions. A discussion, however, is outside the scope of this book and we refer the reader to de Bruin (1980).

6.5.2 Extrapolation

Much of the financial engineering literature uses the Crank–Nicolson method, and many people use it probably for the main reason that it is second-order accurate. However, as we shall see in later chapters, it produces spurious (artificial) oscillations, especially near the strike price and barriers.

In this section we discuss how to 'bootstrap' the accuracy of the implicit Euler method from first-order to second-order accuracy while also avoiding spurious oscillations. We motivate the extrapolated scheme in two ways. Let

- U_k^n be the solution of (6.23a)
- W be the solution of (6.24)

where we have introduced the subscript k in the approximate solution to denote its dependence on k. Then, we can prove (this will be discussed later) that

$$U_k^n = W + Mk + O(k^2) \qquad (6.28)$$

where the constant M does not depend on k. By now taking a scheme with a mesh of size $k/2$ we also see that

$$U_{k/2}^{2n} = W + \frac{Mk}{2} + O(k^2) \qquad (6.29)$$

Some arithmetic shows that

$$V_{k/2}^{2n} \equiv 2U_{k/2}^{2n} - U_k^n = W + O(k^2) \qquad (6.30)$$

Thus, we now get a second-order scheme with little extra effort. We have programmed this method and the C++ code for the scalar case is given in Duffy (2004). We motivate the extrapolated scheme based on Padé matrix approximations and the series form for exponential matrices (based on Lawson and Morris, 1978 and Gourlay and Morris, 1980). Let us for convenience denote the approximate solution by V and drop the dependence on the discrete time level t; we just take any time value t. Applying (6.23a) on a mesh of size k we see that

$$V(t + k) = (I + kA)^{-1}V(t) \qquad (6.31)$$

Alternatively, we can progress from time t to time $t + k$ in two steps, namely from t to $t + k/2$ and then from $t + k/2$ to $t + k$ and this combined step gives:

$$V(t + k) = \left(I + \frac{k}{2}A\right)^{-1}\left(I + \frac{k}{2}A\right)^{-1}V(t) \qquad (6.32)$$

Expanding (6.31) and (6.32) in powers of k gives, respectively,

$$V(t + k) = (I + kA + k^2A^2)V(t) + O(k^3) \qquad (6.33)$$

and

$$V(t + k) = \left(I + kA + \frac{3}{4}k^2 A^2 \right) V(t) + O(k^3) \tag{6.34}$$

If we now multiply equation (6.34) by a factor of 2 and subtract equation (6.33) we get

$$V(t + k) = \left(I + kA + \frac{k^2}{2}A^2 \right) V(t) + O(k^3) \tag{6.35}$$

Comparing this result with the series expansion in equation (6.13) we then get a second-order approximation. This suggests the following algorithm:

$$V^{(1)}(t + k) = (I + kA)^{-1}V(t)$$

$$V^{(2)}(t + k) = \left(I + \frac{k}{2}A \right)^{-1} \left(I + \frac{k}{2}A \right)^{-1} V(t) \tag{6.36}$$

$$V(t + k) = 2V^{(2)} - V^{(1)}$$

We thus have produced the second-order scheme!

Extrapolation techniques in conjunction with the implicit Euler scheme have been applied to the Black–Scholes equation and good results have been obtained: i.e. second-order accuracy and no spurious oscillations. For the details, we refer the reader to Cooney (1999).

6.6   NONLINEAR INITIAL VALUE PROBLEMS

The system (6.11), (6.12) is linear because neither the matrix function $A(t)$ nor the vector function $F(t)$ depends on the unknown solution V. If this is not the case, however, we need a different scheme, which we describe as follows (Dalhquist, 1974). Let us consider the nonlinear IVP:

$$\frac{dy}{dt} = f(t, y), \quad 0 < t \le T$$

$$y(0) = A \tag{6.37}$$

where

$$y = y(t) = {}^t(y_1(t), \dots, y_n(t))$$

$$f = f(t, y) = {}^t(f_1(t, y), \dots, f_n(t, y))$$

$$A = {}^t(a_1, \dots, a_n) \text{ is a constant vector}$$

In this case the vector y is the unknown variable. The function f is a nonlinear vector-valued function and it is not possible to apply the linear methods (such as Crank–Nicolson) to (6.37); whereas for linear problems we can solve a system of linear equations at each time level (using LU decomposition, for example), applying Crank–Nicolson leads to a nonlinear system of equations that must be solved by Newton's method, for example. Instead, we prefer to linearise the IVP (6.37) in some way and then apply well-known finite difference schemes. To this end, we discuss two techniques, namely the predictor–corrector and the Runge–Kutta methods.

Nonlinear problems such as the IVP (6.37) are very important in financial engineering applications. First, they form part of the theory of stochastic differential equations (SDEs).

An SDE is similar to an IVP but has a noise term added on. For a discussion of this topic see Kloeden *et al.* (1994) and for an implementation in C++, see Duffy (2004). Second, nonlinear IVPs arise when we carry out a semi-discretisation of various kinds of nonlinear parabolic partial differential equations. A number of generalisations of the Black–Scholes equation have been proposed in the last few years (for example, passport options, nonlinear volatility and problems with transaction costs) and they lead to nonlinear partial differential equations that are then solved using the solvers in this section.

6.6.1 Predictor–corrector methods

The idea behind predictor–corrector methods is easy. In marching from time level n to time level $n + 1$, we first 'predict' an intermediate and 'rough' solution using some explicit finite difference scheme and we then 'correct' it at time level $n + 1$. The advantage of this approach is that we can approximate a nonlinear IVP by a sequence of simpler (and linear!) finite difference schemes.

In order to motivate the current scheme, let us first discretise (6.37) by the trapezoidal rule

$$y_{n+1} - y_n = \tfrac{1}{2}h[f(t_n, y_n) + f(t_{n+1}, y_{n+1})], \quad n = 0, 1, 2, \ldots \tag{6.38}$$

This is an example of an implicit method because the unknown value of y at time level $n + 1$ appears implicitly on the right-hand side of equation (6.38). Thus we cannot directly solve this problem at time level $n + 1$. If f is a nonlinear function we then have to solve a nonlinear system at each time level because the unknown function lives on both sides of equation (6.38) as it were. This complicates matters somewhat but not all is lost because we modify (6.38) so that the unknown value is removed from the right-hand side. To this end, we propose the following (iterative) algorithm:

- *Step 1*: Calculate an 'intermediate' value (called the predictor) as follows:

$$y_{n+1}^{(0)} = y_n + hf(t_n, y_n) \tag{6.39}$$

Please note that we calculate the predictor by using the explicit Euler method. We now adapt equation (6.38), by using the predicted value on the right-hand side instead of the unknown function to get the approximation

$$y_{n+1}^{(1)} = y_n + \frac{h}{2}[f(t_n, y_n) + f(t_{n+1}, y_{n+1}^{(0)})] \tag{6.40}$$

- *Step 2*: The general iteration is given by

$$y_{n+1}^{(k)} = y_n + \frac{h}{2}[f(t_n, y_n) + f(t_{n+1}, y_{n+1}^{(k-1)})], \quad k = 1, 2, \ldots \tag{6.41}$$

- *Step 3*: We compute the left-hand side of (6.41) until

$$\frac{\|y_{n+1}^{(k)} - y_{n+1}^{(k-1)}\|}{\|y_{n+1}^{(k)}\|} \le \epsilon \text{ for prescribed tolerance } \epsilon \tag{6.42}$$

We conclude with the remark that we need some guarantee that the iterations in equation (6.41) converge to a unique value. A sufficient condition for convergence is that

$$\left\| \frac{\partial f}{\partial y} \right\| h < 2 \tag{6.43}$$

where $\partial f / \partial y$ is a square matrix defined by

$$\frac{\partial f}{\partial y} = \left(\frac{\partial f_i}{\partial y_j} \right), \quad 1 \le i, j \le n$$

and $\| \cdot \|$ is some suitable norm, for example the L_∞ or L_2 norm.

This concludes the basics of the predictor–corrector methods. For a good introduction, see Conte and de Boor (1980). For applications of predictor–corrector methods to stochastic differential equations, see Kloeden *et al.* (1994, 1995).

We have applied predictor–corrector methods to a number of problems and differential equations and we are impressed by its robustness, ease of use and efficiency. We shall apply the method in later chapters for several nonlinear partial differential equations that model financial instruments. The method is not so well known in financial engineering but it is well worth investigating. A discussion of the predictor–corrector method for one-factor stochastic differential equations is given in Duffy (2004).

6.6.2 Runge–Kutta methods

There is a vast literature on Runge–Kutta (RK) methods and their applications to initial value problems (Stoer and Bulirsch, 1980; Conte and de Boor, 1980, Crouzeix, 1975). We give the essentials of these methods in this section. Basically, Runge–Kutta methods are based on the idea of comparing the value of $f(t, y)$ to several strategically chosen points near the solution curve in the interval (t_n, t_{n+1}) and then to combine these values in such a way as to get good accuracy in the computed increment $y_{n+1} - y_n$.

The simplest RK method is called Heun's method:

$$k_1 = hf(t_n, y_n)$$
$$k_2 = hf(t_n + h, y_n + k_1) \tag{6.44}$$
$$y_{n+1} = y_n + \tfrac{1}{2}(k_1 + k_2)$$

This is a second-order scheme, as can be seen from the series

$$y(t, h) = y(t) + c_2(t)h^2 + \sum_{j=3}^{\infty} c_j(t)h^j \tag{6.45}$$

where $y(t, h)$ is the solution of (6.44) at the value t. Notice that we are using h as the time step value. Thus, we can apply Richardson extrapolation to improve the accuracy.

A well-known RK method is the fourth-order method defined as follows:

$$k_1 = hf(t_n, y_n) \tag{6.46a}$$

$$k_2 = hf \left(t_n + \frac{h}{2}, y_n + \frac{k_1}{2} \right) \tag{6.46b}$$

$$k_3 = hf \left(t_n + \frac{h}{2}, y_n + \frac{k_2}{2} \right) \tag{6.46c}$$

$$k_4 = hf(t_n + h, y_n + k_3) \tag{6.46d}$$

$$y_{n+1} = y_n + \tfrac{1}{6}(k_1 + 2k_2 + 2k_3 + k_4) \tag{6.46e}$$

The series for the error term is given by

$$y(x, h) = y(x) + c_4(t)h^4 + \sum_{j=5}^{\infty} c_j(t)h^j \tag{6.47}$$

Again, we can apply Richardson extrapolation to this problem.

6.7   SCALAR INITIAL VALUE PROBLEMS

A special case of an initial value problem is when the number of dimension n in the initial value problem (6.11)–(6.12) is equal to 1. In this case we speak of a scalar problem and it is useful to study these problems if one wishes to get some insights into how finite difference methods work. A numerical and computational discussion of scalar IVP is given in Duffy (2004). In this section we discuss some numerical properties of one-step finite difference schemes for the linear scalar problem:

$$Lu \equiv \frac{du}{dt} + a(t)u = f(t), \quad 0 < t < T$$

$$u(0) = u_0 \tag{6.48}$$

where $a(t) \geq \alpha > 0, \quad \forall t \in [0, T]$

The reader can check that the one-step methods (equations (6.17), (6.18) and (6.19)) can be cast as the general form recurrence relation

$$U^{n+1} = A^n U^n + B^n, \quad n \geq 0 \tag{6.49}$$

Then, using this formula and mathematical induction we can give an explicit solution at any time level as follows:

$$U^n = \left(\prod_{j=0}^{n-1} A^j \right) U^0 + \sum_{v=0}^{n-1} B^v \prod_{j=v+1}^{n-1} A^j, \quad n \geq 1 \quad \text{with} \quad \prod_{j=I}^{j=J} g^j \equiv 1 \text{ if } I > J \tag{6.50}$$

A special case is when the coefficients A and B are constant, that is:

$$U^{n+1} = AU^n + B, \quad n \geq 0 \tag{6.51}$$

Then the general solution is given by

$$U^n = A^n U^0 + B \frac{1 - A^n}{1 - A}, \quad n \geq 0 \tag{6.52}$$

where in equation (6.52) we note that $A^n \equiv n^{th}$ power of constant A and $A \neq 1$.
The proof of this requires the formula for the sum of a series

$$1 + A + \cdots + A^n = \frac{1 - A^{n+1}}{1 - A}, \quad A \neq 1 \tag{6.53}$$

For a readable introduction to difference schemes we refer the reader to Goldberg (1986). Learning finite difference theory for the Black–Scholes equation involves not only understanding the main concepts but also developing skills in basic arithmetic. This is absolutely vital if you wish to become proficient in this area of numerical analysis.

6.7.1 Exponentially fitted schemes

We now introduce a special class of schemes that prove to be very useful in approximating the solution of the Black–Scholes PDE. In particular, these so-called exponentially fitted schemes are able to handle discontinuities (near a strike price and at barriers, for example). In general, a fitted scheme is a modification of the Crank–Nicolson scheme (see equation (6.19)) except that we introduce a new coefficient into the difference equation. In order to find this coefficient we argue as follows: Consider the trivial IVP

$$\frac{du}{dt} + au = 0, \quad a > 0 \text{ constant}$$

$$u(0) = A \tag{6.54}$$

with solution $u(t) = Ae^{-at}$

and we propose the 'fitted' Crank–Nicolson scheme, defined by:

$$\sigma \frac{U^{n+1} - U^n}{k} + a \frac{U^{n+1} + U^n}{2} = 0 \tag{6.55}$$

$$U^0 = A$$

We now demand that the solution of (6.55) should equal the solution of (6.54) at the mesh points. This will determine the value of σ, and some arithmetic shows that

$$\sigma = \frac{ak}{2} \coth \frac{ak}{2} \tag{6.56}$$

where $\coth x = (e^{2x} + 1)/(e^{2x} - 1)$.

This is the famous fitting factor and it has been known since the 1950s (de Allen and Southwell, 1955), elaborated upon by Soviet scientists (Il'in, 1969) and generalised to convection–diffusion equations in Duffy (1980). Based on the fitting factor defined in equation (6.56), we propose the generalised finite difference scheme when the coefficient a in equation (6.54) is variable $a = a(t)$ and non-zero right-hand side $f = f(t)$:

$$\sigma^n \frac{U^{n+1} - U^n}{k} + a^{n+\frac{1}{2}} \frac{U^{n+1} + U^n}{2} = f^{n+\frac{1}{2}}, \quad n \geq 0$$

$$u^0 = A \tag{6.57}$$

$$\sigma^n \equiv \frac{a^{n+\frac{1}{2}} k}{2} \coth \frac{a^{n+\frac{1}{2}} k}{2}$$

A full discussion of this scheme, its applicability to the Black–Scholes equations and its implementation in C++ is given in Duffy (2004). We shall also reuse this fitting factor finite difference schemes for the Black–Scholes equation in later chapters in this book.

6.8   SUMMARY AND CONCLUSIONS

In this chapter we have introduced divided differences as a means of approximating derivatives of smooth functions. They are needed when we approximate the solution of problems involving derivatives of an unknown function. In particular, we shall need them when approximating the one-factor and multi-factor Black–Scholes equation.

We introduced a number of finite difference schemes for linear and nonlinear first-order initial value problems. We have taken this approach for a number of reasons. First, first-order equations are simple enough to understand and we can develop finite difference schemes for them in order to pave the way for later work. Second, the initial value problems in this chapter will resurface in later chapters.

7

An Introduction to the Method of Lines

7.1 INTRODUCTION AND OBJECTIVES

In this chapter we introduce a number of mathematical and numerical techniques that allow us to simplify PDEs. The main techniques we discuss are:

- Rothe's method
- Semi-discretisation methods in general
- Method of lines (MOL).

For general initial boundary value problems (IBVP) we distinguish between the space variable (which forms an n-dimensional space in general) and the scalar time variable. Since these combined variables form an $(n + 1)$-dimensional continuous space, we must approximate the solution of the IBVP on a discrete mesh in the space and time directions. Having decided on this, we are then confronted with the problem of actually producing a finite difference scheme. To this end, we discuss and elaborate the following issues (or action points) relating to the approximate schemes:

A1: How to discretise in the time direction.
A2: How to discretise in the space direction.
A3: Do we discretise in all $n + 1$ directions at once or do we do it in steps?
A4: If we dicretise in steps, do we discretise first in time and then in space, or the other way around?

This is quite a list to work through, but having given answers to the points will mean that we have a good overview of how approximate schemes come to life, what their advantages are and what the consequences are of using a given approximation method.

There are several reasons for studying the method of lines. First, it allows us to approximate an IVBP in space *and* time. The end-result is usually a simpler set of differential equations that may have been solved elsewhere using known and proven techniques. Then we can reapply these numerical methods to approximate the new problem. For example, a one-dimensional parabolic IBVP is discretised in space using centred differences, resulting in a system of first-order ODEs in time. We can solve these ODEs by standard time-marching schemes; we could even resort to a commercial ODE solver! The second reason for using MOL it that it is easy to prove existence and uniqueness results using this approach. The results in this chapter are easily applicable to more complex problems.

7.2 CLASSIFYING SEMI-DISCRETISATION METHODS

Many of the schemes in this book relate to the approximation of initial boundary value problems for PDEs. In general we make a distinction between time and space variables. There are many ways to replace derivatives in the time and space variables. Some scenarios for one-factor models are:

- Centred differences in space and one-step marching scheme in time.
- Exponentially fitted schemes (Duffy, 1980, 2004) in space and one-step marching scheme in time.

For multi-factor models there are a number of options:

- Simultaneous discretisation in all space variables and one-step marching scheme in time.
- Using ADI or splitting schemes in the space variables and one-step marching scheme in time.
- Advanced and modern splitting methods (for example, IMEX schemes).

We shall discuss a number of other competitors to FDM, namely the meshless (or meshfree) method and the finite element method (FEM). These are examples of semi-discretisers:

- FEM discretises in space using locally compact polynomial basis functions and one-step marching schemes in time.
- Meshless uses Rothe's method to discretise in time and then uses radial basis functions (RBFs) to approximate the space derivatives.
- In some cases the meshless method discretises first in the space direction using RBFs and then one-step marching scheme in time.

7.3 SEMI-DISCRETISATION IN SPACE USING FDM

We shall now discuss classic semi-discretisation with finite difference schemes.

7.3.1 A test case

In this case we discretise a parabolic PDE in the space direction only (using centred difference schemes, for instance) while keeping the time variable t continuous. In order to focus our attention we examine the following initial boundary value problem for the one-dimensional heat equation with zero Dirichlet boundary conditions. It is easy to extend the idea to more general cases. The problem is:

$$\frac{\partial u}{\partial t} = \frac{\partial^2 u}{\partial x^2}, \quad 0 < x < 1, \quad t > 0$$

$$u(0, t) = u(1, t) = 0, \quad t > 0 \tag{7.1}$$

$$u(x, 0) = f(x), \quad 0 \le x \le 1$$

We now partition the x interval $(0, 1)$ into J sub-intervals and we approximate (7.1) by the so-called semi-discrete scheme:

$$\frac{du_j}{dt} = h^{-2}(u_{j+1} - 2u_j + u_{j-1}), \quad 1 \le j \le J - 1$$

$$u_0 = u_J = 0, \quad t > 0 \tag{7.2}$$

$$u_j(0) = f(x_j), \quad j = 1, \ldots, J - 1$$

We define the following vectors by:

$$U(t) = {}^t(u_1(t), \ldots, u_{J-1}(t))$$

$$U_0 = {}^t(f(x_1), \ldots, f(x_{J-1}))$$

Then we can rewrite system (7.2) as an ODE system:

$$\frac{dU}{dt} = AU, \quad t > 0$$

$$U(0) = U_0$$

(7.3)

where the matrix A is given by

$$A = h^{-2} \begin{pmatrix} -2 & 1 & & \\ 1 & \ddots & \ddots & 0 \\ 0 & \ddots & \ddots & 1 \\ & & 1 & -2 \end{pmatrix}$$

Where do we go from here? There are a number of questions we would like to ask, for example:

Q1: Does system (7.3) have a unique solution and what are its qualitative properties?
Q2: How accurate is scheme (7.3) as an approximation to the solution of system (7.1)?
Q3: How do we discretise (7.3) in time and how accurate is the discretisation?

We shall discuss Q1 and Q2 in later sections but here we discuss Q3. There are many alternatives ranging from one-step to multi-step methods (see Dahlquist, 1974, for example) and from explicit to implicit methods. We can use other approximate methods such as Runge–Kutta (Stoer and Bulirsch, 1980). In this section however, we concentrate on one-step explicit and implicit theta methods defined in the usual way:

$$\frac{U^{n+1} - U^n}{k} = \theta AU^n + (1 - \theta)AU^{n+1}, \quad 0 \le n \le N - 1, \quad 0 \le \theta \le 1$$

$$U^0 = U_0$$

(7.4)

We can rewrite equations (7.4) in the equivalent form:

$$[I - k(1 - \theta)A]U^{n+1} = (I + k\theta A)U^n$$

(7.5)

or formally as:

$$U^{n+1} = [I - k(1 - \theta)A]^{-1}(I + k\theta A)U^n$$

(7.6)

Some special cases of θ are:

$$\begin{aligned} \theta &= 0, \quad \text{implicit Euler scheme} \\ \theta &= 1, \quad \text{explicit Euler scheme} \\ \theta &= \tfrac{1}{2}, \quad \text{Crank–Nicolson scheme} \end{aligned}$$

(7.7)

When the schemes are implicit we can solve the system of equations (7.4) at each time level $n + 1$ using LU decomposition (for more details, see Duffy, 2004).

7.3.2 Toeplitz matrices

In order to prepare for some general theorems concerning systems similar to (7.3) we look at the constant matrix A that is the coefficient of U. This is an example of a Toeplitz matrix, one that is a band matrix in which each diagonal consists of identical elements although different diagonals may contain different values. A special case is a tridiagonal matrix as follows:

$$
\begin{pmatrix}
b & c & & & \\
a & \ddots & \ddots & & 0 \\
0 & \ddots & \ddots & c \\
& & a & b
\end{pmatrix}
$$

Then (Bronson, 1989; Thomas, 1998, p. 52) the eigenvalues of A are given by:

$$
\lambda_j = b + 2\sqrt{ac}\,\cos\frac{j\pi}{n+1}, \quad j = 1, \ldots, n \tag{7.8}
$$

and the associated eigenvectors are given by:

$$
\mathbf{U}_j = {}^t(u_1, \ldots, u_k, \ldots, u_n)
$$
$$
u_k = 2\left(\sqrt{\frac{a}{c}}\right)^k \sin\frac{kj\pi}{n+1}, \quad k = 1, \ldots, n, \quad j = 1, \ldots, n \tag{7.9}
$$

It is useful to know (7.8) and (7.9) when testing model problems.

7.3.3 Semi-discretisation for convection–diffusion problems

In this section we investigate the semi-discretisation of the one-dimensional convection–diffusion equation (which includes the Black–Scholes as a special case):

$$
-\frac{\partial u}{\partial t} + \sigma(x)\frac{\partial^2 u}{\partial x^2} + \mu(x)\frac{\partial u}{\partial x} + c(x)u = f(x) \tag{7.10}
$$

where

$$
\sigma(x) > 0, \quad \mu(x) > 0, \quad c(x) \leq 0.
$$

We shall define a number of fully discrete schemes for this equation in Parts II and III of this book. In this section however, we discretise in the space direction only and we concentrate on the centred difference and the fitting methods (to be discussed in more detail in Chapter 11). The semi-discrete scheme is:

$$
-\frac{du_j}{dt} + \tilde{\sigma}_j D_+ D_- u_j + \mu_j D_0 u_j + c_j u_j = f_j, \quad 1 \leq j \leq J-1 \tag{7.11}
$$

where

$$
\tilde{\sigma}_j =
\begin{cases}
\sigma(x_j) \equiv \sigma_j & \text{for standard centred difference scheme} \\
\frac{\mu_j h}{2}\coth\frac{\mu_j h}{2\sigma_j} & \text{for fitted scheme}
\end{cases}
$$

and $\mu_j = \mu(x_j)$, $c_j = c(x_j)$, $f_j = f(x_j)$, $1 \leq j \leq J-1$. As already stated, we shall motivate this fitted scheme in more detail in Chapter 11.

As usual, we can write this equation as a vector system as follows:

$$-\frac{dU}{dt} + AU = F$$

$$U(0) = U_0$$

(7.12)

where

$$U = {}^t(u_1, \ldots, u_{J-1})$$

$$A = \begin{pmatrix} \ddots & & & & 0 \\ \ddots & & C_j & \\ \ddots & B_j & & \ddots \\ A_j & & \ddots \\ 0 & & \ddots \end{pmatrix}$$

and

$$A_j = \frac{\tilde{\sigma}_j}{h^2} - \frac{\mu_j}{2h}$$

$$B_j = \frac{-2\tilde{\sigma}_j}{h^2} + c_j$$

$$C_j = \frac{\tilde{\sigma}_j}{h^2} + \frac{\mu_j}{2h}$$

We investigate the matrix A because this determines the behaviour of the solution of (7.12) to a large extent. We take a special example where all the coefficients in (7.10) are constants. Then A is a Toeplitz matrix whose eigenvalues are given by equation (7.8). You can check that the eigenvalues are:

$$\lambda_j = (-2\alpha + c) + 2\sqrt{\alpha^2 - \beta^2} \cos\frac{j\pi}{J}, \quad j = 1, \ldots, J - 1$$

(7.13)

where $\alpha \equiv \tilde{\sigma}/h^2$ and $\beta \equiv \mu/2h$.

A bit of arithmetic shows that the eigenvalues of A are real and non-positive for any range of values of the parameters in equation (7.10) for the fitted scheme. In this case we always have $\alpha > \beta$. For the centred difference scheme we have a different story. In this case the eigenvalues will be real if:

$$A \geq 0 \Leftrightarrow \frac{\tilde{\sigma}_j}{h^2} - \frac{\mu}{2h} \geq 0$$

$$\Leftrightarrow h \leq \frac{2\sigma}{\mu}$$

(7.14)

This is a well-known constraint and the conclusion is: standard difference schemes have matrices with complex eigenvalues. Oscillations can occur if the mesh size is not chosen small enough. A full discussion of the consequences of this fact is given in Duffy (2004 and 2004A).

The reader might be interested in calculating the eigenvectors corresponding to the eigenvectors in (7.13).

7.3.4   Essentially positive matrices

We now give a mathematical discussion of the properties of the general initial value problem:

$$-\frac{dU}{dt} + AU = F \tag{7.15}$$

$$U(0) = U_0$$

We assume for convenience that the matrix A and the vector F are independent of time. We are interested in two aspects of this problem:

- Behaviour of $U(t)$ for large time behaviour
- Numerical approximation of system (7.15).

In this section we shall discuss the first problem based on the results in Varga (1962) and discuss numerical approximations using one-step finite difference schemes.

We now study the stability of the system (7.15) as a function of the right-hand terms and the initial condition. To this end, we must examine the properties of the matrix A. We say that A is irreducible if its directed graph is strongly connected. An equivalent statement is that A has non-vanishing off-diagonal elements. We say that A is an M-matrix (with $a_{ij} \leq 0$ $\forall i \neq j$) if A is non-singular, and a sufficient condition for A to satisfy $A^{-1} > 0$ is that $a_{ij} \leq 0$ $\forall i \neq j$ and $a_{ii} > 0, i = 1, \ldots, J - 1$ (for a proof see Varga, 1962).

Theorem 7.1. *(Limit theorem.) Let A be an irreducible M-matrix having n rows and n columns. Then the unique solution of (7.15) is uniformly bounded in norm for all $t \geq 0$ and satisfies*

$$\lim_{t \to \infty} U(t) = A^{-1}F$$

We are interested in determining the conditions under which spurious oscillations occur in the semi-discrete scheme (7.15). Most of the problems are caused by the eigenvalues of A.

Definition: A real matrix $Q = (q_{ij})$ is said to be essentially positive if $q_{ij} \geq 0$ for $i \neq j$ and Q is irreducible.

The following theorems and definitions are taken from Varga (1962).

Theorem 7.2. *Let Q be an essentially positive matrix. Then Q has a real eigenvalue $\lambda(Q)$ such that*

1. *There exists an eigenvector $x > 0$ corresponding to $\lambda(Q)$.*
2. *If α is another eigenvalue of Q, then $\operatorname{Re} \alpha \leq \lambda(Q)$.*
3. *$\lambda(Q)$ increases when an element of Q increases.*

Theorem 7.3. *(Asymptotic behaviour.) Let Q be an $n \times n$ essentially positive matrix. If $\lambda(Q)$ is the eigenvalue of Theorem 7.2 then*

$$\|\exp(tQ)\| \leq K \exp(t\lambda(Q)), \quad t \to \infty$$

where K is a positive constant independent of t.

Thus $\lambda(Q)$ dictates asymptotic behaviour of $\|\exp(tQ)\|$ for large t.

Definition: Let Q be essentially positive. Then Q is called:

- *Supercritical if $\lambda(Q) > 0$*
- *Critical if $\lambda(Q) = 0$*
- *Subcritical if $\lambda(Q) < 0$*

We now consider (7.15) posed in a slightly different form (in fact, we use the same notation as in Varga, 1962):

$$\frac{dU}{dt} = QU + r \text{ in } (0, T)$$

$$\tag{7.16}$$

$$U(0) = U_0.$$

Theorem 7.4. *(Asymptotic behaviour of solution.) Let Q be essentially positive and non-singular. If Q is supercritical then for a given initial vector U_0 the solution of (7.16) satisfies*

$$\lim_{t \to \infty} \|U(t)\| = \infty.$$

If Q is subcritical then $U(t)$ is uniformly bounded in norm for all $t > 0$ and satisfies

$$\lim_{t \to \infty} U(t) = -Q^{-1}r.$$

We thus see that it is necessary to have negative eigenvalues if we wish to ensure stable asymptotic behaviour of the solution of (7.16).

We give an example in the scalar case to motivate Theorem 7.4. Consider the simple initial value problem

$$\frac{du}{dt} = qu + r, \quad t > 0$$

$$u(0) = A$$

where q and r are constant. By using the integrating factor method, we can show that the solution is given by

$$u(t) = A e^{qt} - \frac{r}{q}[1 - e^{qt}]$$

Thus, if $q < 0$ (the subcritical case) we see that

$$\lim_{t \to \infty} u(t) = -\frac{r}{q}$$

while if $q > 0$ (the supercritical case) the solution is unbounded. Finally, if $q \equiv 0$ the solution is given by

$$u(t) = A + rt \quad \text{(linear growth)}.$$

Many authors use this model problem for testing new difference schemes (Dahlquist, 1974).

7.4 NUMERICAL APPROXIMATION OF FIRST-ORDER SYSTEMS

We shall now discuss linear, semi-linear and general nonlinear problems.

We first consider the system (7.15) on a closed time interval $[0, T]$, and discretise this interval in the usual way.

7.4.1   Fully discrete schemes

We divide the interval $[0, T]$ into N sub-intervals, defined by

$$0 = t_0 < t_1 < \cdots < t_N = T, \quad \text{with } (k = T/N)$$

We replace the continuous time derivative by divided differences. There are many ways to do this (Conte and de Boor, 1980; Crouzeix, 1975). We shall concentrate on so-called two-level schemes, and, to this end, we approximate dU/dt at some time level as follows:

$$\frac{dU}{dt} \cong \frac{U^{n+1} - U^n}{k}, \quad U^n \equiv U(t_n)$$

For the other terms in (7.15) we use weighted averages defined as:

$$\Phi^{n,\theta} \equiv (1 - \theta)\Phi^n + \theta\Phi^{n+1}$$

where $\theta \in [0, 1]$. The discrete scheme is now defined as:

$$-\frac{U^{n+1} - U^n}{k} + AU^{n,\theta} = F \tag{7.17}$$

$$U^0 = U_0$$

Some well-known special cases are now given. Assume for the moment that A and F are constant.

$\theta = 0$: *The explicit Euler scheme*

$$-\frac{U^{n+1} - U^n}{k} + AU^n = F \tag{7.18}$$

$\theta = \frac{1}{2}$: *The Crank–Nicolson scheme*

$$-\frac{U^{n+1} - U^n}{k} + AU^{n,\frac{1}{2}} = F \tag{7.19}$$

$$(U^{n,\frac{1}{2}} \equiv (U^{n+1} + U^n))$$

$\theta = 1$: *The fully implicit scheme*

$$-\frac{U^{n+1} - U^n}{k} + AU^{n,1} = F \tag{7.20}$$

We are interested in determining if the above schemes are stable (in some sense) and whether their solution converges to the solution of (7.15) as $k \to 0$. To this end, we write equation (7.17) in the equivalent form

$$U^{n+1} = CU^n + H \tag{7.21}$$

where the matrix C is given by

$$C = (I - kA\theta)^{-1}[I + kA(1 - \theta)]$$

and

$$H = -k(I - kA\theta)^{-1}F$$

A well-known result (see Varga, 1962) states that the solution of (7.15) is given by

$$U(t) = A^{-1}F + \exp(tA)[U(0) - A^{-1}F].$$

So, in a sense the accuracy of the approximation (7.17) will be determined by how well the matrix C approximates the exponential function of a matrix. We shall now discuss this problem.

Definition: Let $A = (a_{ij})$ be an $n \times n$ real matrix with eigenvalues λ_j, $j = 1, \ldots, n$. The spectral radius $\rho(A)$ is given by

$$\rho(A) = \max|\lambda_j|, \quad j = 1, \ldots, n$$

Definition: The time-dependent matrix $T(t)$ is stable for $0 \le t \le T$ if $\rho[T(t)] \le 1$. It is unconditionally stable if $\rho[T(t)] < 1$ for all $0 \le t \le \infty$. We now state the main result of this section (see Varga, 1962, p. 265).

Theorem 7.5. *Let A be a matrix whose eigenvalues λ_j satisfy $0 < \alpha < \mathrm{Re}\,\lambda_j < \beta \ \forall j = 1, \ldots, n$. Then the explicit Euler scheme (7.18) is stable if*

$$0 \le k \le \min\left(\frac{2\mathrm{Re}\,\lambda_j}{|\lambda_j|^2}\right), \quad 1 \le j \le n \tag{7.22}$$

while the Crank–Nicolson scheme (7.19) and fully implicit scheme (7.20) are both unconditionally stable.

Definition: The matrix $T(t)$ is consistent with $\exp(-tA)$ if $T(t)$ has a matrix power development about $t = 0$ that agrees through at least linear terms with the expansion of $\exp(-tA)$.

We remark that the schemes defined by (7.18), (7.19) and (7.20) have matrices that are consistent with the exponential function.

7.4.2 Semi-linear problems

We now discuss the abstract semi-linear problem:

$$\frac{dU}{dt} + A(t, U) = B(t, U), \quad 0 < t \le T$$

$$U(0) = U_0 \tag{7.23}$$

where

$$A(t, \cdot) : D\,\mathbf{C}\,H \to H, \quad t > 0$$

is a strongly dissipative and maximal operator and H is a real or complex Hilbert space. The operator $B(t, \cdot) : D\,\mathbf{C}\,H \to H$ is a uniformaly Lipschitz continuous operator with Lipschitz contant K.

This is an extremely short discussion as a full treatment is outside the scope of this book. See Hille and Philips (1957) and Zeidler (1990) for more information on a powerful branch of mathematics called Functional Analysis). A special case is the m-factor

Black–Scholes equation where the operator A is a mapping from a Hilbert space of functions to itself:

$$A(t, \cdot) = \sum_{i,j=1}^{m} a_{ij}(x, t) \frac{\partial^2}{\partial x_i \, \partial x_j} + \cdots + \sum_{i=1}^{m} b_i(x, t) \frac{\partial u}{\partial x_i} + c(x, t) \quad (7.24)$$

In this case A is a linear elliptic operator. Furthermore, in the case of the classic Black–Scholes problem the operator B is identically zero. Our aim in this section is to propose some discrete schemes for (7.23) and examine their properties in a Hilbert-space setting. Some special cases are:

- Ordinary differential equations
- Partial differential equations
- Integro-differential equations
- Systems of equations.

We shall give some examples of these equations but first let us examine some schemes for approximating equation (7.23). The explicit scheme is given by

$$\frac{U^{n+1} - U^n}{k} + A(t_n, U^n) = B(t_n, U^n), \quad n \geq 0 \quad (7.25)$$

and the fully implicit method is given by

$$\frac{U^{n+1} - U^n}{k} + A(t_n, U^{n+1}) = B(t_n, U^{n+1}), \quad n \geq 0 \quad (7.26)$$

Finally, the Crank–Nicolson scheme is given by

$$\frac{U^{n+1} - U^n}{k} + A\left(t_{n+\frac{1}{2}}, U^{n+\frac{1}{2}}\right) = B\left(t_{n+\frac{1}{2}}, U^{n+\frac{1}{2}}\right) \quad n \geq 0$$

$$U^{n+\frac{1}{2}} \equiv \tfrac{1}{2}(U^n + U^{n+1}) \quad (7.27)$$

The advantage of the explicit scheme is that it is easy to program but it is only conditionally stable. The other two schemes are unconditionally stable but we must solve a nonlinear system at every time level. Can we find a compromise? The answer is yes. When the system (7.23) is semi-linear (by which we mean that A is linear and B is nonlinear) a ploy is to apply some kind of implicit scheme with respect to the A part and an explicit scheme with respect to the B part. The result is called the semi-implicit method, and one particular case is given by

$$\frac{U^{n+1} - U^n}{k} + A(t_{n+1}, U^{n+1}) = B(t_n, U^n), \quad n \geq 0 \quad (7.28)$$

We can solve this system using standard matrix solvers at each time level since there are no nonlinear terms. We give some examples of this scheme in Chapter 28 where we discuss penalty methods for one-factor and multi-factor American option problems. Of course, we wish to know how good scheme (7.28) is. In general, we should perform a full error analysis, including *consistency, stability* and *convergence*. We summarise the main results here. To this end, we write (7.23) in the more general form:

$$\frac{dU}{dt} = f(t; U, U), \quad 0 < t \leq T$$

$$U(0) = U_0 \quad (7.29)$$

where, for example, the second parameter corresponds to the derivative terms (the A operator), and the third term might correspond to the zero-order terms (the B operator). In this case we assume that the function $f(t; \cdot, v)$ satisfies a Lipschitz condition with respect to the inner product in H, that is

$$\forall t \in [0, T], v \in D$$

$$\langle f(t; u_1, v) - f(t; u_2, v), u_1 - u_2 \rangle \leq K_1 \|u_1 - u_2\|^2 \ \forall u_1, \ u_2 \tag{7.30}$$

where, $K_1 \in \mathbb{R}^1$ and $\| \cdot \|$ is the norm in a Hilbert space H, and $\langle \cdot, \cdot \rangle$ is the inner product in H.

Condition (7.30) is called the one-sided Lipschitz condition. Furthermore,

$$f(t; u, \cdot)$$

is uniformly Lipschitz continuous in the classical sense with constant

$$K_2 > 0 \quad \text{with} \quad \|f(t; u, v_1) - f(t; u, v_2)\| \leq K_2 \|v_1 - v_2\|$$

A particular case is when:

$$f(t; u, v) = A(t, u) + B(t, v) \tag{7.31}$$

where A is dissipative ($K_1 \leq 0$) or strongly dissipative ($K_1 < 0$) and $B(t, \cdot)$ is Lipschitz continuous.

The approximate scheme is defined by:

$$\frac{U^{n+1} - U^n}{k} = f(t_{n+1}; U^{n+1}, U^n) \tag{7.32}$$

We shall discuss several special cases of (7.23) in later chapters.

7.5   SUMMARY AND CONCLUSIONS

We have summarised the main approximate schemes in this book by viewing them as applications of a so-called semi-discretisation process: first discretise in time and then in space (or vice versa). We have also discussed some existence theorems for the semi-discretised set of equations.

The mathematical formalism in this chapter will be useful when we examine specialized problems in quantitative finance in later chapters.

8
General Theory of the Finite
Difference Method

8.1 INTRODUCTION AND OBJECTIVES

In this chapter we analyse difference schemes for initial boundary value problems and initial value problems. We are interested in finding necessary and sufficient conditions for a given finite difference scheme to be a 'good' approximation to some continuous problem. By 'good' we mean that the solution of the difference scheme should have the same qualitative properties as the solution of the continuous problem and that the error between the approximate and exact solutions should be 'small' (when measured in some norm).

The approach taken in this chapter dates from the 1950s and can be attributed to John Von Neumann, the father of the modern computer and one of the mathematical geniuses of the twentieth century. Von Neumann worked on fluid dynamics and military problems and approximated them using finite difference schemes. He used Fourier transform techniques to prove the stability of difference schemes. For a good account of developments, see Richtmyer (1967) – and although the book is somewhat outdated, it is well worth reading.

8.2 SOME FUNDAMENTAL CONCEPTS

The discussion in this and the following sections is based on well-known theory and results. There are many books that deal with the current topics; however, we recommend the works of Smith (1978), Thomas (1998) and Hundsdorfer and Verwer (2003) as important references.

We need to develop some notation. We view a partial differential equation as an operator L from a given space of functions to some other space of functions. For example, we can write the heat equation in the form:

$$Lu \equiv \frac{\partial u}{\partial t} - \frac{\partial^2 u}{\partial x^2} = 0 \qquad (8.1)$$

We wish to distinguish between the derivative term in t and the elliptic part of the operator, as can be seen from heat equation again:

$$\frac{\partial u}{\partial t} + Lu = 0 \qquad (8.2)$$

where $Lu \equiv -\partial^2 u/\partial x^2$ (an elliptic operator).

We can write the general linear parabolic partial differential equation in one-space dimension in the following form:

$$-\frac{\partial u}{\partial t} + Lu = f(x, t) \qquad (8.3)$$

where

$$Lu \equiv \sigma(x,t)\frac{\partial^2 u}{\partial x^2} + \mu(x,t)\frac{\partial u}{\partial x} + b(x,t)u$$

This is the model equation that we use in this part of the book. It encompasses many special cases of interest, of which some examples are:

Diffusion equation

$$Lu \equiv \sigma(x,t)\frac{\partial^2 u}{\partial x^2} \qquad (8.4a)$$

Reaction–diffusion equation

$$Lu \equiv \sigma(x,t)\frac{\partial^2 u}{\partial x^2} + b(x,t)u \qquad (8.4b)$$

Convection equation

$$Lu \equiv \mu(x,t)\frac{\partial u}{\partial x} + b(x,t)u \qquad (8.4c)$$

Convection–diffusion equation

$$Lu \equiv \sigma(x,t)\frac{\partial^2 u}{\partial x^2} + \mu(x,t)\frac{\partial u}{\partial x} + b(x,t)u \qquad (8.4d)$$

Conservation-form equation

$$Lu \equiv \frac{\partial}{\partial x}\left[\sigma(x,t)\frac{\partial u}{\partial x}\right] + b(x,t)u \qquad (8.4e)$$

Since this is a book on option pricing applications we are mainly interested in equation (8.4d). This is called the convection–diffusion equation. The convection term is the first-order term and the diffusion term is the second-order term. It is a model for many kinds of one-factor Black–Scholes equations. For example, the Black–Scholes equation for a standard European call option with continuous dividend D is:

$$-\frac{\partial C}{\partial t} + \frac{1}{2}\sigma^2 S^2 \frac{\partial^2 C}{\partial S^2} + (r - D)S\frac{\partial C}{\partial S} - rC = 0 \qquad (8.5)$$

where C is the option price (the dependent variable). Please note that we use the 'engineering' variable t (starting from $t = 0$) while the financial literature uses the variable t starting from the terminal condition T (see Wilmott, 1998, p. 77).

We now define a discrete operator that is defined at mesh points and where the derivatives are replaced by divided differences, for example the explicit Euler scheme for the heat equation:

$$L_h^k u_j^n \equiv \frac{u_j^{n+1} - u_j^n}{k} - D_+ D_- u_j^n \qquad (8.6)$$

Thus, we have included the steps k and h in the discrete operator to denote its dependence on two meshes. We wish to prove that (8.6) is a good approximation to (8.1). To this end, we discuss a number of general concepts.

8.2.1   Consistency

Let us consider the general initial value problem

$$\frac{\partial u}{\partial t} + Lu = F, \quad -\infty < x < \infty, \quad t > 0 \tag{8.7a}$$

$$u(x, 0) = f(x), \quad -\infty < x < \infty \tag{8.7b}$$

and consider some finite difference scheme

$$L_h^k u_j^n = G_j^n \tag{8.8a}$$

$$u_j^0 = f(x_j) \tag{8.8b}$$

where G_j^n is some approximation to $F(x_j, t_n)$ and L_h^k is a discrete approximation to L

Definition 8.1. The finite difference scheme (8.8a) is pointwise consistent with the partial differential equation (8.7a) if for any function $v = v(x, t)$ the following relationship holds:

$$\left(\frac{\partial v}{\partial t} + Lv - F\right)_j^n - \left[L_h^k v(x_j, t_n) - G_j^n\right] \to 0 \quad \text{as } h, k \to 0 \quad \text{and } (x_j, t_{n+1}) \to (x, t) \tag{8.9}$$

This definition tells us how well the differential equation approximates the finite difference scheme. We can write (8.9) in the equivalent form

$$\left(\frac{\partial}{\partial t} + L - L_k^h\right) v(x_j, t_n) + G_j^n - F_j^n = 0 \tag{8.10}$$

Thus the scheme is consistent (or compatible) with the initial value problem if the terms in (8.10) approach zero as h and k tends to zero. The second term represents approximations to the source term F in equations (8.7) and this tends to zero. It only remains to prove that the first term in (8.10) also tends to zero in general.

Let us take the example of scheme (8.6) that approximates the heat equation (notice that $F = 0$ in this case). Then for the scheme (8.6) we get:

$$\left(\frac{\partial}{\partial t} + L - L_k^h\right) u(x_j, t_n) = \frac{\partial u(x_j, t_n)}{\partial t} - \frac{u(x_j, t_{n+1}) - u(x_j, t_n)}{k}$$
$$- a^2 \left(\frac{\partial^2 u(x_j, t_n)}{\partial x^2} - D_+ D_- u(x_j, t_n)\right) \tag{8.11}$$

Then, by applying Taylor's theorem with an exact remainder we can show that this term is bounded by

$$M(h^2 + k) \tag{8.12}$$

where M depends on the derivatives of u with respect to x and t but is independent of k and h. Thus, scheme (8.6) is consistent with the heat equation.

8.2.2   Stability

We now investigate the concept of stability of finite difference schemes. For the moment, let us take a scheme whose inhomogeneous term is zero. We write a general one-step scheme for an initial value problem in the vector form

$$\mathbf{u}^{n+1} = Q\mathbf{u}^n, \quad n \geq 0$$
$$\mathbf{u}^n = {}^t(\ldots, u^n_{-1}, u^n_0, u^n_1, \ldots)$$
(8.13)

where Q is an operator.

Definition 8.2. The difference scheme (8.13) is said to be stable with respect to the norm $\| \cdot \|$ if there exist positive constants k_0 and h_0 and two non-negative constants K and β such that

$$\|\mathbf{u}^{n+1}\| \leq K e^{\beta t} \|u^n\| \quad \text{for } 0 \leq t = t_{n+1}, \quad 0 < h \leq h_0 \text{ and } 0 < k \leq k_0 \quad (8.14)$$

We now generalise (8.13) to include an inhomogeneous term

$$\mathbf{u}^{n+1} = Q\mathbf{u}^n + k\mathbf{G}^n$$
$$\mathbf{G}^n \equiv {}^t(\ldots, G^n_{-1}, G^n_0, G^n_1, \ldots)$$
(8.15)

Definition 8.3. The difference scheme (8.15) is consistent with the partial differential equation (8.7a) if the solution of (8.7a) satisfies

$$\mathbf{v}^{n+1} = Q\mathbf{v}^n + k\mathbf{G}^n + k\tau^n \quad \text{and} \quad \|\tau^n\| \to 0, \quad \text{as } h, k \to 0 \quad (8.16)$$

where $\mathbf{v}^n$ denotes the vector whose jth component is $u(x_j, t_n)$.

Definition 8.4. The difference scheme (8.15) is said to be accurate of order (p, q) to the given partial differential equation if

$$\|\tau^n\| = O(h^p) + O(k^q) \quad (8.17)$$

We refer to τ^n or $\|\tau^n\|$ as the trunction error.

8.2.3   Convergence

We now discuss the fundamental relationship between consistency and stability.

Theorem 8.1. *(The Lax equivalence theorem.) A consistent, two-level scheme of the form (8.15) for a well-posed linear initial value problem is convergent if and only if it is stable.*

As long as we have a consistent scheme, convergence is synonymous with stability. In short, all we need to prove is that a scheme is consistent (use Taylor's theorem) and stable. As we shall see, there are a few technical methods to prove stability. We discuss the first approach, namely the von Neumann amplification factor method, that is based on the Fourier transform.

8.3   STABILITY AND THE FOURIER TRANSFORM

We give a short introduction to the Fourier transform. We use it to prove the stability of finite difference schemes.

Let us suppose that a function $f(x)$ is a complex-valued function of the real variable x. Furthermore, assume that f is integrable in the following sense:

$$\int_{-\infty}^{\infty} |f(x)| \, dx < \infty \quad (8.18)$$

We then define the Fourier transform of f as follows:

$$\hat{f}(t) = \int_{-\infty}^{\infty} e^{-i2\pi tx} f(x)\,dx, \quad i = \sqrt{-1} \tag{8.19}$$

The transformed function is also complex-valued:

$$\hat{f}(t) = R(t) + iI(t) = |\hat{f}(t)| e^{i\theta(t)}$$

where $|\hat{f}(t)|$ is called the amplitude and θ is called the phase angle, defined as follows

$$\theta = \tan^{-1}(I(t)/R(t))$$
$$|\hat{f}(t)| = \sqrt{R^2(t) + I^2(t)} \tag{8.20}$$

Let us take an example. Define the function $f(x)$ by

$$f(x) = \begin{cases} \beta e^{-\alpha x}, & x \geq 0 \\ 0, & x < 0 \end{cases}$$

Then

$$\hat{f}(t) = \int_{-\infty}^{\infty} e^{-i2\pi tx} f(x)\,dx = \int_0^{\infty} e^{-i2\pi tx} \beta\,e^{-\alpha x}\,dx = \beta \int_0^{\infty} e^{-(\alpha + i2\pi t)x}\,dx$$

$$= \frac{\beta}{\alpha + i2\pi t}$$

$$= \frac{\beta\alpha}{\alpha^2 + (2\pi t)^2} - i\frac{2\pi t\beta}{\alpha^2 + (2\pi t)^2} \tag{8.21}$$

We now introduce the inverse Fourier transform that recovers a function from the transformed function and is defined by

$$f(x) = \int_{-\infty}^{\infty} e^{i2\pi tx} \hat{f}(t)\,dt \tag{8.22}$$

An important relationship between the Fourier transform and its inverse is Parseval's theorem, namely

$$\int_{-\infty}^{\infty} |f(x)|^2\,dx = \int_{-\infty}^{\infty} |\hat{f}(t)|^2\,dt \tag{8.23}$$

In this case we say that the transforms are norm-preserving. The relevance of the Fourier transform to partial differential equations is that these PDEs can be transformed to a simpler problem, this latter problem is solved and then the inverse transform recovers the solution to the original problem. Let us take an example. Consider the initial value problem (Thomas, 1998):

$$\frac{\partial u}{\partial t} = \frac{\partial^2 u}{\partial x^2}, \quad x \in \mathbb{R}, \quad t > 0 \tag{8.24}$$

$$u(x, 0) = f(x), \quad x \in \mathbb{R}$$

Taking the Fourier transform on both sides of the partial differential equation we get

$$\frac{\partial \hat{u}}{\partial t}(\omega, t) \equiv \int_{-\infty}^{\infty} e^{-i2\pi \omega x} \frac{\partial u}{\partial t}(x, t)\, dx$$

$$= \int_{-\infty}^{\infty} \frac{\partial^2 u}{\partial x^2}(x, t) e^{-i2\pi \omega x}\, dx$$

$$= -\omega^2 \int_{-\infty}^{\infty} u(x, t) e^{-i2\pi \omega x}\, dx \tag{8.25}$$

where we have used integration by parts twice and the fact that u and its first derivative in x are zero at plus and minus infinity. We rewrite (8.25) in the equivalent form

$$\frac{\partial \hat{u}}{\partial t}(\omega, t) = -\omega^2 \hat{u}(\omega, t) \tag{8.26}$$

We thus see the PDE is transformed to an ODE in transform space (the space of transformed functions). We define the initial condition for (8.26) as:

$$\hat{u}(\omega, 0) = \int_{-\infty}^{\infty} e^{-i2\pi \omega x} u(x, 0)\, dx$$

$$= \int_{-\infty}^{\infty} e^{-i2\pi \omega x} f(x)\, dx \tag{8.27}$$

The solution of (8.26), (8.27) is then given by

$$\hat{u}(\omega, t) = \hat{u}(\omega, 0) e^{-\omega^2 t} \tag{8.28}$$

Now for the last step; the original solution to IVP (8.24) is realised by using the inverse Fourier transform as follows:

$$u(x, t) = \int_{-\infty}^{\infty} e^{i2\pi \omega x} \hat{u}(\omega, t)\, dw \tag{8.29}$$

and we are finished.

This process is a special case of using transforms in general and a schematic representation is shown in Figure 8.1, which shows how we can use transform methods in general to simplify a given problem.

8.4   THE DISCRETE FOURIER TRANSFORM

We now introduce the discrete variant of the continuous Fourier transform. We apply the discrete Fourier transform (DFT) to a finite difference scheme that will allow us to prove that the scheme is stable (or otherwise).

Let $\mathbf{u} = {}^t(\ldots, u_{-1}, u_0, u_1, \ldots)$ be an infinite sequence of values. Then the DFT (given in Thomas, 1998) is defined as

$$\hat{u}(\xi) = \frac{1}{\sqrt{2\pi}} \sum_{n=-\infty}^{\infty} e^{-in\xi} u_n \tag{8.30}$$

Using this definition we can apply it to the study of finite difference schemes. In particular, we use it to transform an arbitrary finite difference scheme to a much simpler form. But first

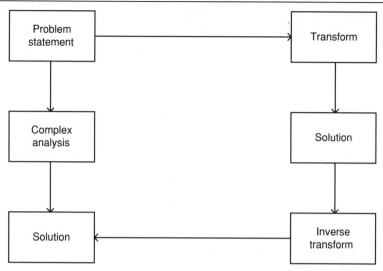

Figure 8.1 Solving a problem

let us take an example of the explicit Euler scheme for the heat equation that we again write in the form

$$u_j^{n+1} = \lambda u_{j-1}^n + (1 - 2\lambda)u_j^n + \lambda u_{j+1}^n \tag{8.31}$$

where $\lambda \equiv ak/h^2$.

Applying the DFT (8.30) to both sides of (8.31) gives the following sequence of results:

$$\frac{1}{\sqrt{2\pi}} \sum_{j=-\infty}^{\infty} e^{-ij\xi} u_j^{n+1} \equiv \hat{u}^{n+1}(\xi)$$

$$= \frac{1}{\sqrt{2\pi}} \left\{ \sum_{j=-\infty}^{\infty} e^{-ij\xi} \left[\lambda u_{j-1}^n + (1 - 2\lambda)u_j^n + \lambda u_{j+1}^n \right] \right\}$$

$$= \frac{\lambda}{\sqrt{2\pi}} \sum_{j=-\infty}^{\infty} e^{-ij\xi} u_{j-1}^n + \frac{1 - 2\lambda}{\sqrt{2\pi}} \sum_{j=-\infty}^{\infty} e^{-ij\xi} u_j^n + \frac{\lambda}{\sqrt{2\pi}} \sum_{j=-\infty}^{\infty} e^{-ij\xi} u_{j+1}^n \tag{8.32}$$

By making a change of variables we can easily prove that

$$\frac{1}{\sqrt{2\pi}} \sum_{j=-\infty}^{\infty} e^{-ij\xi} u_{j\pm 1}^n = \frac{e^{\pm i\xi}}{\sqrt{2\pi}} \sum_{m=-\infty}^{\infty} e^{-im\xi} u_m^n = e^{\pm i\xi} \hat{u}^n(\xi) \quad (m = j \pm 1) \tag{8.33}$$

Using this result in (8.32) we see that, after having done some arithmetic,

$$\hat{u}^{n+1}(\xi) = \lambda e^{-i\xi} \hat{u}^n(\xi) + (1 - 2\lambda)\hat{u}^n(\xi) + \lambda e^{i\xi} \hat{u}^n(\xi)$$

$$= \left[\lambda e^{-i\xi} + (1 - 2\lambda) + \lambda e^{i\xi} \right] \hat{u}^n(\xi)$$

$$= [2\lambda \cos \xi + (1 - 2\lambda)] \hat{u}^n(\xi)$$

$$= \left(1 - 4\lambda^2 \sin^2 \frac{\xi}{2} \right) \hat{u}^n(\xi) \tag{8.34}$$

We thus eliminate the x dependency and this greatly simplifies matters. Continuing, we define the symbol of the difference scheme (8.31) by

$$\rho(\xi) = 1 - 4\lambda^2 \sin^2 \frac{\xi}{2} \tag{8.35}$$

Applying this formula $n + 1$ times gives

$$\hat{u}^{n+1}(\xi) = \rho(\xi)^{n+1} \hat{u}^0(\xi) \tag{8.36}$$

From Thomas (1998) this quantity needs to be less than 1 in absolute value and some tedious but simple arithmetic shows that a sufficient condition is

$$|\rho(\xi)| \le 1 \quad \text{or} \quad \lambda \le \tfrac{1}{2} \tag{8.37}$$

This technique can be applied to more general finite difference schemes.

8.4.1   Some other examples

We conclude this section with some other examples of difference equations whose stability we prove using DFT.

We consider the heat equation for convenience. Some arithmetic shows that its symbol for Crank–Nicolson is given by

$$\rho(\xi) = \frac{1 - 2\lambda \sin^2 \xi/2}{1 + 2\lambda \sin^2 \xi/2} \tag{8.38}$$

The implicit Euler scheme has the symbol:

$$\rho(\xi) = \frac{1}{1 + 4\lambda \sin^2 \xi/2} \tag{8.39}$$

Both symbols have absolute value less than 1 and we conclude that the schemes are unconditionally stable.

As a counterexample, we give an example of a scheme that is not stable. The equation is:

$$\frac{\partial u}{\partial t} - \frac{\partial u}{\partial x} = 0 \tag{8.40}$$

This is wave equation with the wave travelling in the negative x direction with speed equal to 1. We propose upwinding in space, explicit in time scheme:

$$\frac{u_j^{n+1} - u_j^n}{k} - \frac{u_j^n - u_{j-1}^n}{h} = 0 \tag{8.41}$$

Again, some arithmetic shows that

$$\rho(\xi) = 1 + \lambda - \lambda\,e^{-i\xi}, \quad \lambda = \tfrac{k}{h}$$
$$|\rho(\xi)| \le 1 \text{ never satisfied} \tag{8.42}$$

Thus (8.41) is an unconditionally unstable scheme!

Finally, we consider the convection–diffusion equation with constant coefficients

$$\frac{\partial u}{\partial t} + a \frac{\partial u}{\partial x} = \nu \frac{\partial^2 u}{\partial x^2} \tag{8.43}$$

with corresponding difference scheme (centred differences in x, explicit in time)

$$\frac{u_j^{n+1} - u_j^n}{k} + a\frac{u_{j+1}^n - u_{j-1}^n}{2h} = \nu D_+ D_- u_j^n \tag{8.44}$$

The symbol is given by

$$\rho(\xi) = (1 - 2\lambda) + 2\lambda \cos \xi - iR \sin \xi \tag{8.45}$$

where $\lambda = \nu k/h^2$ and $R = ak/h$.

Again, some long-winded arithmetic shows that the symbol has absolute value less than 1 if

$$\frac{R^2}{2} \leq \lambda \leq \tfrac{1}{2} \tag{8.46}$$

See, for example, Thomas (1998) or Richtmyer and Morton (1967).

8.5 STABILITY FOR INITIAL BOUNDARY VALUE PROBLEMS

Up until now we have discussed problems on an infinite interval. We shall now consider problems on a finite space interval, namely initial boundary value problems. In general, schemes that are unstable for an IVP (such as (8.41)) will also be unstable for the corresponding initial boundary value problem. In order to keep things concrete for the moment, we examine the following initial boundary value problem for the heat equation:

$$\begin{aligned}
\frac{\partial u}{\partial t} &= \frac{\partial^2 u}{\partial x^2}, \quad 0 < x < 1, \quad t > 0 \\
u(x, 0) &= f(x), \quad 0 \leq x \leq 1 \\
u(0, t) &= g(t), \quad u(1, t) = h(t), \quad t > 0
\end{aligned} \tag{8.47}$$

along with the compatibility conditions

$$f(0) = g(0), \quad f(1) = h(0)$$

We then propose the Crank–Nicolson scheme

$$\begin{aligned}
u_j^{n+1} - \tfrac{k}{2}D_+ D_- u_j^{n+1} &= u_j^n + \tfrac{k}{2}D_+ D_- u_j^n, \quad j = 1, \ldots, J-1 \\
u_j^0 &= f(x_j), \quad j = 1, \ldots, J-1 \\
u_0^{n+1} &= g(t_{n+1}), \quad u_J^{n+1} = h(t_{n+1}), \quad n \geq 0
\end{aligned} \tag{8.48}$$

Assembling the information in equation (8.48) and assuming zero boundary conditions we can write it in the equivalent matrix form

$$M\mathbf{u}^{n+1} = Q\mathbf{u}^n, \quad n \geq 0 \tag{8.49}$$

where

$$\mathbf{u}^n = {}^t(u_1^n, \ldots, u_{J-1}^n) \tag{8.50}$$

The questions concerning system (8.49) are: Does it have a solution and is it stable? The following discussion attempts to answer these questions in general. To this end, we introduce a useful technique from matrix algebra.

8.5.1 Gerschgorin's circle theorem

In many of the following chapters we shall develop finite difference schemes for one-factor and multi-factor Black–Scholes equations. To this end, it is important to determine if a solution of the resulting matrix system exists and is unique. In the following discussions we assume that A is a real square matrix – that is, one with n rows and n columns:

$$A = (a_{ij}) \quad i,j=1,n$$

Definition 8.5. Let the matrix A have eigenvalues $\lambda_j, \quad j = 1, \ldots, n$. Then

$$\rho(A) \equiv \max_{j=1,\ldots,n} |\lambda_j|$$

is called the spectral radius of the matrix A.

Definition 8.6. The quantity

$$\|A\| = \sup_{x \neq 0} \frac{\|Ax\|}{\|x\|}$$

is the spectral norm of the matrix A, where x is a vector.

It can be shown (Varga, 1962) that

$$\|A\| \geq \rho(A)$$

which gives the relationship between the spectral norm and spectral radius.

We define the quantity

$$\wedge_i \equiv \sum_{\substack{j=1 \\ j \neq i}}^{n} |a_{ij}| \text{ for } 1 \leq i \leq n$$

The following theorem describes the distribution of the eigenvalues of a matrix.

Theorem 8.2. *(Gerschgorin, 1931.) The eigenvalues of the matrix A lie in the union of the disks*

$$|z - a_{ii}| \leq \wedge_i, \quad 1 \leq i \leq n$$

Corollary 8.1. *If A is a square matrix and*

$$\nu \equiv \max_{1 \leq i \leq n} \sum_{j=1}^{n} |a_{ij}|$$

then $\rho(A) \leq \nu$.

Thus, the maximum of the row sums of the moduli of the entries of the matrix A give a simple upper bound for the spectral radius of the matrix A.

Let us take an example. This is the matrix M in equation (8.49):

$$M = \begin{pmatrix} 1+r & -r/2 & & 0 \\ -r/2 & \ddots & \ddots & \\ & \ddots & \ddots & -r/2 \\ 0 & & -r/2 & 1+r \end{pmatrix}$$

and define

$$
Q = \begin{pmatrix}
1-r & r/2 & & 0 \\
r/2 & \ddots & \ddots & \\
& \ddots & \ddots & r/2 \\
0 & & r/2 & 1-r
\end{pmatrix}
$$

where $r = k/h^2$.

$$
\wedge_1 = \wedge_n = \frac{r}{2}
$$

$$
\wedge_j = r, \quad j = 2, \ldots, n-1
$$

We then get

$$
|z - (1+r)| \leq \frac{r}{2} \quad \text{and} \quad |z - (1+r)| \leq r
$$

If the first inequality is satisfied, then the second inequality is also satisfied.
    But then we get

$$
1 \leq z \leq 1 + 2r
$$

We thus see that the eigenvalues of M are always greater than or equal to 1. This implies that the eigenvalues of its inverse are always less than or equal to 1.

Definition 8.7. A Toeplitz matrix is a band matrix in which each diagonal consists of identical elements, although different diagonals may contain different values.

We are particularly interested in tridiagonal Toeplitz matrices. Then the eigenvalues are known (Thomas, 1998; Bronson, 1989), namely:

$$
\begin{pmatrix}
b & c & & 0 \\
a & \ddots & \ddots & \\
& \ddots & \ddots & c \\
0 & & a & b
\end{pmatrix}
\tag{8.51}
$$

where the eigenvalues are defined by

$$
\lambda_j = b + 2\sqrt{ac} \, \cos \frac{j\pi}{n+1}, \quad j = 1, 2, \ldots, n
$$

    This is a useful formula because some difference schemes lead to matrices whose eigenvalues are not real but complex. Oscillatory solutions will appear in such cases.

8.6   SUMMARY AND CONCLUSIONS

We have given an introduction to a number of theoretical issues that help us to determine if a given finite difference scheme is a 'good' approximation to an initial value problem or initial boundary value problem. We discussed consistency, convergence and stability of a difference scheme. In particular, we introduced the 'Lax equivalence theorem', one of the most famous theorems in numerical analysis. Many of the examples centred around the heat equation because we can show how the theory works in this case. In the next two chapters we shall build on our results by examining the convection–diffusion equation and various finite difference schemes that approximate it. Furthermore, we need to investigate the effect of boundary conditions (Dirichlet, Neumann and linearity conditions) on the overall accuracy of the schemes.

Finite Difference Schemes for First-Order Partial Differential Equations

9.1 INTRODUCTION AND OBJECTIVES

In this chapter we develop stable and accurate finite difference schemes for partial differential equations in two independent variables x and t where the derivatives in x and t are both of order 1. In other words, we discuss a number of first-order hyperbolic partial differential equations and we approximate them by explicit and implicit finite difference schemes. We take a model problem in order to motivate these schemes. In later chapters we shall reuse these schemes in larger and more complex applications. Thus, it is important to first master the finite difference schemes for initial value problems and initial boundary value problems for first-order hyperbolic partial differential equations.

The examples in this chapter are found in the physical sciences as well as in financial engineering. We shall need the results from this chapter in later chapters, especially when we investigate the convective terms in the Black–Scholes equation.

9.2 SCOPING THE PROBLEM

There is a vast literature on first-order hyperbolic equations. Much effort has gone into devising robust approximate schemes in application areas such as gas and fluid dynamics, chemical reactor theory and wave phenomena (see Rhee *et al.*, 1986, 1989; Godounov *et al.*, 1979). We consider first-order partial differential equations in two independent variables x and t. The first variable is typically space (or some other dimension) and the second variable usually represents time. The first model problem is an initial value problem (IVP) on an infinite interval:

$$\frac{\partial u}{\partial t} + a\frac{\partial u}{\partial x} = 0, \quad -\infty < x < \infty, \quad t > 0$$

$$u(x, 0) = f(x), \quad -\infty < x < \infty$$

(9.1)

In these equations the constant a can be positive or negative and $f = f(x)$ is some given function that we call the initial condition. System (9.1) is a model for wave propagation in homogeneous media. For example, the solution $u(x, t)$ could represent the concentration of a reactant in a chemical process and a is the linear velocity of the reactant mixture (Rhee *et al.*, 1986). Another example models problems related to multi-phase flow in porous media in reservoir engineering (Peaceman, 1977). In this case $u(x, t)$ is the saturation variable and a is the positive velocity and represents flow in the direction of increasing x. We shall later discuss examples from financial engineering in which the variables x, t and u will take on specific roles, but for the present we shall view (9.1) from a generic perspective.

The second model problem is the so-called initial boundary value problem (IBVP) defined as:

$$\frac{\partial u}{\partial t} + a\frac{\partial u}{\partial x} = 0, \quad 0 < x < 1, \quad t > 0$$

$$u(x, 0) = f(x), \quad 0 \le x \le 1 \tag{9.2}$$

$$u(0, t) = g(t), \quad t \ge 0$$

In this case we assume that $a > 0$ and that a boundary condition $g(t)$ is given when $x = 0$. This is the correct boundary condition because information is coming from left to right. In the case when $a < 0$ the IBVP is formulated as follows:

$$\frac{\partial u}{\partial t} + a\frac{\partial u}{\partial x} = 0, \quad 0 < x < 1, \quad t > 0$$

$$u(x, 0) = f(x), \quad 0 \le x \le 1 \tag{9.3}$$

$$u(1, t) = g(t), \quad t \ge 0$$

The main difference between the IVP (9.1) and IBVP (9.2) or (9.3) is the presence of a boundary condition. This latter condition is needed in many situations. For example, the simplest form of heat exchanger consists of a tube immersed in a bath held at a constant temperature K. If the temperature of the fluid flowing through the tube is $u(x, t)$ at some point from the inlet at $x = 0$, then the IBVP for this case is given by

$$\frac{\partial u}{\partial t} + V\frac{\partial u}{\partial x} = H(K - u), \quad 0 < x < 1, \quad t > 0$$

$$u(x, 0) = f(x), \quad 0 \le x \le 1 \tag{9.4}$$

$$u(0, t) = g(t), \quad t \ge 0$$

where V is the velocity of the fluid, H is some constant, $f(x)$ is the initial temperature distribution and $g(t)$ is the inlet boundary condition. In general, for first-order IBVP we place the boundary condition at $x = 0$ when $a > 0$ (as in equation (9.2)) or at $x = 1$ when $a < 0$ (as in equation (9.3)).

We conclude this section with some examples from financial engineering. The first example is the PDE for an Asian option (Ingersoll, 1987; Wilmott, 1998):

$$-\frac{\partial F}{\partial t} + \frac{1}{2}\sigma^2 S^2 \frac{\partial^2 F}{\partial S^2} + rS\frac{\partial F}{\partial S} + S\frac{\partial F}{\partial A} - rF = 0$$
$$0 < S < \infty, \ 0 < A < \infty, \ 0 < t < T \tag{9.5a}$$

$$F(0, A, t) = 0, \quad t \ge 0 \tag{9.5b}$$

$$F(\infty, A, T) = 1, \quad 0 \le A < \infty \tag{9.5c}$$

$$F(S, \infty, t) = 0, \quad t \ge 0 \tag{9.5d}$$

$$F(S, A, T) = \max\left(S - \frac{A}{T}, 0\right) \tag{9.5e}$$

where the average A is defined by:

$$A = A(T) \equiv \int_0^T S(t)\,dt \tag{9.6}$$

and F is the variable representing the Asian option price.

We see that the equation in the A direction is first order (there is no diffusion term) and thus only one boundary condition needs to be given. We can convince ourselves that the condition at infinity is the right one (in fact, it is similar to equation (9.3)). Thus, system (9.5) is well posed.

The second example is taken from Tavella *et al.* (2000). In this case we examine the Black–Scholes equation:

$$-\frac{\partial V}{\partial t} + \frac{1}{2}\sigma^2 S^2 \frac{\partial^2 V}{\partial S^2} + (r - D)S\frac{\partial V}{\partial S} - rV = 0 \tag{9.7}$$

We investigate the consequences of applying the *linearity boundary condition*

$$\frac{\partial^2 V}{\partial S^2} = 0 \quad \text{when } S = S_{\text{max}} \tag{9.8}$$

where S_{max} is the position of the so-called far field.

In this case the pricing equation (9.7) at $S = 0$ degenerates into the *ordinary differential equation*

$$-\frac{dV}{dt} - rV = 0 \tag{9.9}$$

and it is possible to solve this analytically.

The final example is concerned with the pricing of a zero coupon bond under a Cox–Ingersoll–Ross (CIR) interest-rate model. The pricing equation is given by the parabolic PDE (Tavella *et al.*, 2000)

$$-\frac{\partial B}{\partial t} + \frac{1}{2}\sigma^2 r \frac{\partial^2 B}{\partial r^2} + (a - br)\frac{\partial B}{\partial r} - rB = 0 \tag{9.10}$$

where B is the bond price.

If we let the PDE 'degenerate' to $r = 0$, we get the following boundary condition

$$-\frac{\partial B}{\partial t} + a\frac{\partial B}{\partial r} = 0 \tag{9.11}$$

Thus, on the boundary $r = 0$ we must solve a first-order hyperbolic equation that can be solved numerically, for example.

9.3 WHY FIRST-ORDER EQUATIONS ARE DIFFERENT: ESSENTIAL DIFFICULTIES

Hyperbolic partial differential equations model many kinds of phenomena in the real world – for example, aerodynamics, atmospheric flow, fluid flow in porous media, and more (see Morton, 1996; Dutton, 1986). Hyperbolic equations tend to be more difficult to model than parabolic and elliptic equations. In particular, finding good schemes for nonlinear systems of equations is a non-trivial task (Lax, 1973).

We first take a look at the model initial value problem (9.1). In this case we can conveniently ignore boundary conditions. The reader can check that the solution of (9.1) is given by

$$u(x, t) = f(x - at), \quad -\infty < x < \infty, \quad t > 0 \tag{9.12}$$

Thus, we know what the solution is and we also know that it is constant along the *characteristic curve* $x - at = $ constant. The family of characteristics completely determines the solution at any point (x, t). Furthermore, the form of the solution $u(x, t)$ is the same as that of $f(x)$ except that the form is translated to the right in the case $a > 0$ and to the left in the case $a < 0$.

A special property of the solution of (9.1) is that it contains no *dissipation*. This means that the Fourier modes neither decay nor grow with time. A major challenge when designing finite difference schemes for hyperbolic equations is to design them to be stable while at the same time ensuring that they do not damp out the solution.

Another challenge is to develop schemes that take the *speed of propagation* of the solution u into account. It is intuitively obvious that the numerical schemes should give good approximations to the speed of propagation of the wave forms from the analytic solution.

Finally, *dispersion* is concerned with how the numerical solution loses its form in time. A good discussion of these topics is given in Vichnevetsky and Bowles (1982).

9.3.1 Discontinuous initial conditions

As stated in Thomas (1999), *the solution will only be as smooth as the initial condition*. This is in sharp contrast to parabolic equations where the solution becomes smooth after a certain time even if the initial condition is discontinuous. A simple example is given by defining the initial condition

$$f(x) = \begin{cases} 1 & \text{if } x \leq 0 \\ 0 & \text{if } x > 0 \end{cases} \tag{9.13}$$

Using the exact formula (9.12) we see that the solution $u(x, t)$ will be discontinuous along the lines $x - at = \text{constant}$. The solution in this case is given by

$$u(x, t) = \begin{cases} 1, & x \leq at \\ 0, & x > at \end{cases} \tag{9.14}$$

We conclude that the solution cannot satisfy (9.1) in the classical sense and in this case we must resort to finding a so-called *weak solution*. For a detailed discussion of this topic, see Thomas (1999) and Lax (1973) as this topic is outside the scope of this book.

9.4   A SIMPLE EXPLICIT SCHEME

In this section we introduce a simple finite difference scheme. To this end, we partition (x, t) space by a uniform rectangular mesh and we define the constants h and k to be the mesh sizes in the x and t directions, respectively. In general, we employ one-step methods in the t direction and choose between one-sided or centred differencing in the x direction. We depict the mesh in Figure 9.1.

Let us examine IVP (9.1) again. The first scheme, called Forward in Time, Backward in Space (FTBS), is defined by

$$\frac{u_j^{n+1} - u_j^n}{k} + a\frac{u_j^n - u_{j-1}^n}{h} = 0, \quad a > 0$$

or

$$u_j^{n+1} = (1 - \lambda)u_j^n + \lambda u_{j-1}^n, \quad n \geq 0 \tag{9.15}$$

$$\lambda \equiv \frac{ak}{h}$$

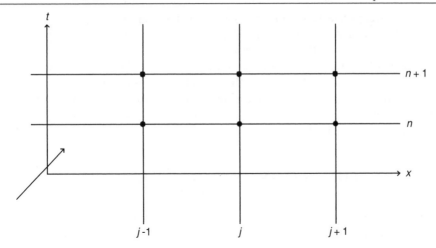

Figure 9.1 Mesh in (x, t) space

Thus, the value at time level $n + 1$ is computed directly from the value at time level n. However, if the parameter λ is greater than 1 the solution may oscillate boundedly or unboundedly. This is a common problem with explicit difference schemes, and we say that (9.15) is conditionally stable. This means that the inequality

$$|\lambda| = \left|\frac{ak}{h}\right| \leq 1 \tag{9.16}$$

must hold if we wish to have a stable and, hence, convergent scheme. Inequality (9.16) is called the Courant–Friedrichs–Lewy (CFL) condition, in honour of the mathematicians who devised it and is one of the most famous inequalities in numerical analysis. It can be shown that the CFL condition is necessary for convergence of the discrete solution to the analytic solution. In fact, we can 'replicate' the CFL inequality by applying the von Neumann stability analysis and examining Fourier modes:

$$u_j^n = \gamma^n\, e^{i\alpha jh}, \quad i = \sqrt{-1} \tag{9.17}$$

Using this representation in the scheme (9.15) gives an expression for the amplification factor as follows:

$$\gamma = (1 - \lambda + \lambda \cos \alpha h) - i\lambda \sin \alpha h$$
$$= 1 - \lambda(1 - \cos \alpha h) - i\lambda \sin \alpha h \tag{9.18}$$

Under the constraint (9.16) you can prove with some artithmetic that

$$|\gamma| \leq 1 \tag{9.19}$$

When the coefficient a in equation (9.1) is negative we advocate the following Forward in Time, Forward in Space (FTFS) scheme

$$\frac{u_j^{n+1} - u_j^n}{k} + a\frac{u_{j+1}^n - u_j^n}{h} = 0, \quad a < 0$$

or $\qquad u_j^{n+1} = (1 + \lambda)u_j^n - \lambda u_{j+1}^n = u_j^n - \lambda\left(u_{j+1}^n - u_j^n\right)$

$$\tag{9.20}$$

Again, we can calculate the amplification factor as before and it will be less than 1 in absolute value if the CFL inequality (9.16) holds. Thus, we must be careful when constructing good schemes; the sign of the coefficient a is important.

The scheme (9.15) uses so-called *backward differencing* (with $a > 0$) while the scheme (9.20) uses *forward differencing* (with $a < 0$). Unstable schemes will result if we use backward differencing with $a < 0$ or forward differencing with $a > 0$. You can convince yourself of this fact by calculating the amplification factors for the schemes. This is also important when working with more complex PDEs.

9.5 SOME COMMON SCHEMES FOR INITIAL VALUE PROBLEMS

We start with a FTCS (Forward in Time, Centred in Space) scheme where the derivative with respect to x is taken at the mesh points $(j - 1)h$ and $(j + 1)h$ and we use explicit Euler in time:

$$\frac{u_j^{n+1} - u_j^n}{k} + a\frac{u_{j+1}^n - u_{j-1}^n}{2h} = 0 \tag{9.21a}$$

Then

$$\gamma(\xi) = 1 - i\,\lambda\sin\xi \left(\lambda = \frac{ak}{h}\right) \quad \text{and} \quad |\gamma(\xi)|^2 \geq 1 \text{ always!} \tag{9.21b}$$

This scheme is thus never stable for any value of the CFL number! We say that this scheme is unconditionally unstable. This is a pity but the situation can be improved somewhat by adding a so-called viscosity term to scheme (9.21) in order to stabilise it. The result is called the Lax–Wendroff scheme and is given by a second-order perturbation of scheme (9.21), namely:

$$u_j^{n+1} = u_j^n - \frac{\lambda}{2}\left(u_{j+1}^n - u_{j-1}^n\right) + \frac{\lambda^2}{2}\left(u_{j+1}^n - 2u_j^n + u_{j-1}^n\right) \tag{9.22}$$

and this scheme is stable if $|\lambda| \leq 1$.

Thus, Lax–Wendroff is a conditionally stable explicit scheme.

We now discuss some implicit schemes. The first scheme, Backward in Time, Backward in Space (BTBS), is given by:

$$\frac{u_j^{n+1} - u_j^n}{k} + a\frac{u_j^{n+1} - u_{j-1}^{n+1}}{h} = 0, \quad a > 0 \tag{9.23a}$$

or

$$u_j^{n+1}(1 + \lambda) = u_j^n + \lambda u_{j-1}^{n+1} \tag{9.23b}$$

This scheme is always stable. The centred difference scheme is given by:

$$\frac{u_j^{n+1} - u_j^n}{k} + a\frac{u_{j+1}^{n+1} - u_{j-1}^{n+1}}{2h} = 0 \tag{9.24}$$

We can show that the amplification factor in this case is

$$\gamma = \frac{1}{1 + \lambda i \sin \alpha h}, \quad |\gamma| < 1 \tag{9.25}$$

and hence the scheme is unconditionally stable.

We conclude this section by applying the Crank–Nicolson scheme to (9.1). It is an implicit scheme and uses averaging in time and centred differences in x:

$$\frac{u_j^{n+1} - u_j^n}{k} + a \frac{u_{j+1}^{n,\frac{1}{2}} - u_{j-1}^{n,\frac{1}{2}}}{2h} = 0 \tag{9.26}$$

where $u_j^{n,\frac{1}{2}} \equiv \frac{1}{2}(u_j^{n+1} + u_j^n)$.

After some lengthy but simple arithmetic we see that the amplification factor is given by:

$$\gamma = \frac{1 - i\beta}{1 + i\beta} \quad \text{where } \beta = \frac{\lambda}{2} \sin \alpha h, \quad \lambda = \frac{ak}{h} \tag{9.27}$$

and hence $|\gamma| = 1$

The Crank–Nicolson scheme is called *neutrally stable* because the absolute value of its amplification factor is exactly equal to 1! Any perturbation (for example, due to round-off errors) could make this value greater than 1. The end-result is possible instability and Gibbs-type oscillation phenomena.

Figure 9.2 is a schematic diagram of the different kinds of schemes for IVP (9.1), based on Peaceman (1977). It shows the stability 'levels' of the different kinds of finite difference schemes of (9.1). You can use this figure as a roadmap.

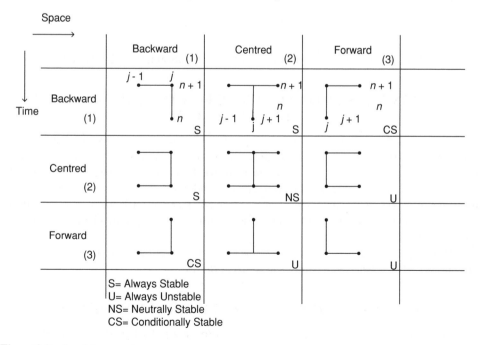

Figure 9.2   Special cases

9.5.1   Some other schemes

We give some other examples of finite difference schemes for first-order hyperbolic partial differential equations. We can use them as well as components or 'building blocks' for schemes for the Black–Scholes equation. We consider the three-level *leapfrog scheme* defined as

$$\frac{u_j^{n+1} - u_j^{n-1}}{2k} + a\frac{u_{j+1}^n - u_{j-1}^n}{2h} = 0 \tag{9.28}$$

This is a second-order accurate scheme with respect to k and h, which makes the scheme appealing. However, it requires two initial values which are usually determined by a two-level scheme. It can be shown (Dautray and Lions, 1983) that the leapfrog scheme is stable if

$$|a|\frac{k}{h} < 1 \tag{9.29}$$

Applying a von Neumann analysis to (9.28) shows that the leapfrog scheme is neutrally stable because the absolute value of its amplification factor is exactly 1.

The following scheme is called the Thomee or box scheme and gets its name from the fact that we take averages in the x and t directions on a box:

$$\frac{u_{j+\frac{1}{2}}^{n+1} - u_{j+\frac{1}{2}}^n}{k} + a\frac{u_{j+1}^{n+\frac{1}{2}} - u_j^{n+\frac{1}{2}}}{h} = 0 \tag{9.30}$$

with

$$u_{j+\frac{1}{2}}^n \equiv \tfrac{1}{2}\left(u_{j+1}^n + u_j^n\right)$$

and

$$u_j^{n+\frac{1}{2}} \equiv \tfrac{1}{2}\left(u_j^{n+1} + u_j^n\right)$$

This is also a second-order scheme in k and h. What is its amplification factor?

9.6   SOME COMMON SCHEMES FOR INITIAL BOUNDARY VALUE PROBLEMS

Having discussed IVP (9.1) in some detail, we now turn our attention to approximating the solution of the IBVP (9.2) using finite differences, starting in section 9.8. In principle the difference schemes that we used to approximate the solution of IVPs can be used for hyperbolic IBVPs under the proviso that we take the boundary conditions into consideration. In particular, for system (9.2) we see that data is given at $x = 0$ and that there is no data at $x = 1$. We must be careful not to destroy accuracy or stability just because we have applied a bad approximation on the boundaries.

In this chapter we discuss two-level schemes. A discussion of three-level schemes is given in Thomas (1998, 1999) and Dautray and Lions (1983).

9.7   MONOTONE AND POSITIVE-TYPE SCHEMES

In general the Lax equivalence theorem also holds for first-order hyperbolic schemes. If the difference scheme is stable and consistent, then it is convergent. We can prove stability by the von Neumann stability analysis, and we can prove consistency by using Taylor expansions

(Richtmyer and Morton, 1967). In this section, however, we take a different approach to proving stability and convergence. In particular, we are interested in *positive schemes* for IVP (9.1). We note that the solution of (9.1) is positive at all points (x, t) if the initial condition $f(x)$ is positive, because the exact solution is given by equation (9.12). We can now ask ourselves the following question: Which finite difference schemes give positive solutions from positive initial data? To this end, we write all two-level difference schemes in the form:

$$u_i^{n+1} = \sum_j c_j u_{i+j}^n \tag{9.31}$$

In this case the index j ranges over some set of integers. Incidentally, all the schemes in this chapter can be written in this form.

Definition 9.1. The scheme (9.31) is of positive type if and only if all the coefficients c_j are non-negative.

Not all schemes are of positive type. For example, the Lax–Wendroff scheme (9.22) is not of positive type.

Definition 9.2. A scheme is called stable if there exists a constant M (independent of k and h) such that

$$\max_i |u_i^n| \le M \max_i |u_i^0| \quad \forall n > 0 \tag{9.32}$$

The added value of positive type schemes is that they produce positive solutions from positive initial conditions. This is appealing because many applications do not allow a solution to become negative. For example, a negative option price in a difference scheme is unacceptable.

An important convergence result for positive type schemes states that the best order possible is 1.

Theorem 9.1. *If the scheme (9.31) is consistent with (9.1) and is of positive type, then it is of order 1 or 'infinity'.*

Another important property of positive type schemes is that they are stable in the max ('pointwise') norm.

Theorem 9.2. *If the scheme (9.31) is consistent with (9.1) and is of positive type, then it is stable in the sense of the inequality in equation (9.32).*

Again, the Lax–Wendroff scheme has order 2 and is not stable in the sense of inequality (9.32).

9.8 EXTENSIONS, GENERALISATIONS AND OTHER APPLICATIONS

There is a vast literature on first-order partial differential equations, much of which is not (yet) of direct relevance to financial engineering. We list certain classes of problems that can be seen as generalisations of the linear, constant-coefficient case in this chapter. Some of these classes will be needed when we discuss one-factor and multi-factor Black–Scholes equations.

You may skip this section on a first reading without loss of continuity.

9.8.1 General linear problems

The most general linear IBVP problem in this context is given by:

$$\frac{\partial u}{\partial t} + a(x, t)\frac{\partial u}{\partial x} = R(x, t), \quad 0 < x < 1, \quad t > 0, \quad a > 0$$

$$u(x, 0) = f(x), \quad 0 \le x < 1 \tag{9.33}$$

$$u(0, t) = g(t), \quad t \ge 0$$

and the finite difference schemes in this chapter can easily be adapted to accommodate the non-constantness in the coefficients.

For example, the FTBS scheme generalisation of (9.15) is:

$$\frac{u_j^{n+1} - u_j^n}{k} + a(x_j, t_n)\frac{u_j^n - u_{j-1}^n}{h} = R(x_j, t_n), \quad 1 \le j \le J, \quad n \ge 0$$

$$u_j^0 = f(x_j), \quad 1 \le j \le J - 1 \tag{9.34}$$

$$u_0^n = g(t_n), \quad n \ge 0$$

Other two-level schemes are defined in a similar fashion and we shall meet them in later chapters.

9.8.2 Systems of equations

In this case the solution is a vector quantity of the form

$$U = {}^t(u_1, \ldots, u_n)$$

$$u_j = u_j(x, t), \quad j = 1, \ldots, n \tag{9.35}$$

and we consider the system of partial differential equations

$$\frac{\partial U}{\partial t} + A\frac{\partial U}{\partial x} = 0 \tag{9.36}$$

where A is a square matrix of order n and is partitioned as follows

$$A = \begin{pmatrix} C & 0 \\ 0 & D \end{pmatrix} \tag{9.37}$$

The matrices C and D are symmetric square matrices of order l and $n - l$, respectively where $0 \le l \le n$. In order to define an IBVP for (9.36) we define initial and boundary conditions.

Intuitively, we need l boundary conditions at $x = 0$ (characteristics going from left to right) and $n - l$ boundary conditions at $x = 1$ (characteristics going from right to left). The initial boundary conditions are given by equations:

$$u(x, 0) = f(x), \quad 0 < x < 1, \quad f = {}^t(f_1, \ldots, f_n)$$

$$u^{\mathrm{I}}(0, t) = \alpha u^{\mathrm{II}}(0, t) + g_0(t), \quad t > 0$$

$$u^{\mathrm{II}}(1, t) = \beta u^{\mathrm{I}}(1, t) + g_1(t), \quad t > 0 \tag{9.38}$$

$$u^{\mathrm{I}} = {}^t(u_1, \ldots, \ldots u_l), \qquad u^{\mathrm{II}} = {}^t(u_{l+1}, \ldots, u_n)$$

where $g_0 \in \mathbb{R}^l$, $g_1 \in \mathbb{R}^{n-l}$, and α and β are matrices.

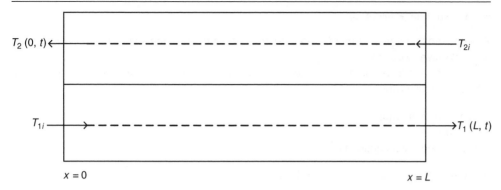

Figure 9.3   Countercurrent heat exchange *r*

Systems of the form (9.36) have been extensively studied and various approximate schemes advocated for them (see Dupont and Todd, 1973; Duffy, 1977; Friedrichs, 1958; Gustafsson *et al.*, 1972).

Let us take an example. The background to the example is somewhat technical (Rhee *et al.*, 1986) but it does illustrate how systems of first-order equations are proposed. We consider a so-called countercurrent heat exchanger depicted in Figure 9.3.

In this case the system consists of two temperature 'waves', one travelling from $x = 0$ to $x = L$ and the other variable from $x = L$ to $x = 0$. The system of equations is given by

$$\frac{\partial T_1}{\partial t} + V_1 \frac{\partial T_1}{\partial x} = H_1(T_2 - T_1)$$

$$\frac{\partial T_2}{\partial t} - V_2 \frac{\partial T_2}{\partial x} = H_2(T_1 - T_2)$$

(9.39)

where the (positive) constant coefficients V_1 and V_2 are velocities of the streams in the exchanger.

The initial and boundary conditions are:

$$T_1(x, 0) = T_{10}(x) \tag{9.40a}$$

$$T_2(x, 0) = T_{20}(x) \tag{9.40b}$$

$$T_1(0, t) = T_{1i}(t) \tag{9.40c}$$

$$T_2(L, t) = T_{2i}(t) \tag{9.40d}$$

where the functions on the right-hand side of equations (9.40) are given.

The relevance of hyperbolic systems to financial engineering is that such systems appear in systems of Black–Scholes equations, for example chooser and compound options (see Wilmott, 1998, p. 185) and convertible bonds with credit risk (see Ayache, 2002). In all cases we can formally arrive at a first-order system by setting the volatilities to zero. It is obvious that the finite difference schemes should be good approximations in this limiting case.

9.8.3   Nonlinear problems

A problem is nonlinear if one or more coefficients in the problems are functions of x, t and the (unknown) solution u.

We recognise three major categories of nonlinear functions, each of which is important in financial engineering:

- Semilinear equations
- Quasilinear equations
- Highly nonlinear equations.

A semilinear equation has the general form

$$\frac{\partial u}{\partial t} + a \frac{\partial u}{\partial x} + f(u) = 0 \tag{9.41}$$

where $f(u)$ is some nonlinear function of u. This kind of equation will be introduced when we discuss the approximate of American-style option problems using so-called penalty methods (see Nielson *et al.*, 2002). An example of a quasilinear equation has the general form

$$\frac{\partial u}{\partial t} + a(u) \frac{\partial u}{\partial x} = 0 \tag{9.42}$$

Finally, highly nonlinear equations are discussed in Wilmott (1998) where they are used to model the short-term interest rate using non-probabilistic methods. The defining equations are:

$$\frac{\partial V}{\partial t} + c \left(\frac{\partial V}{\partial r} \right) \left(\frac{\partial V}{\partial r} \right) - rV = 0$$

$$V(r, T) = known\ function$$

$$V(r, t_i^-) = V(r, t_i^+) + K \tag{9.43}$$

$$c(x) = \begin{cases} c^+, & x < 0 \\ c^-, & x > 0 \end{cases}$$

Again, good schemes need to be devised for this class of problem.

9.8.4   Several independent variables

Multi-factor pricing equations have first-order convection components. For example, a two-factor model will have the following generic form for its convection component:

$$\frac{\partial u}{\partial t} + a \frac{\partial u}{\partial x} + b \frac{\partial u}{\partial y} = 0 \tag{9.44}$$

In this case the coefficients a and b may be either positive or negative. We need to provide an initial condition of the form

$$u(x, y, 0) = f(x, y) \tag{9.45}$$

As in the discussion that has gone before we can consider initial value problems as well as initial boundary value problems for model (9.44). These topics will be discussed later. The options are:

- Discretise simultaneously with respect to x, y and t
- Approximate the two-dimensional problem as a sequence of simpler one-dimensional problems.

The second option implies the use of so-called alternating direction implicit (ADI) or operator splitting methods.

9.9 SUMMARY AND CONCLUSIONS

In this chapter we have introduced a number of finite difference schemes to approximate the convective (or advective) component of the Black–Scholes equation. This component is more difficult to approximate than simple diffusion equations and for this reason we must pay special attention to issues such as boundary conditions, stability and convergence.

We have analysed finite difference schemes for first-order problems in some depth for a number of reasons. First, they have not had much exposure in the quantitative finance literature and readers may not be certain of what does or does not constitute a good scheme. For instance, we have already given an example of a scheme that looks good (see scheme (9.21)) but which is always unconditionally unstable! Second, a good understanding of the theory in this chapter is essential when modelling one-factor and multi-factor PDEs, in particular those with convective terms. In particular, we shall need to investigate the relationship between convective and diffusion terms. Finally, some pricing applications can be modelled by PDEs that 'evolve' or reduce into a first-order PDE and we must be able to construct suitable schemes that degrade gracefully. For example, in certain bond pricing problems the time-dependent volatility may decrease exponentially to zero as we approach the maturity date. We then have a so-called singular perturbation problem and special schemes are needed in this case.

10

FDM for the One-Dimensional Convection–Diffusion Equation

10.1 INTRODUCTION AND OBJECTIVES

In this chapter we introduce standard difference schemes for parabolic differential equations containing second-order terms (diffusion) and first-order terms (convection or advection). In particular, this chapter contains details concerning finite difference schemes for the one-dimensional convection–diffusion equation. We focus on the special issues:

- Time-independent and time-dependent convection–diffusion equations
- Using standard finite difference schemes for convection–diffusion equations
- How to approximate Dirichlet, Neumann, Robin and linearity boundary conditions
- Setting up the linear system of equations
- Analysing the stability of the approximate schemes
- Approximating the derivatives of the solution
- Nasty and problematic cases (for example, discontinuous initial conditions).

The added value of this approach is that the transition to the one-factor and multi-factor Black–Scholes equation will be easy to realise.

In this book we are mainly interested in linear second-order BVP, and to this end we deal with the problem defined by

$$Lu \equiv -u'' + p(x)u' + q(x)u = r(x) \tag{10.1}$$

We now approximate this BVP using finite differences. There are two aspects to this problem. First, we must approximate the derivatives appearing in (10.1) using divided differences and second we have the added challenge of approximating the dependent variable or its first order derivative on the boundaries $x = a$ and $x = b$.

The first issue is addressed by defining a sub-division of the interval (a, b) into J equal sub-intervals

$$a = x_0 < x_1 < \cdots < x_{J-1} < x_J = b$$
$$h = x_j - x_{j-1}, \qquad j = 1, \ldots, J$$

We then use centred-differencing at each discrete mesh point and to this end we define the discrete operator

$$L_h u_j \equiv -\left(\frac{u_{j+1} - 2u_j + u_{j-1}}{h^2}\right) + p(x_j)\left(\frac{u_{j+1} - u_{j-1}}{2h}\right) + q(x_j)u_j \tag{10.2}$$

We now come to the problem of how to tackle the boundary conditions. There are two main options, namely

- Dirichlet condition: function u known at a and b
- Neumann condition: first derivative of u known at a or b.

We could also have hybrid boundary conditions in which case we would have Dirichlet boundary conditions at one end and Neumann boundary conditions at the other. Let us first look at Dirichlet boundary conditions for both continuous and discrete solutions:

$$u(a) = u_0 = \alpha$$
$$u(b) = u_J = \beta$$

(10.3)

Where α and β are given constants.

Theorem 10.1. *Let the coefficients $p(x)$ and $q(x)$ in (10.1) satisfy*

$$|p(x)| \le P^*, \quad 0 < Q_* \le q(x) \le Q^* \quad \text{for } a \le x \le b,$$

where P^*, Q_* and Q^* are positive constants, and suppose that the mesh size h satisfies

$$h \le \frac{2}{P^*}$$

(10.4)

Then the finite difference scheme (10.2) with boundary conditions (10.3) has a unique solution.

Remark. We may wonder what happens to the finite difference scheme if the condition in (10.4) is not satisfied. This situation occurs if the convection coefficient $p(x)$ becomes very large (of the order of 10 000, for example). Then the mesh size has to be chosen very small to ensure boundedness of the solution. In this case we speak of convection-dominated problems and these are common in fluid dynamics applications.

10.2   APPROXIMATION OF DERIVATIVES ON THE BOUNDARIES

In some cases we may wish to define Neumann boundary conditions. In these cases the dependent variable's first-order derivative is known on the boundary. We approximate the derivative by some kind of divided difference. The main options are:

- One-sided difference scheme (with first-order accuracy)
- Centred-difference scheme with ghost point (second-order accuracy).

To be specific, let us consider the Robin boundary condition at $x = a$ while keeping Dirichlet boundary condition at $x = b$:

$$\alpha_0 u(a) + \alpha_1 u'(a) = \alpha$$

(10.5)

The first-order approximation is given by

$$\alpha_0 u_0 + \frac{\alpha_1}{h} (u_1 - u_0) = \alpha$$

or

$$(\alpha_0 h - \alpha_1) u_0 + \alpha_1 u_1 = \alpha h$$

(10.6)

This approximation destroys the second-order accuracy of scheme (10.2). In order to resolve this problem we introduce a ghost or fictitious point, one step length to the left of a. The boundary condition (10.5) is now approximated by a centred-difference scheme

$$\alpha_0 u_0 + \frac{\alpha_1}{2h} (u_1 - u_{-1}) = \alpha$$

or

$$2h\alpha_0 u_0 + \alpha_1 (u_1 - u_{-1}) = 2\alpha h$$

(10.7)

Then we have the *ansatz* or assumption that the differential equation (10.1) is satisfied at $x = a$ (we call this continuity to the boundary) and thus the difference approximation (10.2) is valid at that point as well:

$$-\left(\frac{u_1 - 2u_0 + u_{-1}}{h^2}\right) + p(x_0)\left(\frac{u_1 - u_{-1}}{2h}\right) + q(x_0)u_0 = r(x_0) \qquad (10.8)$$

We can now eliminate the value at the ghost point from equations (10.7) and (10.8) and we can then produce a linear system that we solve using *LU* decomposition. Assuming Dirichlet boundary conditions at $x = b$, the unknown vector U has the components

$$U = {}^t(u_0, u_1, \ldots, u_{J-1})$$

This vector has thus one extra component compared with the vector for the problem with Dirichlet boundary conditions at both end-points!

We conclude this section with a convergence theorem.

Theorem 10.2. *Let $p(x)$ and $q(x)$ satisfy*

$$|p(x)| \le P^*, \qquad 0 < Q_* \le q(x) \le Q^*, \quad a \le x \le b$$

and suppose that h satisfies the inequality

$$h \le \frac{2}{P^*}$$

Let $\{u_j\}_{j=0}^J$ and $u(x)$ be the solutions of the discrete BVP (10.2) and continuous BVP (10.1), respectively, where both problems have boundary conditions in (10.3).
Set

$$M = \max(1, 1/Q_*)$$

Then

$$|u_j - u(x_j)| \le M \max |\tau_j(u)|, \quad 0 \le j \le J$$

where

$$\tau_j(u) = -[D_+ D_- u(x_j) - u''(x_j)] + p(x_j)[D_0 u(x_j) - u'(x_j)]$$
$$= \frac{-h^2}{12}[u'''(\xi_j) - 2p(x_j)u''(\eta_j)] \quad 0 \le j \le J \; \xi_j, \eta_j \in [x_{j-1}, x_{j+1}]$$

Furthermore, if u has four continuous derivatives, then

$$|u_j - u(x_j)| \le M\frac{h^2}{12}(M_4 + 2P^* M_3) \quad 0 \le j \le J$$

where

$$M_k = \max_{a \le x \le b} \left|\frac{du^k}{dx^k}\right|, \quad k = 3, 4.$$

This result states that the finite difference scheme is second-order accurate.

10.3   TIME-DEPENDENT CONVECTION–DIFFUSION EQUATIONS

We now generalise the equations and results from section 10.1 to the time-dependent convection–diffusion problem

$$-\frac{\partial u}{\partial t} + Lu = f(x, t), \quad a < x < b, \quad t > 0 \tag{10.9}$$

where

$$Lu(x, t) \equiv \sigma(x, t)\frac{\partial^2 u}{\partial x^2} + \mu(x, t)\frac{\partial u}{\partial x} + b(x, t)u$$

The initial and boundary conditions are:

$$u(x, 0) = f(x), \quad a \leq x \leq b$$

$$u(a, t) = g(t), \quad u(b, t) = h(t), \quad t > 0$$

There are different ways to discretise (10.9), namely

- Discretise in x and t simultaneously (fully discrete schemes)
- Discretise in x and keep t continuous (Method of Lines)
- Discretise in t and keep x continuous (Rothe's method).

The choice will be determined by a number of factors that we shall explain in this chapter.

10.4   FULLY DISCRETE SCHEMES

We use the usual notation for meshes in the x and t directions. For example, h is the mesh size in the x direction while k is the mesh size in the t direction. Define the operator

$$L_k^h w_j^n \equiv \sigma_j^n D_+ D_- w_j^n + \mu_j^n D_0 w_j^n + b_j^n w_j^n, \quad 1 \leq j \leq J - 1, \quad n \geq 0$$

for some mesh function w_j^n where

$$\left.\begin{array}{l} \sigma_j^n = \sigma(x_j, t_n) \\ \mu_j^n = \mu(x_j, t_n) \\ b_j^n = b(x_j, t_n) \\ f_j^n = f(x_j, t_n) \end{array}\right\} \quad 1 \leq j \leq J - 1, \quad n \geq 0$$

Then, based on the first-order schemes in previous chapters, we can define a number of fully discrete schemes as follows:

- *Implicit Euler scheme*

$$-\frac{u_j^{n+1} - u_j^n}{k} + L_k^h u_j^{n+1} = 0 \tag{10.10}$$

- *Explicit Euler scheme*

$$-\frac{u_j^{n+1} - u_j^n}{k} + L_k^h u_j^n = 0 \tag{10.11}$$

- *Crank–Nicolson scheme*

This is the average of schemes (10.10) and (10.11) defined as

$$-\frac{u_j^{n+1} - u_j^n}{k} + \tfrac{1}{2}\left(L_k^h u_j^{n+1} + L_k^h u_j^n\right) = 0 \tag{10.12}$$

This equation, in the context of the financial engineering literature, seems to be the de-facto standard finite difference scheme for the one-factor Black–Scholes equation. It is not a perfect scheme and the author has discussed some its shortcomings in Duffy (2004A).

Summarising these problems, we note:

- The Crank–Nicolson method is second-order accurate on uniform meshes only.
- It produces spurious oscillations and possibly spikes for problems with non-smooth initial and boundary conditions, and for problems where the compatibility conditions between boundary and initial conditions are not satisfied.
- It reduces to a neutrally stable method when the diffusion coefficient is small. This has the implication that the accuracy of the results will be compromised due to possible rounding errors.
- It gives terrible results near the stike price for approximations to the first and second derivatives in the space direction. In pricing applications, this translates to the statement that the Crank–Nicolson method gives bad approximations to the delta and gamma of the option price.

10.5   SPECIFYING INITIAL AND BOUNDARY CONDITIONS

No finite difference scheme would be complete without specifying its associated initial and boundary conditions. Let us examine system (10.9) again and let us approximate it using scheme (10.10).

The continuous initial conditions in (10.9) are approximated by

$$u_j^0 = f(x_j), \quad 1 \le j \le J - 1 \tag{10.13}$$

Thus, in order to specify a well-defined problem we use one of the schemes (10.10), (10.11) or (10.12) in combination with (10.13) and with the boundary conditions

$$u_0^n = g(t_n), \qquad u_J^n = h(t_n), \quad n \ge 0 \tag{10.14}$$

Thus, this system can be solved at each time level using LU decomposition, for example.

10.6   SEMI-DISCRETISATION IN SPACE

This approach entails approximating the derivatives in the x direction only. Applied to system (10.9) a semi-discrete scheme looks like

$$-\frac{du_j}{dt} + \sigma_j(t)D_+D_-u_j(t) + \mu_j(t)D_0u_j(t) + b_j(t)u_j(t) = f_j(t), \tag{10.15}$$

where $\sigma_j(t) \equiv \sigma(x_j, t)$, etc.

We can then write (10.15) as a vector system:

$$\frac{dU}{dt} + A(t)\,U = F(t), \quad t > 0$$

$$U(0) = U_0$$

(10.16)

We can now discretise (10.16) using the methods from Chapter 6.

10.7   SEMI-DISCRETISATION IN TIME

Let us recall the parabolic initial boundary value problem (10.9). We can apply discretisation in t using different schemes. Let us examine the implicit Euler scheme:

$$-\frac{U^{n+1}(x) - U^n(x)}{k} + LU^{n+1}(x) = f^{n+1}(x), \quad n \geq 0$$

(10.17)

where

$$LU^{n+1}(x) \equiv \sigma(x, t_{n+1})\frac{d^2 U^{n+1}}{dx^2} + \mu(x, t_{n+1})\frac{dU^{n+1}}{dx} + b(x, t_{n+1})U^{n+1}$$

$$f^{n+1}(x) = f(x, t_{n+1})$$

with boundary conditions

$$U^n(a) = g(t_n), \qquad U^n(b) = h(t_n), \quad n \geq 0$$

and initial condition

$$U^0(x) = f(x), \quad a \leq x \leq b$$

System (10.17) is now an ordinary differential equation and it is solved from level n to level $n + 1$.

10.8   CONCLUSIONS AND SUMMARY

We have introduced a number of standard finite difference schemes that approximate the solution of convection–diffusion equations in one space dimension. Such equations contain both a diffusion term and a convection term and they model the Black–Scholes equation. We also discuss how to approximate Dirichlet and Neumann boundary conditions and assemble the system of equations that we solve at each time level.

11

Exponentially Fitted Finite
Difference Schemes

11.1 INTRODUCTION AND OBJECTIVES

In this chapter we introduce robust finite difference schemes that are suitable for a range of applications in financial engineering. In particular, the schemes can be applied to one-factor and multi-factor Black–Scholes equations. They are called exponentially fitted finite difference schemes (Duffy, 1980). The schemes use the implicit Euler scheme for time marching and hence do not suffer from the spurious oscillation problems that we witness with the Crank–Nicolson method, for example. This chapter is important for a number of reasons:

- It provides a robust, accurate and easy to program finite difference scheme for a general one-factor Black–Scholes equation. The volatility and other terms may be functions of S and t.
- The finite difference scheme resolves many of the oscillation problems that we see with some standard schemes. Furthermore, some authors have resolved these problems by mapping the Black–Scholes PDE (which is linear) into a nonlinear finite difference scheme (for example, the Van Leer method (see Zvan *et al.*, 1997)). This scheme must be solved by some iterative method at each time level, which slows down performance.
- The fitted scheme gives good approximations to the first and second derivatives (in Black–Scholes, called delta and gamma) with no wiggly oscillations near the strike price.
- We prove stability of the fitted scheme by using the discrete Maximum Principle and M matrices. This is an improvement on the somewhat outdated von Neumann stability analysis (this technique is, strictly speaking, only valid for linear initial value problems with constant coefficients).

In short, this chapter paves the way for a discussion of the Black–Scholes equation and its approximation using robust finite differences schemes.

11.2 MOTIVATING EXPONENTIAL FITTING

We first discuss some issues in quantative finance in order to motivate exponentially fitted methods. Exponential fitting is a technique that we can apply to both ordinary and partial differential equations. In many cases we know that the solution contains terms involving the exponential function. However, we do not know the exact form and we must guess a solution or try to approximate the solution in some way. For example, the exact formula for the price of a standard European option on stock paying no dividend is given by

$$C = SN(d_1) - Ke^{-rT}N(d_2) \tag{11.1}$$

where

$$d_1 = \frac{\ln(S/K) + (r + \sigma^2/2)T}{\sigma\sqrt{T}}$$

$$d_2 = \frac{\ln(S/K) + (r - \sigma^2/2)T}{\sigma\sqrt{T}} = d_1 - \sigma\sqrt{T}$$

$$N(x) = \frac{1}{\sqrt{2\pi}} \int_{-\infty}^{x} e^{-\frac{z^2}{2}}\, dz$$

$$n(x) = \frac{dN(x)}{dx} = \frac{1}{\sqrt{2\pi}} e^{-x^2/2}$$

(see Haug, 1998). Here we see exponential terms in both time T and asset variable S. In general it is not possible to find an exact solution for more complicated problems.

We discuss two specific cases: the first technique is used in the financial engineering literature to guess an 'approximate exact solution' to the original differential equation. The second technique mimics exponential behaviour by creating special finite difference equations that contain so-called fitting factors (see Duffy, 1980 and 2004). In a sense we speak of continuous and discrete fitting.

11.2.1 'Continuous' exponential approximation

We take an example to show what we mean. Consider the partial differential equation that describes a zero coupon bond price P (Van Deventer and Imai, 1997; Wilmott, 1998):

$$\frac{\partial P}{\partial t} + \frac{1}{2}\sigma^2 \frac{\partial^2 P}{\partial r^2} + [\alpha(t) + \lambda\sigma]\frac{\partial P}{\partial r} - rP = 0 \tag{11.2}$$

with the final condition

$$P(r, T, T) = 1 \tag{11.3}$$

(this is because the value of a zero coupon bond is equal to 1 at maturity). In this case we are using the extended Merton SDE for the short-term interest rate:

$$dr = \alpha(t)\, dt + \sigma\, dZ \tag{11.4}$$

where $\alpha(t)$ = drift rate

σ = instantaneous standard deviation of interest rates

Z = standard Wiener process with mean 0 and standard deviation 1.

In Van Deventer and Imai (1997) the authors take an educated guess in order to postulate a solution of (11.2) in a form assuming that the price P closely approximate the Merton model, as follows (called an *ansatz*):

$$P(r, t, T) = e^{-r\tau + G(t,T)}, \quad \tau = T - t \tag{11.5}$$

We can verify from equation (11.2) that the function G satisfies the ordinary differential equation

$$\frac{dG}{dt} + \frac{1}{2}\sigma^2\tau^2 - [\alpha(t) + \lambda\sigma]\tau = 0 \tag{11.6}$$

by using the relationships

$$\frac{\partial P}{\partial r} = -\tau P$$

$$\frac{\partial^2 P}{\partial r^2} = \tau^2 P$$

$$\frac{\partial P}{\partial t} = \left(r + \frac{dG}{dt} \right) P$$

and substituting these three partial derivatives into the differential equation (11.2). Now, integrating the ordinary differential equation (11.6) between the limits t and T, and using the easy-to-verify relationships

$$G(T, T) = 0 \quad (\text{since } P(r, T, T) = 1)$$

$$\frac{1}{2}\sigma^2 \int_t^T (T - s)^2 \, ds = \frac{\sigma^2 \tau^3}{6} \tag{11.7}$$

$$\lambda \sigma \int_t^T (T - s) \, dS = \frac{\lambda \sigma \tau^2}{2}$$

we see that the solution of (11.6) is given by

$$G(t, T) = -\frac{\lambda \sigma \tau^2}{2} + \frac{1}{6}\sigma^2 \tau^3 - \int_t^T \alpha(s)(T - s) \, ds \tag{11.8}$$

Hence using the ansatz we can now write the solution of (11.2) in the explicit form

$$P(r, t, T) = \exp\left[-r\tau - \frac{\lambda \sigma \tau^2}{2} + \frac{1}{6}\sigma^2 \tau^3 - \int_t^T \alpha(s)(T - s) \, ds \right] \tag{11.9}$$

We now give an objective critique of the above analysis. This approach may work in isolated cases but in general we refrain from this approach in this book for the following reasons:

- It would seem that the ansatz is mathematically unfounded. I have seen no justification and the approach is very difficult to scale to multi-factor, nonlinear problems containing discontinuities.
- Having arrived at the solution equation (11.9) we still have to approximate the integral term, either analytically or numerically. Thus, the fact that we have produced a closed solution does not mean that our work is finished.

On the other hand, this technique gives us some insight into the financial model.

11.2.2   'Discrete' exponential approximation

In this section we examine a boundary value problem and attempt to fit the exponential terms (which are the most difficult terms to approximate) by a specially designed finite difference scheme. To this end, let us begin with a homogeneous second-order ordinary differential equation with constant coefficients:

$$\frac{d^2 u}{dx^2} + a\frac{du}{dx} + bu = 0 \tag{11.10}$$

It is known that the general solution of (11.10) is a sum of exponentials whose coefficients are roots of the so-called auxiliary equation

$$m^2 + am + b = 0 \quad \text{(roots } \alpha_1, \, \alpha_2)$$ (11.11)

Thus, depending on these roots, the general solution is given by one of the following equations:

Real Roots, $\alpha_1 \neq \alpha_2$:

$$u = c_1 \, e^{\alpha_1 x} + c_2 \, e^{\alpha_2 x}$$ (11.12a)

Real Roots, $\alpha_1 = \alpha_2 = \alpha$:

$$u = (c_1 + c_2 x) \, e^{\alpha x}$$ (11.12b)

Complex Roots, $\alpha_1 = A + iB, \quad \alpha_2 = A - iB$

$$u = e^{Ax}(c_1 \cos Bx + c_2 \sin Bx)$$ (11.12c)

where c_1 and c_2 are (undetermined) constants.

Some authors have developed special finite difference schemes that closely approximate the general solution of (11.10) at mesh points. For example, Roscoe (1975) defines difference schemes that are in some sense the discrete analogues of the solutions in equations (11.12) and the schemes achieve accurate and oscillation-free approximation to one-dimensional and two-dimensional convection–diffusion equations. In fact, for the boundary value problem:

$$\frac{\mathrm{d}^2 u}{\mathrm{d}x^2} - \epsilon \left(\tfrac{1}{2} - x \right) \frac{\mathrm{d}u}{\mathrm{d}x} = 0, \quad 0 < x < 1$$

$$u(0) = 0, \qquad u(1) = 1$$ (11.13)

with exact solution given by

$$u(x) = \frac{\displaystyle\int_0^x e^{\frac{1}{2}\epsilon y(1-y)} \, \mathrm{d}y}{\displaystyle\int_0^1 e^{\frac{1}{2}\epsilon y(1-y)} \, \mathrm{d}y}$$

The standard schemes such as upwinding, downwinding and centred differencing give terrible answers at $x = 0.5$ for certain large values of ϵ. In fact, the solution exhibits spurious oscillations at these points while the so-called unified difference representation (UDR) in Roscoe (1975) does not suffer from these schemes. The scheme is given by:

$$U_{j+1} - (1 + e^{w(x_j)}) \, U_j + e^{w(x_j)} U_{j-1} = 0$$

$$w(x) \equiv \epsilon \left(\frac{1}{2} - x \right)$$ (11.14)

The reason why standard-difference schemes are not good is because the convection term $w(x)$ changes sign at $x = 0.5$ and for this reason we call (11.13) a turning-point problem. This kind of equation can occur in financial applications when the drift term changes sign.

We now introduce another fitting difference scheme (based on Il'in, 1969) which is also the foundation for a number of schemes for the Black–Scholes equation. To this end, we consider the second-order equation

$$\sigma \frac{\mathrm{d}^2 u}{\mathrm{d}x^2} + \mu \frac{\mathrm{d}u}{\mathrm{d}x} = 0$$ (11.15)

where σ and μ are constants.

We now define the so-called fitted centred-difference equation:

$$\rho D_+ D_- U_j + \mu D_0 U_j = 0, \quad 1 \le j \le J - 1 \tag{11.16}$$

where the fitting factor ρ is chosen in such a way that the discrete and exact solutions have the same values at mesh points. If we insert the exact solution of (11.15) into equation (11.16) we can convince ourselves that

$$\rho \equiv \frac{\mu h}{2} \coth \frac{\mu h}{2\sigma} \tag{11.17}$$

This scheme is a faithful representation of the exact solution. For example, let us suppose that the coefficient σ tends to zero. Then by using the limits:

$$\lim_{\sigma \to 0} \frac{\mu h}{2} \coth \frac{\mu h}{2\sigma} = \begin{cases} +\mu h/2, & \mu > 0 \\ -\mu h/2, & \mu < 0 \end{cases} \tag{11.18a}$$

$$\lim_{\mu \to 0} \frac{\mu h}{2} \coth \frac{\mu h}{2\sigma} = 1 \tag{11.18b}$$

we see that the 'reduced' difference schemes are:

$$\frac{\mu}{h}(U_{j+1} - U_j) = 0, \quad \mu > 0$$

$$\frac{\mu}{h}(U_j - U_{j-1}) = 0, \quad \mu < 0 \tag{11.19}$$

We thus get the correct upwinding or downwinding depending on the sign of μ. Many standard schemes have to be modified in order to get the correct winding. Il'in's scheme takes care of these problems automatically!

What happens next? We usually have to solve boundary value problems with non-constant coefficients, as in the following case with Dirichlet boundary conditions:

$$\sigma(x)\frac{d^2 u}{dx^2} + \mu(x)\frac{du}{dx} + b(x)u = f(x), \quad x \in (A, B) \tag{11.20}$$

$$u(A) = \alpha, \qquad u(B) = \beta$$

We now approximate the solution of (11.20) by the generalisation of the scheme (11.16), namely

$$\rho_j D_+ D_- U_j + \mu_j D_0 U_j + b_j U_j = f_j, \quad 1 \le j \le J - 1$$

$$U_0 = \alpha, \qquad U_J = \beta \tag{11.21}$$

where

$$\rho_j \equiv \frac{\mu_j h}{2} \coth \frac{\mu_j h}{2\sigma_j}, \qquad \sigma_j \equiv \sigma(x_j), \qquad \mu_j \equiv \mu(x_j), \qquad f_j \equiv f(x_j), \qquad b_j \equiv b(x_j)$$

Theorem 11.1. *(Convergence.) Let u and U be the solutions of (11.20) and (11.21), respectively. Then*

$$|u(x_j) - U_j| \le Mh, \quad j = 0, \ldots, J$$

where the constant M is independent of h, μ and σ.

We say that scheme (11.21) is uniformly convergent irrespective of the relative sizes of the coefficients μ and σ. In order to improve the accuracy of the scheme we can use extrapolation. We take two approximate solutions on mesh sizes h and $h/2$:

$$U_j \equiv U_j^h = u(x_j) + A_1 h + A_2 h^2 + \cdots$$

$$U_{2j} \equiv U_{2j}^{h/2} = u(x_j) + A_1 \frac{h}{2} + A_2 \frac{h^2}{4} + \cdots \tag{11.22}$$

Then the discrete scheme defined by

$$V_{2j}^{h/2} \equiv 2U_{2j}^{h/2} - U_j^h = u(x_j) + B_2 h^2 \tag{11.23}$$

is a second-order approximation to the solution of (11.20). This estimate is borne out in theory and in numerical experiments. So, we calculate the solution on two consecutive meshes and use (11.23).

11.2.3   Where is exponential fitting being used?

Fitted schemes have been in use for more than fifty years. In 1955 de Allen and Southwell used a novel finite difference representation to solve certain fluid dynamics problems. They derived an 'exact' difference scheme in much the same way as we have motivated in previous sections. This scheme involved exponential terms that were not suitable from the point of view of the human relaxer, and probably, as a consequence, the schemes were not developed further at that time.

One of the first articles that analysed fitted schemes from a numerical analysis viewpoint was Il'in (1969), in which the two-point boundary value problem (11.20) was approximated by the fitted scheme (11.21). The scheme was generalised to one-factor convection–diffusion equations by the author (Duffy, 1980) and consequently applied to the Black–Scholes equation in Cooney (1999). More information on fitting methods can be found in the specialised monographs by Morton (1996) and Farrell *et al.* (2000).

11.3   EXPONENTIAL FITTING AND TIME-DEPENDENT CONVECTION–DIFFUSION

We now come to the central theme of this chapter. We examine an initial boundary value problem with Dirichlet boundary conditions for the one-factor Black–Scholes, written in general form:

$$Lu \equiv -\frac{\partial u}{\partial t} + \sigma(x,t)\frac{\partial^2 u}{\partial x^2} + \mu(x,t)\frac{\partial u}{\partial x} + b(x,t)u = f(x,t) \text{ in } D$$

$$u(x,0) = \varphi(x), \quad x \in \Omega \tag{11.24}$$

$$u(A,t) = g_0(t), \qquad u(B,t) = g_1(t), \quad t \in (0,T)$$

where $\Omega = (A, B)$ and $D = \Omega \times (0, T)$.

We introduce and apply exponentially fitted schemes to the problem (11.24) and discuss the stability and convergence properties using the discrete maximum principle. As always, we partition the space and time intervals as follows:

$$A = x_0 < x_1 < \cdots < x_J = B \quad (h = x_j - x_{j-1})$$

$$0 = t_0 < t_1 < \cdots < t_N = T \quad (k = T/N)$$

We also approximate derivatives by divided differences, and to this end we define the following discrete operators:

$$L_k^h U_j^n \equiv -\frac{U_j^{n+1} - U_j^n}{k} + \rho_j^{n+1} D_+ D_- U_j^{n+1} + \mu_j^{n+1} D_0 U_j^{n+1} + b_j^{n+1} U_j^{n+1} \quad (11.25)$$

Here we use the notation

$$\varphi_j^{n+1} = \varphi(x_j, t_{n+1}) \text{ in general}$$

and a similar notation for the other coefficients. Furthermore,

$$\rho_j^{n+1} \equiv \frac{\mu_j^{n+1} h}{2} \coth \frac{\mu_j^{n+1} h}{2\sigma_j^{n+1}}$$

We are now in a position to define the exponentially fitted scheme:

$$\begin{aligned} L_k^h U_j^n &= f_j^{n+1}, \quad j = 1, \dots, J-1, \quad n = 0, \dots, N-1 \\ U_0^n &= g_0(t_n), \quad U_J^n = g_1(t_n), \quad n = 0, \dots, N \\ U_j^0 &= \varphi(x_j), \quad j = 1, \dots, J-1 \end{aligned} \quad (11.26)$$

What is going on here? Well, in the x direction we use the Il'in fitting scheme while in the time direction we use the implicit Euler method. As we shall see later, the method is first-order accurate in both k and h. The difference between (11.26) and traditional finite difference schemes is the presence of the fitting factor. Accuracy can be improved by extrapolation (as already described in section 11.2.2) and this process will give us second-order accuracy.

In general, the fitted scheme combines fitting in space and implicit Euler in time.

11.4   STABILITY AND CONVERGENCE ANALYSIS

In this section we examine the scheme (11.26) from a numerical analysis viewpoint. In particular, we ask the questions:

- Does the scheme always produce realistic output from input?
- Is the solution bounded by the input?
- How close is the approximate solution to the exact solution?
- How does the scheme (11.26) perform compared to the Crank–Nicolson method?

The first result states that positive input data leads to a positive solution at all space and time.

Lemma 11.1. *Let the discrete function w_j^n satisfy $L_k^h w_j^n \leq 0$ in the interior of the mesh with $w_j^n \geq 0$ on the boundary Γ. Then*

$$w_j^n \geq 0, \quad \forall j = 0, \dots, J, \quad n = 0, \dots, N.$$

The next result gives an estimate for the growth of the solution of (11.26) in terms of its input data.

Lemma 11.2 (Uniform stability.) *Let $\left\{ U_j^n \right\}$ be the solution of scheme (11.26) and suppose that*

$$\max |U_j^n| \leq N \text{ for all } j \text{ and } n$$

$$\max |f_j^n| \leq N \text{ for all } j \text{ and } n$$

Then

$$\max_j |U_j^n| \leq -\frac{N}{\beta} + \text{m in } \overline{D}, \quad \text{where } b(x, t) \leq \beta < 0$$

We have thus proved stability by application of the discrete maximum principle. The result is general and is valid for problems with non-constant coefficients, discontinuous coefficients, and Neumann and Robin boundary conditions. The following result tells us how accurate our exponentially fitted scheme is (we state the essential conclusions), see Duffy (1980).

Theorem 11.2. *Let u and U_j^n be the solution of (11.24) and (11.26), respectively. Then*

$$|u(x_j, t_n) - U_j^n| \le M(h + k).$$

where M is independent of h, k, σ and μ.

Remark. We say that scheme (11.26) is uniformly convergent because the accuracy does not depend on the relative sizes of the coefficients σ and μ in the original problem.

We now discuss the detailed issues of numerical accuracy and performance of scheme (11.26). All code has been written in C++. Extensive tests have been carried out in Cooney (1999) and Mirani (2002). We compare fitting with a number of other schemes:

S1: Implicit Euler in time, standard centred differencing in x
S2: Duffy exponential fitting (11.26)
S3: Crank–Nicolson (standard)
S4: Fitted Crank–Nicolson (CN in time, fitting in x).

We give the discrete operators corresponding to the above schemes. The notation remains the same as before:

Implicit Euler scheme (no fitting)

$$L_k^h U_j^n = -\frac{U_j^{n+1} - U_j^n}{k} + \sigma_j^{n+1} D_+ D_- U_j^{n+1} + \mu_j^{n+1} D_0 U_j^{n+1} + b_j^{n+1} U_j^{n+1}$$

Crank–Nicolson scheme:

$$L_k^h U_j^n = -\frac{U_j^{n+1} - U_j^n}{k} + \sigma_j^{n+\frac{1}{2}} D_+ D_- U_j^{n+\frac{1}{2}} + \mu_j^{n+\frac{1}{2}} D_0 U_j^{n+\frac{1}{2}} + b_j^{n+\frac{1}{2}} U_j^{n+\frac{1}{2}}$$

where

$$\sigma_j^{n+\frac{1}{2}} = \sigma \left(x_j, t_{n+\frac{1}{2}} \right)$$

$$\mu_j^{n+\frac{1}{2}} = \mu \left(x_j, t_{n+\frac{1}{2}} \right)$$

$$b_j^{n+\frac{1}{2}} = b \left(x_j, t_{n+\frac{1}{2}} \right)$$

$$U_j^{n+\frac{1}{2}} \equiv \frac{1}{2} \left(U_j^{n+1} + U_j^n \right)$$

Fitted Crank–Nicolson scheme:

$$L_k^h U_j^n = -\frac{U_j^{n+1} - U_j^n}{k} + \rho_j^{n+\frac{1}{2}} D_+ D_- U_j^{n+\frac{1}{2}} + \mu_j^{n+\frac{1}{2}} D_0 U_j^{n+\frac{1}{2}} + b_j^{n+\frac{1}{2}} U_j^{n+\frac{1}{2}}$$

We first examine the performance of the different schemes. In principle we are interested in the relative performance. We have taken meshes of size 500×500 and 1000×1000 and compared the different schemes with these as benchmarks (Cooney, 2000). The results are presented in Table 11.1 (units are seconds). The code was run on, at the time, (2000) a state-of-the art Pentium machine.

Table 11.1 Comparison of finite difference schemes

Scheme	500×500	1000×1000
Fully implicit	1.750000	7.210938
Fitted Duffy	2.281250	9.539062
Crank–Nicolson	1.851562	7.632812
Fitted Crank–Nicolson	2.406250	10.015625
Van Leer flux limiter	3.320312	13.250000

Table 11.2 Execution time ratios for the numerical schemes

Scheme	Ratio
Fully implicit	1.00
Crank–Nicolson	1.06
Fitted Duffy	1.31
Fitted Crank–Nicolson	1.38
Van Leer flux limiter	1.87

The results in Table 11.1 include writing the output data to an ASCII file. This file was then used as input to the package gnuplot. We see that the implicit Euler scheme performs best while the Van Leer method is slowest (this is because the Van Leer is a nonlinear scheme and we must apply the Newton–Raphson iterative method at each time level to find the solution).

We now wish to compare the relative performance of the different schemes (Cooney, 2000). The results are shown in Table 11.2.

We now discuss accuracy. The two Crank–Nicolson schemes produce spurious oscillations at the strike price (or where the initial condition is not smooth) and for large values of x (or for large values of S in the case of the Black–Scholes equation). The Van Leer scheme is the most accurate of all the schemes.

11.5 APPROXIMATING THE DERIVATIVES OF THE SOLUTION

An important requirement in option pricing and hedging applications is the approximation of the option's sensitivities (or 'Greeks' are they are also known. The main Greeks are (V is the option price):

$$
\begin{aligned}
\text{Delta} \qquad & \Delta = \frac{\partial V}{\partial S} \\[6pt]
\text{Gamma} \qquad & \Gamma = \frac{\partial \Delta}{\partial S} = \frac{\partial^2 V}{\partial S^2} \\[6pt]
\text{Theta} \qquad & \Theta = -\frac{\partial V}{\partial t} \\[6pt]
\text{Rho} \qquad & \rho = \frac{\partial V}{\partial r} \\[6pt]
\text{Strike} \qquad & \frac{\partial V}{\partial K} \\[6pt]
\text{Vega} \qquad & \frac{\partial V}{\partial \sigma}
\end{aligned}
\tag{11.27}
$$

Table 11.3   Error measure

Scheme	Sol	Δ	Γ	Θ
Fully implicit	1.05e-05	0.0030627	1.017440	0.809263
Fitted Duffy	1.05e-05	0.0.003080	0.947018	0.809278
Crank–Nicolson	1.64e-05	0.0237210	5.142210	5.313600
Fitted Crank–Nicolson	1.54e-05	0.0151708	5.413000	9.628910

(Hull, 2000). For certain kinds of options we have exact formulae (see Haug, 1998) but in general we must resort to numerical techniques to approximate them. Our interest here lies in approximating the delta and gamma of an option. We use divided differences of the solution V of the fitted scheme as estimates of delta and gamma:

$$\Delta \sim \frac{V_{j+1} - V_{j-1}}{2h}$$

$$\Gamma \sim \frac{V_{j+1} - 2V_j + V_{j-1}}{h^2}$$

(11.28)

We compare a number of these schemes in the region of the strike price K ('at-the-money') and the results are shown in Table 11.3.

The finite difference schemes are less dependable when we try to approximate the other sensitivities.

11.6   SPECIAL LIMITING CASES

In some applications the coefficient $\sigma(x, t)$ can become very small, in which case we have essentially a first-order hyperbolic equation. The question now is: If we let $\sigma(x, t)$ tend to zero, will we get a scheme that is the same or similar to an upwinding or downwinding scheme? To answer this question, we use the limits (see equation (11.18)) for the fitting factor. We then get the difference schemes:

$$\mu > 0, \quad -\frac{U_j^{n+1} - U_j^n}{k} + \mu_j^{n+1} \frac{(U_{j+1}^{n+1} - U_j^{n+1})}{h} + b_j^{n+1} U_j^{n+1} = f_j^{n+1}$$

$$\mu < 0, \quad -\frac{U_j^{n+1} - U_j^n}{k} + \mu_j^{n+1} \frac{(U_j^{n+1} - U_{j-1}^{n+1})}{h} + b_j^{n+1} U_j^{n+1} = f_j^{n+1}$$

These are just the standard upwind or downwind schemes that we met in Chapter 9! Thus, the fitting scheme degenerates into a stable upwinding/downwinding scheme for a first-order hyperbolic partial differential equation. This is reassuring.

11.7   SUMMARY AND CONCLUSIONS

We have introduced a robust finite difference scheme that is suitable for awkward convection–diffusion equations and that we have applied to the Black–Scholes equation. It gives good approximations to problems with small volatility and/or large drift terms and also gives accurate results for the full spectrum of values of these functions. Second, it gives accurate results near points where the initial condition (payoff function) is discontinuous or has discontinuous derivatives, for example, at-the-money. In fact it gives good results for the delta (first derivative in space), in contrast to some traditional methods (for example, Crank–Nicolson) where spurious oscillations and spikes can and do occur. Finally, the method is first-order accurate in time and space and we can produce a second-order scheme by Richardson extrapolation.

Part III
Applying FDM to One-Factor
Instrument Pricing

12
Exact Solutions and Explicit Finite Difference Method for One-Factor Models

12.1 INTRODUCTION AND OBJECTIVES

In this chapter we discuss some simple finite difference schemes for the one-factor Black–Scholes partial differential equation for plain options with no early exercise. This is a well-known problem in the literature and has an exact solution. The schemes in this chapter use the explicit Euler scheme in time.

In order to reduce the scope we restrict our attention to calculating the price C of a standard European call option. Furthermore, we wish to calculate the values of some of its senstivities (the so-called Greeks), for example:

$$
\begin{aligned}
\text{Delta} &= \Delta_C = \frac{\partial C}{\partial S} \\
\text{Gamma} &= \Gamma_C = \frac{\partial^2 C}{\partial S^2} = \frac{\partial \Delta_C}{\partial S} \\
\text{Vega} &= \frac{\partial C}{\partial \sigma} \\
\text{Theta} &= \Theta_C = -\frac{\partial C}{\partial t}
\end{aligned}
\tag{12.1}
$$

For European options we can give an exact formula for the call price and its sensitivities (Cox *et al.*, 1985) and we use these values as benchmarks against which to test our finite difference schemes. We have not listed all possible sensitivities in (12.1) and the interested reader can find formulae for all major ones in Haug (1998).

We discuss constructing a simple algorithm to calculate the option price and its sensitivities by perturbing one parameter (such as the strike price K or expiry time T) in a given interval. We shall then get a range of values that can be displayed in Excel for example (see Duffy, 2004). This is the basis for a Risk Engine. We then introduce two finite difference schemes for the one-factor Black–Scholes equation by approximating the derivatives in the underlying variable by centred differences in S, and the derivative in t by the explicit Euler scheme. We examine accuracy by comparing the exact and approximate solutions. Furthermore, we investigate the problem of calculating the option delta and gamma based on the approximate solution.

12.2 EXACT SOLUTIONS AND BENCHMARK CASES

We introduce the generalised Black–Scholes formula to calculate the price of a call option on some underlying asset. In general the call price is a function

$$
C = C(S, K, T, r, \sigma)
\tag{12.2}
$$

where S = asset price
         K = strike (exercise) price
         T = exercise (maturity) date
         r = risk-free interest rate
         σ = constant volatility

We can view the call option price C as a vector function because it maps a vector of parameters into a real value. The exact formula for C is given by:

$$C = S\,e^{(b-r)T} N(d_1) - K e^{-rT} N(d_2) \tag{12.3}$$

where $N(x)$ is the standard cumulative normal (Gaussian) distribution function defined by

$$N(x) = \frac{1}{\sqrt{2\pi}} \int_{-\infty}^{x} e^{-y^2/2}\,\mathrm{d}y \tag{12.4}$$

and

$$d_1 = \frac{\ln(S/K) + (b + \sigma^2/2)T}{\sigma\sqrt{T}}$$
$$d_2 = \frac{\ln(S/K) + (b - \sigma^2/2)T}{\sigma\sqrt{T}} = d_1 - \sigma\sqrt{T} \tag{12.5}$$

The cost-of-carry parameter b has specific values depending on the kind of security in question (Haug, 1998):

$b = r$ is the Black–Scholes stock option model

$b = r - q$ is the Morton model with continuous dividend yield q

$b = 0$ is the Black–Scholes futures option model

$b = r - R$ is the Garman and Kohlhagen currency option model, where R is the foreign
    risk-free interest rate.

Thus, we can find the price of a plain call option by using formula (12.3). Furthermore, it is possible to differentiate C with respect to any of the parameters to produce a formula for the option sensitivities. For example, some tedious differentiation allows us to prove that:

$$\Delta_C \equiv \frac{\partial C}{\partial S} = e^{(b-r)T} N(d_1)$$

$$\Gamma_C \equiv \frac{\partial^2 C}{\partial S^2} = \frac{\partial \Delta_C}{\partial S} = \frac{n(d_1)\,e^{(b-r)T}}{S\sigma\sqrt{T}}$$

$$\text{Vega}_C \equiv \frac{\partial C}{\partial \sigma} = S\sqrt{T}\,e^{(b-r)T}\,n(d_1) \tag{12.6}$$

$$\Theta_C \equiv -\frac{\partial C}{\partial T} = -\frac{S\sigma\,e^{(b-r)T} n(d_1)}{2\sqrt{T}} - (b-r)S\,e^{(b-r)T} N(d_1) - rK\,e^{-rT} N(d_2)$$

In the appendix (section 12.8) we have developed the formula for option Vega for the benefit of those readers who would like to see how it is derived in a step-by-step fashion. Thus, not only do we have exact formulae for C but we also have exact formulae for its sensitivities. We can then determine how C varies as a function of the change in one or more of the option's parameters. In particular, we are interested in delta and gamma for problems where there is no exact solution, and in these cases we resort to finite difference schemes. Of course, we need some assurance that our approximations are accurate.

12.3   PERTURBATION ANALYSIS AND RISK ENGINES

From the previous section we know how to calculate the price of a call option and its sensitivities for specific values of the defining parameters. What we would now like to do is calculate these functions for a *range of values* of the parameters. The ability to do this would be the first step on the way to creating a risk engine for options. At this stage we create arrays of values and display them on a screen or save them to a database. We could also produce line drawings in two dimensions or surface plots in thee dimensions. In two dimensions, for example, we would like to plot C and its sensitivities as a function of one of the parameters. Some specific examples of what we would like to do are (Cox *et al.*, 1985):

- Value of C as a function of the asset price S
- Value of C as a function of the expiry date T
- Value of C as a function of the volatility σ
- Value of C as a function of the interest rate r.

The same set of questions can be applied to each of the call's sensitivities. In general, we draw a function on an X–Y axis, where X is the range of the independent variable (one of the parameters in (12.2)) and Y is the value of C or one of its sensitivities.

Viewing this problem from an algorithmic and data-processing point of view we model it as an activity that produces an array of values. The input consists of two pieces; first, the function (for example, for C or its sensitivities) and, second, the specific parameter (for example, S) in which we are also interested.

A good example of what we mean is to calculate the vector of values of C with the following parameter values (Cox *et al.*, 1985, p. 217):

$K = 50$
$T = 0.4$
$r = 1.06$ (expressed in annualised terms)
$\sigma = 3$ (expressed in annualised terms)
$b = r$ (Black–Scholes stock option).

The special parameter in this case is S, and we shall generate the call price in the range [0, 100] at 25 evenly distributed discrete values of S. We realise this kind of output using finite difference schemes, for example. We provide some examples of C++ code on the accompanying CD.

12.4   THE TRINOMIAL METHOD: PREVIEW

It seems like a good idea to motivate explicit finite difference schemes for the one-factor Black–Scholes equation by giving a short introduction to the trinomial method. We shall discuss this method in more detail in Chapter 13. We can discuss the stability of finite difference schemes by using probabilistic heuristics without having to go into more difficult numerical analysis techniques. Explicit schemes are easy to program (no matrix inversion needed) and to this end we see them as a good way to learn and to experiment with finite difference schemes. The trinomial method is an improvement on the binomial method in a number of ways. First, it models the real world better because there are three possible asset price movements during each time interval. Second, it has better stability properties than the binomial method. We focus in this section on the Black–Scholes equation and its relationship with the trinomial method:

$$-\frac{\partial C}{\partial t} + \frac{1}{2}\sigma^2 S^2 \frac{\partial^2 C}{\partial S^2} + rS\frac{\partial C}{\partial S} - rC = 0 \tag{12.7}$$

Notice that time increases from $t = 0$ to $t = T$! (Note that some authors let t vary from $t = T$ to $t = 0$ and the finite difference schemes differ somewhat from the schemes in this section, for example Hull, 2000). We employ centred differencing in S and the explicit Euler scheme in time to produce the fully discrete scheme:

$$C_j^{n+1} = \alpha_j C_{j-1}^n + \beta_j C_j^n + \gamma_j C_{j+1}^n, \quad j = 1, \ldots, J - 1 \tag{12.8}$$

where α_j, β_j and γ_j are easily calculated.

In order to complete the specification of this problem we must provide initial and boundary conditions. We give them in continuous/discrete pairs for convenience:

$$C(S, 0) = \max(S - K, 0) \quad \text{(call option)}$$
$$C_j^0 = \max(S_j - K, 0), \quad j = 1, \ldots, J - 1 \tag{12.9}$$

and

$$C(0, t) = 0$$
$$C_0^n = 0, \quad n = 0, \ldots, N \tag{12.10a}$$

and

$$C(S, t) \sim S \text{ as } S \to \infty$$
$$C_J^n = S_J, \quad n = 0, \ldots, N \tag{12.10b}$$

Equations (12.10) represent Dirichlet boundary conditions and since we are working on an infinite domain in the continuous problem we must truncate it to a finite domain in the discrete problem.

Equations (12.8), (12.9) and (12.10) constitute a discrete system of equations that we can solve at every time level n from $n = 0$ to $n = N$. The basic algorithm that computes the values is as follows:

Init:

- Calculate the initial value based on equation (12.9)
- Calculate the arrays of coefficients α, β, γ in equation (12.8)
- $n = 0$

Continue:

- Calculate new vector at time level $n + 1$ using equation (12.8)
- If $(n < N)$ then
- go to Continue

You can then choose how to program this algorithm in your favourite programming language. It is interesting to note that Hull (2000) discusses a variant of equation (12.8) in which the reaction term is evaluated at the new time level $n + 1$ rather than at the level n, namely:

$$-\frac{C_j^{n+1} - C_j^n}{k} + \frac{1}{2}\sigma^2 S_j^2 D_+ D_- C_j^n + r S_j D_0 C_j^n - r C_j^{n+1} = 0 \qquad (12.11)$$

It is possible to rewrite equation (12.11) in a form similar to equation (12.8) and, as we shall now see it has slightly better stability properties than scheme (12.8). In fact, scheme (12.11) is a kind of mixed implicit–explicit scheme.

12.4.1 Stability of the trinomial method

We have already discussed stability for finite difference schemes using both von Neumann stability and the maximum principle. Another interesting way of analysing the stability of scheme (12.8) is from a probability perspective (Hull, 2000). We can interpret the coefficients as probabilities:

- α the probability that the stock price decreases from jh to $(j - 1)h$
- β the probability that the stock price remains unchanged at jh
- γ the probability that the stock price increases from jh to $(j + 1)h$

To this end, in order to examine stability, we prefer the more general form of the Black–Scholes equation:

$$-\frac{\partial C}{\partial t} + \sigma(S, t)\frac{\partial^2 C}{\partial S^2} + \mu(S, t)\frac{\partial C}{\partial S} + b(S, t)C = 0 \qquad (12.12)$$

and we approximate it as before by an explicit Euler scheme:

$$-\frac{C_j^{n+1} - C_j^n}{k} + \sigma_j^n D_+ D_- C_j^n + \mu_j^n D_0 C_j^n + b_j^n C_j^n = 0 \qquad (12.13)$$

We examine this scheme from the viewpoint of positivity arguments. In particular, we rewrite (12.13) in the form

$$C_j^{n+1} = \alpha_j^n C_{j-1}^n + \beta_j^n C_j^n + \gamma_j^n C_{j+1}^n \qquad (12.14)$$

where

$$\alpha_j^n \equiv \left(\frac{\sigma_j^n}{h^2} - \frac{\mu_j^n}{2h}\right) k$$

$$\beta_j^n \equiv 1 + kb_j^n - \frac{2k\sigma_j^n}{h^2} \quad (b_j^n \le 0)$$

$$\gamma_j^n \equiv \left(\frac{\sigma_j^n}{h^2} + \frac{\mu_j^n}{2h}\right) k$$

and we wish to choose the mesh sizes h and k such that the coefficients in (12.14) are always positive. We see that this scheme has the same form as (12.8). In this case we can deduce that a positive solution at level n will also be positive at time level $n + 1$ and hence will be stable, albeit it at a cost in performance. On the other hand, we may be pleasantly surprised that the performance of explicit schemes, even with small mesh sizes, is acceptable, especially on modern 32-bit and 64-bit computers. Of course, we have to back up any claims that we make.

Examining the coefficients in (12.14) we see that they are positive if the following constraints are satisfied:

$$\frac{\sigma_j^n}{h^2} - \frac{\mu_j^n}{2h} \geq 0 \Rightarrow h \leq \frac{2\sigma_j^n}{\mu_j^n} \tag{12.15}$$

and

$$1 + kb_j^n - \frac{2k\sigma_j^n}{h^2} \geq 0 \Rightarrow k \leq \frac{1}{\left[\left(2\sigma_j^n/h^2\right) - b_j^n\right]} \tag{12.16}$$

We must thus determine the minimum values for h and k for each problem that we tackle. In the case of the Black–Scholes equation, for example, we get the following constraints:

$$h \leq \frac{\sigma^2 S_j}{r} \tag{12.17}$$

and

$$k \leq \frac{1}{(\sigma^2 j^2 + r)} \tag{12.18}$$

12.5   USING EXPONENTIAL FITTING WITH EXPLICIT TIME MARCHING

It is possible to use exponential fitting in S and explicit Euler in t to produce a scheme that is similar to (12.13) except the Il'in fitting operator appears in the coefficients (we have already discussed this scheme in Chapter 11). Some useful features of the scheme are:

- It is stable independently of the size of the mesh size h. Constraint (12.15) is always satisfied and is thus insensitive to the relative sizes of the diffusion and drift terms.
- It is conditionally stable when the volatility approaches zero. The resulting upwinding scheme must satisfy the CFL stability condition. On the other hand, formally setting the volatility to zero for the explicit Euler scheme (12.13) we arrive at a scheme that is only neutrally stable.

The exponentially fitted scheme for the PDE (12.7) is thus:

$$-\frac{C_j^{n+1} - C_j^n}{k} + \rho_j D_+ D_- C_j^n + r S_j \, D_0 C_j^n - r C_j^n = 0 \tag{12.19}$$

where

$$\rho_j = \frac{a_j h}{2} \coth \frac{a_j h}{2\sigma_j} \quad \text{and} \quad a_j = r S_j \quad \text{and} \quad \sigma_j = \frac{1}{2}\sigma^2 S_j^2$$

12.6   APPROXIMATING THE GREEKS

It is important to calculate an option's sensitivities. First, the delta measures the absolute change in the option price with respect to a small change in the price of the underlying asset:

$$\Delta_C = \frac{\partial C}{\partial S} \tag{12.20}$$

The delta represents the hedge ratio, the number of options to write or to buy in order to create a risk-free portfolio. The delta varies from zero for deep out-of-the money options to one for deep in-the-money calls. This is clear if we examine the payoff function. However, the delta is not continuous at the strike price K because it is zero to the left of K and one to the right of K for a call option. We thus expect problems near K, and this is borne out in practice by the appearance of so-called spurious or non-physical oscillations (see Duffy, 2004A) when we use Crank–Nicolson time averaging.

Approximation of the delta takes place by using divided differences, as discussed in Chapter 6. We can choose between forward, backward or centred difference schemes. For example, we use centred differences in the interior of the domain while we use one-sided divided differences at the boundaries:

$$\text{Discrete delta } D_j^n = \frac{C_{j+1}^n - C_{j-1}^n}{2h}, \quad 1 \le j \le J - 1$$

$$= \frac{C_1^n - C_0^n}{h} \quad (j = 1)$$

$$= \frac{C_J^n - C_{J-1}^n}{h} \quad (j = J) \tag{12.21}$$

This approach gives good results in combination with fitted schemes.

The gamma measures the change in delta:

$$\Gamma_C = \frac{\partial^2 C}{\partial S^2} = \frac{\partial \Delta_C}{\partial S} \tag{12.22}$$

It is greatest for at-the-money options and it is nearly zero for deep in-the-money or deep out-of-the-money. The gamma gives us an indication of the vulnerability of the hedge ratio. We approximate formula (12.22) for the gamma by using the divided differences:

$$\text{Discrete gamma } G_j^n = \frac{D_{j+1}^n - D_{j-1}^n}{2h}, \quad 1 \le j \le J - 1, \tag{12.23}$$

where D_j^n is the discrete delta function.

Similarly, we can calculate the derivative of C with respect to r:

$$\rho_C = \frac{\partial C}{\partial r} \tag{12.24}$$

Exact formulae are known for this quantity (Haug, 1998). For a call option with zero and non-zero cost-of-carry these are:

$$\rho_C = TK\, e^{-rT}\, N(d_2) \quad (b \ne 0)$$

$$\rho_C = -TC \quad (b = 0) \tag{12.25}$$

One possible formula to approximate Rho is given by the divided difference:

$$\text{Rho (discrete)} = \frac{C_j^{n+1} - C_j^n}{k} \tag{12.26}$$

In general, an exact option price eludes us and we then resort to finite differences to find an approximate solution.

12.7 SUMMARY AND CONCLUSIONS

This was the first chapter of Part III of the book and it is here that we used finite difference schemes to find option prices and their corresponding sensitivities (in particular, delta and gamma). We focus mainly on European call option modelling because closed solutions are known and we can use these solutions as a benchmark when testing the accuracy of finite difference schemes. There are two reasons for including this chapter: first, the schemes are easy to understand and to implement and, second, they are in fact the same as the trinomial method – a method that is well established in the literature. Finite difference schemes for the Black–Scholes equations are discussed in Duffy (2004), including C++ source code and techniques for approximating option sensitivities as formulated in this chapter. You can consider this chapter as an introduction to finite difference schemes for option pricing problems.

12.8 APPENDIX: THE FORMULA FOR VEGA

We shall work out the formula for the Vega of a call option for those readers who wish to refresh their mathematics in the area of differential calculus. For more information on calculus, see, for example, Widder (1989). Before we embark on calculating Vega, we must do some preliminary work. First, let $n(x)$ be the derivative of the normal cumulative distribution function. Then

$$n(x) = \frac{dN(x)}{dx} = \frac{1}{\sqrt{2\pi}} e^{-x^2/2}$$

and, furthermore, you can check that the following are true:

(1) $\frac{\partial N(x)}{\partial \eta} = n(x)\frac{\partial x}{\partial \eta}$ for $\eta = \sigma$, S or T
(2) $n(d_2) = n(d_1) \, S \, e^{bT}/K$

Then the formula for the Vega is calculated using the following sequence of steps:

$$\text{Vega} = \frac{\partial C}{\partial \sigma}$$

$$= \frac{\partial}{\partial \sigma} \left[S e^{(b-r)T} N(d_1) - K e^{-rT} N(d_2) \right]$$

$$= S e^{(b-r)T} \frac{\partial}{\partial \sigma} N(d_1) - K e^{-rT} \frac{\partial}{\partial \sigma} N(d_2)$$

$$= S e^{(b-r)T} n(d_1) \frac{\partial d_1}{\partial \sigma} - K e^{-rT} n(d_2) \frac{\partial d_2}{\partial \sigma}$$

$$= S e^{(b-r)T} n(d_1) \frac{\partial d_1}{\partial \sigma} - K e^{-rT} \left[\frac{n(d_1) S e^{br}}{K} \right] \frac{\partial d_2}{\partial \sigma}$$

$$= S e^{(b-r)T} n(d_1) \left[\frac{\partial d_1}{\partial \sigma} - \frac{\partial d_2}{\partial \sigma} \right]$$

$$= S e^{(b-r)T} n(d_1)\sqrt{T}$$

This is the same answer as in Haug (1998).

Here we have used the fact that

$$\frac{\partial d_2}{\partial \sigma} = \frac{\partial d_1}{\partial \sigma} - \sqrt{T}$$

because of the relationship $d_2 = d_1 - \sigma\sqrt{T}$.

13

An Introduction to the Trinomial Method

13.1 INTRODUCTION AND OBJECTIVES

In this chapter we give a short introduction to the trinomial method. Discussing the trinomial method and its relationship with finite difference methods will hopefully help some readers to appreciate the relevance and importance of the finite difference method in financial engineering.

We begin with the trinomial method for a standard European option. We then compare the method with some other methods and show that the trinomial method is fact an instance of an explicit finite difference scheme. We also show how the method is applied to pricing barrier options. We include this chapter for comparison with finite difference schemes. It is not as relevant to the tenor of this book as the other chapters.

13.2 MOTIVATING THE TRINOMIAL METHOD

We can use the trinomial method for one-factor option models. In general terms we build up a trinomial tree of asset prices (the forward induction step) using the stochastic differential equation (SDE) for the asset price. We build the tree up to the maturity date. Having done that we calculate, starting from the payoff function at maturity, the option prices using discounted expectations (the backwards induction phase).

We take a step-by-step approach to explaining the trinomial method. To this end, we assume that the geometric Brownian motion model holds for the asset price behaviour (Clewlow and Strickland, 1998; Hull, 2000):

$$dS = (r - D)S \, dt + \sigma S \, dW \tag{13.1}$$

where r = risk-free interest rate

   D = continuous dividend yield

   σ = volatility

   W = Brownian motion

We now define the new variable $x = \ln S$. We then get the modified SDE:

$$dx = v \, dt + \sigma dW, \qquad v = r - D - \tfrac{1}{2}\sigma^2 \tag{13.2}$$

We thus get a modified SDE and this is what we use in the subsequent discussion. We now model (13.2) in a special way (see Figure 13.1). Let us consider what happens to the price x in a small interval of time Δt. We assume that x can take one of three values in this interval: it can go up or down by an amount Δx, or it can stay the same. Each transition is associated with a corresponding probability, as shown in Figure 13.1, namely an up, down and no change. We must find values for these probabilities and this is based on a financial argument, namely the relationship between the continuous time and the trinomial process by equating the mean and

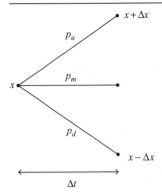

$x + \Delta x$

p_u

p_m

x

p_d

$x - \Delta x$

Δt

Figure 13.1   Trinomial tree model

variance over the time interval Δx and equating the sum of the probabilities to 1:

$$E[\Delta x] = p_u(\Delta x) + p_m(0) + p_d(-\Delta x) = v\Delta t$$

$$E[\Delta x^2] = p_u(\Delta x^2) + p_m(0) + p_d(\Delta x^2) = \sigma^2 \Delta t + v^2 \Delta t^2 \qquad (13.3)$$

$$p_u + p_m + p_d = 1$$

Let us define the following 'convenience' parameters:

$$\alpha = \frac{v\Delta t}{\Delta x} \quad \text{and} \quad \beta = \frac{\sigma^2 \Delta t + v^2 \Delta t}{\Delta x^2}$$

then a bit of arithmetic shows that

$$p_u = \frac{\alpha + \beta}{2}, \qquad p_d = \frac{\beta - \alpha}{2}, \qquad p_m = 1 - \beta$$

We now embark on the mechanics of the trinomial method. To this end, we prefer to use the index n to represent time and j to represent the index for the underlying (much of the literature uses the indices i and j, which I personally find confusing). If S is the price at time $n = 0$, then the price at level j is given by:

$$S_j^n = S\,e^{j\Delta x}$$

We compute the array using a vector Sarr:

$$\text{Sarr}[-N] = S\,e^{-N\Delta x}$$

$$\text{Sarr}[j] = \text{Sarr}[j - 1]e^{\Delta x}, \quad j = -N + 1, \ldots, N \qquad (13.4)$$

Here N is the number of sub-divisions of the interval $(0, T)$ where T is the maturity date, that is $N\Delta t = T$. We model call options with price C and its discrete values will be denoted in the same way as the stock price S, namely C_j^n.

The value of the call option is known at the maturity date, and the continuous and discrete variants are given by:

$$C(S, T) = \max(S - K, 0)$$

$$C_j^N = \max(S_j^N - K, 0) \qquad (13.5)$$

Finally, we compute the call option value at time n as discounted expectations in a risk-neutral world based on the call option values at time $n + 1$ as follows:

$$C_j^n = e^{-r\Delta t}(p_u C_{j+1}^{n+1} + p_m C_j^{n+1} + p_d C_{j-1}^{n+1}) \tag{13.6}$$

where the probabilities are defined as above. Summarising this process as a computational algorithm:

1. Create the trinomial tree structure
2. Initialise the call option values in the tree using formula (13.4)
3. Compute the vector payoff, equation (13.5)
4. Compute the call values at previous time steps using equation (13.6).

Steps 1 and 2 correspond to the forward induction step while 3 and 4 constitute the backward induction step. We can now easily compute this algorithm in C++ if desired.

13.3   TRINOMIAL METHOD: COMPARISONS WITH OTHER METHODS

The binomial and trinomial methods are both examples of lattice methods. Although the binomial method is very popular it does have a number of shortcomings.

There is evidence to show that the binomial method with one underlying variable does not always produce accurate numerical results, and in this case the trinomial method is preferred (Boyle, 1986). However, we must realise that the trinomial method is an example of an explicit finite difference scheme and the conclusion is that it is only conditionally stable. To this end, we now show that the standard explicit finite difference scheme for the Black–Scholes PDE is equivalent to performing discounted expectations in a trinomial tree. Let us first consider the Black–Scholes PDE:

$$-\frac{\partial C}{\partial t} = \tfrac{1}{2}\sigma^2 \frac{\partial^2 C}{\partial x^2} + v\frac{\partial C}{\partial x} - rC \tag{13.7}$$

We are marching from the maturity date down to time zero (as done in Hull, 2000) and we construct the explicit finite difference approximation to (13.7) as follows:

$$-\frac{C_j^{n+1} - C_j^n}{\Delta t} = \tfrac{1}{2}\sigma^2 \frac{C_{j+1}^{n+1} - 2C_j^{n+1} + C_{j-1}^{n+1}}{\Delta x^2} + v\frac{C_{j+1}^{n+1} - C_{j-1}^{n+1}}{2\Delta x} - rC_j^{n+1} \tag{13.8}$$

Rearranging terms we get the following representation:

$$C_j^n = p_u C_{j+1}^{n+1} + p_m C_j^{n+1} + p_d C_{j-1}^{n+1} \tag{13.9}$$

where

$$p_u = A + B$$
$$p_m = 1 - 2A - r\Delta t$$
$$p_d = A - B$$

and

$$A = \frac{\Delta t \sigma^2}{2\Delta x^2}, \quad B = \frac{\Delta t v}{2\Delta x}$$

This scheme is similar to taking discounted expectations. In general the free term is evaluated at time level n (implicit) (see Hull, 2000; Clewlow and Strickland, 1998). Of course the probabilities in equation (13.9) should be positive, and this leads to restrictions on the step size Δt.

We mention finally that the trinomial method can be used to find an approximate solution for American options. This is quite easy because it is a variation of the European case and is well documented in the literature. In particular, we must check that the free boundary condition remains valid and hence we must have, for an American put option,

$$C_j^n = \max(C_j^n, S_j^n - K) \tag{13.10}$$

at each time level. In general, the relationship between the steps in time and S is given by (Clewlow and Strickland, 1998):

$$\Delta x = \sigma\sqrt{3\Delta t}$$

If this relationship is not satisfied then we will get negative values for the option price, something that is not possible, neither physically nor financially.

13.3.1   A general formulation

The trinomial method can be applied to a range of products such as equities, currencies, interest rates or any other quantity that can be described as a stochastic differential equation (see Wilmott, 1998, p. 140 for an elegant presentation). Let us examine the general SDE:

$$dy = A(y, t)dt + B(y, t)dx$$
$$y = \text{Real-valued function} \tag{13.11}$$
$$x = \text{Brownian motion}$$

Furthermore, A and B are given functions. They are nonlinear in general.

As before, the variable y can rise, fall or remain at the same value in the interval Δt. Let:

$$\varphi^+(y, t) = \text{probability of a rise}$$
$$\varphi^-(y, t) = \text{probability of a fall} \tag{13.12}$$

Then the mean of the change in y in the given time step is:

$$(\varphi^+ - \varphi^-)\Delta y,$$

where $\Delta y = $ jump size in y and the variance is given by

$$[\varphi^+(1 - \varphi^+ + \varphi^-)^2 + (1 - \varphi^+ - \varphi^-)(\varphi^+ - \varphi^-)^2 + \varphi^-(1 + \varphi^+ - \varphi^-)^2]\Delta y^2$$

Now, from equation (13.11) the mean and variance in the continuous-time variant are approximately:

$$A(y, t)\Delta t$$
$$B(y, t)^2\Delta t \tag{13.13}$$

Equating like-terms we choose:

$$\varphi^+(y, t) = \frac{1}{2}\frac{\Delta t}{\Delta y^2}[B(y, t)^2 + A(y, t)\Delta y]$$

$$\varphi^-(y, t) = \frac{1}{2}\frac{\Delta t}{\Delta y^2}[B(y, t)^2 - A(y, t)\Delta y]$$
(13.14)

This is a powerful result because it allows us to create a trinomial tree for any SDE. The reader might like to check that the specific case in equation (13.9) is consistent with equation (13.14). As mentioned in Wilmott, the scheme is only conditionally stable and we must have a constraint of the form $\Delta y = O(\sqrt{\Delta t})$.

13.4 THE TRINOMIAL METHOD FOR BARRIER OPTIONS

We now discuss the application of the trinomial method to barrier option pricing. It is known that the binomial method gives erroneous answers for non-constant barriers or multiple barriers (Boyle and Lau, 1994). A major challenge is aligning the location of the barriers with the layers of nodes in the lattice. In Chapters 14 and 15 we shall develop robust and accurate finite difference schemes that can price barrier options, but in this chapter we show how to achieve the same results with trinomial lattices, albeit with more effort. The results are based on Ritchken (1995). We assume that the SDE holds:

$$dS = \mu S dt + \sigma S dW$$
(13.15)

Taking logarithmic terms on each side of (13.15) gives:

$$S(t + \Delta t) = S(t)e^{\mu\Delta t + \sigma W}, \qquad W \sim N(0, \Delta t)$$
(13.16)

We now define the term

$$\xi(t) = \mu\Delta t + \sigma W$$

$$\xi(t) = \begin{cases} \lambda\sigma\sqrt{\Delta t} \text{ with probability } p_u \\ 0 \text{ with probability } p_m \\ -\lambda\sigma\sqrt{\Delta t} \text{ with probability } p_d \end{cases}$$

where λ is the 'stretch' parameter and we must approximate in the interval $[0, \Delta t]$ by the following discrete random variable, defined by:

$$\ln S(t + \Delta t) = \ln S(t) + \mu\Delta t + \sigma W$$
(13.17)

where the probabilities are given by:

$$p_u = \frac{1}{2\lambda^2} + \frac{\mu\sqrt{\Delta t}}{2\lambda\sigma}$$

$$p_m = 1 - 1/\lambda^2$$
(13.18)

$$p_d = \frac{1}{2\lambda^2} - \frac{\mu\sqrt{\Delta t}}{2\lambda\sigma}$$

The factor λ controls the 'gap' between layers of prices on the lattice; when it is equal to 1 we revert to the binomial method. For barrier options we choose λ such that the barrier is hit exactly. We take the example of a down-and-out call option and H is the value of the knock-out barrier. We need to compute the number of consecutive down moves that lead to the lowest layer of nodes just above the barrier H. This is the largest integer smaller than the following value:

$$\eta = \frac{\ln(S_0/H)}{\sigma\sqrt{\Delta t}} \quad \text{when } \lambda = 1; \qquad \eta_0 < \eta$$

Then

$$\lambda = \frac{\ln(S_0/H)}{\eta_0\sigma\sqrt{\Delta t}}$$

Using this value of λ will give us a layer of nodes that coincides with the barrier. We note that this approach has been applied to other kinds of barrier options (Ritchken, 1995):

- Barrier options with exponential barrier
- Complex barrier options
- Multiple barriers
- Problems when the underlying is very close to the barrier
- Extensions to higher dimensions.

A discussion of these problems is outside the scope of this book. However, Chapter 14 discusses finite difference methods for double barrier option problems and it is the author's opinion that FDM is easier to apply than the trinomial method for this type of problem.

13.5   SUMMARY AND CONCLUSIONS

We have given an introduction to the trinomial method for one-factor models. The material is well known but we have included it because we wish to view it as a special kind of explicit finite difference scheme. In fact, the finite difference method is more powerful because it uses a rectangular grid instead of an oddly shaped lattice.

14
Exponentially Fitted Difference Schemes for Barrier Options

14.1 INTRODUCTION AND OBJECTIVES

In this chapter we apply the exponentially fitted finite difference schemes to an important class of one-factor options, namely barrier options. A barrier option is one that comes into existence or becomes worthless if the underlying asset reaches some prescribed value before expiry. In this case we speak of a single barrier. It is possible to define double barrier options in which case there is both a lower and an upper barrier. We shall give a compact overview of the different kinds of barrier options. The main goals in this chapter are:

- Describing all barrier option problems by a parabolic initial boundary value problem (IBVP) based on Black–Scholes PDE with Dirichlet boundary conditions
- Approximating the IBVP by robust finite difference schemes.

We concentrate on well-behaved barriers, that is barriers that are defined by either constant or sufficiently smooth functions. In the next chapter we shall treat barrier option problems with intermittent, exponentially increasing, decreasing and other time-dependent barriers. Furthermore, in this chapter we assume continuous monitoring. Thus, having posed the problem as a well-defined IBVP we then apply to it the exponentially fitted finite difference scheme as described in Duffy (1980) and Cooney (1999).

We focus on exponentially fitted difference schemes and compare them to a number of other solutions, for example the exact solution (Haug, 1998) and numerical solutions using the finite element method (see Topper, 1998, 2005).

14.2 WHAT ARE BARRIER OPTIONS?

Barrier options are options where the payoff depends on whether the underlying asset's price reaches a given level during a certain period of time before the expiry date. Barrier options are the most popular of the exotic options. There are two kinds of barriers:

- *In barrier:* This is reached when the asset price S hits the barrier value H before maturity. In other words, if S never hits H before maturity then the payout is zero.
- *Out barrier:* This is similar to a plain option except that the option is knocked out or becomes worthless if the asset price S hits the barrier H before expiration. This is an option that is knocked out if the underlying asset touches a lower boundary L or upper boundary U, prior to maturity.

The above examples were based on constant values for U and L. In other words, we assume that the values of U and L are time-independent. This is a major simplification; in general U and L are functions of time, $U = U(t)$ and $L = L(t)$. In fact, these functions may even be discontinuous at certain points. For more detailed information, see Haug (1998).

14.3 INITIAL BOUNDARY VALUE PROBLEMS FOR BARRIER OPTIONS

In this chapter we concentrate on one-factor barrier options described by the following partial differential equation:

$$-\frac{\partial V}{\partial t} + \frac{1}{2}\sigma^2 S^2 \frac{\partial^2 V}{\partial S^2} + rS\frac{\partial V}{\partial S} - rV = 0 \tag{14.1}$$

In contrast to plain options we now need to specify two boundary conditions at finite values of S. For a double barrier option this is not a problem because two finite boundaries are specified:

$$\begin{aligned} V(A,t) &= g_0(t), \quad 0 < t < T \\ V(B,t) &= g_1(t), \quad 0 < t < T \end{aligned} \tag{14.2}$$

where g_0 and g_1 are given functions of t.

Here A and B are specific values of the underlying S and we assume that these barriers are constant for the moment. In Chapter 15 we shall discuss problems with time-dependent barriers $L(t)$ and $U(t)$ that are defined in boundary conditions as:

$$\begin{aligned} V(L(t),t) &= g_0(t), \quad 0 < t < T \\ V(U(t),t) &= g_1(t), \quad 0 < t < T \end{aligned} \tag{14.3}$$

For single barriers (we are only given one barrier) we have to decide on how to define the other barrier! Given a positive single barrier we then can choose between $S = 0$ or some large value for S. A more analytical technique can be used to find this far-field boundary condition.

There are a number of scenarios when working with single barrier options. For example, we view a single up-and-out barrier as a double barrier option with rebate of value 0 at the down-and-out barrier (that is, when $S = 0$). In this case the company whose stock is being modelled is probably bankrupt and is therefore unable to recover (Jarrow and Turnbull, 1996). Another example is a down-and-out call option in which case we need to truncate the semi-infinite domain. In this case we take the boundary conditions as follows:

$$V(S_{\max}, t) = S_{\max} - Ke^{-r(T-t)} \tag{14.4}$$

where $S_{\max}$ is 'large enough'.

The payoff function is the initial condition for equation (14.1) and is given by:

$$V(S, 0) = \max(S - K, 0) \tag{14.5}$$

We shall now examine how to approximate barrier option problems by finite difference methods.

14.4 USING EXPONENTIAL FITTING FOR BARRIER OPTIONS

The exponentially fitted schemes were developed specifically for boundary layer problems and convection–diffusion equations whose solutions have large gradients in certain regions of the domain of interest (see Il'in, 1969; Duffy, 1980). In particular, the schemes are ideal for approximating the solution of IBVP that describe barrier options. We have already analysed these schemes in Chapter 11. In this chapter we now use exponential fitting in the space (S) direction and implicit Euler time marching in the t direction. If needed, we can employ extrapolation techniques in order to promote accuracy. For convenience, we write the Black–Scholes equation (14.1) in the more general and convenient form

$$LV \equiv -\frac{\partial V}{\partial t} + \sigma(S, t)\frac{\partial^2 V}{\partial S^2} + \mu(S, t)\frac{\partial V}{\partial S} + b(S, t)V = 0 \tag{14.6}$$

where $\sigma(S, t) = \frac{1}{2}\sigma^2 S^2$

$\mu(S, t) = rS$

$b(S, t) = -r.$

The corresponding fitted scheme is now defined as:

$$L_k^h V_j^n \equiv -\frac{V_j^{n+1} - V_j^n}{k} + \rho_j^{n+1} D_+ D_- V_j^{n+1}$$

$$+ \mu_j^{n+1} D_0 V_j^{n+1} + b_j^{n+1} V_j^{n+1} = 0, \quad 1 \le j \le J - 1 \tag{14.7}$$

where

$$\rho_j^n \equiv \frac{\mu_j^n h}{2} \coth \frac{\mu_j^n h}{2\sigma_j^n}$$

We must define the discrete variants of the initial condition (14.5) and boundary conditions (14.2) and we realise them as follows:

$$V_j^0 = \max(S_j - K, 0), \quad 1 \le j \le J - 1 \tag{14.8}$$

and

$$\left.\begin{array}{l} V_0^n = g_0(t_n) \\ V_J^n = g_1(t_n) \end{array}\right\} \quad 0 \le n \le N \tag{14.9}$$

The system (14.7), (14.8), (14.9) can be cast as a linear matrix system:

$$A^n U^{n+1} = F^n, \quad n \ge 0 \quad \text{with } U^0 \text{ given} \tag{14.10}$$

and we solve this system using LU decomposition, for example. A discussion of this topic with algorithms and implementation in C++ can be found in Duffy (2004). We now compare the accuracy and performance of the fitted Duffy scheme by comparing it and benchmarking it with several other approaches:

- Exact solutions (Haug, 1998)
- Finite element method (Topper, 1998, 2005)
- Trinomial method and explicit finite difference schemes.

In general, our schemes compare favourably. Let us discuss some examples. The test cases are taken from Topper (1998) and Haug (1998).

Table 14.1   Performance

Mesh size	Time
11 × 11	0.02 sec
55 × 55	0.16 sec
110 × 110	0.54 sec
1100 × 1100	49 sec

14.4.1   Double barrier call options

We consider an up-and-out :: down-and-out call option with continuous monitoring, and we supply the following data:

- Strike price K 100
- Down-and-out barrier 75
- Up-and-out barrier 130
- Rebates none
- Interest rate r 0.1
- Volatility 0.2
- Maturity T 1 year.

In this case we see that there are no rebates, making the option worthless if the stock price hits either barrier before maturity.

In Table 14.1 we give the timing results from Duffy fitting. We carried out the experiments at the time on a 400-Mhz Pentium II machine and the execution times were as follows (in the year 1999). At the moment of writing (2005) these processing times are drastically improved.

14.4.2   Single barrier call options

We now discuss an up-and-out call option with a given rebate. We model this as a double barrier with rebate 0 at the down-and-out barrier $S = 0$:

- Strike price K 100
- Up-and-out barrier 110
- Rebates 10
- Interest rate r 0.05
- Volatility 0.2
- Maturity T 0.5 year

Table 14.2 compares the exact solution in Topper (1998) with the fitting scheme.

14.5   TIME-DEPENDENT VOLATILITY

We now discuss the accuracy of the fitted scheme when the volatility is non-constant. We are assuming a term structure of volatility. In particular, it has the simple linear form:

$$\sigma(t) = at + b \tag{14.11}$$

Table 14.2

Stock-price	Topper	Duffy (55 × 55)	Duffy (1100 × 1100)
80	0.43223	0.43123	0.43222
90	2.10253	2.09175	2.10248
100	5.60968	5.59806	5.60968
105	7.79972	7.79342	7.79967
109	9.56930	9.56490	9.56929

Table 14.3

Problem	Initial volatility	Ending volatility	a	b
1	0.25	0.25	0	0.25
2	0.177	0.306	−0.129	0.306
3	0.306	0.177	0.129	0.177

This form is related to the term structure of volatility. Some exact solutions are known for barrier options with a linear volatility model. We consider three problems, as shown in Table 14.3. Here we have constant, decreasing and increasing volatilities. The data for this problem is:

- Asset price 95
- Strike price K 100
- Down-and-out barrier 90
- Rebates 10
- Interest rate r 0.1
- (Volatility is now a function)
- Maturity T 1 year

We compare finite element (FEM), trinomial and fitting methods and the results are shown in Table 14.4. Here we see that the methods converge to slightly different values, but the FEM and fitting methods agree most.

Table 14.4

Problem	Topper (Trinomial)	Topper (FE)	Duffy (110 × 110)	Duffy (1100 × 1100)
1	5.9968	5.9969	5.9960	5.9968
2	6.4566	6.4632	6.4628	6.4642
3	5.7286	5.7169	5.7160	5.7167

14.6   SOME OTHER KINDS OF EXOTIC OPTIONS

We shall now discuss some other kinds of exotic options.

14.6.1 Plain vanilla power call options

We continue with an analysis of exponentially fitted schemes by examining a class of options whose payoff at maturity depends on the power of the asset. There are two main sub-categories:

- Symmetric power call

$$V(S, T) = \max((S - K)^p, 0) \tag{14.12}$$

- Asymmetric power call

$$V(S, T) = \max(S^p - K, 0) \tag{14.13}$$

We formulate the boundary conditions as follows:

$$V(0, t) = 0$$
$$V(1000, t) = S^p - K e^{-rt} \tag{14.14}$$

The first boundary condition states that the option is worthless at $S = 0$ while the second boundary condition states that the option is deep in-the-money. Again, we have truncated the domain of interest.

Here, p is some number ($p = 1$ corresponds to a 'normal' option), and exact solutions are known for such problems (see Zhang, 1998). We concentrate on asymmetric power call options in this section given the following data:

- Asset price 555
- Strike price K 550
- Interest rate r 0.06
- Volatility 0.15
- Dividend yield 0.04
- Maturity T 0.5 year

The results of the fitting scheme and the FEM scheme are shown in Table 14.5, with p ranging from $p = 0.96$ to $p = 1.05$.

Table 14.5

p	0.96	0.97	0.98	0.99	1.00
Topper	0.17614	1.01010	4.08800	12.21638	28.29032
Duffy	0.17621	1.01023	4.08816	12.21617	28.28956

p	1.01	1.02	1.03	1.04	1.05
Topper	53.39500	86.29781	124.81669	167.30009	213.01648
Duffy	53.39503	86.29759	124.81687	167.30023	213.01652

14.6.2 Capped power call options

Capped power options are traded in the marketplace. The major difference with non-capped power calls lies in the payoff:

- Symmetric capped power call

$$V(S, T) = \min[\max[(S - K)^p, 0], \ C]$$ (14.15)

- Asymmetric capped power call

$$V(S, T) = \min[\max(S^p - K, 0), \ C]$$ (14.16)

where C is the floor value.

We take the example with

$$V(0, t) = 0$$
$$V(1000, t) = 50$$
$$C = 50$$

with the same data as in the previous sub-section. Table 14.6 compares FEM, Monte Carlo and fitting schemes for this problem for the asymmetric case, while Table 14.7 shows the results for the symmetric case with $p = 2$ and the stock price varies from out-of-the-money to in-the-money.

Table 14.6

p	0.96	0.97	0.98	0.99	1.00
Monte Carlo	0.163	0.909	3.442	9.327	18.887
Topper (FE)	0.165	1.008	3.434	9.332	18.886
Duffy (FDM)	0.165	0.907	3.437	9.325	18.879

p	1.01	1.02	1.03	1.04	1.05
Monte Carlo	29.897	39.098	44.745	47.327	48.219
Topper (FE)	29.839	39.084	44.736	47.326	48.224
Duffy (FDM)	29.897	39.091	44.735	47.323	48.222

Table 14.7

S	500	550	555	560	600
Monte Carlo	8.47390	23.50052	25.15097	26.78109	37.98719
Topper (FE)	8.46219	23.51419	25.16434	26.79323	37.97783
Duffy (FDM)	8.45895	23.50785	25.15838	26.78773	37.97530

In these cases, we see that fitting and Monte Carlo give similar values.

14.7 COMPARISONS WITH EXACT SOLUTIONS

As another endorsement of the exponentially fitted schemes and their ability to approximate the price of call and put barrier options, we compare the exact solutions in Haug (1998) with ours. Let us take an example:

- Asset price 100
- Strike price K (will be a range of values)

Table 14.8   Down-and-out call option

σ	K	H	Haug	Duffy	σ	K	H	Haug	Duffy
0.25	90	95	9.0246	9.0246	0.25	90	100	3.0000	3.0000
0.30	90	95	8.8334	8.8336	0.30	90	100	3.0000	3.0000
0.25	100	95	6.7924	6.7922	0.25	100	100	3.0000	3.0000
0.30	100	95	7.0285	7.0286	0.30	100	100	3.0000	3.0000
0.25	110	95	4.8759	4.8755	0.25	110	100	3.0000	3.0000
0.30	110	95	5.4137	5.4137	0.30	110	100	3.0000	3.0000

Table 14.9   An up-and-out call option

σ	K	H	Haug	Duffy	σ	K	H	Haug	Duffy
0.25	90	105	2.6789	2.6787	0.30	100	105	2.4389	2.4389
0.30	90	105	2.6341	2.6339	0.25	110	105	2.3453	2.3453
0.25	100	105	2.3580	2.3579	0.30	110	105	2.4315	2.4315

Table 14.10   Down-and-out put option

σ	K	H	Haug	Duffy	σ	K	H	Haug	Duffy
0.25	90	95	2.2798	2.2798	0.25	90	100	3.0000	3.0000
0.30	90	95	2.4170	2.4170	0.30	90	100	3.0000	3.0000
0.25	100	95	2.2947	2.2946	0.25	100	100	3.0000	3.0000
0.30	100	95	2.4258	2.4257	0.30	100	100	3.0000	3.0000
0.25	110	95	2.6252	2.6250	0.25	110	100	3.0000	3.0000
0.30	110	95	2.6246	2.6244	0.30	110	100	3.0000	3.0000

- Interest rate r 0.08
- Volatility (will be a range of values)
- Dividend (cost-of-carry) 0.04
- Maturity T 0.5 year
- Rebate 3.

In the current case Haug (1998, Table 2-9, p. 72) varies the strike price K and the boundary H as well as the volatility. The results in Table 14.8 allows us to compare Haug and fitting (we take a right boundary $S = 200$, boundary condition as in equation (14.4) and a 200 × 200 mesh for fitting).

Again, the agreement between the two sets of values is good.

In Table 14.9 we provide the results for an up-and-out call option. In Table 14.10 we provide the results for a down-and-out put. In this case we use the initial conditions

$$V(S, 0) = \max (K - S, 0) \tag{14.17}$$

with the right-hand boundary condition

$$V(S_{\max}, t) = 0 \quad (S_{\max} \equiv 200) \tag{14.18}$$

Table 14.11   An up-and-out put option

σ	K	H	Haug	Duffy	σ	K	H	Haug	Duffy
0.25	90	105	3.7760	3.7757	0.30	100	105	5.8032	5.8032
0.30	90	105	4.2293	4.2290	0.25	110	105	7.5187	7.5187
0.25	100	105	5.4932	5.4931	0.30	110	105	7.5649	7.5650

In Table 14.11 we provide the results for an up-and-out put option. In this case we take the left-hand boundary condition

$$V(0, t) = K e^{-(r-d)(T-t)} \tag{14.19}$$

where d is the dividend.

Finally, we discuss Table 2-10, p. 75 of Haug (1998) where data is provided for up-and-out and down-and-out call options. Let L denote the lower boundary and U the upper boundary. Haug (1998) uses the parameters

$$\begin{aligned} \delta_1 &= \text{curvature of lower boundary} \\ \delta_2 &= \text{curvature of upper boundary} \end{aligned} \tag{14.20}$$

We take these values to be zero in this chapter, and deploy the following data:

- Asset price 100
- Strike price K
- Interest rate r 0.1
- Volatility (will be a range of values)

The results are shown in Tables 14.12 to 14.14.

Table 14.12 $L = 50$ and $U = 150$

σ	T	Haug	Duffy	σ	T	Haug	Duffy
0.15	0.25	4.3515	4.3511	0.15	0.5	7.9336	7.9332
0.25	0.25	6.1644	6.1641	0.25	0.5	7.9336	7.9332
0.35	0.25	7.0373	7.0370	0.35	0.5	6.5088	6.5087

Table 14.13 $L = 70$ and $U = 130$

σ	T	Haug	Duffy	σ	T	Haug	Duffy
0.15	0.25	4.3139	4.3133	0.15	0.5	5.9697	5.9689
0.25	0.25	4.8293	4.8288	0.25	0.5	4.0004	4.0002
0.35	0.25	3.7765	3.7762	0.35	0.5	2.2563	2.2562

Table 14.14 $L = 90$ and $U = 110$

σ	T	Haug	Duffy	σ	T	Haug	Duffy
0.15	0.25	1.2055	1.2051	0.15	0.5	0.5537	0.5535
0.25	0.25	0.3098	0.3098	0.25	0.5	0.0441	0.0441
0.35	0.25	0.0477	0.0477	0.35	0.5	0.0011	0.0011

14.8   OTHER SCHEMES AND APPROXIMATIONS

There are other popular finite difference schemes that are used to approximate the price of barrier options:

- Binomial method (not discussed in this book)
- Trinomial method (as discussed in Chapter 13)

Boyle and Lau (1994) reported that the binomial method is very unstable ('bumpy') when used to price barrier options. A major problem is how to approximate the barrier at each time level. The data structure for the binomial method is a lattice – not the most symmetric of structures at the best of times – while, on the other hand, the datastructures for FDM are rectangular. The binomial method is conditionally stable and stability is assured if

$$h = \sqrt{k} \quad \text{or} \quad k = h^2 \tag{14.21}$$

Use of the trinomial method is a better solution than use of the binomial method. Again, it is equivalent to an explicit finite difference scheme. It will produce negative and non-physical values if the time step k is not small enough.

We mention that there are other analytical techniques for finding the value of a barrier option:

- Infinite series, single or double integral solution (Kunitomo and Ikeda, 1992)
- Laplace transforms (Geman and Yor, 1996)
- Method of images (Rich, 1994; Lo, 1997).

While it is very interesting to examine these methods, a treatment of these topics is outside the scope of this book.

14.9   EXTENSIONS TO THE MODEL

We have deliberately restricted the scope in this chapter because we wish to demonstrate the applicability of fitting schemes. In particular, we did not examine:

- Discrete monitoring
- In-barriers; here the rebate is the output from a plain vanilla calculation
- Support for boundaries with variable curvature
- Support for time-dependent barriers
- Intermittent and partial barriers – in this case a barrier may be defined in one part of the domain and not in other parts
- American or Asian barrier options.

We shall examine some of these issues in the next chapter.

14.10   SUMMARY AND CONCLUSIONS

In this chapter we examined the application of the exponentially fitted finite difference schemes to approximate the price of barrier options (see Duffy, 1980). We have compared our results with Monte Carlo, FEM (Topper, 1998), exact solutions (Haug, 1998) and the trinomial method. We can conclude that our method is robust and produces accurate results. Although not mentioned, we can obtain accurate values for delta and gamma with this method.

The numerical experiments and results confirm the mathematical findings on exponentially fitted schemes in Duffy (1980). The method in this chapter can be applied to Black–Scholes equations with time-dependent coefficients

$$-\frac{\partial V}{\partial t} + \tfrac{1}{2}\sigma^2(t)S^2\frac{\partial^2 V}{\partial S^2} + [r(t) - d(t)]S\frac{\partial V}{\partial S} - r(t)V = 0$$

For example, we could model interest rate behaviour by a function that has been perturbed from some equilibrium level to which it returns via an exponential decay

$$r(t) = r_\infty + [r(0) - r_\infty]\exp(-ct)$$

where c is some constant.

15
Advanced Issues in Barrier
and Lookback Option Modelling

15.1 INTRODUCTION AND OBJECTIVES

In Chapter 14 we applied exponentially fitted finite difference schemes to finding good approximate solutions to the partial differential equations that describe one-factor barrier options with continuous monitoring. We also assumed that the barriers were constant throughout the life of the option.

In this chapter we discuss a number of advanced features that have to do with barrier option pricing. First, we model problems with time-dependent (non-constant) barriers. These problems can be reduced to a modified PDE on a fixed domain and we can then solve this new problem using the schemes from Chapter 14. Second, we investigate how to apply finite difference schemes to barrier option problems with discrete monitoring. Furthermore, we discuss a result by Broadie *et al.* (1997) on how to modify the barrier boundary so that the problem can be posed as a problem with continuous monitoring. Finally, we discuss some complex barrier option classes and give guidelines on how to apply FDM to finding approximations to them.

15.2 KINDS OF BOUNDARIES AND BOUNDARY CONDITIONS

In this section we discuss time-dependent barriers. A regular barrier option subjects investors to barrier exposure throughout the life of the option. Time-dependent barrier options are hybrids between regular barrier options and ordinary options.

In Chapter 14 we assumed that the boundaries associated with the PDE for barrier options were 'flat', that is, we had boundary conditions of the form

$$V(A, t) = g_0(t), \ 0 < t < T$$
$$V(B, t) = g_1(t), \ 0 < t < T$$

(15.1)

where A and B are the constant barriers (see Figure 15.1). On the boundaries we need to specify boundary conditions. In general, it is possible and common to define time-dependent boundary conditions

$$V(L(t), t) = g_0(t), \ 0 < t < T$$
$$V(U(t), t) = g_1(t), \ 0 < t < T$$

(15.2)

where g_0 and g_1 are given functions of t (see Figure 15.2). In this case we assume that the functions $L(t)$ (lower absorbing boundary) and $U(t)$ (upper absorbing boundary) are well behaved for the moment. We need to make this more precise.

There are different kinds of barrier options that are characterised by the form of the barrier functions. A 'protected' barrier option is one where the barrier clause is only effective part of the time. A 'rainbow' barrier option is one where the barrier clause refers to the price

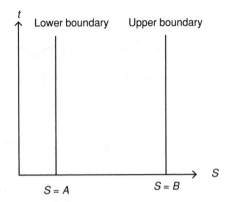

Figure 15.1   Fixed boundaries

of a second stock while a 'Parisian' option is cancelled or knocked out some time after the stock exceeds a threshold. It is obvious that these types must be modelled properly using the PDE/FDM approach.

Let us assume, as another way of looking at the problem, that we are pricing an up-and-out call option and that the stock price satisfies a SDE whose solution is given by:

$$S_t = S_0 \exp(\sigma B_t + \alpha t) \tag{15.3}$$

where B_t = standard Brownian motion

σ = volatility

S_0 = initial stock price $\equiv S(0)$

r = interest rate > 0

$\alpha = r - \dfrac{1}{2}\sigma^2.$

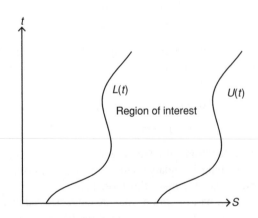

Figure 15.2   Time-dependent boundaries

We can describe the boundary in terms of the underlying Brownian motion. To this end, define the function

$$f(t) = \sigma^{-1}\{\log[U(t)/S_0] - \alpha t\}$$

Now, the up-and-out option is cancelled if and only if the Brownian motion B_t ever hits $f(t)$. For a double barrier option, we see that the contract is cancelled if

$$B_t \notin (g(t), f(t)) \quad \text{for some } 0 \le t \le T$$

where

$$g(t) = \sigma^{-1}\{\log[L(t)/S_0] - \alpha t\}$$

There are various kinds of barriers:

- Constant barriers
- Exponential barriers
- Linear boundaries

Problems involving constant or exponential barriers have known analytic solutions (Kunitomo and Ikeda, 1992; Geman and Yor, 1996). We have also discussed these in Chapter 14.

In general, we must examine the IBVP describing barrier options from a number of perspectives; for example, under which conditions does the problem have a unique solution and what is the smoothness of the solution? Two crucial questions must be addressed:

- What is the smoothness of the barrier functions $L(t)$ and $U(t)$?
- What are the compatibility conditions between the initial and boundary conditions?

Some authors assume that the functions $L(t)$ and $U(t)$ are four time continuously differentiable (see Bobisud, 1967). Furthermore, the compatibility conditions between boundary and initial conditions state that

$$\begin{aligned} g_0(0) &= \varphi(A) \\ g_1(0) &= \varphi(B) \end{aligned} \tag{15.4}$$

where g_0 and g_1 are boundary conditions and φ is the initial condition, as discussed in previous chapters.

These conditions may or may not be valid for a given problem. Lack of compatibility will influence the accuracy of the finite difference scheme near the corners.

Given a problem with time-dependent barriers we can transform this problem to one with constant barriers by a change of variables (Bobisud, 1967). To this end, define the variable z by

$$z = \frac{S - L(t)}{U(t) - L(t)} \tag{15.5}$$

where S is the underlying price.

This transforms (S, t) space into (z, t) space and we can then apply the techniques of Chapter 14 to the IBVP in (z, t) space. Of course, the Black–Scholes PDE in S will need to be transformed into a PDE in z and t. We leave this as an exercise in partial differentiation but we shall come back to this issue when we discuss free boundary value problems and American options.

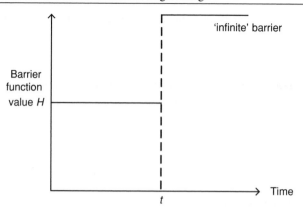

Figure 15.3   Discontinuous barrier function

In equation (15.5) we see that the barriers should not touch each other (otherwise we get division by zero) and should be smooth in some sense. Unfortunately, not all barrier option problems have this property – for example, barrier options with partial barriers, where we can experience jumps in the boundary. We can then expect minor hiccups at best, and wrong answers at worst.

A good example of a problem with a discontinuous barrier is the Front-End Barrier Call Option (see Hui, 1997). The barrier H for this type exists from option start time to some time t in the future. It behaves as a regular barrier in this region. The option then becomes an ordinary option after the barrier period t (see Figure 15.3). Similarly we can define the Rear-End Barrier Call Option where the option is an ordinary option before the barrier date t. Then, after that date up to expiration T, it is a regular barrier option.

15.3 DISCRETE AND CONTINUOUS MONITORING

In practice most, if not all, barrier options traded in markets are discretely monitored. Thus, fixed times for monitoring of the barrier must be specified (usually daily closings). There are legal and financial reasons why discretely monitored barrier options are preferred to continuously monitored barrier options.

15.3.1 What is discrete monitoring?

We have discussed barrier options in Chapter 14 where we have assumed that the price of the underlying was continuously monitored. In real markets, the asset price is monitored at discrete time instances

$$D \equiv \left\{ t_k^* \right\}_{k=0}^{K} \subset \{t_n\}_{n=0}^{N} \tag{15.6}$$

where $t_0 = 0$ and $t_N = T$.

Thus, we are assuming that the set of monitoring dates is a subset of the set of 'full' discrete time points (consisting of $N + 1$ points) in the interval $[0, T]$ where T is the expiry time. The analytical solution of discrete barrier options involves the evaluation of multidimensional integrals. Attempting to evaluate such integrals is not feasible. For a discussion of analytical methods in combination with simulation techniques for barrier options, see Steinberg (2003).

In this section we focus on the application of finite difference schemes to the problem of barrier option pricing in the presence of discrete monitoring points. We concentrate on one kind of barrier option, namely out-options. In-options can then be handled through an in–out parity argument.

Consider a discretely monitored up-and-out call $V(t, S)$ with monitoring date set D, as in equation (15.6), and consider the barrier constraint

$$
\begin{aligned}
V^-(t_k^*, S_j) &= BC[V^+(t_k^*, S_j)] \\
&\equiv \begin{cases} 0, & \text{if } S_j \geq h(t_k^*)H, \quad j = 0, \ldots, J \\ V^+(t_k^*, S_j), & \text{if } S_j < h(t_k^*)H, \quad j = 0, \ldots, J \end{cases}
\end{aligned}
\tag{15.7}
$$

where H is the barrier and $h(t)$ is a time-dependent positive function that allows the barrier to move in time (Foufas *et al.*, 2004). A special case is when the barrier is a flat constant and equation (15.7) then takes the simpler form

$$
V^-(t_k, S_j) = \begin{cases} 0, & S_j \geq H, \quad j = 0, \ldots, J \\ V^+(t_k^*, S_j), & S_j < H, \quad j = 0, \ldots, J \end{cases}
\tag{15.8}
$$

where

$$
V^-(t, S) \equiv \lim_{\epsilon \to 0} V(t - \epsilon, S) \ (\epsilon > 0)
\tag{15.9}
$$
$$
V^+(t, S) \equiv \lim_{\epsilon \to 0} V(t + \epsilon, S) \ (\epsilon > 0)
$$

We thus see that the option price V can experience a jump at the monitoring dates and it is obvious that it is not continuous at such dates. We can thus expect a problem with 'standard' FDM and FEM schemes that assume continuity of the solution. For example, using the Crank–Nicolson method in time leads to large 'spikes' in the solution (Tavella *et al.*, 2000). It is well-known that Crank–Nicolson has its problems but these are even more pronounced when the solution is discontinuous.

15.3.2   Finite difference schemes and jumps in time

We now discuss how to approximate Black–Scholes in the presence of discrete barriers. We pose the question: can we adapt the finite difference schemes from Chapter 14 to allow them to cater for jumps? Based on the experiences from the previous sub-section we propose solving the following more general PDE

$$
-\frac{\partial V}{\partial t} + \sigma(t, S) \frac{\partial^2 V}{\partial S^2} + \mu(t, S) \frac{\partial V}{\partial S} - rV = 0
\tag{15.10}
$$

by the scheme that uses centred differencing in S and implicit Euler in time:

$$
\begin{aligned}
&-\frac{V_j^{n+1} - V_j^n}{k} + \sigma_j^n D_+ D_- V_j^{n+1} + \mu_j^n D_0 V_j^{n+1} - r V_j^{n+1} = 0 \\
&V_{j+}^n = V_{j-}^n, \quad t_n \in D \\
&V_{j+}^n = BC(V_{j-}^n), \quad t_n \in D \\
&V_{j+}^0 = \max(S - K, 0)
\end{aligned}
\tag{15.11}
$$

where we use the discrete analogues of 'jumps' as defined in (15.8). In general, we march from $t = 0$ to $t = T$ while taking into account jumps in time at the special monitoring points.

Please note that the system has now been written in the 'engineer's' form (we speak of initial condition instead of terminal condition).

15.3.3 Lookback options and jumps

As a final example, we examine lookback options. A lookback option has a payoff that depends on the maximum or minimum of the underlying stock price over some given period in time. Let us denote the maximum price of the asset in the interval $[0, T]$ as M; then the payoff of put and call options is given by the floating strike (lookback strike option)

$$\begin{aligned} \text{payoff} &= \max[M - S(T), 0] \quad \text{(put)} \\ \text{payoff} &= \max[S(T) - M, 0] \quad \text{(call)} \end{aligned} \tag{15.12}$$

and the put and call option payoffs for the fixed strike (lookback rate)

$$\begin{aligned} \text{payoff} &= \max(K - M, 0) \quad \text{(put)} \\ \text{payoff} &= \max(M - K, 0) \quad \text{(call)} \end{aligned} \tag{15.13}$$

(see Wilmott, 1998, p. 232).

We now concentrate on fixed strike lookbacks. As in Wilmott *et al.* (1993) we define the variables

$$\xi = S/M$$
$$V(S, M, t) = Mu(\xi, t),$$

where $u(\xi, t)$ is a new dependent variable.

The PDE for u in the new independent variable ξ and t then reads

$$\frac{\partial u}{\partial t} + \frac{1}{2}\sigma^2 \xi^2 \frac{\partial^2 u}{\partial \xi^2} + (r - d)\,\xi \frac{\partial u}{\partial \xi} - ru = 0 \tag{15.14}$$

The final condition becomes

$$u(\xi, T) = U_T := \begin{cases} \max(\xi - 1, 0), & \text{for a call option} \\ \max(1 - \xi, 0), & \text{for a put option} \end{cases} \tag{15.15}$$

The jump condition across sampling dates $t_k^* \in D$ is similar to the case for Barrier options and is given by

$$u^-(t_k^*) = JC[u^+(t_k^*)] := \begin{cases} \max(\xi, 1)u^+(\min(\xi, 1), t_k^*), & \text{for a put option} \\ \min(\xi, 1)u^+(\max(\xi, 1), t_k^*), & \text{for a call option} \end{cases} \tag{15.16}$$

The boundary condition at 0 is given by

$$\begin{aligned} u(0, t) &= e^{-r(T-t)} \quad \text{(put)} \\ u(0, t) &= 0 \quad \text{(call)} \end{aligned} \tag{15.17}$$

while at $\xi = 1$ we have the Robin condition $\partial u/\partial \xi = u$.

All further algorithmic details, as discussed for barrier options, remain the same.

15.4 CONTINUITY CORRECTIONS FOR DISCRETE BARRIER OPTIONS

It is obvious from the previous section that approximating barrier option prices when discrete monitoring is used is, in effect, more difficult than when continuous monitoring is used. In general, it is not possible to find closed solutions to discrete problems but our intuition tells us that the discrete price converges to the continuous price as the monitoring frequency increases, thus suggesting that the continuous price may be used as a naive approximation in some way. In Broadie *et al.* (1997) a result is given that allows us to adjust the continuous formula to obtain a good approximation to the discrete price. In short, the authors apply a continuity correction to the barrier.

The main result is as follows:

Theorem 15.1. *Let $V_m(H)$ be the price of a discretely monitored knock-in or knock-out down call or up put with barrrier H, where m is the number of monitoring points. Let $V(H)$ be the price of the corresponding continuously monitored barrier option.*

Then

$$V_m(H) = V(He^{\pm\beta\sigma\sqrt{T/m}}) + O\left(\frac{1}{\sqrt{m}}\right)$$

where we apply

$$+ \quad \text{if } H > S_0$$
$$- \quad \text{if } H < S_0$$

where $S_0 \equiv$ inital asset value.

Furthermore,

$$\beta = \frac{-\varphi\left(\frac{1}{2}\right)}{\sqrt{2\pi}} \approx 0.5826,$$

where φ is the Riemann zeta function.

In this theorem we assume that the barrier is monitored at times nk, $n = 0, 1, \ldots, m$ where $k = T/m$ (thus m is the number of monitoring points).

The results in Broadie *et al.* (1997) have been extended to more cases and a simpler proof to the above theorem has been given in Kou (2003).

The conclusion is that we can apply the methods of Chapter 14 to discretely monitored barrier option problems by realigning the boundary and solving the problem as a continuously monitored barrier option. This might be a pragmatic approach in some cases.

15.5 COMPLEX BARRIER OPTIONS

In Chapter 14 we proposed the exponentially fitted scheme for calculating the price of single and double barrier option problems with continuous monitoring while, in the first four sections of the current chapter, we introduced FDM schemes that enabled us to take jumps into account. We now conclude this chapter by discussing how complex barrier problems can be modelled using these kinds of schemes.

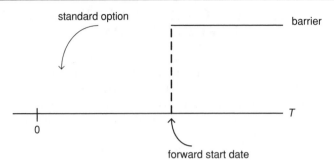

Figure 15.4   Forward starting barrier option

What is a complex barrier option? In general terms, this is an option that has a 'barrier structure' that cannot be described as a single double barrier (Nelken, 1995; Zhang, 1998; Carr and Chou, 1997):

- *Partial barrier options:* The barrier is active only in some time interval, and disappears at some prescribed time. In general, the payoff at expiry may be a function of the spot price at the time that the barrier disappears. An analytical solution for partial barrier options is known (use of the cumulative bivariate normal distribution is given in Carr and Chou, 1997).
- *Double barrier options:* There are two barriers, namely an upper and lower barrier. We have already discussed finite difference schemes for this class of problems.
- *Lookback options:* In this case the payoff depends on the maximum or minimum of the value of the underlying during the lookback period. This period is contained in the interval between the valuation date and the expiry date. We have already proposed finite difference schemes in the current chapter for this class of problems.
- *Forward starting barrier options:* The barrier is active only in the latter period of the option's life. The barrier level may be fixed beforehand or it may be defined as a function of the current underlying date at the so-called forward start date (see Figure 15.4 for a visual cue). Furthermore, the payoff may be a function of the spot price at the time that the barrier becomes active.
- *Rolling options:* These are options that are defined by a sequence of barriers. When each barrier is reached the option strike price is lowered (for calls) or raised (for puts). Rolling options are a subclass of barrier options because they are knocked out only at the last barrier. There are two main kinds of rolling barrier options, namely *roll-down* where all barriers are below the initial spot price, and *roll-up* where all barriers are above the initial spot price.
- *Rachet options:* A rachet option (also known as moving strike option or cliquet option) consists of a sequence of forward starting options where the strike price for the next maturity date is set to be equal to a (positive) constant times the underlying value of the previous maturity date. The exact formula for rachet calls and puts is known (see, for example, Haug, 1998, p. 37).

In general, we are interested in approximating the option price by using finite difference schemes. Exact solutions can be found for one-factor problems with constant coefficients but life soon becomes difficult as, for example, we progress to two-factor problems with time-dependent coefficients and non-constant boundaries.

We shall now discuss how to approach the problem of pricing complex barrier options using finite difference schemes, and a major objective is to flesh out the algorithms that describe how to use the schemes. We first take an example of a so-called front-end single barrier option (Steinberg, 2003). This option is a barrier option from the start of the option to some prespecified time $t < T$, where T is the maturity date. Thus, the option behaves as a down-and-out barrier option to time t and then as an ordinary call option after that. The strategy is as follows: first, solve the Black–Scholes equation from t to T (for example, we could give the analytical solution or we could employ an approximate scheme to find the option price). Second, we use the option value at time t as the initial (actually terminal) condition for the barrier option problem and we can then use our finite difference schemes. Again, we can use the exact formula for such problems (Haug, 1998) or we can apply the finite difference schemes from Chapter 14.

The procedure in the general case is to solve the Black–Scholes equation, starting from the maturity date T to the first 'type' change (for example, barrier to no barrier) and progressively down to time zero. At each date we must recalculate the payoff.

15.6   SUMMARY AND CONCLUSIONS

In this chapter we have introduced a number of topics that are concerned with barrier option pricing. In particular, we focused on time-dependent barriers, discrete monitoring, approximating discrete barriers by continuous ones and finally finite differences to finding approximate solutions to these problems.

When modelling barrier options with discrete monitoring dates, the conclusion is that it is not so much more difficult than modelling such options with continuous monitoring; you do a semi-discretisation in FEM or FDM, for example, and then discretise the corresponding ODE while taking the jumps into account. However, we must model the discrete monotoring dates explicitly in our algorithm schemes, and this procedure can be generalised to lookback and Asian options.

16
The Meshless (Meshfree) Method in Financial Engineering

16.1 INTRODUCTION AND OBJECTIVES

In this chapter we give a short overview of a modern method that is a competitor of the finite difference method (FDM) and the finite element method (FEM). In particular, we discuss the meshless method that attempts to resolve some of the shortcomings of FDM and FEM. First, FDM and FEM schemes are difficult to construct and solve, even in two and three dimensions. Second, they achieve low-order, polynomial accuracy only. Third, they do not scale easily to n-dimensional problems and this can result in these methods being unsuitable for multi-asset derivative problems, for example. Finally, the computational complexity grows exponentially. The meshless method, on the other hand, does not suffer from these problems. In fact, it is 'dimension blind' in the sense that it can be applied to n-dimensional problems with ease. Furthermore, it is easy to program and to understand. To this end, we give an introduction to the meshless method and apply it to convection–diffusion and Black–Scholes equations.

16.2 MOTIVATING THE MESHLESS METHOD

In order to motivate the meshless method we take the one-dimensional heat equation as our model problem:

$$\frac{\partial u}{\partial t} = \frac{\partial^2 u}{\partial x^2}, \quad 0 < x < L, \quad t > 0 \tag{16.1}$$

We now describe what we are going to do; first, we discretise (16.1) in t by applying the explicit Euler scheme (this is Rothe's method) while still keeping the variable x continuous. Then we approximate the solution of the resulting ordinary differential equation (ODE) by using special functions that satisfy the ODE exactly.

In particular, a semi-discretisation of equation (16.1) in time using explicit Euler gives us the system of ordinary differential equations:

$$\frac{U^{n+1}(x) - U^n(x)}{k} = \frac{d^2 U^n(x)}{dx^2}, \quad 0 < x < L, \quad n = 0, \dots, N-1$$

$$U^0(x) \quad \text{given}, \quad 0 < x < L \tag{16.2}$$

or in the differential operator form:

$$H_+ U^{n+1}(x) = H_- U^n(x), \quad 0 < x < L, \quad n = 0, \dots, N-1 \tag{16.3}$$

where we define the operators as

$$H_+ \equiv 1$$

$$H_- \equiv 1 + k\frac{d^2}{dx^2}$$

As usual, we have partitioned the interval $(0, T)$ into N equal sub-intervals of length k. We now assume a solution of (16.3) in the form

$$U^n(x) \simeq \sum_{j=1}^{J} \lambda_j^n \varphi(r_j), \quad 0 < x < L \tag{16.4}$$

where r_j is the Eucliden distance between point x and x_j, $r_j = \sqrt{(x - x_j)^2}$ and $(x_j)_{j=1}^{J}$ are given or known collocation points.

In particular letting the value x be a specific collocation point we get the expression:

$$U^n(x_i) \simeq \sum_{j=1}^{J} \lambda_j^n \varphi(r_{ij}), \tag{16.5}$$

where $r_{ij} = \sqrt{(x_i - x_j)^2}$.

We approximate the ODE (16.3) at each collocation point by inserting the expression (16.5) into equation (16.3), giving the identity:

$$\sum_{j=1}^{J} \lambda_j^{n+1} H_+ \varphi(r_{ij}) = \sum_{j=1}^{J} \lambda_j^n H_- \varphi(r_{ij}), \quad 1 \le i \le J \tag{16.6}$$

or in matrix form:

$$A U^{n+1} = B^n, \quad n \ge 0 \tag{16.7}$$

where $U^n = {}^t(\lambda_1, \ldots, \lambda_J)$ (unknowns)

$A = (H_+ \varphi(r_{ij}))_{1 \le i, j \le J}$

$B = {}^t(B_1, \ldots, B_J)$

where

$$B_i^n = \sum_{j=1}^{J} \lambda_j^n H_- \varphi(r_{ij}), \quad i = 1, \ldots, J$$

We can then use a matrix solver such as Gaussian elimination with partial pivoting, for example, to solve the above system of equations.

Some initial remarks are in order:

- The so-called radial basic function (RBF) φ (unspecified as of yet) is defined on the whole region of interest, in contrast to FEM where we use piecewise polynomials with compact support.
- The matrix A in (16.7) is dense in general. This means that all its values must be stored in memory, again in contrast to FDM and FEM where we usually encounter tridiagonal, band or even sparse matrices. The matrix A is sometimes called the stiffness matrix. More dramatically, it is often ill-conditioned and we must use regularisation techniques to solve system (16.7).
- No mesh is needed in the meshless method. We do, however, have to determine the collocation points where the ODE (16.7) is evaluated. This has potential advantages that add to the understandability of the method, thus making it easier to program.

16.3 AN INTRODUCTION TO RADIAL BASIS FUNCTIONS

Before we discuss more complex examples we give an introduction to radial basis functions (or RBF for short). Radial basis functions are a special class of functions. Their characteristic feature is that they increase or decrease monotonically from a central point. We give the first example of such a function in one dimension. This is the Gaussian RBF with centre c and radius r:

$$\varphi(x) = \exp\left[-\frac{(x-c)^2}{r^2}\right] \tag{16.8}$$

This function decreases monotonically with distance from the centre c. Another function is the multiquadric (MQ) RBF defined by the formula:

$$\varphi(x) = \frac{\sqrt{r^2 + (x-c)^2}}{r} \tag{16.9}$$

This function increases monotonically with distance from the centre c. We thus see that Gaussian functions are 'local' in the sense that they decrease to zero as we move from the centre while the multiquadric RBF has a global response. Other popular RBFs are:

TPS (Thin Plate Shell): $\varphi(\mathbf{x}, \mathbf{x}_j) = \varphi(r_j) = r_j^4 \log(r_j)$

MQ: $\varphi(\mathbf{x}, \mathbf{x}_j) = \varphi(r_j) = \sqrt{c^2 + r_j^2}$

Cubic: $\varphi(\mathbf{x}, \mathbf{x}_j) = \varphi(r_j) = r_j^3$

Gaussian: $\varphi(\mathbf{x}, \mathbf{x}_j) = \varphi(r_j) = e^{-c^2 r_j^2}$
$$\tag{16.10}$$

where $r_j = \|\mathbf{x} - \mathbf{x}_j\|$ in the Euclidean norm.

16.4 SEMI-DISCRETISATIONS AND CONVECTION–DIFFUSION EQUATIONS

In general, we are interested in convection–diffusion equations and their applications to the Black–Scholes equation. The meshless method is quite general and can be applied to elliptic, hyperbolic and integro-differential equations as well as to integral equations and ordinary differential equations.

In this section we concentrate on the general convection–diffusion equation in n dimensions:

$$\frac{\partial u(\mathbf{x}, t)}{\partial t} = K \Delta u(\mathbf{x}, t)t + \mathbf{v} \cdot \nabla u(\mathbf{x}, t) \quad \mathbf{x} \in \Omega \subset R^n, \ t > 0 \tag{16.11}$$

with Robin boundary conditions:

$$c_1 u(\mathbf{x}, t) + \mathbf{c}_2 \cdot \nabla u(\mathbf{x}, t) = f(\mathbf{x}, t), \quad \mathbf{x} \in \partial\Omega, \ t > 0 \tag{16.12}$$

and initial conditions:

$$u(\mathbf{x}, 0) = u_0(\mathbf{x}), \quad t = 0 \tag{16.13}$$

Using Rothe's method we discretise first in time using Crank–Nicolson averaging. We then get the ODE:

$$u(\mathbf{x}, t + k) - u(\mathbf{x}, t) = \frac{k}{2}[K \Delta u(\mathbf{x}, t + k) + K \Delta u(\mathbf{x}, t)$$
$$+ \mathbf{v} \cdot \nabla u(\mathbf{x}, t + k) + \mathbf{v} \cdot \nabla u(\mathbf{x}, t)] \qquad (16.14)$$

Define the following terms (n = 3):

$$u^n = u(\mathbf{x}, t_n), \qquad t_{n+1} = t_n + k$$

$$\alpha = -\frac{Kk}{2}, \qquad \beta = {}^t[\beta_x, \beta_y, \beta_z] = -\frac{k}{2}\mathbf{v} \qquad (16.15)$$

$$\eta = \frac{Kk}{2}, \qquad \xi = {}^t[\xi_x, \xi_y, \xi_z] = \frac{k}{2}\mathbf{v}$$

and the operators

$$H_+ \equiv 1 + \alpha \Delta + \beta \cdot \nabla$$
$$H_- \equiv 1 + \eta \Delta + \xi \cdot \nabla \qquad (16.16)$$

Then we can pose equation (16.14) in the following equivalent form:

$$H_+ u^{n+1} = H_- u^n \quad \text{(Semi-discrete scheme)} \qquad (16.17)$$

and we can solve this using the same strategy that we used for the heat equation in section 16.2 except that we use multidimensional radial basis functions. The problem (16.11)–(16.13) has been solved in Boztosun and Chirafi (2002) using the meshless method. Some general conclusions are:

- When compared with the standard FDM scheme, both FDM and RBF solutions are in good agreement with the exact solution for diffusion-dominated problems. However, for convection-dominated problems the FDM displayed oscillations and signs of numerical diffusion. Thus, sharp gradients within the solution are smeared, resulting in inaccuracies. The RBF solution, on the other hand, gives good results even in the convection-dominated case.
- On performance, BBF is slower than FDM because it generates a dense matrix whereas FDM generates a tridiagonal matrix.
- When comparing the methods for a given accuracy, the RBF is much better than FDM. A typical example is as follows (Boztosun and Chirafi, 2002); let's say we wish to have an accuracy of 0.006. Then the following results are valid; for RBF we have CPU time of 1.6 seconds and we need 100 collocation nodes, while with FDM we have CPU time of 60.8 seconds with 500 nodes approximately.

The meshless method uses random points as collocation nodes. Meshless works where the traditional FDM fails. We note finally that is it possible to discretise a convection–diffusion equation in space first by using RBFs. This will give us a system of ODEs that we can subsequently solve in the usual way. For an example, see Cao and Traw-Cong (2003).

16.5 APPLICATIONS OF THE ONE-FACTOR BLACK–SCHOLES EQUATION

We now discuss the application of the meshless method to approximate the solution of the one-factor Black–Scholes equation (Koc *et al.*, 2003). We shall examine the one-factor Black–Scholes equation

$$-\frac{\partial V}{\partial t} + \tfrac{1}{2}\sigma^2 S^2 \frac{\partial^2 V}{\partial S^2} + rS\frac{\partial V}{\partial S} - rV = 0 \tag{16.18}$$

with terminal condition

$$V(S, T) = \begin{cases} \max(K - S, 0) & \text{for a put} \\ \max(S - K, 0) & \text{for a call} \end{cases}$$

and we approximate the solution $V(S, t)$ of system (16.18) by a linear combination of radial basis functions

$$V(S, t) \cong \sum_{j=1}^{J} \lambda_j(t)\varphi(S, S_j), \quad S \in \Omega \subset \mathbb{R}^1 \tag{16.19}$$

where J is the number of data points, λ is the time-dependent unknown quantity and φ is the radial basis function. We first discretise (16.18) using Crank–Nicolson averaging to give the ODE:

$$-\frac{V^{n+1}(S) - V^n(S)}{k} + \tfrac{1}{2}\sigma^2 S^2 \frac{\mathrm{d}^2 V^{n+1/2}}{\mathrm{d}S^2} + rS\frac{\mathrm{d}V^{n+1/2}}{\mathrm{d}S} - rV^{n+1/2} = 0 \tag{16.20}$$

where $V^{n+1/2} \equiv \tfrac{1}{2}(V^{n+1} + V^n)$ or, in the equivalent form,

$$H_+ V^{n+1}(S) = H_- V^n(S) \tag{16.21}$$

where

$$H_- = 1 + \alpha\left(\tfrac{1}{2}\sigma^2 S^2 \frac{\mathrm{d}^2}{\mathrm{d}s^2} + rS\frac{\mathrm{d}}{\mathrm{d}s} - r\right)$$

$$H_+ = 1 - \alpha\left(\tfrac{1}{2}\sigma^2 S^2 \frac{\mathrm{d}^2}{\mathrm{d}S^2} + rS\frac{\mathrm{d}}{\mathrm{d}S} - r\right)$$

and

$$\alpha = k/2$$

We can then calculate the discrete option price at each time level as follows:

$$\sum_{j=1}^{J} \lambda_j^{n+1} H_+ \varphi(S_{ij}) = \sum_{j=1}^{J} \lambda_j^n H_- \varphi(S_{ij}) \tag{16.22}$$

The authors in Koc *et al.* (2003) used the following test data for a standard European option:

$$K = 10, \quad r = 0.05, \quad \sigma = 0.20, \quad T = 0.5, \quad \text{Spatial domain is } [0, 30]$$

The number of time steps N is 100. The authors compared the option price and its delta using TPS, MQ, Cubic and Gaussian. In general, the MQ and TPS radial functions were the most accurate. For example, if the number of collocation nodes is $J = 121$, then the accuracy was

TPS	0.00013971
MQ	0.00013637

CUBIC	0.06190414
GAUSSIAN	0.00464602

The approximations to the delta were:

TPS	0.00008954
MQ	0.00017647
CUBIC	0.63676377
GAUSSIAN	0.00379306

The relative error in these experiments was defined as

$$\epsilon(t) \equiv \frac{1}{J-1}\sum_{j=1}^{J}|V(S_j,t)_{\text{RBF}} - V(S_j,t)| \qquad (16.23)$$

Concluding, the meshless method gives accurate results for the TPS and MQ RBFs when compared to the FDM. Finally, expressions for some option sensitivities are given as follows by differentiation of expression (16.19):

$$\frac{\partial V}{\partial S} = \sum_{j=1}^{J}\lambda_j(t)\frac{d\varphi}{dS}(S,S_j) \quad \text{(Delta)} \qquad (16.24a)$$

$$\frac{\partial^2 V}{\partial S^2} = \sum_{j=1}^{J}\lambda_j(t)\frac{d^2\varphi}{dS^2}(S,S_j) \quad \text{(Gamma)} \qquad (16.24b)$$

$$\frac{\partial V}{\partial t} = \sum_{j=1}^{J}\frac{d\lambda_j(t)}{dt}\varphi(S,S_j) \quad \text{(Theta)} \qquad (16.24c)$$

16.6 ADVANTAGES AND DISADVANTAGES OF MESHLESS

We conclude this chapter with a short summary of the advantages and disadvantages of the meshless method. The advantages are:

- Simple and straightforward; easy to implement.
- It is 'dimension-blind'; for example, a three-dimensional problem is not much more difficult than a one-dimensional problem.
- It can achieve the same accuracy as FDM but with less effort.

The perceived disadvantages at the moment of writing are:

- Error analysis is often difficult or impractical; in this sense the full mathematical basis of the meshless method has yet to be established. This is a new area of research.

- The resulting matrix system based on collocation points can be ill-conditioned and hence may be difficult to invert. We must then use regularisation techniques (see Golub and Van Loan, 1996).
- We do not yet have a body of work on how accurate the meshless method is for the Black–Scholes equation and its generalisations.

16.7 SUMMARY AND CONCLUSIONS

We have given an introduction to a new technique to approximate the solution of convection–diffusion problems in general and Black–Scholes equation in particular. It is called meshless (or meshfree) and could become a major competitor to such accepted methods as FDM and FEM. It is easy to understand and to implement, gives accurate results for the option price and its sensitivities and is 'dimension-blind', meaning that it scales easily to multi-factor derivatives problem. The meshless method has been applied to 2- and 3-factor asset problems and the convergence is somewhat better than that achieved using the splitting method. Finally, for a given tolerance, performance of meshless also seems to be better in general.

17
Extending the Black–Scholes Model:
Jump Processes

17.1 INTRODUCTION AND OBJECTIVES

The Black–Scholes model assumes that the probability distribution of the stock price at any given future time is lognormal. If this assumption is not true we shall get biases in the prices produced by the model. If the true distribution is different from the lognormal distribution we shall underprice or overprice call and put options, depending on the distributions' tails (Hull, 2000). A number of models have been proposed to resolve these shortcomings:

• Model the volatility as a stochastic process (for example, the Heston model).
• Models where the company's equity is assumed to be an option on its asset.
• Models where the stock price may experience occasional jumps rather than continuous changes, as happened on 19 and 20 October 1987, for example (Bates, 1991).

In this chapter we concentrate on the third of these models and introduce a partial integro-differential equation (PIDE) that models contingent claims for stocks with jumps. Examining these equations from a theoretical and numerical point of view will necessitate the introduction of new techniques.

In this chapter we shall discuss the following topics:

• Stochastic models for a number of processes that model stock behaviour with jumps.
• Setting up PIDEs that model contingent claims on stock.
• A discussion and comparison of several techniques that approximate PIDEs.

Informally, we can describe a PIDE as:

$$\text{PIDE} = \text{PDE} + \text{an integral term}$$

The PDE term is usually a convection–diffusion equation while the integral term involves the (unknown) option price evaluated over an infinite or semi-infinite interval.

In Appendix 1 we give some background information on integrals and integral equations.

17.2 JUMP–DIFFUSION PROCESSES

There is evidence to suggest that the geometric Brownian motion model for stock price behaviour does not always model real stock behaviour. In particular, financial instruments do not follow a lognormal random walk (see, for example, Bates, 1991; Wilmott, 1998). Jumps can appear at random times and to this end a number of alternative models have been proposed, for example, the jump diffusion (Poisson) model (see Merton, 1976).

The Poisson process is a special case of a so-called counting process. In general, a random process $X(t)$ is said to be a counting process if $X(t)$ represents the total number of events that have occurred in the time interval $(0, t)$. A counting process must satisfy the following conditions:

1. $X(t) \geq 0$, $X(0) = 0$
2. $X(t)$ is integer-valued
3. $X(s) < X(t)$ if $s < t$
4. $X(t) - X(s)$ equals the number of events that have occurred in the interval (s, t)

A Poisson process $X(t)$ is a counting process with rate or intensity $\lambda > 0$ if

1. $X(0) = 0$
2. $X(t)$ has independent and stationary increments
3. $P[X(t + dt) - X(t) = 1] = \lambda\, dt + O(dt)$, P = probability
4. $P[X(t + dt) - X(t) \geq 2] = O(dt)$ when $O(dt)$ is a function that tends to zero faster than dt, that is:

$$\lim_{dt \to 0} \frac{O(dt)}{dt} = 0$$

(Hsu, 1997). In the current context we prefer to define a Poisson process dq as follows:

$$dq = \begin{cases} 0, & \text{with probability } 1 - \lambda\, dt \\ 1, & \text{with probability } \lambda\, dt \end{cases} \tag{17.1}$$

where λ = Poisson arrival intensity.

Thus, there is a probability $\lambda\, dt$ of a jump in q in the time step dt. The Poisson process models many kinds of arrival patterns and its applications are numerous, for example in queuing systems, inventory control applications and telecommunications. It also models the behaviour of underlying assets in real options modelling, for example:

- Energy prices (Pilipović, 1998)
- Oil and natural gas prices
- Business models (Mun, 2002).

These quantities can exhibit peaks and spikes; for example, in one case the unit price of natural gas jumped from 30 euros to more than 1500 euros in one day during a period of short supply. Fortunately, the price dropped again shortly afterwards. With shares, however, the price plummeted, as was witnessed in October 1987.

We now introduce the modified stochastic differential equation that models jumps:

$$\frac{dS}{S} = \mu\, dt + \sigma\, dz + (\eta - 1)\, dq \tag{17.2}$$

where S = underlying stock price
μ = drift rate
σ = volatility
dz = increment of Gauss–Wiener process
dq = Poisson process with arrival rate λ
$\eta - 1$ = impulse function producing a jump from S to $S\eta$
$K = E(\eta - 1)$, expected relative jump size.

In other words, the arrival of a jump is random and this is part of the stochastic differential equation for S. We thus have two sources of uncertainty. In short, the term dz corresponds to the usual Brownian motion while the term dq corresponds to exceptional (and infrequent) events. Two special cases of (17.2) are geometric Brownian motion and pure jump diffusion, the latter being defined by the equation

$$\frac{dS}{S} = (\eta - 1)\,dq$$

In the case of equation (17.2) the path followed by S is continuous most of the time while finite negative or positive jumps will appear at discrete points in time. Based on the SDE (17.2) the resulting PIDE for a contingent claim $V(S, t)$ that depends on S is given by (Merton, 1976):

$$\frac{\partial V}{\partial \tau} = \tfrac{1}{2}\sigma^2 S^2 \frac{\partial^2 V}{\partial S^2} + (r - \lambda K)S\frac{\partial V}{\partial S} - rV + \left[\lambda \int_0^\infty V(S\eta)g(\eta)\,d\eta - \lambda V\right] \quad (17.3)$$

where $\tau = T - t =$ time to expiry

   $\eta =$ jump amplitude and the function g satisfies

   $g(\eta) \geq 0$ and $\int_0^\infty g(\eta)\,d\eta = 1$

We rewrite equation (17.3) in the form:

$$\frac{\partial V}{\partial \tau} = \tfrac{1}{2}\sigma^2 S^2 \frac{\partial^2 V}{\partial S^2} + (r - \lambda K)S\frac{\partial V}{\partial S} - (r + \lambda)V + \lambda \int_0^\infty V(S\eta)g(\eta)\,d\eta \quad (17.4)$$

We now must think about this problem in more detail. In particular, we are interested in approximating the solution of this problem using finite difference schemes. Some questions and problems arise:

- The integral term in the PIDE is on a semi-infinite interval; how are we to put a semi-infinite interval into the computer? How are we going to approximate the integral term? In some cases the integrand may contain singularities.
- The PDE part of the PIDE is also defined on a semi-infinite interval. It too must be truncated, but how? Furthermore, we are now confronted by two truncated intervals and how should they be chosen so as they do not destroy accuracy?
- Can we apply standard finite difference schemes (Euler, Crank–Nicolson, fitting) in combination with numerical integration techniques to produce stable and accurate approximations?
- How can we avoid producing a dense system of equations when we approximate the integral term on a bounded interval?
- How do we compare one method with another one? For example, is Crank–Nicolson really better than implicit Euler even though the former method may produce spurious oscillations?

17.2.1   Convolution transformations

We rewrite the integral term in equation (17.4) so that it is formulated in convolution (or Faltung) form (Tricomi, 1957; Zemanian, 1987). To this end, we define a change of variables of (S, η) to (x, y) as follows:

$$y = \log \eta, \qquad x = \log S$$

Then

$$F(S) \equiv \int_0^\infty V(S\eta)g(\eta)\,d\eta$$

$$= \int_{-\infty}^\infty \overline{V}(x+y)\overline{f}(y)\,dy$$

where

$$\overline{V}(y) \equiv V(e^y), \qquad \overline{f}(y) = g(e^y)e^y$$

We can perform another change of variables from y to t to describe the integral in a form that is common in the mathematical literature:

$$t = -y, \qquad f(t) = \overline{f}(-t)$$

This gives the new form:

$$F(x) = \int_{-\infty}^\infty \overline{V}(x-t)f(t)\,dt$$

In more general terms we can write the transform in the following form:

$$F(x) = \int_{-\infty}^\infty G(x-t)f(t)\,dt$$

This latter equation is in fact an example of a convolution transform. This expression is a mapping that transforms $f(t)$ into $F(x)$ with kernel $G(x-t)$. A detailed study of these transforms is given in Zemanian (1987). In particular, a function-theoretic approach determines the conditions under which $F(x)$ is a smooth function, given certain assumptions on the kernel G. This is important in relation to the PIDE (17.4) where we are also interested in the regularity (smoothness) of the solution. Extensive use is made of delta functions and distribution theory in Zemanian (1987). It is interesting to note that the one-sided Laplace transform (often used in financial engineering applications – see, for example, Fu *et al.*, 1998; Craddock *et al.*, 2000; Fusai, 2004) can be viewed as a special kind of convolution integral.

17.3   PARTIAL INTEGRO-DIFFERENTIAL EQUATIONS AND FINANCIAL APPLICATIONS

There are two main formulations for the PIDE, depending on how we wish to describe the integral term. In order to reduce the cognitive overload we define the elliptic operator (written in a slightly more generic form) as:

$$Lu \equiv \tilde{\sigma}\frac{\partial^2 u}{\partial x^2} + \mu\frac{\partial u}{\partial x} - (r+\lambda)u \tag{17.5}$$

Then the PIDE (17.4) can be written in the new form:

$$\frac{\partial u}{\partial t} = Lu + \lambda\int_0^\infty u(xy,t)g(y)\,dy \tag{17.6}$$

or as

$$\frac{\partial u}{\partial t} = Lu + \lambda\int_{-\infty}^\infty u(x+y,t)g(y)\,dy \tag{17.7}$$

depending on how you transform the original PIDE.

It does not really matter which form you take, but we should be aware of these two options when we consider the numerical methods for these equations. Since we are using the 'engineer's' time we need to augment the PIDE by an initial condition:

$$u(x, 0) = \psi(x), \quad -\infty < x < \infty \quad \text{or} \quad 0 < x < \infty \tag{17.8}$$

The corresponding boundary conditions are always an issue in these kinds of problems and we use the following one corresponding to equation (17.6), for example:

$$\frac{\partial u}{\partial t} - ru = 0 \quad \text{as } x \to 0$$

$$\frac{\partial^2 u}{\partial x^2} = 0 \quad \text{as } x \to \infty \tag{17.9}$$

We shall have similar boundary conditions in the infinite interval case.

17.4 NUMERICAL SOLUTION OF PIDE: PRELIMINARIES

We now begin our study of the finite difference schemes for approximating the solution of the problem (17.7), (17.8) and (17.9). The situation is complicated by the fact that the unknown solution appears in the differential equation and in the integral term. In general, we then must construct two meshes, namely one for the PDE and one for the integral term. These meshes do not necessarily have to coincide but things become messy in this case because we have to use some kind of interpolation when we construct the discrete systems of equations. It is easier to use the same mesh for both the differential and integral terms.

Another potential problem is that the discrete system of equations can result in a dense matrix. In the pure PDE we get a band matrix of some kind (for example, a tridiagonal system) but again the integral term confuses things. We shall see how to avoid this problem.

Finally, the PDE is defined on an semi-infinite interval and we must truncate this to a finite interval. However, the integral term in equation (17.7) is also defined on an infinite interval and this must always be truncated. This issue is discussed in La Chioma (2003) and we give the main results here. In general, the procedure is to choose two finite values A and B such that the difference between the infinite and truncated integrals is less than a given tolerance:

$$\left| \int_{-\infty}^{\infty} f(x)\,dx - \int_{A}^{B} f(x)\,dx \right| < \epsilon$$

Then we can approximate the truncated integral by some kind of Newton–Cotes integration method:

$$\int_{A}^{B} f(x)\,dx \approx \frac{B - A}{N} \sum_{j=0}^{N} w_j f(x_j)$$

where $\{w_j\}$ is some set of weights.

In the current problem we have a specific integrand (kernel), namely a probability density function of the form

$$g(y) \equiv \Gamma_\delta(y) = \frac{1}{\sqrt{2\pi}\,\delta} \exp\left(-\frac{y^2}{2\delta^2}\right)$$

This function goes to zero very quickly and we only look at this when it values are greater than a given tolerance ϵ. Then we have the inequalities:

$$\Gamma_\delta(y) \geq \epsilon$$

$$\Leftrightarrow -\sqrt{-2\,\delta^2 \log(\epsilon\delta\sqrt{2\pi})} \leq y \leq \sqrt{-2\,\delta^2 \log(\epsilon\,\delta\sqrt{2\pi})}$$

In the above context we then choose the limits of integration as:

$$A = +\sqrt{-2\,\delta^2 \log(\epsilon\delta\sqrt{2\pi})}$$
$$B = -A$$

We now propose the modified form of equation (17.7)

$$\frac{\partial u}{\partial t} = Lu + \lambda \int_A^B u(x+y,t)\Gamma_\delta(y)\,dy \tag{17.10}$$

We now have a PIDE whose integrand is defined on a bounded interval.

17.5   TECHNIQUES FOR THE NUMERICAL SOLUTION OF PIDEs

In recent years there has been a lot of interest in PIDEs for financial derivatives problems. In Tavella (2000) a discussion is given on how to approximate such problems using finite difference methods.

We discuss some methods in this section. We first introduce some notation in order to promote the understandability of the PIDE (17.10):

$$L^{h,k} = \text{fully discrete approximate to } L \text{ (PDE term)}$$

$$I^h = \text{discrete approximation to the integral term } I(u) \text{ (integral term)}$$

In the time dimension, we apply exclusively one-step methods and we can then choose between fully explicit, fully implicit and Crank–Nicolson variants.

In the following discussion we suppress the dependence of the discrete solution on the index corresponding to the S direction. This makes the schemes more readable.

17.6   IMPLICIT AND EXPLICIT METHODS

A simple approach is to apply the so-called θ-method to both the PDE and integral terms:

$$\frac{U^{n+1} - U^n}{k} = \theta_1 L^{h,k}(U^n) + (1-\theta_1)L^{h,k}(U^{n+1})$$

$$+ \theta_2 I^h(U^n) + (1-\theta_2)I^h(U^{n+1}), \quad 0 \leq \theta_j \leq 1, \quad j = 1, 2 \tag{17.11}$$

This system of equations leads to a dense matrix system in general because the integral terms also contain the unknown solution at time level $n+1$ and the specific numerical integration technique uses its values at a finite (and possibly large) number of points in the integration domain. This can be remedied by approximating the integral term only at the known time level n. For example, using Crank–Nicolson for the PDE term and integral evaluation at level n leads to the equation:

$$\frac{U^{n+1} - U^n}{k} = \tfrac{1}{2}\left[L^{h,k}(U^n) + L^{h,k}(U^{n+1})\right] + I^h(U^n) \tag{17.12}$$

This is an interesting scheme because it is a tridiagonal matrix system and it has been proved that this scheme is stable (see Cont and Voltchkova, 2003) when the integral is evaluated using the trapezoidal rule. The authors prove stability and accuracy of the scheme (17.12) using the so-called viscosity method. This is needed because the Lax Equivalence Principle is no longer valid due to the fact that solutions of the PIDE may be non-smooth and higher-order derivatives may not exist. There exist more modern techniques and these should be applied whenever possible as Cont and Voltchkova (2003) and other articles have shown.

17.7   IMPLICIT–EXPLICIT RUNGE–KUTTA METHODS

It is obvious that the coupling between the differential and integral terms in equation (17.10) complicates the discovery of suitable numerical schemes and their subsequent analysis. It would be nice if we could split the problem in some way to enable us to solve several simpler sub-problems. To this end, we introduce a method that splits the PIDE in such a way that one part is implicit in time and the other part is explicit in time. The method is called the implicit–explicit (IMEX) and the rationale behind it is to split a scheme into its stiff and non-stiff parts (see Hundsdorfer, 2003 for a good introduction to IMEX methods). In the current case we define the following 'components' of the PIDE.

$$\frac{\partial u}{\partial t} = \sigma \frac{\partial^2 u}{\partial x^2} + \mu \frac{\partial u}{\partial x} + bu + \lambda \left[\int_{-\infty}^{\infty} u(x+y,t)\Gamma_\sigma(y)\,dy - u(x,t) \right] \qquad (17.13)$$

where

$$\frac{\partial u}{\partial t} = H(u) + G(u)$$

$$H(u) = \text{convection (advection) integral term}$$

$$= \mu \frac{\partial u}{\partial x} + \lambda \left[\int_{-\infty}^{\infty} u(x+y,t)\Gamma_\sigma(y)\,dy - u(x,t) \right]$$

$$G(u) = \text{diffusion/reaction term} = \sigma \frac{\partial^2 u}{\partial x^2} + bu$$

In this case we use explicit time-stepping for the convection (advection) term $H(u)$ and implicit time-stepping for the diffusion term $G(u)$. Then one particular IMEX scheme for this problem becomes

$$\frac{U^{n+1} - U^n}{k} = H(U^n) + \theta\, G(U^n) + (1-\theta)G(U^{n+1}), \ \theta \geq \tfrac{1}{2} \qquad (17.14)$$

Here we see that the Euler method is combined with an A-stable θ method (Hunsdorfer and Verwer, 2003). A generalisation of this method is given in Briani *et at.* (2004) where the authors propose a multi-step extension of equation (17.14). Thus, we can now solve (17.14) with the techniques that we developed for PDEs.

17.8   USING OPERATOR SPLITTING

Operator splitting methods are a powerful technique for partitioning a problem into simpler problems. In general, an n-dimensional problem is split into a series of one-dimensional problems using this method. In the current context, operator splitting has been applied to integro-differential equations for the neutron transport problem (see Yanenko, 1971, p. 99). We already know that the PIDE (17.10) has a differential and an integral form:

$$\frac{\partial u}{\partial t} = Lu + Iu \tag{17.15}$$

Based on this remark we split the problem into two sub-problems, which we write as (in an intuitive/semi-formal form):

$$\frac{\partial u}{\partial t} = Iu \quad \text{and} \quad \frac{\partial u}{\partial t} = Lu \tag{17.16}$$

Based on Yanenko (1971) we propose the following splitting scheme:

$$
\left.
\begin{aligned}
&\text{(a)} \quad \frac{U^{n+\frac{1}{2}} - U^n}{k} = I^h(\alpha\, U^{n+\frac{1}{2}} + \beta U^n) \\[2ex]
&\text{(b)} \quad \frac{U^{n+1} - U^{n+\frac{1}{2}}}{k} = L^{h,k}(\alpha\, U^{n+1} + \beta U^{n+\frac{1}{2}})
\end{aligned}
\right\}
\quad \alpha \geq 0, \quad \beta \geq 0, \quad \alpha + \beta = 1 \quad (17.17)
$$

We can choose different sets of values of α and β to give us implicit or explicit schemes in both (17.17a) and (17.17b). For example, we could take an explicit scheme for (17.17a) and the exponentially fitted implicit-in-time scheme for (17.17b):

$$
\left.
\begin{aligned}
&\text{(a)} \quad \frac{U^{n+\frac{1}{2}} - U^n}{k} = I^h(U^n) \\[2ex]
&\text{(b)} \quad \frac{U^{n+1} - U^{n+\frac{1}{2}}}{k} = L_E^{h,k}(U^{n+1})
\end{aligned}
\right\}
\quad L_E^{h,k} \equiv \text{(Duffy) exponential fitting operator} \quad (17.18)
$$

These schemes have first-order accuracy in general.

17.9 SPLITTING AND PREDICTOR–CORRECTOR METHODS

We now discuss the following problem: Can we devise a scheme that has the computational ease of the explicit Euler scheme while at the same time achieving high-order accuracy? We answer this question by appealing to the predictor–corrector method that is used in the approximation of the solutions of initial value problems (see Conte and de Boor, 1980, p. 379) and that we have applied it with success to financial engineering applications, in particular the numerical solution of stochastic differential equations (Duffy, 2004). Let us recall how predictor–corrector works for the initial value problem:

$$\frac{du}{dt} = f(t, u), \quad 0 < t < T$$

$$u(0) = A \tag{17.19}$$

$$u(t) = {}^t(u_1(t), \ldots, u_n(t))$$

If we apply the standard trapezoidal rule to (17.19) we get the scheme:

$$\frac{u_{n+1} - u_n}{k} = \frac{1}{2}[f(t_n, u_n) + f(t_{n+1}, u_{n+1})] \tag{17.20}$$

One problem with this scheme is that it is nonlinear since the function $f(t, u)$ is in general a nonlinear function of u. Hence the system (17.20) cannot be solved without resorting to some nonlinear solver such as Newton–Raphson, for example. In order to resolve this problem we define predictor and corrector solutions as follows:

$$u_{n+1}^{(0)} = u_n + kf(t_n, u_n) \quad \text{(Explicit Euler)}$$

$$u_{n+1}^{(1)} = u_n + \frac{k}{2}[f(t_n, u_n) + f(t_{n+1}, u_{n+1}^{(0)})] \quad \text{(Modified Trapezoidal rule)}$$

(17.21)

This is the essence of predictor–corrector method. In general, we define the iterative scheme:

$$u_{n+1}^{(j)} = u_n + \frac{k}{2}[f(t_n, u_n) + f(t_{n+1}, u_{n+1}^{(j-1)})], \quad j = 1, 2, \ldots$$

(17.22)

and the stopping criterion for a given tolerance TOL is given by

$$\frac{\|u_{n+1}^{(j)} - u_{n+1}^{(j-1)}\|}{\|u_{n+1}^{(j)}\|} \le \text{TOL}$$

(17.23)

in some suitable norm (for example, the max norm).

We now apply the predictor–corrector method to generalise the scheme (17.18a). We define

$$U_{n+1}^{(0)} = U_n + kI^h(U_n)$$

(17.24)

and

$$U_{n+1}^{(1)} = U_n + \frac{k}{2}[I^h(U_n) + I^h(U_{n+1}^{(0)})]$$

More generally, we have

$$U_{n+1}^{(j)} = U_n + \frac{k}{2}[I^h(U_n) + I^h(U_{n+1}^{(j-1)})], \quad j = 1, 2, \ldots$$

with the same stopping criteria as in inequality (17.23). Summarising, we have produced a scheme that allows us to get as good an approximation as we like to the integral term (17.18a) while we can continue using our favourite finite difference scheme for the PDE term (17.18b).

17.10 SUMMARY AND CONCLUSIONS

We have introduced a number of finite difference schemes for European-style options with a jump-diffusion term. This is a relatively new area of research in financial engineering and a number of numerical techniques have been proposed to approximate the solution of the partial integro-differential equation (PIDE) that models contingent claims depending on an underlying asset with jumps. For more background information, see Appendix 1 for an introduction to integral equations and their numerical approximation. Some conclusions on the advantages and disadvantages of the finite difference methods are:

- *Explicit and implicit:* Easy to implement as it builds on well-known schemes. Conditionally stable. First-order accurate.
- *IMEX:* Robust, modern schemes. Ability to handle stiff problems. Second and higher order accuracy. This is a specialised area of research.
- *Operator splitting:* Reliable and robust. Watch out for the errors induced by splitting. You may not always get second-order accuracy.
- *Predictor–Corrector:* A good performer, as has been proved in many applications.

Part IV

FDM for Multidimensional Problems

18
Finite Difference Schemes
for Multidimensional Problems

18.1 INTRODUCTION AND OBJECTIVES

This is the first chapter of Part IV. It is here that we introduce finite difference schemes in two space variables (two-factor problems). The resulting system of equations can become quite large and special matrix solvers must be devised to solve the resulting linear system of equations. The complexity is due to the fact that we are discretising in all directions simultaneously. We can avoid solving a large system at each time level if we use an explicit time-marching scheme but then the scheme will only be conditionally stable and this may constrain the time mesh size k to be small.

The main goal of this chapter is to introduce finite difference schemes for a number of prototypical partial differential equations. We discuss the relevance of the schemes to the Black–Scholes equation; however, the main applications to financial engineering will appear in Part V of this book.

After having read and studied this chapter you should have a good understanding of finite difference schemes for two-factor partial differential equations. This chapter can be seen as a warming-up session to n-factor PDEs in quantitative finance.

18.2 ELLIPTIC EQUATIONS

The Black–Scholes equation (in n dimensions) is a parabolic partial differential equation of the form

$$\frac{\partial u}{\partial t} = Lu \tag{18.1}$$

where the operator L is defined by

$$Lu \equiv \sum_{i,j=1}^{n} a_{ij}(x)\frac{\partial^2 u}{\partial x_i \partial x_j} + \sum_{i=1}^{n} b_i(x)\frac{\partial u}{\partial x_i} + c(x)u \tag{18.2}$$

$$x = {}^t(x_1, \ldots, x_n) \in \mathbb{R}^n$$

For the moment we assume that the coefficients in (18.2) are independent of t. We shall see later how to approximate equation (18.2) by finite difference schemes. To this end, we shall solve a system of equations at each time level and the solvers that are used are based on results from elliptic equations (see the classic work Varga, 1962, and a more recent work Thomas, 1999). For a modern and definitive treatment of matrix computational problems, see Golub and Van Loan (1996).

Definition 18.1. The operator L is elliptic if for each point x in n-dimensional space the following inequality holds:

$$0 < \lambda(x) \, \|\xi\|^2 \le \sum_{i,j=1}^{n} a_{ij}(x) \, \xi_i \, \xi_j \le \Lambda(x) \, \|\xi\|^2 \tag{18.3}$$

where

$$\xi = {}^t(\xi_1, \ldots, \xi_n)$$
$$\lambda(x) = \text{ smallest eigenvalue of matrix } (a_{ij}) \quad i, j = 1, \ldots, n$$
$$\Lambda(x) = \text{ largest eigenvalue of matrix } (a_{ij}) \quad i, j = 1, \ldots, n \tag{18.4}$$
$$\|\xi\|^2 \equiv \sum_{i=1}^{n} |\xi_i|^2$$

We now give some examples of elliptic operators in two space dimensions. First, we define the Laplace differential operator by:

$$\Delta u \equiv \nabla^2 u \equiv \frac{\partial^2 u}{\partial x^2} + \frac{\partial^2 u}{\partial y^2} \tag{18.5}$$

This leads to two well-known equations

$$\Delta u = f \text{ (Poisson equation)}$$
$$\Delta u = 0 \text{ (Laplace equation)} \tag{18.6}$$

We notice that the so-called cross-term (the second derivative term with one contribution by each of x and y) is not present in the Laplacian operator. In financial engineering applications, however, this term is present and it represents the correlation between the underlying assets.

We take an example of a two-factor interest rate model (Wilmott, 1998, ch. 37):

$$-\frac{\partial Z}{\partial t} + \tfrac{1}{2}w^2 \frac{\partial^2 Z}{\partial r^2} + \rho wq \frac{\partial^2 Z}{\partial r \partial l} + \tfrac{1}{2}q^2 \frac{\partial^2 Z}{\partial l^2} + (u - \lambda_r w)\frac{\partial Z}{\partial r} + (p - \lambda_l q)\frac{\partial Z}{\partial l} - rZ = 0 \tag{18.7}$$

where $r = $ spot interest rate
$l = $ another independent variable, for example the long rate
$\rho = $ correlation between dW_1 and dW_2 (appearing in SDEs)
$Z = $ price of a zero coupon bond
$\lambda_r, \ \lambda_l = $ market prices of risk for factors r and l

and the stochastic processes r and l are defined by the pair of SDEs:

$$dr = u \, dt + w \, dW_1$$
$$dl = p \, dt + q \, dW_2 \tag{18.8}$$
$$dW_j = \text{ standard geometric Brownian motion}, \quad j = 1, 2$$

The question is whether the time-independent part of equation (18.7) is elliptic. In this case the relevant coefficients in inequality (18.3) have the specific values:

$$a_{11} = \tfrac{1}{2}w^2$$
$$a_{12} = \tfrac{1}{2}\rho wq$$
$$a_{21} = \tfrac{1}{2}\rho wq \quad (= a_{12})$$
$$a_{22} = \tfrac{1}{2}q^2$$

(18.9)

and

$$A = (a_{ij})_{1 \le i,j \le 2} = \tfrac{1}{2}\begin{pmatrix} \omega^2 & \rho wq \\ \rho wq & q^2 \end{pmatrix}$$

(18.10)

A bit of 'nitty-gritty' arithmetic shows that the eigenvalues of A are given by:

$$\lambda_{\pm} = \frac{(\omega^2 + q^2) \pm \sqrt{(\omega^2 + q^2)^2 - 4\omega^2 q^2(1 - \rho^2)}}{2}$$

(18.11)

and are real if

$$\rho \le 1$$

(18.12)

which is the case in financial engineering; the correlation coefficient ρ is always in the range $[-1, 1]$. You can check this result by using calculus.

We now discuss how to approximate elliptic problems using finite difference techniques. In many cases in financial engineering the domain in which the equation is defined is a rectangle. To this end we partition the domain into a number of boxes of equal or unequal size. Furthermore, we approximate derivatives in the different directions by the analogues of the one-dimensional divided differences:

$$\Delta_x^2 U_{ij} = h^{-2}(U_{i+1,j} - 2U_{i,j} + U_{i-1,j})$$

and

$$\Delta_y^2 U_{ij} = h^{-2}(U_{i,j+1} - 2U_{i,j} + U_{i,j-1})$$

(18.13)

For convenience we have chosen the mesh sizes in the x and y directions to be the same (we denote this common length by h).

In order to motivate the use of finite difference schemes for elliptic boundary value problems we examine the following Poisson problem on a unit square in two dimensions with Dirichlet boundary conditions:

$$\Delta u = f \text{ in } R = (0, 1) \times (0, 1)$$
$$u = g \text{ on } \partial R$$

(18.14)

where ∂R is the boundary of R.

Then letting I and J denote the number of sub-divisions in the x and y directions, respectively we propose the following scheme:

$$\Delta_x^2 U_{ij} + \Delta_y^2 U_{ij} = f_{ij}, \quad i = 1, \ldots, I - 1, \quad j = 1, \ldots, J - 1$$

(18.15)

with discrete boundary conditions

$$
\begin{aligned}
u_{0j} &= g_{0j}, \quad j = 0, \ldots, J \\
u_{Ij} &= g_{Ij}, \quad j = 0, \ldots, J \\
u_{i0} &= g_{i0}, \quad i = 1, \ldots, I-1 \\
u_{iJ} &= g_{iJ}, \quad i = 1, \ldots, I-1
\end{aligned}
\tag{18.16}
$$

Then we pose system (18.15)–(18.16) in the following matrix form:

$$
\begin{aligned}
AU &= F \\
A &= (a_{ij})_{L \times L}, \qquad U = {}^t(u_1, \ldots, u_L) \\
F &= {}^t(f_1, \ldots, f_L), \qquad L = (I-1) \times (J-1)
\end{aligned}
\tag{18.17}
$$

The matrix A has a special structure. In particular, it is positive definite, has thus an inverse and hence the problem (18.15), (18.16) has a unique solution (see Thomas, 1999).

18.2.1   A self-adjoint elliptic operator

We now discuss a slightly more general form of equation (18.6), namely the self-adjoint semi-linear equation

$$
\frac{\partial}{\partial x}\left[\sigma_1(x, y)\frac{\partial u}{\partial x}\right] + \frac{\partial}{\partial y}\left[\sigma_2(x, y)\frac{\partial u}{\partial y}\right] + f(x, y, u) = 0, \quad 0 < x < L, \quad 0 < y < M
\tag{18.18}
$$

with Neumann boundary conditions

$$
\begin{aligned}
\frac{\partial u}{\partial x} &= 0, \quad x = 0, \quad x = L \\
\frac{\partial u}{\partial y} &= 0, \quad y = 0, \quad y = M
\end{aligned}
\tag{18.19}
$$

This problem occurs in many physical applications (see Peaceman, 1977). We now define non-uniform meshes in the x and y directions and to this end we adopt the following notation:

$$
\begin{aligned}
x_{i\pm\frac{1}{2}} &= \tfrac{1}{2}(x_i + x_{i\pm1}) \\
y_{j\pm\frac{1}{2}} &= \tfrac{1}{2}(y_j + y_{j\pm1}) \\
\Delta x_i &\equiv x_{i+\frac{1}{2}} - x_{i-\frac{1}{2}} \\
\Delta y_j &\equiv y_{j+\frac{1}{2}} - y_{j-\frac{1}{2}} \\
a_{i+\frac{1}{2},j} &\equiv \frac{\sigma_1(x_{i+\frac{1}{2}}, y_j)\Delta y_j}{x_{i+1} - x_i} \\
b_{i,j+\frac{1}{2}} &\equiv \frac{\sigma_2(x_i, y_{j+\frac{1}{2}})\Delta x_i}{y_{j+1} - y_j} \\
a_{i-\frac{1}{2},j} &= \frac{\sigma_1(x_{i-\frac{1}{2}}, y_j)\Delta y_j}{x_i - x_{i-1}} \\
b_{i,j-\frac{1}{2}} &= \frac{\sigma_2(x_i, y_{j-\frac{1}{2}})\Delta x_i}{y_j - y_{j-1}}
\end{aligned}
\tag{18.20}
$$

We approximate the separate terms in equation (18.18) as follows:

$$\frac{\partial}{\partial x}\left[\sigma_1(x_i, y_j)\frac{\partial u}{\partial x}\right]_{i,j} \approx \frac{\sigma_1(x_{i+\frac{1}{2}}, y_j)\frac{u_{i+1,j} - u_{i,j}}{x_{i+1} - x_i} - \sigma_1(x_{i-\frac{1}{2}}, y_j)\frac{u_{i,j} - u_{i-1,j}}{x_i - x_{i-1}}}{\Delta x_i} \quad (18.21)$$

in the x direction, and

$$\frac{\partial}{\partial y}\left[\sigma_2(x_i, y_j)\frac{\partial u}{\partial y}\right]_{i,j} \approx \frac{\sigma_2(x_i, y_{j+\frac{1}{2}})\frac{u_{i,j+1} - u_{i,j}}{y_{j+1} - y_j} - \sigma_2(x_i, y_{j-\frac{1}{2}})\frac{u_{i,j} - u_{i-1,j}}{y_j - y_{j-1}}}{\Delta y_j} \quad (18.22)$$

in the y direction. Combining these terms and doing a bit of rearranging we can pose the problem in matrix form, as in system (18.17), that is

$$a_{i+\frac{1}{2},j}(u_{i+1,j} - u_{i,j}) - a_{i-\frac{1}{2},j}(u_{i,j} - u_{i-1,j}) + b_{i,j+\frac{1}{2}}(u_{i,j+1} - u_{i,j})$$
$$- b_{i,j-\frac{1}{2}}(u_{i,j} - u_{i,j-1}) + \Delta x_i \Delta y_j f(x_i.y_j, u_{i,j}) = 0 \quad (18.23)$$

This leads us to the discussion on how to actually solve the system (18.17).

18.2.2   Solving the matrix systems

In general the matrix A in equation (18.17) is sparse. This means that many of the entries in the matrix are not needed and that a small percentage of the entries will be used. For this reason we need efficient storage structures for such matrices. Discussion of the actual mechanics can be found in Dahlquist (1974) and Duff *et al.* (1990). In most of our applications the matrix will be sparse but it is also broadly banded.

It is not our intention to give an exhaustive overview of the different solvers for elliptic problems of the form (18.17). A good overview can be found in Thomas (1999) and an overview of solvers with applications in financial engineering can be found in Tavella *et al.* (2000, p. 98). For more detailed information on the actual implementation of these solvers, we refer to Golub and Van Loan (1996). We shall also discuss the so-called residual correction methods that are very popular for elliptic systems (Varga, 1962; Thomas, 1999). To this end, let **U** be the solution of (18.17) and let **W** be some approximation to **U**. We define the quantities

$$\text{Algebraic error } \mathbf{e} = \mathbf{U} - \mathbf{W}$$

$$\text{Residual error } \mathbf{r} = \mathbf{F} - A\mathbf{W}$$

We use both of these errors (with respect to some norm). We see that these two errors are related by the residual equation

$$A\mathbf{e} = A(\mathbf{U} - \mathbf{W}) = \mathbf{F} - A\mathbf{W} = \mathbf{r}$$

From this last equation we obtain a correction equation defined by

$$\mathbf{U} = \mathbf{W} + \mathbf{e} = \mathbf{W} + A^{-1}\mathbf{r}$$

Continuing, we define the residual correction method to approximate the inverse of the matrix A as follows using the residual correction method:

$$\mathbf{W}_{k+1} = \mathbf{W}_k + B\mathbf{r}_k, \quad k \geq 0 \quad (18.24)$$

where $$\mathbf{r}_k = \mathbf{F} - A\mathbf{W}_k, \quad k \geq 0$$

Specific values of the matrix B lead to the following specific schemes:

Richardson:

$$B = I \text{ (identity matrix)}$$

$$\mathbf{W}_{k+1} = \mathbf{W}_k + \mathbf{r}_k, \quad k \geq 0 \text{ and } B \text{ is some aproximation to } A^{-1} \qquad (18.25)$$

We thus compute $\mathbf{r}$ and we use the correction equation to find $\mathbf{U}$. Other approaches: in this case we decompose A into

$$A = L + D + U$$

where L and U are the triangular matrices representing the elements below and above the diagonal, respectively while D is the diagonal matrix of A. Some special choices are:

Jacobi:

$$B = D^{-1}$$

Gauss–Seidel:

$$B = (L + D)^{-1}$$

Successive over-relaxation:

$$B = \omega(I + \omega D^{-1}L)D^{-1} = \omega(D + \omega L)^{-1}$$

where ω is some parameter.

The corresponding algorithms for these schemes are discussed in Thomas 1999. In general, we do not often use these methods as we prefer to use ADI and splitting methods, as we shall see in later chapters.

18.2.3   Exact solutions to elliptic problems

In general, it is not possible to find a closed solution for elliptic boundary value problems. However, we may wish to test the accuracy of a finite difference scheme and it is then useful to have some solution to benchmark against. To this end, we give a crash course in the Separation of Variables technique for two-dimensional problems (see Kreider *et al.*, 1966; Tolstov, 1962). We first examine Laplace's equation on a rectangular region with Dirichlet boundary conditions:

$$\frac{\partial^2 u}{\partial x^2} + \frac{\partial^2 u}{\partial y^2} = 0, \quad 0 < x < L, \ 0 < y < M \qquad (18.26a)$$

$$u(0, y) = u(L, y) = 0, \quad 0 < y < M \qquad (18.26b)$$

$$u(x, M) = 0, \qquad u(x, 0) = f(x), \ 0 < x < L \qquad (18.26c)$$

We then seek a solution $u(x, y)$ of the boundary value problem (18.26) by using the *ansatz* (assumption)

$$u(x, y) = XY, \qquad X = X(x), \qquad Y = Y(y)$$

Plugging this representation into equation (18.26a) we get

$$\frac{d^2 Y}{dy^2} / Y - \frac{d^2 X}{dx^2} / X = \lambda$$

$$\frac{d^2 X}{dx^2} + \lambda X = 0$$

$$\frac{d^2 Y}{dy^2} - \lambda Y = 0$$

where λ is a constant.

From equations (18.26b) and (18.26c) we see that

$$X(0) = X(L) = 0$$

$$Y(0) = Y(M) = 0$$

We then get the representation

$$X_n(x) = A_n \frac{\sin n\pi x}{L}, \quad n = 1, 2, \ldots$$

$$\lambda = \lambda_n = \left(\frac{n\pi}{L}\right)^2$$

Using this fact in the ordinary differential equation for Y gives us

$$\frac{d^2 Y}{dy^2} - \frac{n^2 \pi^2}{L^2} Y = 0$$

that has the solution (containing two constants to be determined via $Y(0) = Y(M) = 0$)

$$Y_n(y) = B_n \sinh \frac{n\pi y}{L} + C_n \cosh \frac{n\pi y}{L}$$

$$B_n = -\cosh \frac{n\pi M}{L}, \quad C_n = \sin \frac{n\pi}{L} M$$

Using the formula

$$\sinh \alpha \cosh \beta - \cosh \alpha \sinh \beta = \sinh(\alpha - \beta)$$

gives us the general expression

$$Y_n(y) = \sinh \frac{n\pi}{L}(M - y)$$

and hence

$$u(x, y) = \sum_{n=1}^{\infty} A_n \sinh \frac{n\pi x}{L} \sinh \frac{n\pi}{L}(M - y)$$

There is only one unknown term left, and using equation (18.26)(c)

$$u(x, 0) = \sum_{n=1}^{\infty} A_n \sinh \left(\frac{n\pi M}{L}\right) \sinh \frac{n\pi x}{L} = f(x)$$

$$A_n = \frac{2}{\sinh(n\pi M/L)} \int_0^L f(x) \sin \left(\frac{n\pi x}{L}\right) dx$$

Finally, the exact solution of the boundary value problem (18.26) is given by

$$u(x, y) = \frac{2}{L} \sum_{n=1}^{\infty} \frac{\int_0^L f(x) \sin(n\pi x/L)\, dx}{\sinh(n\pi M/L)} \sin\left(\frac{n\pi x}{L}\right) \sinh \frac{n\pi}{L}(M - y)$$

This solution is valid when f is sufficiently smooth. In particular, if the function f and its first derivative are piecewise continuous in the interval $[0, L]$, then the formal solution is uniformly and absolutely convergent to the exact solution in $[0, L] \times [0, M]$. The Separation of Variables technique that we discussed above can be applied to more general boundary conditions, for example Neumann, Robin and the following non-homogeneous Dirichlet boundary conditions:

$$u(0, y) = f_1(y), \qquad u(L, y) = f_2(y), \quad 0 < y < M$$

$$u(x, 0) = f_3(x), \qquad u(x, M) = f_4(x), \quad 0 < x < L$$

For further details, see Tolstov (1962).

18.3   DIFFUSION AND HEAT EQUATIONS

The heat equation is probably one of the most famous equations in mathematical physics. In two dimensions it is given by

$$\frac{\partial u}{\partial t} = \frac{\partial^2 u}{\partial x^2} + \frac{\partial^2 u}{\partial y^2} \tag{18.27}$$

This equation is usually defined on a bounded, semi-infinite or infinite two-dimensional region. On the boundaries we defined boundary conditions as well as an associated initial condition. For example, on a bounded rectangle $[0, L] \times [0, M]$ we define the Dirichlet boundary conditions on one part of the boundary and Neumann boundary conditions on the other part:

$$u(x, 0, t) = 0, \quad 0 < x < L$$
$$u(x, M, t) = 0, \quad 0 < x < L \tag{18.28a}$$

$$\frac{\partial u}{\partial x}(0, y, t) = 0, \quad 0 < y < M$$
$$\frac{\partial u}{\partial x}(L, y, t) = 0, \quad 0 < y < M \tag{18.28b}$$

Finally, we prescribe the initial condition

$$u(x, y, 0) = f(x, y), \quad 0 \le x \le L, \quad 0 \le y \le M \tag{18.29}$$

We call equations (18.27), (18.28) and (18.29) the initial boundary value problem (IBVP) for the heat equation. We are interested in finding stable and accurate finite difference schemes for this problem. In general, we employ centred difference schemes in the x and y directions while for time discretisation we use the theta methods (its special cases are the explicit Euler, implicit Euler and Crank–Nicolson schemes). We first discretise (18.27) by the explicit Euler scheme:

$$\frac{U_{i,j}^{n+1} - U_{i,j}^n}{k} = \Delta_x^2 U_{i,j}^n + \Delta_y^2 U_{i,j}^n \tag{18.30}$$

This is a time-marching scheme from level n (where the value is known) to level $n + 1$ (where the value is unknown). Rearranging terms gives us the following explicit formula:

$$U_{i,j}^{n+1} = \lambda U_{i-1,j}^n + r U_{i,j}^n + \lambda U_{i+1,j}^n + \lambda U_{i,j-1}^n + \lambda U_{i,j+1}^n$$

$$= r U_{i,j}^n + \lambda (U_{i-1,j}^n + U_{i+1,j}^n + U_{i,j-1}^n + U_{i,j+1}^n) \tag{18.31}$$

where $\lambda = k/h^2$ and $r = 1 - 4\lambda$.

We now examine the discrete scheme from the following perspective: given that the discrete solution is positive at time level n, can we find sufficient conditions that ensure that the solution is also positive at level $n + 1$? Examining equation (18.31) allows us to conclude that this constraint is:

$$r \geq 0 \Leftrightarrow \frac{k}{h^2} \leq \tfrac{1}{4}$$

Of course, we do not want to get negative solutions from positive input. Negative values are non-physical (on 'non-financial').

We can also apply the von Neumann stability analysis technique to the scheme (18.30) to get the same constraint as above. Let (see Peaceman, 1977)

$$\epsilon_{ij}^n = \gamma^n \exp(i\alpha i h) \exp(i\beta j h), \quad i = \sqrt{-1}$$

Then constructing the terms

$$\Delta_x^2 \epsilon_{ij}^n + \Delta_y^2 \epsilon_{ij}^n$$

and noting that

$$\cos \alpha h - 1 = 2 \sin^2 \frac{\alpha h}{2}$$

and then doing a little arithmetic, we see that

$$\gamma = 1 - 4\lambda \sin^2 \frac{\alpha h}{2} - 4\lambda \sin^2 \frac{\beta h}{2}$$

For stability, we must have

$$-1 \leq \gamma \leq 1$$

and this leads to the same constraint as before. This is a requirement for stability. Of course, the positivity argument is more intuitive than the von Neumann analysis.

The (fully) implicit method is given by:

$$\frac{U_{i,j}^{n+1} - U_{i,j}^n}{k} = \Delta_x^2 U_{i,j}^{n+1} + \Delta_y^2 U_{i,j}^{n+1} \tag{18.32}$$

and rearranging gives us

$$U_{i,j}^{n+1}(1 + 4\lambda) = \lambda (U_{i-1,j}^n + U_{i+1,j}^n + U_{i,j-1}^n + U_{i,j+1}^n) \tag{18.33}$$

Again, we see that positive values at level n give us positive values at level $n + 1$ irrespective of the relative sizes of k and h. We say that this scheme is unconditionally stable. It is sometimes called a monotonic scheme. Some arithmetic shows that the amplification factor is:

$$\gamma = \frac{1}{1 + 4\lambda \sin^2(\alpha h/2) + 4\lambda \sin^2(\beta h/2)} \tag{18.34}$$

This is always less than 1 in absolute value.

Finally, the Crank–Nicolson scheme is given by:

$$\frac{U_{i,j}^{n+1} - U_{i,j}^n}{k} = \Delta_x^2 U_{i,j}^{n+\frac{1}{2}} + \Delta_y^2 U_{i,j}^{n+\frac{1}{2}} \tag{18.35}$$

where

$$U_{i,j}^{n+\frac{1}{2}} \equiv \tfrac{1}{2}(U_{i,j}^{n+1} + U_{i,j}^n)$$

This scheme is not positive in the above sense but it is unconditionally stable. The von Neumann symbol is given by:

$$\gamma = \frac{1 - i\beta}{1 + i\beta} \tag{18.36}$$

where

$$\beta = 2\lambda \sin^2 \frac{\alpha h}{2} + 2\lambda \sin^2 \frac{\beta h}{2}$$

What is the absolute value of γ?

18.3.1 Exact solutions to the heat equation

We can apply the Separation of Variables technique to find a solution to the IBVP (18.27), (18.28) and (18.29) in the form of a bi-orthogonal Fourier series. The details are discussed in Kreider *et al.* (1966) and Tolstov (1962) and we summarise the main results here. To this end, we seek a solution in the form:

$$u(x, y, t) = X(x)Y(y)T(t)$$

The components are given by

$$Y_n(y) = A_n \sin \frac{n\pi y}{M}, \quad n = 1, 2, \ldots,$$

$$X_m(x) = B_m \cos \frac{m\pi x}{L}, \quad m = 0, 1, 2, \ldots$$

$$T = \exp\left[-\pi^2 \left(\frac{m^2}{L^2} + \frac{n^2}{M^2}\right)t\right]$$

Then

$$u(x, y, t) = \sum_{\substack{m=0 \\ n=1}}^{\infty} u_{mn}(x, y, t)$$

where

$$u_{mn}(x, y, t) = A_{mn} \cos \frac{m\pi x}{L} \sin \frac{n\pi y}{M} e^{-\pi^2 \left(\frac{m^2}{L^2} + \frac{n^2}{M^2}\right)t}$$

We find the constant term in this last equation by using the initial condition (18.29) and some integration. When $t = 0$ we get:

$$f(x, y) = \sum_{\substack{m=0 \\ n=1}}^{\infty} A_{mn} \cos \frac{m\pi x}{L} \sin \frac{n\pi y}{M}$$

where the coefficients are given by:

$$A_{0n} = \frac{2}{LM} \int_0^M \int_0^L f(x, y) \sin\left(\frac{n\pi y}{M}\right) dx\, dy \quad (m = 0)$$

$$A_{mn} = \frac{4}{LM} \int_0^M \int_0^L f(x, y) \cos\left(\frac{m\pi x}{L}\right) \sin\left(\frac{n\pi y}{M}\right) dx\, dy \quad (m > 0)$$

You can use this example in benchmarks to test the effectiveness of FDM schemes.

18.4   ADVECTION EQUATION IN TWO DIMENSIONS

First-order hyperbolic equations have been extensively studied in the literature. We motivate the theory by providing some appropriate examples. To start, let us examine the scalar first-order hyperbolic equation (initial value problem)

$$\frac{\partial u}{\partial t} + a\frac{\partial u}{\partial x} + b\frac{\partial u}{\partial y} = 0, \quad -\infty < x < \infty, \quad -\infty < y < \infty \tag{18.37}$$

with the associated initial condition

$$u(x, y, 0) = f(x, y) \tag{18.38}$$

We assume that

$$a > 0, \quad b > 0$$

The solution of the initial value problem (18.37), (18.38) is then given by

$$u(x, y, t) = f(x - at, y - bt) \tag{18.39}$$

Thus, as in the one-dimensional case the solution consists of translating the initial condition in the appropriate direction. The constant coefficients a and b are called the speed of propagation in the x and y directions, respectively. The curve through the point (x, y, t) defined by the equations

$$x - at = x_0$$
$$y - bt = y_0 \tag{18.40}$$

is called a characteristic curve. Here x_0 and y_0 are arbitrary points.

First-order hyperbolic equations are a bit more tricky than the heat equations and other second-order parabolic equations. Some of the reasons are:

- Since the equation is first order only in x and y we need just one boundary condition at one of the boundaries in the domain of dependence. But the question is: Where do we place the boundary condition?
- Centred difference schemes do not necessarily produce stable results.

- Unlike parabolic equations (where discontinuities in the initial conditions are smoothed after a short time), discontinuities propagate through the domain of dependence when we model hyperbolic equations. Furthermore, for some kinds of nonlinear hyperbolic equations the solution may become discontinuous after a finite time, even if the initial conditions are continuous.
- The imposition of boundary conditions can be tricky, especially for systems (Friedrichs, 1958).

Let us start with an example and suppose that we discretise equation (18.37) using explicit Euler in time and centred differencing in the x and y directions:

$$\frac{U_{i,j}^{n+1} - U_{i,j}^{n}}{k} + \frac{a}{2h_1}\left(U_{i+1,j}^{n} - U_{i-1,j}^{n}\right) + \frac{b}{2h_2}\left(U_{i,j+1}^{n} - U_{i,j-1}^{n}\right) = 0 \qquad (18.41)$$

where h_1 and h_2 are the steplengths in the x and y directions, respectively.

The symbol for this operator and its absolute value are given by

$$\gamma = 1 - i\left(R_x \sin \xi + R_y \sin \eta\right) \quad \left(R_x = \frac{ak}{h_1}, \quad R_y = \frac{bk}{h_2}\right) \qquad (18.42)$$

$$|\gamma|^2 = 1 + R_x^2 \sin^2 \xi + R_y^2 \sin^2 \eta \geq 1$$

(see for example, Thomas, 1998, 1999). We thus see that this harmless looking scheme is unconditionally unstable! The problem is that some centred difference schemes are not suitable for this kind of problem. Instead, the first-order upwinding schemes produce better results as we shall now see. The scheme is:

$$\frac{U_{i,j}^{n+1} - U_{i,j}^{n}}{k} + \frac{a}{h_1}\left(U_{i,j}^{n} - U_{i-1,j}^{n}\right) + \frac{b}{h_2}\left(U_{i,j}^{n} - U_{i,j-1}^{n}\right) = 0 \qquad (18.43)$$

Calculation shows that the symbol is

$$\gamma = \gamma(\xi, \eta) = 1 - R_x(1 - e^{-i\xi}) - R_y(1 - e^{-i\eta}) \qquad (18.44)$$

and that it is less than 1 in absolute value if

$$0 \leq R_x + R_y \leq 1, \qquad R_x \geq 0, \quad R_y \geq 0 \qquad (18.45)$$

We now try to derive the same result on the basis of positivity arguments. From equation (18.43) the value at level $n + 1$ can be written in terms of the solution at level n as follows:

$$U_{i,j}^{n+1} = \left(1 - \frac{ak}{h_1} - \frac{bk}{h_2}\right)U_{i,j}^{n} + \frac{a}{h_1}U_{i-1,j}^{n} + \frac{b}{h_2}U_{i,j-1}^{n} \qquad (18.46)$$

We would like to define sufficient conditions for the right-hand side of equation (18.46) to be positive. This criterion thus leads to the inequality:

$$1 - \frac{ak}{h_1} - \frac{bk}{h_2} \geq 0 \quad \text{or} \quad R_x + R_y \leq 1 \qquad (18.47)$$

and this is precisely the inequality in equations (18.45). First-order hyperbolic problems are important in the Black–Scholes environment because we need to model them in Asian option problems and basket option models, for example. This section has given insight into FDM for these problems.

18.4.1   Initial boundary value problems

A new challenge arises when we wish to approximate the solution of first-order hyperbolic initial boundary value problems. The theory is well developed (see, for example, Friedrichs, 1958) and knowing where to place the boundary conditions is important when we model Asian options and the convective terms in the Black–Scholes PDE, for example. Let us consider equation (18.37) in the rectangle:

$$0 \le x \le L$$
$$0 \le y \le M \tag{18.48}$$

When a and b are positive, the boundary conditions are specified at the 'incoming' boundaries, thus:

$$u(0, y, t) = g(y, t), \quad 0 \le y \le M, \quad t > 0$$
$$u(x, 0, t) = h(x, t), \quad 0 \le x \le L, \quad t > 0 \tag{18.49}$$

If we use one-sided upwinding schemes to solve this problem, then everything works fine. If we use centred difference schemes (for example, the scheme in equation (18.41) but with Crank–Nicolson in time) we have to provide a numerical boundary condition on the boundaries that do not have analytic boundary conditions. This has been a source of errors when modelling Asian options in the past (see Mirani, 2002b). A solution to this problem is to use upwinding schemes. A thorough treatment of numerical boundary conditions is given in Thomas (1999).

18.5   CONVECTION–DIFFUSION EQUATION

A convection–diffusion equation in n dimension contains both diffusion and convection terms and these equations have received much attention in the engineering literature in the last 50 years because they model many kinds of physical problems such as the Navier–Stokes equation and its specialisations. In financial engineering we view the Black–Scholes equation as an instance of a convection–diffusion equation:

$$\frac{\partial C}{\partial t} + \frac{1}{2} \sum_{i,j=1}^{n} \frac{\partial^2 C}{\partial S_i \, \partial S_j} \rho_{ij} \sigma_i \sigma_j + \sum_{i=1}^{n} r S_i \frac{\partial C}{\partial S_i} - rC = 0 \tag{18.50}$$

In this case we have n underlying assets and C is the contingent claim. We note the presence of cross-terms if the assets are correlated and our resulting finite difference schemes must produce accurate approximations to these terms.

An example of equation (18.50) is with $n = 2$. In this case we model an option with more than one underlying asset. In particular, we can model the following kinds of options (see Clewlow and Strickland, 1998; Zhang, 1998):

- The difference of two assets (spread option)
- Options on the maximum or minimum of two assets

In this case the partial differential equation (a specialisation of equation (18.50)) is given by:

$$-\frac{\partial C}{\partial t} = (r - D_1)S_1\frac{\partial C}{\partial S_1} + (r - D_2)S_2\frac{\partial C}{\partial S_2}$$

$$+ \frac{1}{2}\sigma_1^2 S_1^2 \frac{\partial^2 C}{\partial S_1^2} + \frac{1}{2}\sigma_2^2 S_2^2 \frac{\partial^2 C}{\partial S_2^2} + \rho\sigma_1 S_1 \sigma_2 S_2 \frac{\partial^2 C}{\partial S_1 \partial S_2} - rC \qquad (18.51)$$

We discuss multi-asset options in more detail in Chapter 24.

As in Clewlow (1998), we can transform this equation to the simpler form

$$-\frac{\partial C}{\partial t} = v_1\frac{\partial C}{\partial x_1} + v_2\frac{\partial C}{\partial x_2} + \frac{1}{2}\sigma_1^2\frac{\partial^2 C}{\partial x_1^2} + \frac{1}{2}\sigma_2^2\frac{\partial^2 C}{\partial x_2^2} + \rho\sigma_1\sigma_2\frac{\partial^2 C}{\partial x_1 \partial x_2} - rC \quad (18.52)$$

where $v_1 = r - D_1 - \frac{1}{2}\sigma_1^2$ and $v_2 = r - D_2 - \frac{1}{2}\sigma_2^2$

By the change of variables

$$x_1 = \ln(S_1)$$

$$x_2 = \ln(S_2)$$

where $v_1 = r - D_1 - \frac{1}{2}\sigma_1^2$ and $v_2 = r - D_2 - \frac{1}{2}\sigma_2^2$.

In general, we prefer not to use these transformations but instead tackle the original PDE (18.50) 'head-on' as it were.

18.6 SUMMARY AND CONCLUSIONS

In this chapter we have given an introduction to finite difference schemes for parabolic partial differential equations in two space variables. This corresponds to two-factor models in financial engineering applications. The focus in this chapter is on explaining the essential models and difficulties that we need to understand when approximating the solution of multi-factor problems. To this end, we have adopted a 'building-block' approach by proposing useful schemes for the heat equation, convection equations and convection–diffusion equations. The knowledge that we gain here will be extremely useful in later chapters of this book, not only for the theory but also applications to financial instrument pricing. Much of the financial literature makes use of the schemes in this chapter.

19

An Introduction to Alternating Direction
Implicit and Splitting Methods

19.1 INTRODUCTION AND OBJECTIVES

In this chapter we introduce a class of finite difference schemes that are suitable for multi-factor Black–Scholes equations. In general, finite difference schemes tend to become more difficult to set up, understand and implement as the dimensionality of the space increases. Is there a way to resolve this 'curse of dimensionality'? We discuss how to resolve this problem in this and the next chapter by decomposing a multidimensional problem into a number of simpler sub-problems. Our interest is in applying and reusing the schemes from previous chapters if possible. Some typical applications are:

- Asian options (payoff depends on the underlying S and the average price of S over some prescribed period)
- Multi-asset options (for example, basket options and options with two or more underlyings)
- Convertible bonds (bond price is a function of the underlying S and the (stochastic) interest rate r)
- Multidimensional interest rate models.

We now give a short introduction to the origins of alternating direct implicit (ADI) and splitting methods. Like much of numerical analysis, many techniques were developed during the 1960s when the digital computer was introduced to model many kinds of industrial, scientific and military problems. Some examples are:

- Reservoir engineering (Peaceman, 1977)
- Solving the heat equations in several dimensions (Douglas *et al.*, 1955)
- Problems in hydrodynamics and elasticity (Yanenko, 1971).

The ADI method – pioneered in the United States by Douglas, Rachford, Peaceman, Gunn and others – has a number of advantages. First, explicit difference methods are rarely used to solve initial boundary value problems owing to their poor stability problems. Implicit methods have superior stability properties but unfortunately they are difficult to solve in two and more dimensions. Consequently, ADI methods became an alternative because they can be programmed by solving a simple tridiagonal system of equations.

During the period that ADI was being developed a number of Soviet scientists (most notably Yanenko, Marchuk, Samarskii and D'Yakanov) were developing splitting methods (also known as fractional step or locally one-dimensional (LOD) methods) for solving time-dependent partial differential equations in two and three dimensions.

The ADI method is popular in the financial literature. However, there are many interpretations on how to use it and how to split a Black–Scholes equation into simpler one-dimensional problems. We hope that this chapter and the subsequent chapters will help to resolve some issues such as:

- The approximation of cross derivatives
- Using Crank–Nicolson with ADI
- How to split a multi-factor PDE
- Algorithms for ADI schemes (Thomas, 1998).

19.2   WHAT IS ADI, REALLY?

In general, ADI is a method that approximates the solution of an initial boundary value problem by a sequence of simpler problems. In order to motivate what ADI is we consider the prototype example, namely the heat equation:

$$\frac{\partial u}{\partial t} = \frac{\partial^2 u}{\partial x^2} + \frac{\partial^2 u}{\partial y^2} \tag{19.1}$$

In Chapter 18 we approximated this equation by centred difference schemes (recall the notation for divided differences in that chapter):

$$\frac{U_{ij}^{n+1} - U_{ij}^n}{k} = \Delta_x^2 U_{ij}^{n+1} + \Delta_y^2 U_{ij}^{n+1} \tag{19.2}$$

The disadvantage of this scheme is that we must solve a large system of equations at each time level. In Chapter 18 we discussed a number of iterative schemes to solve such problems. In this chapter, however, we propose schemes that allow us to simplify scheme (19.2) in some way while still keeping the schemes stable and accurate. We now modify equation (19.2) somewhat so that it becomes implicit in the x direction and explicit in the y direction:

$$\frac{U_{ij}^{n+1} - U_{ij}^n}{k} = \Delta_x^2 U_{ij}^{n+1} + \Delta_y^2 U_{ij}^n \tag{19.3}$$

In this case we can solve problem (19.3) since it can be cast as a tridiagonal system that can subsequently be solved using LU decomposition, for example (Duffy, 2004). However, we must determine if it is stable (be it unconditionally (absolutely) or conditionally). To prove stability, we can employ the following techniques:

- Von Neumann stability analysis
- Positivity and maximum principle analysis.

We examine the positivity argument first. We rewrite system (19.3) as follows:

$$-\lambda U_{i-1,j}^{n+1} + (1 + 2\lambda)\, U_{ij}^{n+1} - \lambda\, U_{i+1,j}^{n+1}$$
$$= \lambda U_{i,j-1}^n + (1 - 2\lambda)\, U_{ij}^n + \lambda\, U_{i,j+1}^n \quad (\lambda \equiv k/h^2) \tag{19.4}$$

We wish to find sufficient conditions to ensure that the right-hand side of (19.4) is positive at time level $n + 1$, assuming that the discrete solution at time level n is positive. We then get the condition

$$1 - 2\lambda \geq 0 \Leftrightarrow \lambda = \frac{k}{h^2} \leq \tfrac{1}{2} \tag{19.5}$$

We get the same condition if we apply von Neumann stability analysis. Continuing, we write (19.4) in the matrix form

$$MU^{n+1} = BU^n \quad \text{or} \quad U^{n+1} = M^{-1}BU^n \tag{19.6}$$

where M and B are matrices.

The solution at time level $n + 1$ is positive because both the inverse of M and the matrix B are positive matrices, and since the product of positive matrices is positive we get the result. The matrix B is positive because the constraint (19.5) must be satisfied, and the inverse of M is positive because M is an M-matrix, that is:

$$M = (m_{ij}), \quad i, j = 1, \ldots, n$$

$$m_{ii} > 0,$$

$$m_{ij} \leq 0, \quad i \neq j$$

(see Morton, 1996; Duffy, 2004).

So we see that the scheme (19.3) is only conditionally stable, and this is unacceptable. Can we improve on this situation? To answer this question, let us consider consecutive applications of this scheme at two time 'legs': the first leg is implicit in x and explicit in y while the second leg is explicit in x and implicit in y. The new scheme moves from the time level n to a somewhat 'fictitious' time level $n + \frac{1}{2}$ and then to time level $n + 1$. The full scheme is:

$$\frac{U_{ij}^{n+\frac{1}{2}} - U_{ij}^n}{k/2} = \Delta_x^2 U_{ij}^{n+\frac{1}{2}} + \Delta_y^2 U_{ij}^n \tag{19.7a}$$

$$\frac{U_{ij}^{n+1} - U_{ij}^{n+\frac{1}{2}}}{k/2} = \Delta_x^2 U_{ij}^{n+\frac{1}{2}} + \Delta_y^2 U_{ij}^{n+1} \tag{19.7b}$$

The hope is that even though the scheme at each leg is only conditionally stable there might be a chance that the full scheme that marches the solution from time level n to time level $n + 1$ will be stable. The scheme alternates between what are essentially one-dimensional implicit schemes, thus the name alternating direction implicit (ADI). In general, the increase in the error due to the presence of the explicit term in a given leg is balanced by the error decrease in the implicit scheme in the next leg. To verify this statement, we use von Neumann stability analysis to prove unconditional stability of scheme (19.7). We assume an equal step length h in the x and y directions for convenience only. Let

$$\epsilon_{ij}^n = \gamma^n \exp(i\alpha ih) \exp(i\beta jh)$$

Then after using the results

$$\Delta_x^2 \epsilon_{ij}^n = -\frac{4}{h^2} \sin^2 \frac{\alpha h}{2}$$

$$\Delta_y^2 \epsilon_{ij}^n = -\frac{4}{h^2} \sin^2 \frac{\beta h}{2}$$

we get the following expressions for the growth factors:

$$\frac{\gamma^{n+\frac{1}{2}}}{\gamma^n} = \frac{1-\alpha_1}{1+\alpha_2}$$

$$\frac{\gamma^{n+1}}{\gamma^{n+\frac{1}{2}}} = \frac{1-\alpha_2}{1+\alpha_1}$$

where

$$\alpha_1 = 4\lambda \sin^2 \frac{\beta h}{2}$$

$$\alpha_2 = 4\lambda \sin^2 \frac{\alpha h}{2}$$

and

$$\lambda = \frac{k}{2h^2}$$

Hence

$$\frac{\gamma^{n+1}}{\gamma^n} = \frac{1-\alpha_2}{1+\alpha_1} \cdot \frac{1-\alpha_1}{1+\alpha_2}$$

We thus see that the growth factor γ from n to $n+1$ is less than 1 in absolute value. Hence, scheme (19.7) is unconditionally stable. This scheme, which is known as the **Peaceman–Rachford scheme**, is second-order accurate in time and space (see, for example, Thomas, 1998).

Please note that we have not yet discussed boundary conditions but shall need to incorporate them into these ADI schemes. We discuss this issue later.

19.3   IMPROVEMENTS ON THE BASIC ADI SCHEME

We introduce some variations on the basic ADI scheme.

19.3.1   The D'Yakonov scheme

In this section we discuss some modifications of the original scheme (19.7) in order to improve computational efficiency. First, we eliminate the solution at time level $n+\frac{1}{2}$ by using equation (19.7a) to get the scheme:

$$\left(1 - \frac{k}{2}\Delta_x^2\right)\left(1 - \frac{k}{2}\Delta_y^2\right) U_{ij}^{n+1} = \left(1 + \frac{k}{2}\Delta_x^2\right)\left(1 + \frac{k}{2}\Delta_y^2\right) U_{ij}^n \tag{19.8}$$

This equation suggests another splitting by the so-called **D'Yakonov scheme**, which we define as follows:

$$\left(1 - \frac{k}{2}\Delta_x^2\right) U_{ij}^* = \left(1 + \frac{k}{2}\Delta_x^2\right)\left(1 + \frac{k}{2}\Delta_y^2\right) U_{ij}^n$$

$$\left(1 - \frac{k}{2}\Delta_y^2\right) U_{ij}^{n+1} = U_{ij}^* \tag{19.9}$$

This set of equations is easy to solve: we apply LU decomposition at each leg and note that the matrix in the matrix system is tridiagonal.

19.3.2 Approximate factorization of operators

We now discuss a technique that allows us to factor a given difference operator in two dimensions into the product of two one-dimensional operators. Let us again take the example of the Crank–Nicolson scheme for the two-dimensional heat equation (19.1):

$$\frac{U_{ij}^{n+1} - U_{ij}^{n}}{k} = \tfrac{1}{2}(\Delta_x^2 U_{ij}^{n+1} + \Delta_y^2 U_{ij}^{n+1} + \Delta_x^2 U_{ij}^{n} + \Delta_y^2 U_{ij}^{n}) \qquad (19.10)$$

We write this equation in the equivalent form

$$(1 - L_x - L_y)U_{ij}^{n+1} = (1 + L_x + L_y)U_{ij}^{n} \qquad (19.11)$$

where

$$L_x \equiv (k/2)\Delta_x^2 \quad \text{and} \quad L_y \equiv (k/2)\Delta_y^2$$

We now factor the terms on both sides of equation (19.11) by using the formula

$$(1 - L_x)(1 - L_y) = 1 - L_x - L_y - L_x L_y$$

$$(1 + L_x)(1 + L_y) = 1 + L_x + L_y + L_x L_y$$

We then get the so-called approximate factorisation scheme by neglecting the cross terms:

$$(1 - L_x)(1 - L_y)U_{ij}^{n+1} = (1 + L_x)(1 + L_y)U_{ij}^{n} \qquad (19.12)$$

This scheme is second order in k, and the idea can be generalised to more complex PDEs.

As a more general example, let us now examine the heat equation in m dimensions:

$$\frac{\partial u}{\partial t} = \sum_{j=1}^{m} \frac{\partial^2 u}{\partial x_j^2} \qquad (19.13)$$

and its approximation by the n-dimensional difference scheme

$$\frac{U^{n+1} - U^{n}}{k} = LU^{n+1}$$

$$L = \sum_{j=1}^{m} L_j \quad \text{(discrete operator)} \qquad (19.14)$$

$$L_j = \frac{\Delta_+ \Delta_-}{h_j^2}$$

where Δ_+ and Δ_- are the forward and backward approximations to the first derivative of a function in the direction j.

This is the m-dimensional equivalent of the difference scheme (19.2). Please note that, for convenience, we have suppressed the subscripts that show dependence on the spatial mesh points. We then write equations (19.14) in the form:

$$(I - kL)U^{n+1} = U^{n} \qquad (19.15)$$

We now factor the operator $I - kL$ by producing a second-order accurate approximation (Yanenko, 1971):

$$(1 - kL_1)(1 - kL_2) \ldots (1 - kL_m) = 1 - kL + k^2 \Phi \tag{19.16}$$

where

$$\Phi = \sum_{i<j} L_i L_j - k \sum_{i<j<k} L_i L_j L_k + \cdots + (-1)^m k^{m-2} L_1 \ldots L_m$$

Based on this expression we now propose a modified form of scheme (19.15):

$$\prod_{j=1}^{m}(1 - kL_j)U^{n+1} = U^n \tag{19.17}$$

The splitting scheme, based on the so-called upper operator in (19.17), is now defined as:

$$(1 - kL_1)U^{n+1/m} = U^n$$
$$(1 - kL_2)U^{n+2/m} = U^{n+1/m}$$
$$\ldots \tag{19.18}$$
$$(1 - kL_m)U^{n+1} = U^{n+(m-1)/m}$$

As an application of this scheme, we now examine the convection–diffusion equation:

$$\frac{\partial u}{\partial t} + A\frac{\partial u}{\partial x} + B\frac{\partial u}{\partial y} = v\left(\frac{\partial^2 u}{\partial x^2} + \frac{\partial^2 u}{\partial y^2}\right) \tag{19.19}$$

We assume that this problem is to be solved in a rectangular region

$$D = \{(x, y) : 0 < x < 1, \quad 0 < y < 1\}$$

However, we do not worry about boundary conditions just yet. Furthermore, we assume that all the coefficients appearing in (19.19) are constant. We define the divided differences:

$$\Delta_x U_{ij} = \tfrac{1}{2h}(U_{i+1,j} - U_{i-1,j})$$

$$\Delta_y U_{ij} = \tfrac{1}{2h}(U_{i,j+1} - U_{i,j-1})$$

Let us consider the two-level difference scheme depending on a single parameter β

$$\frac{U_{ij}^{n+1} - U_{ij}^n}{k} + A\beta\Delta_x U_{ij}^{n+1} + A(1 - \beta)\Delta_x U_{ij}^n + B\beta\Delta_y U_{ij}^{n+1} + B(1 - \beta)\Delta_y U_{ij}^n \tag{19.20}$$
$$= \beta(v\Delta_x^2 U_{ij}^{n+1} + v\Delta_y^2 U_{ij}^{n+1}) + (1 - \beta)(v\Delta_x^2 U_{ij}^n + v\Delta_y^2 U_{ij}^n) \quad (0 \leq \beta \leq 1)$$

We write this longwinded expression in the more compact form

$$(1 + k\beta L_x + k\beta L_y)U_{ij}^{n+1} = [1 - k(1 - \beta)L_x - k(1 - \beta)L_y]U_{ij}^n \tag{19.21}$$

where $L_x \equiv A\Delta_x - v\Delta_x^2$ and $L_y \equiv B\Delta_y - v\Delta_y^2$.
As before, we factor out as follows:

$$(1 + k\beta L_x)(1 + k\beta L_y) = (1 + k\beta L_x + k\beta L_y) + k^2\beta^2 L_x L_y$$

which leads us to the approximate factorisation scheme:

$$(1 + k\beta L_x)(1 + k\beta L_y)U_{ij}^{n+1} = (1 - k(1 - \beta)L_x - k(1 - \beta)L_y)U_{ij}^n$$
$$\equiv L_3 U_{ij}^n \tag{19.22}$$

As before, we can implement this scheme as a two-stage algorithm:

$$(1 + k\beta L_x)U_{ij}^* = L_3 U_{ij}^n$$
$$(1 + k\beta L_y)U_{ij}^{n+1} = U_{ij}^* \tag{19.23}$$

Some remarks:

- The scheme can be generalised to more general convection–diffusion problems than those proposed in equation (19.19) – for example, coefficients that depends on both space and time and equations having inhomogeneous terms.
- The scheme can be generalised to higher dimensions as we saw with the m-dimensional heat equation in this section.
- The technique can be applied to system of equations.
- Of course convection-dominated problems will impact the stability of the schemes. In this case we could use the exponentially fitted schemes (see Chapter 11) in each leg of the approximate factorisation scheme, for example.

19.3.3   ADI classico for two-factor models

In the previous section we introduced an approximate factorisation (AF) method for splitting a problem into a sequence of simpler one-dimensional problems. In this section we discuss the original Peaceman–Rachford ADI for equation (19.19). The two-leg scheme is given by:

$$\frac{U^{n+\frac{1}{2}} - U_{ij}^n}{k} + A\Delta_x U_{ij}^{n+\frac{1}{2}} + B\Delta_y U_{ij}^n = \nu(\Delta_x^2 U_{ij}^{n+\frac{1}{2}} + \Delta_y^2 U_{ij}^n) \tag{19.24a}$$

$$\frac{U_{ij}^{n+1} - U_{ij}^{n+\frac{1}{2}}}{k} + A\Delta_x U_{ij}^{n+\frac{1}{2}} + B\Delta_y U_{ij}^{n+1} = \nu(\Delta_x^2 U_{ij}^{n+\frac{1}{2}} + \Delta_y^2 U_{ij}^{n+1}) \tag{19.24b}$$

As before, the scheme is implicit in x and explicit in y in the first leg, while it is explicit in x and implicit in y in the second leg. The method is unconditionally stable and has second-order accuracy, that is of order

$$O(k^2 + h^2)$$

where k is the step-size in time and h is the step-size in both the x and y directions. We can use LU decomposition with tridiagonal matrices to solve system (19.24).

19.4   ADI FOR FIRST-ORDER HYPERBOLIC EQUATIONS

For completeness, we discuss the use of ADI and AF methods for first-order hyperbolic problems. We take the model initial value problem:

$$\frac{\partial u}{\partial t} + a\frac{\partial u}{\partial x} + b\frac{\partial u}{\partial y} = 0, \quad (x, y) \in D = (0, 1) \times (0, 1), \quad t > 0$$
$$u(x, y, 0) = f(x, y), \quad (x, y) \in D \tag{19.25}$$

The two-dimensional Crank–Nicolson scheme (averaging in time) and centred differences in space is given by:

$$\frac{U_{ij}^{n+1} - U_{ij}^n}{k} + a\Delta_x U_{ij}^{n+\frac{1}{2}} + b\Delta_y U_{ij}^{n+\frac{1}{2}} = 0 \qquad (19.26)$$

where

$$U_{ij}^{n+\frac{1}{2}} \equiv \tfrac{1}{2}(U_{ij}^n + U_{ij}^{n+1})$$

$$\Delta_x U_{ij}^n = \tfrac{1}{2h}(U_{i+1,j}^n - U_{i-1,j}^n)$$

$$\Delta_y U_{ij}^n = \tfrac{1}{2h}(U_{i,j+1}^n - U_{i,j-1}^n)$$

Rearranging terms leads to the following representation (step size is h in the x and y directions):

$$\left(1 + \frac{\lambda_x}{2}\Delta_x + \frac{\lambda_y}{2}\Delta_y\right) U_{ij}^{n+1} = \left(1 - \frac{\lambda_x}{2}\Delta_x - \frac{\lambda_y}{2}\Delta_y\right) U_{ij}^n \qquad (19.27)$$

where $\lambda_x = ak/h$ and $\lambda_y = bk/h$.

We now apply the same techniques as in the previous section to produce the following approximate scheme:

$$\left(1 + \frac{\lambda_x}{2}\Delta_x\right)\left(1 + \frac{\lambda_y}{2}\Delta_y\right) U_{ij}^{n+1} = \left(1 - \frac{\lambda_x}{2}\Delta_x\right)\left(1 - \frac{\lambda_y}{2}\Delta_y\right) U_{ij}^n \qquad (19.28)$$

This is the so-called **Beam–Warming scheme** and we usually write in the computational form:

$$\left(1 + \frac{\lambda_x}{2}\Delta_x\right) U_{ij}^* = \left(1 - \frac{\lambda_x}{2}\Delta_x\right)\left(1 - \frac{\lambda_y}{2}\Delta_y\right) U_{ij}^n$$

$$\left(1 + \frac{\lambda_y}{2}\Delta_y\right) U_{ij}^{n+1} = U_{ij}^* \qquad (19.29)$$

Some arithmetic shows that the symbol of this scheme is:

$$\gamma(\xi, \eta) = \frac{(1 - i\frac{\lambda_x}{2}\sin\xi)(1 - i\frac{\lambda_y}{2}\sin\eta)}{(1 + i\frac{\lambda_x}{2}\sin\xi)(1 + i\frac{\lambda_y}{2}\sin\eta)} \qquad (19.30a)$$

and

$$|\gamma(\xi, \eta)|^2 = 1 \qquad (19.30b)$$

The Beam–Warming scheme is a second-order, unconditionally stable scheme, and hence convergent.

Finally, by subtracting the term

$$\left(1 + \frac{\lambda_x}{2}\Delta_x\right)\left(1 + \frac{\lambda_y}{2}\Delta_y\right) U_{ij}^n$$

from each side of equation (19.28), we can us to write the scheme in the computational form:

$$\left(1 + \frac{\lambda_x}{2}\Delta_x\right)\Delta U_{ij}^* = (-\lambda_x\Delta_x - \lambda_y\Delta_y)U_{ij}^n$$

$$\left(1 + \frac{\lambda_y}{2}\Delta_y\right)\Delta U_{ij} = \Delta U_{ij}^* \qquad (19.31)$$

where $\Delta U_{ij} = U_{ij}^{n+1} - U_{ij}^n$.

This is called the delta formulation (Thomas, 1998).

Finally, we discuss a so-called locally one-dimensional or LOD scheme for the initial value problem (19.25). The idea is that we break up the equation into two one-dimensional equations and approximate each one by a well-known finite difference scheme. In this case we use the implicit Euler scheme in time and centred differences in space:

$$\frac{U_{ij}^{n+\frac{1}{2}} - U_{ij}^n}{k} + a\Delta_x U_{ij}^{n+\frac{1}{2}} = 0$$

$$\frac{U_{ij}^{n+1} - U_{ij}^{n+\frac{1}{2}}}{k} + b\Delta_y U_{ij}^{n+1} = 0 \qquad (19.32)$$

We rewrite this scheme in the computational form:

$$(1 + \lambda_x\Delta_x)U_{ij}^{n+\frac{1}{2}} = U_{ij}^n$$

$$(1 + \lambda_y\Delta_y)U_{ij}^{n+1} = U_{ij}^{n+\frac{1}{2}} \qquad (19.33)$$

An analysis of this scheme allows us to conclude the following (see Thomas, 1998, p. 247):

- It is unconditionally stable for solving IVP (19.25)
- It is first-order accurate in time, that is $O(k)$
- It is second-order accurate in space, that is $O(h_1^2 + h_2^2)$.

19.5   ADI CLASSICO AND THREE-DIMENSIONAL PROBLEMS

We have already seen that ADI produces a conditionally stable scheme on each leg, but this potential instability gets balanced out at the next leg. Of course, if there is an uneven number of legs we will get unstable schemes! Take for example, the innocent-looking scheme for approximating the three-dimensional heat equation

$$\frac{U^{n+1/3} - U^n}{k/3} = \Delta_x^2 U^{n+1/3} + \Delta_y^2 U^n + \Delta_z^2 U^n$$

$$\frac{U^{n+2/3} - U^{n+1/3}}{k/3} = \Delta_x^2 U^{n+1/3} + \Delta_y^2 U^{n+2/3} + \Delta_z^2 U^{n+1/3} \qquad (19.34)$$

$$\frac{U^{n+1} - U^{n+2/3}}{k/3} = \Delta_x^2 U^{n+2/3} + \Delta_y^2 U^{n+2/3} + \Delta_z^2 U^{n+1}$$

In this equation we have suppressed dependence on the space variable for readability reasons. It has been proved that this scheme is not unconditionally stable (Yanenko, 1971). There are a number of solutions to this problem. First, the Douglas–Rachford scheme is

$$\frac{U^{n+1/3} - U^n}{k} = \Delta_x^2 U^{n+1/3} + \Delta_y^2 U^n + \Delta_z^2 U^n$$

$$\frac{U^{n+2/3} - U^{n+1/3}}{k} = \Delta_y^2 (U^{n+2/3} - U^n) \qquad (19.35)$$

$$\frac{U^{n+1} - U^{n+2/3}}{k} = \Delta_z^2 (U^{n+1} - U^n)$$

Furthermore, the simplest splitting scheme for this problem is:

$$\frac{U^{n+1/3} - U^n}{k} = \Delta_x^2 U^{n+1/3}$$

$$\frac{U^{n+2/3} - U^{n+1/3}}{k} = \Delta_y^2 U^{n+2/3} \qquad (19.36)$$

$$\frac{U^{n+1} - U^{n+2/3}}{k} = \Delta_z^2 U^{n+1}$$

Another problem with the standard ADI method is that it is not applicable to problems with mixed derivatives:

$$\frac{\partial u}{\partial t} = \sum_{i,j=1}^{m} a_{ij} \frac{\partial^2 u}{\partial x_i \partial x_j} \qquad (19.37)$$

even in the case $m = 2$ because an explicit operator breaches the stability of the scheme (Yanenko, 1971). This is bad news for two-factor Black–Scholes problems where we have correlation between the underlying assets. We shall resolve this problem in the next chapter.

19.6   THE HOPSCOTCH METHOD

For the sake of completeness we give an introduction to the Hopscotch method (Gourlay, 1970). We focus on the heat equation (19.1) for convenience. The basic idea is to divide the mesh points in the two-dimensional x–y mesh (ih, jh) as follows:

$$i + j \text{ odd}$$
$$i + j \text{ even}$$

The Hopscotch consists of two 'sweeps'. In the first sweep (and subsequent odd-numbered sweeps) the mesh points that are marked by a diamond (see Figure 19.1), that is for which $i + j$ is odd, are calculated based on current values (time level n) at the neighbouring points. We use a FTCS scheme defined as follows:

$$\frac{U_{ij}^{n+1} - U_{ij}^n}{k} = \Delta_x^2 U_{ij}^n + \Delta_y^2 U_{ij}^n \quad \text{for} \quad (i + j) \text{ odd} \qquad (19.38)$$

For the second sweep at the same time level $n + 1$ the same calculation is used at nodes marked with a circle, as shown in Figure 19.1. This second sweep is fully implicit. The scheme is:

$$\frac{U_{ij}^{n+1} - U_{ij}^n}{k} = \Delta_x^2 U_{ij}^{n+1} + \Delta_y^2 U_{ij}^{n+1} \quad (i + j) \text{ even} \qquad (19.39)$$

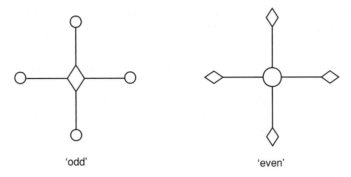

'odd'   'even'

Figure 19.1   Hopscotch mesh points

From this equation we can find the value at time level $n + 1$ as follows:

$$U_{ij}^{n+1} = \frac{\left[U_{ij}^n + k\frac{U_{i+1,j}^{n+1}+U_{i-1,j}^{n+1}}{h_x^2} + k\frac{U_{i,j+1}^{n+1}+U_{i,j-1}^{n+1}}{h_y^2} \right]}{\left[1 + \frac{2k}{h_x^2} + \frac{2k}{h_y^2} \right]} \tag{19.40}$$

In the second and subsequent even-numbered time steps, the roles of the diamonds and circles are interchanged.

Some remarks on the Hopscotch method are in order.

- It can be applied to convection–diffusion equations and the scheme is unconditionally stable if upwind (one-sided) differencing is used for approximating the first-order derivative terms (see Gourlay, 1970).
- The method is 3 to 4 times as fast as the Peaceman–Rachford method owing to the absence of tridiagonal inversions.
- The method has been applied to problems with cross derivatives, but this fact is not well documented in the literature.
- How would you apply Hopscotch to problems in three space dimensions? (The neighbouring points live in a cube.)

The devil is in the details. It seems that the Hopscotch method is not widely used in practice. We have some anecdotal evidence of its use in quantitative finance applications.

A discussion of the Hopscotch methods for convection–diffusion equations is given in Hunsdorfer and Verwer (2003).

19.7   BOUNDARY CONDITIONS

When solving initial boundary value problems for the heat equation we must model the bounded or unbounded region in which the equation is defined. In particular, we must describe the conditions on the solution at the boundary of the region. There are five main issues that we must address:

- The shape or geometry of the region
- The kinds of boundary conditions (Dirichlet, Neumann, Robin, linearity)
- How to approximate the boundary conditions
- How to incorporate the boundary conditions into the ADI or splitting equations

- Ensuring that the boundary condition approximation does not adversely affect the stability and accuracy of the difference scheme.

We now give a brief discussion of each of these topics. We focus on creating the algorithm for the two-dimensional heat equation in a rectangular region with Dirichlet boundary conditions. We extend the technique to more general PDEs later.

In general, it would seem that ADI and splitting methods are better suited to rectangular regions than to non-rectangular regions, because it is more difficult to approximate function values and their derivatives on curved boundaries than on horizontal or vertical boundaries. (see Greenspan, 1966).

We shall now discuss the case of Dirichlet boundary conditions. To this end, we consider the heat equation (19.1). We rewrite the ADI equations (19.7) by grouping known terms on the right-hand side of the equations and unknown terms on the left-hand side:

$$\left(1 - \frac{k}{2}\Delta_x^2\right) U_{ij}^{n+\frac{1}{2}} = \left(1 + \frac{k}{2}\Delta_y^2\right) U_{ij}^n \tag{19.41a}$$

$$\left(1 - \frac{k}{2}\Delta_y^2\right) U_{ij}^{n+1} = \left(1 + \frac{k}{2}\Delta_x^2\right) U_{ij}^{n+\frac{1}{2}} \tag{19.41b}$$

In general, there is not much difficulty involved if we wish to calculate the boundary values of the approximate solution at times n and $n + 1$. The real challenge is to determine suitable boundary conditions for the intermediate value $n + \frac{1}{2}$ in equations (19.41). To this end, we add the left-hand side of equation (19.41)(a) to the right-hand side of equation (19.41b) and vice versa. This give use a formula for the intermediate solution in terms of the solution at time levels n and $n + 1$:

$$U_{ij}^{n+\frac{1}{2}} = \frac{1}{2}\left(1 - \frac{k}{2}\Delta_y^2\right) U_{ij}^{n+1} + \frac{1}{2}\left(1 + \frac{k}{2}\Delta_y^2\right) U_{ij}^n \tag{19.42}$$

This formula allows us to find the appropriate boundary values. For example, in the x directions these will be:

$$i = 0: \quad U_{0j}^{n+\frac{1}{2}} = \frac{1}{2}\left(1 - \frac{k}{2}\Delta_y^2\right) g[0, jh_2, (n + 1)k] + \frac{1}{2}\left(1 + \frac{k}{2}\Delta_y^2\right) g\,(0, jh_2, nk)$$

$$\tag{19.43}$$

$$i = I: \quad U_{Ij}^{n+\frac{1}{2}} = \frac{1}{2}\left(1 - \frac{k}{2}\Delta_y^2\right) g[1, jh_2, (n + 1)k] + \frac{1}{2}\left(1 + \frac{k}{2}\Delta_y^2\right) g\,(1, jh_2, nk)$$

We can find the corresponding boundary conditions in the y direction by plugging in special index values of $(j = 0, j = J)$ in equations (19.42). Equations (19.43) are second-order (in time) accurate approximations to the boundary condition. An alternative solution is to use the (again) second-order approximation

$$U_{0j}^{n+\frac{1}{2}} = g\left[0, jh_2, \left(n + \tfrac{1}{2}\right)k\right]$$

$$U_{Ij}^{n+\frac{1}{2}} = g\left[1, jh_2, \left(n + \tfrac{1}{2}\right)k\right] \tag{19.44}$$

Thus, you may choose between (19.43) and (19.44) as each gives second-order accuracy. It is also possible to handle Neumann boundary conditions in conjunction with ADI. A full treatment of these topics is given in Thomas (1998).

19.8   SUMMARY AND CONCLUSIONS

We have given an introduction to alternating direction implicit (ADI) methods that are used in engineering, science and finance to solve multidimensional partial differential equations. These methods are based on the decomposition of a multidimensional problem into a series of one-dimensional problems. We then solve each sub-problem using the techniques for one-factor equations, as already discussed in earlier chapters of this book.

We have included this chapter for a number of reasons. First, there is growing interest in ADI, as can be seen in the financial literature, and it is probably a good idea to present the essence of the method for a simple but important model problem, namely the two-dimensional heat equation and the convection–diffusion equation. There is some evidence to show that splitting methods give better results than ADI for two-factor Black–Scholes equations. Third, ADI and splitting methods are easy to understand and to implement and are sometimes preferable to direct methods.

20
Advanced Operator Splitting Methods: Fractional Steps

20.1 INTRODUCTION AND OBJECTIVES

Splitting methods were developed in the 1950s and 1960s by Soviet scientists. In this chapter we apply the splitting method to the two-dimensional heat equation and from there we move to more challenging problems such as:

- Modelling cross-derivative terms
- Applications to three and higher dimensions
- Predictor–corrector methods in conjunction with splitting.

A detailed analysis of splitting methods can be found in the definitive monograph, Yanenko (1971). ADI and operator splitting were introduced in Duffy (2004).

20.2 INITIAL EXAMPLES

We examine the two-dimensional heat equation:

$$\frac{\partial u}{\partial t} = \frac{\partial^2 u}{\partial x^2} + \frac{\partial^2 u}{\partial y^2} \tag{20.1}$$

The idea behind operator splitting is to reduce equation (20.1) into two one-dimensional problems. We then approximate each sub-problem by implicit or explicit schemes. Thus, we are thinking intuitively of two one-dimensional partial differential equations:

$$\frac{\partial v}{\partial t} = \frac{\partial^2 v}{\partial x^2} \quad \text{and} \quad \frac{\partial w}{\partial t} = \frac{\partial^2 w}{\partial y^2} \tag{20.2}$$

where the functions v and w are deliberately unspecified. In general we take centred differencing in space and explicit or implicit time marching in time. For example, using explicit Euler we get the two-leg scheme

$$\frac{\tilde{U}_{ij} - U_{ij}^n}{\Delta t} = \triangle_x^2 U_{ij}^n$$
$$\frac{U_{ij}^{n+1} - \tilde{U}_{ij}}{\Delta t} = \triangle_y^2 \tilde{U}_{ij} \tag{20.3}$$

where we have used the notation of $\tilde{U}$ for the intermediate value.

Let us assume for convenience that the mesh size in the x and y directions is the same, namely h. We wish to examine the stability of this scheme. We expect it to be conditionally stable only, and we can prove this using either von Neumann stability analysis or the maximum principle. Using the former method we see that the amplification factor is given by

(in much the same way as in Chapter 19)

$$\frac{\gamma^{n+1}}{\gamma^n} = \left(1 - 4\lambda \sin^2 \frac{\alpha h}{2}\right)\left(1 - 4\lambda \sin^2 \frac{\beta h}{2}\right), \qquad \lambda = \frac{k}{h^2} \qquad (20.4)$$

This leads to the constraint:

$$\frac{k}{h^2} \leq \tfrac{1}{2} \qquad (20.5)$$

Now, the implicit splitting scheme is defined by:

$$\frac{\tilde{U}_{ij} - U_{ij}^n}{\Delta t} = \Delta_x^2 \tilde{U}_{ij}$$

$$\frac{U_{ij}^{n+1} - \tilde{U}_{ij}}{\Delta t} = \Delta_y^2 U_{ij}^{n+1} \qquad (20.6)$$

This scheme is unconditionally stable. In fact each leg is stable, a property not shared by the ADI schemes. Finally, it is possible to define a splitting method in conjunction with Crank–Nicolson time marching:

$$\frac{\tilde{U}_{ij} - U_{ij}^n}{k} = \tfrac{1}{2}(\Delta_x^2 \tilde{U}_{ij} + \Delta_x^2 U_{ij}^n)$$

$$\frac{U_{ij}^{n+1} - \tilde{U}_{ij}}{k} = \tfrac{1}{2}(\Delta_y^2 U_{ij}^{n+1} + \Delta_y^2 \tilde{U}_{ij}) \qquad (20.7)$$

Having motivated splitting we now discuss a number of important issues that will be useful when we model multi-factor Black–Scholes problems.

20.3 PROBLEMS WITH MIXED DERIVATIVES

The standard ADI method is not good at approximating mixed derivatives and a number of workarounds have been suggested by researchers and practitioners in financial engineering (Bhar *et al.*, 2000; Andreasen, 2001). The splitting method is better and to this end we examine the problem:

$$\frac{\partial u}{\partial t} = Lu$$

$$Lu \cong \sum_{i,j=1}^{2} a_{ij} \frac{\partial^2 u}{\partial x_i \partial x_j} \qquad (20.8)$$

$$a_{11} a_{22} - a_{12}^2 > 0, \quad a_{11} > 0, \quad a_{22} > 0$$

a_{ij} constant

In Yanenko (1971) the following scheme is proposed:

$$\frac{\tilde{U}_{ij} - U_{ij}^n}{\Delta t} = a_{11}\Delta_x^2 \tilde{U}_{ij} + a_{12}\Delta_x \Delta_y U_{ij}^n$$

$$\frac{U_{ij}^{n+1} - \tilde{U}_{ij}}{\Delta t} = a_{21}\Delta_x \Delta_y \tilde{U}_{ij} + a_{22}\Delta_y^2 U_{ij}^{n+1} \qquad (20.9)$$

This scheme is stable and convergent (see Yanenko, 1971) and it resolves the problems that ADI methods show for this equation.

We shall see later how to use scheme (20.9) in multi-factor Black–Scholes problems. Yanenko has also produced a scheme for the three-dimensional heat conduction equation:

$$\frac{\partial u}{\partial t} = \sum_{i,j=1}^{3} a_{ij} \frac{\partial^2 u}{\partial x_i \, \partial x_j} \tag{20.10}$$

The proposed scheme is:

$$\frac{U^{n+\frac{1}{6}} - U^n}{k} = \tfrac{1}{2}\Lambda_{11} U^{n+\frac{1}{6}} + \Lambda_{12} U^n$$

$$\frac{U^{n+\frac{2}{6}} - U^{n+\frac{1}{6}}}{k} = \Lambda_{21} U^{n+\frac{1}{6}} + \tfrac{1}{2}\Lambda_{22} U^{n+\frac{2}{6}}$$

$$\frac{U^{n+\frac{3}{6}} - U^{n+\frac{2}{6}}}{k} = \tfrac{1}{2}\Lambda_{11} U^{n+\frac{3}{6}} + \Lambda_{13} U^{n+\frac{2}{6}}$$

$$\frac{U^{n+\frac{4}{6}} - U^{n+\frac{3}{6}}}{k} = \Lambda_{31} U^{n+\frac{3}{6}} + \tfrac{1}{2}\Lambda_{33} U^{n+\frac{4}{6}} \tag{20.11}$$

$$\frac{U^{n+\frac{5}{6}} - U^{n+\frac{4}{6}}}{k} = \tfrac{1}{2}\Lambda_{22} U^{n+\frac{5}{6}} + \Lambda_{23} U^{n+\frac{4}{6}}$$

$$\frac{U^{n+1} - U^{n+\frac{5}{6}}}{k} = \Lambda_{32} U^{n+\frac{5}{6}} + \tfrac{1}{2}\Lambda_{33} U^{n+1}$$

where

$$\Lambda_{jj} u \sim a_{jj} \frac{\partial^2 u}{\partial x_j^2}, \quad j = 1, 2, 3$$

$$\Lambda_{i,j} u \sim a_{ij} \frac{\partial^2 u}{\partial x_i \partial x_j}, \quad i \neq j, \quad i, j = 1, 2, 3$$

This scheme is consistent with PDE (20.10) and is stable provided that the matrix $B = (b_{ij})$ is positive definite, where $b_{ij} = a_{ij}, i \neq j$ and $b_{ii} = a_{ii}/2$.

This scheme can be generalised to more general differential operators that appear in the financial engineering literature, for example currency options that depend on the spot exchange rate and two activity rates (Carr, 2004, private communication). We conclude our discussion of mixed derivatives by proving a result concerning the approximation of the mixed derivative by divided differences:

$$\frac{\partial^2 u}{\partial x \partial y}(x_i, y_j) \sim \frac{1}{4 h_x h_y} (u_{i+1,j+1} - u_{i+1,j-1} - u_{i-1,j+1} + u_{i-1,j-1}) \tag{20.12}$$

The steps in the proof are given as follows:

$$\Delta_x \Delta_y u_{ij} = \frac{1}{2 h_y} \Delta_x (u_{i,j+1} - u_{i,j-1})$$

$$= \frac{1}{4 h_x h_y} [(u_{i+1,j+1} - u_{i-1,j+1}) - (u_{i+1,j-1} - u_{i-1,j-1})]$$

$$= \frac{1}{4 h_x h_y} (u_{i+1,j+1} - u_{i-1,j+1} - u_{i+1,j-1} + u_{i-1,j-1}) \tag{20.13}$$

as was to be shown. Summarising, scheme (20.11) could be one leg of a splitting scheme for Black–Scholes. The other leg could be a convective PDE.

20.4 PREDICTOR–CORRECTOR METHODS (APPROXIMATION CORRECTORS)

These are methods that are based on predictor–corrector methods for initial value problems for ordinary differential equations (Conte and de Boor, 1980). Again, let us examine the three-dimensional heat equation:

$$\frac{\partial u}{\partial t} = \sum_{j=1}^{3} \frac{\partial^2 u}{\partial x_j^2} \tag{20.14}$$

The following scheme is then unconditionally stable and second-order accurate (for a proof, see Yanenko, 1971, p. 29):

$$\frac{U^{n+1/6} - U^n}{k/2} = \Delta_x^2 U^{n+1/6} + \Delta_y^2 U^n + \Delta_z^2 U^n \tag{20.15a}$$

$$\frac{U^{n+2/6} - U^{n+1/6}}{k/2} = \Delta_y^2 (U^{n+2/6} - U^n) \tag{20.15b}$$

$$\frac{U^{n+3/6} - U^{n+2/6}}{k/2} = \Delta_z^2 (U^{n+3/6} - U^n) \tag{20.15c}$$

$$\frac{U^{n+1} - U^n}{k} = \Delta_x^2 U^{n+1/6} + \Delta_y^2 U^{n+2/6} + \Delta_z^2 U^{n+3/6} \tag{20.15d}$$

In this case we have defined three predictors and the 'final' corrector that represents the desired approximate solution at time level $n + 1$. This is thus called a stabilising corrections scheme. The scheme is unconditionally stable and of second-order accuracy in both time and space.

One final example of a predictor–corrector method is given by:

$$\frac{U^{n+1/6} - U^n}{k/2} = \Delta_x^2 U^{n+1/6} \tag{20.16a}$$

$$\frac{U^{n+2/6} - U^{n+1/6}}{k/2} = \Delta_y^2 U^{n+2/6} \tag{20.16b}$$

$$\frac{U^{n+3/6} - U^{n+2/6}}{k/2} = \Delta_z^2 U^{n+3/6} \tag{20.16c}$$

$$\frac{U^{n+1} - U^n}{k} = (\Delta_x^2 + \Delta_y^2 + \Delta_z^2) U^{n+3/6} \tag{20.16d}$$

Again, we have three predictors and one corrector. Again, this scheme is unconditionally stable and second-order accurate. This scheme can be generalised to more general partial differential equations, for example convection–diffusion equations and equations with mixed derivatives. Furthermore, the scheme is easy to implement and has good stability and convergence properties.

20.5   PARTIAL INTEGRO-DIFFERENTIAL EQUATIONS

The splitting technique has been applied to the solution of partial integro-differential equations (PIDEs) by Yanenko, Marchuk and others. For example, consider the PIDE for the kinetic theory equation:

$$\frac{\partial u}{\partial t} + \sum_{k=1}^{m-1} u_k \frac{\partial u}{\partial x_k} + \sigma u = \frac{\sigma_s}{4\pi} \int u(x, y, t)\, dy + f(x, y, t) \qquad (20.17)$$

Now let

$$\wedge_1 = \text{approximation to } \sigma I + \frac{\sigma s}{4\pi} \int u\, dy$$

$$\wedge_2 = \text{approximation to } \sum_{k=1}^{m-1} u_k \frac{\partial u}{\partial x_k}$$

$$\overline{f} = \text{approximation to } f$$

where the integral term is taken on some interval (it may be bounded, infinite or semi-infinite). Then the splitting scheme is defined by:

$$\frac{U^{n+1/2} - U^n}{k} = \wedge_1(\alpha U^{n+1/2} + \beta U^n) + \overline{f}$$

$$\frac{U^{n+1} - U^{n+1/2}}{k} = \wedge_2(\alpha U^{n+1} + \beta U^{n+1/2}) \qquad (20.18)$$

where

$$\alpha \geq 0, \quad \beta \geq 0, \quad \alpha + \beta = 1$$

$$\wedge_2 = \wedge_{21} + \cdots + \wedge_{2,m-1}$$

$$\wedge_{2j} = \text{approximation to the differential operator } u_j \frac{\partial}{\partial x_j}, \quad j = 1, \dots, m-1$$

A so-called complete splitting is defined in Yanenko (1971) in which the first-order terms in equation (20.17) are split.
Then the complete splitting scheme is given by:

$$\frac{U^{(n+1)/m} - U^n}{k} = \wedge_1(\alpha U^{(n+1)/m} + \beta U^n) + \overline{f}$$

$$\frac{U^{n+(j+1)/m} - U^{n+j/m}}{k} = \wedge_{2j}(\alpha U^{n+(j+1)/m} + \beta U^{n+j/m}) \quad j = 1, \dots, m-1 \quad (20.19)$$

We can choose between different marching schemes in each leg of this scheme, for example explicit in the first leg and fully implicit in the second leg when $m = 2$:

$$\frac{U^{n+1/2} - U^n}{k} = \wedge_1 U^n \begin{pmatrix} \alpha = 0 \\ \beta = 1 \end{pmatrix} \qquad (20.20a)$$

$$\frac{U^{n+1} - U^n}{k} = \wedge_{21} U^{n+1} \begin{pmatrix} \alpha = 1 \\ \beta = 0 \end{pmatrix} \qquad (20.20b)$$

We can thus solve the problem as a sequence of one-dimensional problems. We note finally that splitting methods can be applied to integral and algebraic equations. A discussion is outside the scope of this book.

20.6   MORE GENERAL RESULTS

We conclude our discussion of splitting methods with some general schemes for general PDEs and PIDEs. Consider the general PIDE initial value problem in m dimensions:

$$\frac{\partial u}{\partial t} = Lu$$

$$u(x, 0) = u_0(x) \tag{20.21}$$

where L is an integro-differential operator of the form

$$L = L_1 + L_2 + \cdots + L_m \tag{20.22}$$

and the individual operators are approximated by some finite difference schemes:

$$L_1 \sim \wedge_{10} + \wedge_{11}$$

$$L_2 \sim \wedge_{20} + \wedge_{21} + \wedge_{22}$$

$$\cdots$$

$$L_m \sim \wedge_{20} + \cdots + \wedge_{mm} \tag{20.23}$$

The splitting method is defined by:

$$\frac{U^{n+1/m} - U^n}{k} = \wedge_{10} U^n + \wedge_{11} U^{n+1/m}$$

$$\frac{U^{n+2/m} - U^{n+1/m}}{k} = \wedge_{20} U^n + \wedge_{21} U^{n+1/m} + \wedge_{22} U^{n+2/m}$$

$$\cdots \tag{20.24}$$

$$\frac{U^{n+1} - U^{n+(m-1)/m}}{k} = \wedge_{m0} U^n + \wedge_{m1} U^{n+1/m} + \cdots + \wedge_{mm} U^{n+1}$$

where $\wedge_{sr} = 0$ if $r < s - 1$.

It is possible to prove convergence of this scheme if the discrete operators are commutative.

20.7   SUMMARY AND CONCLUSIONS

We have given an introduction to splitting methods. These are similar to ADI methods but are somewhat easier to understand and to apply in practice. Furthermore, splitting solves problems with cross derivatives well and it can be applied to multi-factor problems, PIDE and applications where classical ADI methods fail (Levin, 1999, private communication).

Modern Splitting Methods

21.1 INTRODUCTION AND OBJECTIVES

In this short chapter we deal with a number of emerging techniques and schemes that are useful for approximating initial boundary value problems in financial engineering. Some of the topics to be discussed are:

- Systems of Black–Scholes equations and their numerical approximation
- ADI and operator splitting schemes for systems of PDEs
- A new kind of splitting: implicit–explicit (IMEX) schemes

This chapter can be skipped on a first reading of this book.

21.2 SYSTEMS OF EQUATIONS

We shall examine systems of partial differential equations. In order to reduce the scope we shall look at parabolic systems in two dimensions. In general, nonlinear systems of equations occur in many application areas such as weather prediction, oil reservoir simulation, groundwater flow and computational aerodynamics. In financial engineering we see applications to chooser options (Wilmott, 1998) and leveraged knock-in options (Tavella *et al.*, 2000). In this section we examine systems of parabolic equations of the form:

$$\frac{\partial \mathbf{v}}{\partial t} = B_1 \frac{\partial^2 \mathbf{v}}{\partial x^2} + B_2 \frac{\partial^2 \mathbf{v}}{\partial y^2} + A_1 \frac{\partial \mathbf{v}}{\partial x} + A_2 \frac{\partial \mathbf{v}}{\partial y} + C_0 \mathbf{v} \tag{21.1}$$

where

$$\mathbf{v} = {}^t(v_1, \ldots, v_n), \qquad v_j = v_j(x, y, t), \quad j = 1, \ldots, n$$

and B_1, B_2, A_1, A_2 and C_0 are $n \times n$ matrices.

This is a general system and there are special sub-cases that have been extensively studied in the literature. One special case is the class of first-order hyperbolic systems of the form:

$$\frac{\partial \mathbf{v}}{\partial t} = A_1 \frac{\partial \mathbf{v}}{\partial x} + A_2 \frac{\partial \mathbf{v}}{\partial y} + C_0 \mathbf{v} \tag{21.2}$$

A discussion of this kind of problem is outside the scope of this book. For more information, see Thomas (1998). Instead, we examine parabolic systems of the form (21.1).

Definition 21.1. The system (21.1) is said to be parabolic if for all

$$\omega = {}^t(\omega_1, \omega_2) \in \mathbb{R}^2 \text{ the eigenvalues } \lambda_j(\omega), \, j = 1, \ldots n \text{ of the matrix}$$
$$-\omega_1^2 B_1 - \omega_2^2 B_2 \text{ satisfy } \Re\lambda_j(\omega) \le \delta|\omega|^2$$

for $j = 1, \ldots, n$ for some $\delta > 0$ independent of ω.

Definition 21.2. The matrices B_1 and B_2 are said to be simultaneously diagonisable if there exists a matrix S such that $D_1 = SB_1S^{-1}$ and $D_2 = SB_2S^{-1}$ are both diagonal matrices.

We reduce the scope for the moment by examining the system:

$$\frac{\partial \mathbf{v}}{\partial t} = A\frac{\partial^2 \mathbf{v}}{\partial x^2} + B\frac{\partial^2 \mathbf{v}}{\partial y^2} \tag{21.3}$$

where we assume that A and B are both positive definite and simultaneously diagonalisable. We propose a number of schemes for this problem where we assume that the notation in the scalar case carries over to the vector case. The first FTCS scheme uses explicit time marching and centred differencing in space:

$$\frac{\mathbf{U}_{ij}^{n+1} - \mathbf{U}_{ij}^n}{k} = A\Delta_x^2 \mathbf{U}_{ij}^n + B\Delta_y^2 \mathbf{U}_{ij}^n \tag{21.4}$$

Let μ_j and v_j ($j = 1, \ldots, n$) be the eigenvalues of A and B, respectively. Then the condition $\mu_j r_x + v_j r_y \le \frac{1}{2}$ where $r_x = k/h_x^2$, $r_y = k/h_y^2$ is both necessary and sufficient for convergence of the difference scheme (21.4) to the solution of (21.3).

We now discuss the applicability of the Crank–Nicolson scheme to the system (21.3). It is given by:

$$\frac{\mathbf{U}_{ij}^{n+1} - \mathbf{U}_{ij}^n}{k} = \frac{1}{2}\left\{ A\Delta_x^2 \mathbf{U}_{ij}^{n+1} + B\Delta_y^2 \mathbf{U}_{ij}^{n+1} + A\Delta_x^2 \mathbf{U}_{ij}^n + B\Delta_y^2 \mathbf{U}_{ij}^n \right\} \tag{21.5}$$

By taking the discrete Fourier transform of equation (21.5) it can be shown that this scheme is unconditionally stable (see Thomas, 1998, for details).

21.2.1 ADI and splitting for parabolic systems

The finite difference scheme (21.5) is quite expensive at run-time in terms of memory usage and processing time, and for this reason we investigate the option of applying ADI methods. The ADI scheme with implicit Euler time stepping is given by:

$$\frac{\mathbf{U}_{ij}^{n+1/2} - \mathbf{U}_{ij}^n}{k} = A\Delta_x^2 \mathbf{U}_{ij}^{n+1/2} + B\Delta_y^2 \mathbf{U}_{ij}^n$$

$$\frac{\mathbf{U}_{ij}^{n+1} - \mathbf{U}_{ij}^{n+1/2}}{k} = A\Delta_x^2 \mathbf{U}_{ij}^{n+1/2} + B\Delta_y^2 \mathbf{U}_{ij}^{n+1} \tag{21.6}$$

On the other hand, the splitting scheme with implicit Euler time stepping is given by:

$$\frac{\mathbf{U}_{ij}^{n+1/2} - \mathbf{U}_{ij}^n}{k} = A\Delta_x^2 \mathbf{U}_{ij}^{n+1/2}$$

$$\frac{\mathbf{U}_{ij}^{n+1} - \mathbf{U}_{ij}^{n+1/2}}{k} = B\Delta_y^2 \mathbf{U}_{ij}^{n+1} \tag{21.7}$$

In short, these equations are the equivalents of the scalar schemes in Chapters 19 and 20.

21.2.2 Compound and chooser options

A compound option is an option on an option. It gives the holder the right to buy (call) or sell (put) another option. If we exercise the option we shall then own a call or put option that will then give us the right to buy or sell the underlying. We say that the compound option is of second order because it gives the holder rights over another derivative. A chooser option is similar to a compound option because it gives the holder the right to buy a further option (Wilmott, 1998). However, in this case the holder can choose to receive a call or put. The value C_h of a chooser option depends on two other options, as seen by the following parabolic system:

$$\frac{\partial C_h}{\partial t} + \tfrac{1}{2}\sigma^2 S^2 \frac{\partial^2 C_h}{\partial S^2} + rS\frac{\partial C_h}{\partial S} - rC_h = 0$$

$$\frac{\partial V_1}{\partial t} + \tfrac{1}{2}\sigma^2 S^2 \frac{\partial^2 V_1}{\partial S^2} + rS\frac{\partial V_1}{\partial S} - rV_1 = 0 \qquad (21.8)$$

$$\frac{\partial V_2}{\partial t} + \tfrac{1}{2}\sigma^2 S^2 \frac{\partial^2 V_2}{\partial S^2} + rS\frac{\partial V_2}{\partial S} - rV_2 = 0$$

where C_h = price of chooser option

        V_1 = underlying option

        V_2 = underlying option.

This is an uncoupled system of equations and can be posed in the form (21.1). The coupling between the different variables in system (21.8) is seen at the expiry of the chooser option:

$$C_h(S, T) = \max[V_1(S, T) - K_1, V_2(S, T) - K_2] \qquad (21.9)$$

where T = expiry date of chooser option

        K_1 = strike price of option V_1

        K_2 = strike price of option V_2.

The price of a chooser option can be calculated as the sum of two suitable vanilla options. But it is also interesting to view it from a PDE point of view.

With compound options, on the other hand, we have two steps. First, we price the 'underlying' option and then the compound option. To this end, let the underlying option have payoff $F(S)$ at time T:

$$\frac{\partial V}{\partial t} + \tfrac{1}{2}\sigma^2 S^2 \frac{\partial^2 V}{\partial S^2} + rS\frac{\partial V}{\partial S} - rV = 0$$

$$V(S, T) = F(S) \qquad (21.10)$$

Now suppose that the compound option can be exercised at time $T_C < T$ with a given payoff $G[V(S, T_C)]$. Then the PDE for the compound option $C(S, t)$ is given by:

$$\frac{\partial C}{\partial t} + \tfrac{1}{2}\sigma^2 S^2 \frac{\partial^2 C}{\partial S^2} + rS\frac{\partial C}{\partial S} - rC = 0$$

$$C(S, T_C) = G[V(S, T_C)] \qquad (21.11)$$

For example, a call option on a call option with exercise prices K for the underlying and K_C for the compound option gives the payoffs:

$$F(S) = \max(S - K, 0)$$
$$G(S) = \max(V - K_C, 0)$$

(21.12)

It is possible to approximate the solution of system (21.11) by finite differences. The process involves schemes for approximating V and then C. This might be overkill because exact solutions are known (see Haug, 1998, p. 43), but for some problems an exact solution may not be known.

21.2.3 Leveraged knock-in options

In Tavella (2000) an example is given of a standard knock-in barrier put option that has no value until the spot price touches a barrier B, at which time the option becomes a standard put option. In order to price the knock-in we can add another Black–Scholes equation that gives the value of the standard option that the knock-in option becomes when knocked in:

$$\frac{\partial V_{sp}}{\partial t} + \frac{1}{2}\sigma^2 S^2 \frac{\partial^2 V_{sp}}{\partial S^2} + (r - D_0)S\frac{\partial V_{sp}}{\partial S} - rV_{sp} = 0$$

$$\frac{\partial V_{ki}}{\partial t} + \frac{1}{2}\sigma^2 S^2 \frac{\partial^2 V_{ki}}{\partial S^2} + (r - D_0)S\frac{\partial V_{ki}}{\partial S} - rV_{ki} = 0$$

(21.13)

where V_{sp} = standard put option price

V_{ki} = knock-in option

D_0 = dividend.

At expiration the payoff conditions are given by:

$$V_{sp}(S, T) = \max(K - S, 0)$$
$$V_{ki}(S, T) = V_{sp}(S, T), \quad S \le B \text{ (knock-in condition)}$$
$$V_{ki}(S, T) = 0, \quad S > B$$

(21.14)

The domain of integration needs to be truncated and the corresponding boundary conditions are:

$$\frac{\partial^2 V_{sp}}{\partial S^2} = \frac{\partial^2 V_{ki}}{\partial S^2} = 0 \quad \text{at } S = S_{min}$$

(21.15)

or

$$V_{sp} = V_{ki} = 0 \quad \text{at } S = S_{max}$$

The systems in this section can be modelled using standard finite difference scheme, ADI and splitting methods. We omit the details. Please note that there are no mixed derivative terms in (21.13).

21.3   A DIFFERENT KIND OF SPLITTING: THE IMEX SCHEMES

Until now we have carried out so-called dimensional splitting, but many problems can be split into two parts, one of which is stiff and the other non-stiff.

In this section we give a brief introduction to IMEX methods. They have this name because part of the scheme uses implicit time differencing while the other part uses explicit time differencing. Let us take the simple convection–diffusion equation for motivational purposes:

$$\frac{\partial u}{\partial t} = \sigma \frac{\partial^2 u}{\partial x^2} + \mu \frac{\partial u}{\partial x} \quad \sigma, \mu > 0 \quad \text{constant} \tag{21.16}$$

We now carry out a semi-discretisation of problem (21.16) by applying centred differencing in the space direction. The scheme is:

$$\frac{du_j}{dt} = \sigma D_+ D_- u_j + \mu D_0 u_j, \quad 1 \leq j \leq J - 1 \tag{21.17}$$

or in matrix form

$$\frac{dU}{dt} = AU + BU, \quad U = {}^t(u_1, \ldots, u_{J-1})$$

$$A = \frac{\sigma}{h^2} \begin{pmatrix} -2 & 1 & & 0 \\ 1 & \ddots & \ddots & \\ & \ddots & \ddots & 1 \\ 0 & & 1 & -2 \end{pmatrix}$$

$$B = \frac{\mu}{2h} \begin{pmatrix} 0 & +1 & & 0 \\ -1 & \ddots & \ddots & \\ & \ddots & \ddots & +1 \\ 0 & & -1 & 0 \end{pmatrix} \tag{21.18}$$

In other words, we have decomposed the term in the ODE into a stiff (diffusive) and a non-stiff (convective) term. We now fully discretise scheme (21.18) in time by using explicit Euler for the convection term and the θ method for the diffusion term, as follows:

$$\frac{U^{n+1} - U^n}{k} = (1 - \theta)AU^n + \theta AU^{n+1} + BU^n \tag{21.19}$$

where $0 \leq \theta \leq 1$.

This is the simplest example of what we call the IMEX-θ method. We generalise it to the nonlinear semi-discrete scheme:

$$\frac{dU}{dt} = F[t, U(t)] = F_0[t, U(t)] + F_1[t, U(t)] \tag{21.20}$$

where F_0 is the non-stiff term (convection, for example) and F_1 is the stiff term (diffusion and reaction, for example).

The corresponding IMEX-θ method is given by:

$$U^{n+1} = U^n + k[F_0(t_n, U^n) + (1 - \theta)F_1(t_n, U^n) + \theta F_1(t_{n+1}, U^{n+1})] \tag{21.21}$$

We shall see some examples of scheme (21.21) when we examine finite difference schemes for American option problems.

This method has more favourable truncation errors than methods based on operator splitting with fractional steps. The big challenge, however, is to examine the stability properties of the scheme (Hundsdorfer and Verwer, 2003). A disadvantage of this method is that explicit Euler is not well suited to convection problems and first-order accuracy may not be good enough. We should then resort to IMEX multi-step methods, but that topic is outside the scope of this book.

21.4   APPLICABILITY OF IMEX SCHEMES TO ASIAN OPTION PRICING

We shall examine Asian option pricing in Chapter 23 where we discuss ADI and splitting methods. For the moment, let us accept that the two-factor PDE governing the option behaviour is given by:

$$-\frac{\partial u}{\partial t} + L_S u + L_I u = 0 \qquad (21.22)$$

where the elliptic and hyperbolic operators are given by

$$L_S u \equiv \tfrac{1}{2}\sigma^2 S^2 \frac{\partial^2 u}{\partial S^2} + rS\frac{\partial u}{\partial S} - ru$$

$$L_I u \equiv S\frac{\partial u}{\partial I} \qquad (21.23)$$

respectively. Of course, we could solve this problem using operator splitting (as we have seen in Chapters 19 and 20) but this has its own problems:

- The act of splitting introduces so-called splitting errors
- Numerical boundary conditions are difficult to approximate and have caused us many headaches in the past.

For these reasons the IMEX schemes are an improvement (Hundsdorfer and Verwer, 2003; Briani *et al.*, 2004). The motivation is to split a semi-discretised scheme into its stiff and non-stiff components. The former group usually corresponds to diffusion, and reaction–diffusion equations while the latter group corresponds to convection (advection) equations. Looking at the operators in (21.22) we see that we have two possible candidates for the IMEX scheme. To this end, let us discretise (21.22) in the S and I directions using centred differencing. The discrete schemes are then:

$$\frac{\mathrm{d}u_{ij}}{\mathrm{d}t} = \tilde{L}_S u_{ij} + \tilde{L}_I u_{ij} \qquad (21.24)$$

where the discrete operators are defined:

$$\tilde{L}_S u_{ij} \equiv \tfrac{1}{2}\sigma^2 S_i^2 D_+ D_-^{(S)} u_{ij} + rS_i D_0^{(S)} u_{ij}^{(S)} - rS_i$$

$$\tilde{L}_I u_{ij} \equiv S_i D_0^{(I)} u_{ij}^{(I)} \qquad (21.25)$$

We can write the semi-discrete schemes in the vector form (as in Hundsdorfer and Verwer, 2003, p. 383):

$$\frac{\mathrm{d}U}{\mathrm{d}t} = F[t, U(t)] = F_0[t, U(t)] + F_1[t, U(t)] \qquad (21.26)$$

where F_0 = non-stiff term (I direction)

F_1 = stiff term (S direction).

In fact the terms in (21.26) can be nonlinear in general but in the current situation they will be linear, in which case we get a simpler form of (21.26), namely:

$$\frac{dU}{dt} = A_1 U + A_2 U \tag{21.27}$$

Scheme (21.21) can then be used in this case.

We see IMEX methods as an active area of reseach in the coming years.

21.5 SUMMARY AND CONCLUSIONS

We have given an overview of a number of special problems in option pricing, for example applications where we must deal with systems of Black–Scholes equations. Furthermore, we also introduced some new schemes that compete with the current FDM 'establishment'. We feel that it is necessary to give these schemes some air space and we expect to see more development work in this area in the future.

Part V
Applying FDM to Multi-Factor
Instrument Pricing

22

Options with Stochastic Volatility: The Heston Model

22.1 INTRODUCTION AND OBJECTIVES

Until now we have assumed that the volatility is either constant (as in the original Black–Scholes formulation) or is some deterministic function of time and of the underlying assets. The Black–Scholes model has been successful in explaining stock option prices but is less robust in other areas such as foreign currency option pricing. In particular, since the model assumes that volatility is uncorrelated with spot returns it cannot capture important skewness effects.

In this chapter we examine a model that was proposed in Heston (1993). The original article was devoted to finding a closed-form solution for the price of a European call option on an asset that has stochastic volatility. Both the asset and the volatility are modelled by separate stochastic differential equations (SDEs). Based on these SDEs we describe the partial differential equation that models the behaviour of a contingent claim on the asset. We describe the boundary conditions and initial condition that, together with the PDE, describes a well-defined initial boundary value problem.

Since the PDE for the Heston model contains two factors and since it has cross derivatives we shall investigate the applicability of operator splitting schemes to solving this problem. We thus ignore ADI methods in this chapter. A further complication is that the boundary conditions associated with the Heston model can be complex (for example, in one case we have a first-order hyperbolic PDE in two space variables, in which case we have to devise finite difference schemes on the boundaries.

In this chapter we shall need all our PDE skills, and knowledge of FDM (splitting and exponential fitting), to devise good scheme for the Heston model.

22.2 AN INTRODUCTION TO ORNSTEIN–UHLENBECK PROCESSES

We start with some stochastics theory. Those readers for whom this material is known may wish to skip this section. We need three types of stochastic process

$$\{Y_t : t \geq 0\}$$

It is called

- *Stationary* if $\forall\, t_1 < t_2 < \cdots < t_N$ and $h > 0$, $(Y_{t_1}, Y_{t_2}, \ldots, Y_{t_N})$ and $(Y_{t_1+h}, \ldots Y_{t_N+h})$ are identically distributed, that is, time shifts leave joint probabilities unchanged
- *Gaussian* if $(Y_{t_1}, Y_{t_2}, \ldots, Y_{t_N})$ is multi-variate normally distributed
- *Markovian* if $P(Y_{t_N} \leq y \mid Y_{t_1}, Y_{t_2}, \ldots, Y_{t_N-1}) = P(Y_{t_N} \leq y \mid Y_{t_N-1})$, that is, the future is determined only by the present and not by the past.

A stochastic process is an Ornstein–Uhlenbeck (OU) process or a Gauss–Markov process if it is stationary, Gaussian, Markovian and continuous in probability (Uhlenbeck and Ornstein, 1930; Wang and Uhlenbeck, 1945). A fundamental theorem (see Doob, 1942) states that the stochastic process satisfies the following linear SDE:

$$dX_t = -\rho(X_t - \mu)\,dt + \sigma\,dW_t \tag{22.1}$$

where $\{W_t : t \geq 0\}$ is a Brownian motion with unit variance and ρ, μ and σ are constants.

Furthermore, we have the moments:

$$E(X_t) = \mu, \quad \text{Cov}(X_s, X_t) = \frac{\sigma^2}{2\rho}\,e^{-\rho|s-t|} \tag{22.2}$$

in the unconditional (strictly stationary) case and

$$E(X_t | X_0 = c) = \mu + (c - \mu)\,e^{-\rho t}$$

$$\text{Cov}(X_s, X_t | X_0 = c) = \frac{\sigma^2}{2\rho}(e^{-\rho|s-t|} - e^{-\rho(s+t)}) \tag{22.3}$$

in the conditional (asymptotically stationary) case, where X_0 is constant. The Brownian motion process is a special case of the Ornstein–Uhlenbeck process.

One final remark: let

$$f(x, t) \equiv \frac{d}{dx}P\,[X(t) \leq x] \tag{22.4}$$

be the probability density function of the OU process. Then this function satisfies the Fokker–Planck equation, namely:

$$\frac{\partial f}{\partial t} = \frac{\partial^2 f}{\partial x^2} + \frac{\partial}{\partial x}(xf) \tag{22.5}$$

(Øksendal 1998, p. 159). We shall see that OU processes are used in the Heston model.

22.3 STOCHASTIC DIFFERENTIAL EQUATIONS AND THE HESTON MODEL

Since there are two factors in the Heston model we need two SDEs. First, the spot asset price satisfies the SDE:

$$dS_t = \mu S_t\,dt + \sqrt{v(t)}S_t\,dW_t^{(1)} \tag{22.6}$$

where $S_t = $ spot price

$W_t^{(1)} = $ a Wiener process

$v(t) = $ variance

$\mu = $ (risk neutral) drift.

Second, the variance $v(t)$ satisfies an OU process defined by the SDE:

$$d\sqrt{v(t)} = -\beta\sqrt{v(t)}\,dt + \sigma\,dW_t^{(2)}$$

It can be shown that:

$$dv(t) = \kappa \left[\theta - v(t)\right] dt + \sigma \sqrt{v(t)} \, dW_t^{(2)} \tag{22.7}$$

where $\sigma =$ volatility of the volatility

$0 < \theta =$ long-term variance

$\theta < \kappa =$ rate of mean reversion

$W_t^{(2)} =$ a Wiener process and ρ is the correlation value.

The correlation between the two Wiener processes is given by:

$$dW_t^{(1)} dW_t^{(2)} = \rho \, dt \tag{22.8}$$

In general, an increase in ρ generates an asymmetry in the distribution while a change of volatility of variance σ results in a higher kurtosis. Finally (as discussed in Heston, 1993) the PDE for a contingent claim U is given by:

$$\frac{\partial U}{\partial t} + L_s U + L_v U + \rho \sigma v S \frac{\partial^2 U}{\partial S \partial v} = 0$$

where

$$L_s U \equiv \tfrac{1}{2} v S^2 \frac{\partial^2 U}{\partial S^2} + r S \frac{\partial U}{\partial S} - r U = 0$$

$$L_v U \equiv \tfrac{1}{2} \sigma^2 v \frac{\partial^2 U}{\partial v^2} + \{K \left[\theta - v(t)\right] - \lambda(S, v, t)\} \frac{\partial U}{\partial v} \tag{22.9}$$

and λ is the market price of volatility risk.

Let us pause to examine system (22.9) from a mathematical viewpoint. We see that the PDE is a convection–diffusion equation in two variables and there is a mixed derivative term appearing in the equation. From a PDE and FDM point of view, (22.9) is now well known.

In order to complete the jigsaw we need to define boundary conditions and a terminal condition for this PDE.

22.4 BOUNDARY CONDITIONS

We now discuss how to augment the PDE (22.9) by a variety of boundary conditions and let us focus on standard European options. In general, we must define boundary conditions at the following points:

$$S \to 0, \quad S \to \infty$$

$$v \to 0, \quad v \to \infty \tag{22.10}$$

Thus, we give some kind of boundary condition at each of these four points (intuitively, we need four conditions because integrating the second derivatives in S and v in the PDE (22.9) gives us four constants that can be found from the four conditions in conditions (22.10)). We now look at some particular examples of boundary conditions.

22.4.1   Standard European call option

This is the formulation as first mentioned in Heston (1993). When $S = 0$ we consider the call to be worthless; when S becomes very large we use a Neumann boundary condition which more or less is the same as a linearity boundary condition. When the volatility is 0 we assume that the PDE (22.9) is satisfied on the line $v = 0$; in this case some of the terms in (22.9) fall away. Finally, when v is very large we assume that the option behaves as a standard European option. Summarising, the boundary conditions become:

$$U(0, v, t) = 0 \quad (S = 0) \tag{22.11}$$

$$\frac{\partial U}{\partial S}(\infty, v, t) = 1 \quad (S = \infty) \tag{22.12}$$

$$\frac{\partial U}{\partial t} + rS\frac{\partial U}{\partial S} - rU + K\theta\frac{\partial U}{\partial v} = 0 \quad (v = 0) \tag{22.13}$$

$$U(S, \infty, t) = S \quad (v = \infty) \tag{22.14}$$

These conditions are easy to approximate numerically, with the exception of (22.13) which we must handle with kid gloves. The boundary conditions (22.11) to (22.14) are those as specified in Heston (1993). Other variations have also been discussed in the literature.

22.4.2   European put options

We define the boundary conditions for a put option (Ikonen and Toivanen, 2004):

$$U(0, v, t) = K \tag{22.15}$$

$$\frac{\partial U}{\partial S}(\infty, v, t) = 0 \tag{22.16}$$

$$U(S, 0, t) = \max(K - S, 0) \tag{22.17}$$

$$\frac{\partial U}{\partial v}(S, \infty, t) = 0 \tag{22.18}$$

These boundary conditions are easy to approximate as we have seen in previous chapters. Of course, we must use far-field conditions and decide between one-sided or two-sided approximations to the derivatives on the boundary. Having done that, we can then apply operator splitting methods to solve the problem.

22.4.3   Other kinds of boundary conditions

Another vision and interpretation on how to define boundary conditions for the Heston model is given in Zvan et al. (1998). They let the PDE be satisfied at the boundaries in three of the four cases. The full set is given by:

$$\frac{\partial U}{\partial t} - rU + L_v U = 0 \quad (S = 0) \tag{22.19}$$

$$\left.\begin{aligned} U &= S \text{ (call)} \\ U &= 0 \text{ (put)} \end{aligned}\right\} \quad (S \to \infty) \tag{22.20}$$

$$\frac{\partial U}{\partial t} + rS\frac{\partial U}{\partial S} - rU + K\theta\frac{\partial U}{\partial v} = 0 \quad (v \to 0) \tag{22.21}$$

$$\frac{\partial U}{\partial t} + \frac{1}{2}vS^2\frac{\partial^2 U}{\partial S^2} + rS\frac{\partial U}{\partial S} - rU = 0 \quad (v \to \infty) \tag{22.22}$$

As before, some of the boundary conditions (for example, equation (22.22)) may have an exact solution. If this is not possible we must resort to a finite difference scheme, for example. It is also possible to integrate barrier options into the Heston model (see Faulhaber, 2002).

22.5 USING FINITE DIFFERENCE SCHEMES: PROLOGUE

We have now set up the initial boundary value problem (IBVP) for the Heston model – that is, equations (22.9), (22.11), (22.12), (22.13) and (22.14) – in conjunction with the following initial condition (payoff function) for the call option:

$$U(S, v, 0) = \max{(S - K, 0)} \tag{22.23}$$

In order to reduce the scope we restrict our attention to splitting methods. We deal with the most challenging problems in some detail. In particular, the following issues deserve our attention:

- How to approximate the mixed derivative terms
- How to approximate the boundary condition (22.13); boundary conditions (22.11), (22.12) and (22.14) are easy at this stage in the game.

22.6 A DETAILED EXAMPLE

We now discuss the application of the splitting method to the Heston problem. For convenience, we concentrate on first-order accurate methods in the time direction, but the ideas can be extended to give second-order methods. In order to ease the burden of understanding and holding in short-term memory, a myriad of symbols and equations, we adopt some new notation. To this end, we define the operators:

$$L_S U \equiv A\frac{\partial^2 U}{\partial S^2} + B\frac{\partial U}{\partial S} + CU$$

$$L_v U \equiv D\frac{\partial^2 U}{\partial v^2} + E\frac{\partial U}{\partial v} \tag{22.24}$$

$$F \equiv \rho\sigma vS \quad \text{(coefficient of cross term)}$$

when the coefficients A, B, C, D, E and F have obvious meaning.

Formally, our splitting scheme is given by the following set of equations:

$$-\frac{\partial U}{\partial t} + L_S U + F\frac{\partial^2 U}{\partial S\,\partial v} = 0$$

$$-\frac{\partial U}{\partial t} + L_v U = 0 \tag{22.25}$$

Note: We are now using a forward equation in time in the respective directions. This is why there is a minus sign in front of the derivative with respect to t.

Furthermore, we approximate the elliptic operators in (22.24) by their finite difference equivalents:

$$
\begin{aligned}
\tilde{L}_S U_{ij}^n &= A_{ij}^n D_+ D_-^{(S)} U_{ij}^n + B_{ij}^n D_0^{(S)} U_{ij}^n + C_{ij}^n U_{ij}^n \\
\tilde{L}_v U_{ij}^n &= D_{ij}^n D_+ D_-^{(v)} U_{ij}^n + E_{ij}^n D_0^{(v)} U_{ij}^n
\end{aligned}
\tag{22.26}
$$

We are now ready to formulate the splitting scheme. The first leg calculates a solution at level $n + \frac{1}{2}$ given the solution at level n:

$$
-\frac{U_{ij}^{n+\frac{1}{2}} - U_{ij}^n}{k} + \tilde{L}_S U_{ij}^{n+\frac{1}{2}} + \frac{1}{2} F_{ij}^n D_0^{(S)} D_0^{(v)} U_{ij}^n = 0
\tag{22.27}
$$

with $n \geq 0$, $1 \leq i \leq I - 1$, $1 \leq j \leq J - 1$.

The second leg brings us from level $n + \frac{1}{2}$ to level $n + 1$:

$$
-\frac{U_{ij}^{n+1} - U_{ij}^{n+\frac{1}{2}}}{k} + \tilde{L}_v U_{ij}^{n+1} + \frac{1}{2} F_{ij}^n D_O^{(S)} D_0^{(v)} U_{ij}^{n+1/2} = 0
\tag{22.28}
$$

with $n \geq 0$, $1 \leq i \leq I - 1$, $1 \leq j \leq J - 1$.

Please note how we have approximated the mixed derivative terms as advocated in Yanenko (1971), namely in an explicit way.

We now come to the approximation of the boundary conditions for this problem. We concentrate on condition (22.13) because it is new and the other conditions have already been discussed in previous chapters. We write (22.13) in the more convenient form:

$$
-\frac{\partial U}{\partial t} + \alpha \frac{\partial U}{\partial S} + \beta \frac{\partial U}{\partial v} + bU = 0 \quad (v = 0)
\tag{22.29}
$$

where the new coefficients are defined by:

$$
\begin{aligned}
\alpha &= rS, & \alpha &> 0 \\
b &= -r, & b &< 0 \\
\beta &= K\theta, & \beta &> 0
\end{aligned}
$$

We mention that the signs of the coefficients α and β determine where the information in the system is coming from. This is shown in Figure 22.1 for the four different cases. Our current situation corresponds to case (a). Thus, information at some node (i, j) is coming from 'upwind' nodes such as $(i + 1, i)$, $(i, j + 1)$ and $(i + 1, j + 1)$, for example. This regime must be mirrored by the finite difference schemes for (22.13). We thus choose the correct scheme in space and we can choose between the following kinds of time marching:

- Explicit Euler scheme (conditionally stable)
- Implicit Euler (unconditionally stable).

Of course, we could take time-averaging schemes (Crank–Nicolson) to produce second-order accuracy, but this is outside the scope of this chapter.

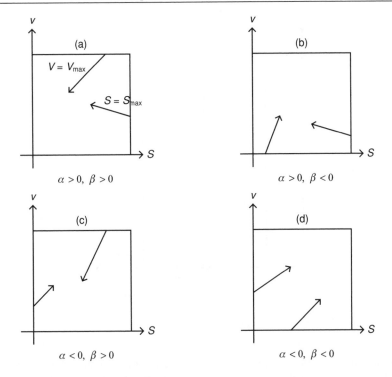

Figure 22.1 Direction of information flow (2d case)

Looking at Figure 22.2 we see that we must approximate (22.13) when $j = 0$. Taking into account the upwinding effects we then propose the following scheme:

$$-\frac{U_{i,0}^{n+1} - U_{i,0}^n}{k} + \alpha_{i,0}\frac{U_{i+1,0}^n - U_{i,0}^n}{h_1} + \beta_{i,0}\frac{U_{i,1}^n - U_{i,0}^n}{h_2} + bU_{i,0}^n = 0 \qquad (22.30)$$

Some arithmetic and rearranging shows that:

$$U_{i,0}^{n+1} = (1 - \lambda_1 - \lambda_2 + bk)U_{i,0}^n + \lambda_1 U_{i+1,0}^n + \lambda_2 U_{i,1}^n \qquad (22.31)$$

where

$$\lambda_1 = \frac{\alpha_{i,0}k}{h_1} > 0 \quad \text{and} \quad \lambda_2 = \frac{\beta_{i,0}k}{h_2} > 0$$

Appealing to the discrete maximum principle by examining the right-hand side of equation (22.31) we know that the values at level n and at the nodes $(i, 1)$ and $(i + 1, 0)$ are non-negative; we also know that there is just one sufficient condition to make the right-hand side positive, namely (taking $b = 0$ for convenience):

$$1 - \lambda_1 - \lambda_2 \geq 0 \quad \text{or} \quad k \leq \frac{1}{\alpha/h_1 + \beta/h_2} \qquad (22.32)$$

When $b \neq 0$ we get a slightly different estimate.

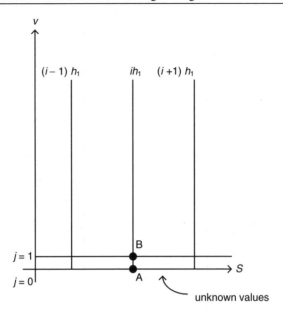

Figure 22.2 Approximating on the boundary

This is the same conditions as in Thomas (1998). Thus, the scheme (22.30) is conditionally stable and this allows us to define what is essentially the Dirichlet boundary conditions on $v = 0$.

We now consider the implicit Euler scheme. In space it is exactly the same as (22.31) except that readings are taken at time level $n + 1$:

$$-\frac{U_{i,0}^{n+1} - U_{i,0}^{n}}{k} + \alpha_{i,0}\frac{U_{i+1,0}^{n+1} - U_{i,0}^{n+1}}{h_1} + \beta_{i,0}\frac{U_{i,1}^{n+1} - U_{i,0}^{n+1}}{h_2} + bU_{i,0}^{n+1} = 0 \quad (22.33)$$

Some arithmetic shows that:

$$-U_{i,0}^{n+1} + U_{i,0}^{n} + \lambda_1\left(U_{i+1,0}^{n+1} - U_{i,0}^{n+1}\right) + \lambda_2\left(U_{i,1}^{n+1} - U_{i,0}^{n}\right) + bkU_{i,0}^{n+1} = 0$$

and thus

$$U_{i,0}^{n+1} = \frac{U_{i,0}^{n} + \lambda_1 U_{i+1,0}^{n+1} + \lambda_2 U_{i,1}^{n+1}}{1 + \lambda_1 + \lambda_2 - bk} \quad (22.34)$$

Appealing to the maximum principle and monotonicity, we see that the solution at time level $n + 1$ is positive because all data on the right-hand side of (22.34) is positive (notice that $b < 0$). Summarising, we solve this problem using splitting and incorporating the appropriate boundary conditions in S and v.

22.7 SUMMARY AND CONCLUSIONS

We have discussed the Heston stochastic model in this chapter. First, it addresses a non-trivial pricing problem, namely an option pricing problem with stochastic volatility. We formulate this model as a parabolic initial boundary value problem. The PDE part of the problem contains two independent factors (the underlying S and the volatility v) as well as a mixed derivative in S and v that models correlation effects. Furthermore, we experience a mixture of Dirichlet, Neumann and other boundary conditions that describe the solution.

We apply the operator splitting method to approximate the Heston model and we employ schemes that are first order in space and time. On one boundary, on which a first-order, two-factor hyperbolic problem is defined, we discuss both explicit-in-time and implicit-in-time upwinding schemes. Having done that, we can assemble the system of equations that we then solve by standard matrix techniques at each time level.

The results in this chapter made extensive use of the finite difference schemes from previous chapters.

Finite Difference Methods for Asian Options and other 'Mixed' Problems

23.1 INTRODUCTION AND OBJECTIVES

In this short chapter we introduce the partial differential equations and the corresponding initial boundary value problems that model Asian options. An Asian option is a contract that gives the holder the right to buy an asset based on its average price over some prescribed period of time (Wilmott *et al.*, 1993). The PDE formulation is a two-factor model; the first independent variable is the underlying asset while the second variable is an average of the underlying asset over a prescribed period.

Our interest in Asian options lies in determining which finite difference schemes are appropriate for this kind of problem. In general, the PDE for an Asian option consists of two parts: the first part is based on the underlying S and is a standard convection–diffusion equation (the standard one-factor Black Scholes model), while the second part (based on the continuously sampled arithmetic average I or A) is a first-order hyperbolic equation (thus containing no diffusion term) and hence we need only one boundary condition for this direction (Ingersoll, 1987).

We conclude this chapter with a short discussion of a Cheyette two-factor interest rate model (Cheyette, 1992; Andreasen, 2001). The PDE models for these problems are similar in structure to the PDE models for Asian options because they have a random part (convection–diffusion) and a deterministic part (modelled as a first-order hyperbolic PDE).

We discuss only the most fundamental issues pertaining to Asian options in this chapter. We do not include topics such as discrete monitoring or early exercise features, for example.

23.2 AN INTRODUCTION TO ASIAN OPTIONS

In general we can sample either continuously or discretely. The first alternative is to take the continuously sampled arithmetic average of the underlying asset in some time interval, namely:

$$I = I(t) = \int_0^t S(\tau)\,d\tau \tag{23.1}$$

The other continuous formulation is given by:

$$A(t) = \frac{I(t)}{t} = \frac{1}{t}\int_0^t S(\tau)\,d\tau \tag{23.2}$$

The PDE that models the Asian option is given by:

$$\frac{\partial V}{\partial t} + \tfrac{1}{2}\sigma^2 S^2 \frac{\partial^2 V}{\partial S^2} + rS\frac{\partial V}{\partial S} + S\frac{\partial V}{\partial I} - rV = 0 \tag{23.3}$$

while in the second case the PDE is given by:

$$\frac{\partial V}{\partial t} + \tfrac{1}{2}\sigma^2 S^2 \frac{\partial^2 V}{\partial S^2} + rS\frac{\partial V}{\partial S} + \frac{1}{t}(S - A)\frac{\partial V}{\partial A} - rV = 0 \tag{23.4}$$

Both PDEs have the same structure from a mathematical point of view: informally we can write:

Asian PDE == one-factor Black–Scholes PDE + First-order hyperbolic PDE

In both cases the first-order PDE component in equations (23.3) and (23.4) can be written in the generic form:

$$\frac{\partial V}{\partial t} + a(S, y, t)\frac{\partial V}{\partial y} = 0 \quad (y = I \text{ or } A) \tag{23.5}$$

We have studied this equation in great detail in this book. We know that it is a wave equation and we know what the boundary condition should be, as a function of the sign of the coefficient $a(S, y, t)$. In particular, we have proposed and analysed robust and accurate finite difference schemes for solving equations such as (23.5).

23.3 MY FIRST PDE FORMULATION

We examine the PDE (23.3) and we consider the so-called similarity reduction technique by defining a new variable R as $R = I/S$ and the function H by (Wilmott *et al.*, 1993):

$$V(S, R, t) = SH(R, t)$$

Please note that we are now using the engineer's t variable in this and future sections in this chapter!

You can check that the function H satisfies the following PDE:

$$-\frac{\partial H}{\partial t} + \tfrac{1}{2}\sigma^2 R^2 \frac{\partial^2 H}{\partial R^2} + (1 - rR)\frac{\partial H}{\partial R} = 0 \tag{23.6}$$

The initial/terminal condition for H is now:

$$H(R, 0) = \frac{V(S, R, 0)}{S(0)} = g(S(0), I(0)) \tag{23.7}$$

where g is some function.

Now for the tricky part. At large values of R the value of H is zero:

$$\lim_{R \to \infty} H(R, t) = 0 \tag{23.8}$$

while when $R = 0$ the PDE degenerates into the first-order hyperbolic PDE:

$$-\frac{\partial H}{\partial t} + \frac{\partial H}{\partial R} = 0 \tag{23.9}$$

We now discuss how to find an approximation to the initial boundary value problem defined by equations (23.6), (23.7), (23.8) and (23.9). In this case we use implicit Euler in time and some kind of centred difference scheme (for example, the standard scheme or exponential fitting) in the R direction. This gives the difference scheme for equation (23.6):

$$-\frac{H_j^{n+1} - H_j^n}{k} + L_k^h H_j^{n+1} = 0, \quad 1 \le j \le J - 1, \quad n \ge 0 \tag{23.10}$$

where L_k^h is some approximation to the time-independent terms in (23.6).

We must define a far-field point and the boundary condition at this point is:

$$H_J^n = 0, \quad n \geq 0 \tag{23.11}$$

When $R = 0$ we have to take upwinding/downwinding into consideration. Then:

$$-\frac{H_0^{n+1} - H_0^n}{k} + \frac{H_1^{n+1} - H_0^{n+1}}{h} = 0, \quad n \geq 0 \tag{23.12}$$

(It might be worth investigating the possibility of finding an exact solution to (23.9) instead of using (23.12).) Finally, the initial condition is given by:

$$H_j^0 = g(S_j, I_j), \quad 1 \leq j \leq J - 1 \tag{23.13}$$

We can now formulate this problem as a matrix system at each time level:

$$\left.\begin{aligned}
AU^{n+1} = F^n, \quad n \geq 0, \\
U^0 \text{ given by equation (23.13)}
\end{aligned}\right\} \tag{23.14}$$

where $U^n = {}^t(H_0^n, \ldots, H_{J-1}^n)$ and A is a positive-definite matrix and hence this problem has a unique solution.

23.4   USING OPERATOR SPLITTING METHODS

It may not always be possible to find a similarity solution and we then must devise other methods. To this end, we have already discussed operator splitting methods and their applications to two-factor and multi-factor problems. In general, the PDE in each separate dimension was of convection–diffusion type. In the case of the Asian option PDE, however, the PDE in the I (or A) direction is now a first-order hyperbolic PDE. Formally, the splitting of the original PDE in equation (23.3) takes the form:

$$-\frac{\partial V}{\partial t} + \frac{1}{2}\sigma^2 S^2 \frac{\partial^2 V}{\partial S^2} + rS\frac{\partial V}{\partial S} - rV = 0 \tag{23.15a}$$

$$-\frac{\partial V}{\partial t} + S\frac{\partial V}{\partial I} = 0 \tag{23.15b}$$

We thus need to approximate both of these PDEs using the finite difference method. In general, we can choose between explicit and implicit time-marching in time in each PDE in (23.15). Futhermore, in the S and I directions we can choose from a variety of 'spatial' discretisations; for example, for (23.15a) we can choose from:

- Traditional centred differencing
- Duffy exponentially fitted schemes
- Reduce (23.15a) to a first-order system and approximate V and its delta to second-order accuracy (for example, using the Keller box scheme (Keller, 1971)).

In the I direction there are also many suitable finite difference schemes, for example:

- Upwinding/downwinding schemes
- Centred difference schemes
- Other schemes (for example, Lax–Wendroff scheme)
- The Method of Characteristics (MOC)
- Analytical solution.

The combination of the discretisation types for equations (23.15) will determine the stability and accuracy of the resulting schemes. For example, some schemes are unconditionally stable, some are conditionally stable while other schemes are unconditionally unstable. These issues have already been discussed in this book. Furthermore, first-order or second-order accuracy in any of the directions S, I or t is possible.

In order to focus on one specific finite difference scheme, let us examine the partial differential equation (23.3) in conjunction with the boundary conditions (two for the S direction and one for the I direction!), for example:

$$V(0, I, t) = g_0(I, t), \ 0 < I < I_M$$
$$V(S_M, I, t) = g_1(I, t), \ 0 < I < I_M \tag{23.16}$$
$$V(S, I_M, t) = h_0(S, t), \ 0 < S < S_M$$

where S_M, I_M are far-field values in the S and I directions respectively and g_o, g and h_0 are known functions along with some payoff function that we describe as the initial condition:

$$V(S, I, 0) = V_0(S, I) \tag{23.17}$$

We now propose using the exponentially fitted scheme with implicit Euler for the approximation of (23.15a) (we know that this scheme is uniformly accurate to first order in time and space) while we take an upwinding scheme in I and implicit Euler in time in (23.15b) (this scheme is first-order accurate in I and t). Finally, splitting the PDE (23.3) into two separate PDEs also introduces a splitting error. The proposed schemes are thus:

$$-\frac{\tilde{V}_{ij} - V_{ij}^n}{k} + L_k^h \tilde{V}_{ij} = 0, \quad 1 \le i \le I - 1, \quad j \text{ fixed} \tag{23.18a}$$

$$-\frac{V_{ij}^{n+1} - \tilde{V}_{ij}}{k} + S_i \frac{V_{i,j+1}^{n+1} - V_{ij}^{n+1}}{h} = 0, \quad 1 \le j \le J - 1, \quad i \text{ fixed} \tag{23.18b}$$

while the discrete boundary conditions (corresponding to (23.16)) at each time level are:

$$V_{0j}^n = g_0(I_j, t_n), \ \ 0 \le j \le J$$
$$V_{Ij}^n = g_1(I_j, t_n), \ \ 0 \le j \le J \tag{23.19}$$
$$V_{iJ}^n = h_0(S_i, t_n), \ \ 0 \le i \le I$$

where g_0, g_1 and h_0 are known functions.

Finally, the discrete initial conditions (corresponding to (23.17)) are:

$$V_{ij}^0 = V_0(S_i, I_j) \tag{23.20}$$

Other operator splitting schemes can be proposed if, for example, you wish to get second-order accuracy. The example in this section is of use in itself but it also gives guidelines on applying different finite difference schemes to Asian option problems.

23.4.1   For sake of completeness: ADI methods for Asian option PDEs

In Duffy (2004) we discussed the applicability of the ADI method for Asian option PDEs. We used centred differences to approximate all derivatives, including the first-order derivative in I. Be warned! We must define numerical boundary conditions with this scheme and avoiding boundary errors is non-trivial (for a discussion of these problems, see Thomas, 1999). We pose the PDE (23.3) in more neutral and generic form:

$$-c\frac{\partial V}{\partial t} + \epsilon\frac{\partial^2 V}{\partial S^2} + a\frac{\partial V}{\partial S} + \alpha\frac{\partial V}{\partial I} - bV = f \tag{23.21}$$

With ADI, as we already know, we march from time level n to time level $n + \frac{1}{2}$ and then from time level $n + \frac{1}{2}$ to time level $n + 1$. In this case we use exponential fitting in all space variables and implicit Euler in time. The first leg is given by the scheme:

$$-c_{ij}^{n+\frac{1}{2}}\frac{V_{ij}^{n+\frac{1}{2}} - V_{ij}^{n}}{\frac{1}{2}k} + \sigma_{ij}^{n+\frac{1}{2}}\frac{V_{i+1j}^{n+\frac{1}{2}} - 2V_{ij}^{n+\frac{1}{2}} + V_{i-1j}^{n+\frac{1}{2}}}{h^2}$$

$$+ a_{ij}^{n+\frac{1}{2}}\frac{V_{i+1j}^{n+\frac{1}{2}} - V_{i-1j}^{n+\frac{1}{2}}}{2h} + \alpha_{ij}^{n+\frac{1}{2}}\frac{V_{ij+1}^{n} - V_{ij-1}^{n}}{2m}$$

$$- b_{ij}^{n+\frac{1}{2}}V_{ij}^{n+\frac{1}{2}} = f_{ij}^{n+\frac{1}{2}} \tag{23.22}$$

The second leg is given by:

$$-c_{ij}^{n+1}\frac{V_{ij}^{n+1} - V_{ij}^{n+\frac{1}{2}}}{\frac{1}{2}k} + \sigma_{ij}^{n+1}\frac{V_{i+1j}^{n+\frac{1}{2}} - 2V_{ij}^{n+\frac{1}{2}} + V_{i-1j}^{n+\frac{1}{2}}}{h^2}$$

$$+ a_{ij}^{n+1}\frac{V_{i+1j}^{n+\frac{1}{2}} - V_{i-1j}^{n+\frac{1}{2}}}{2h} + \alpha_{ij}^{n+1}\frac{V_{ij+1}^{n+1} - V_{ij-1}^{n+1}}{2m}$$

$$- b_{ij}^{n+1}V_{ij}^{n+\frac{1}{2}} = f_{ij}^{n+1} \tag{23.23}$$

Each of these legs can be solved using LU decomposition, as shown in Duffy (2004).

We prefer operator splitting to ADI mainly because it is conceptually easier to understand and is easier to program. It is computationally somewhat more efficient than ADI because there are less terms to evaluate at each leg. Finally we have seen that it is giving better results than ADI for complex problems.

23.5   CHEYETTE INTEREST MODELS

An interesting example is the problem of modelling the volatility structure of the continuously compounded forward rates in the Heath, Jarrow, Morton (HJM) framework (Andreasen, 2001; Cheyette, 1992). In Andreasen (2001) the author produces the PDE:

$$\frac{\partial V}{\partial t} + \frac{1}{2}\eta^2\frac{\partial^2 V}{\partial x^2} + (-Kx + y)\frac{\partial V}{\partial x} + (\eta^2 - 2Ky)\frac{\partial V}{\partial y} - rV = 0 \tag{23.24}$$

We remark that this equation has the same basic format as the PDE (23.3). We do not go into the financial relevance of the parameters in (23.24).

Defining the operators:

$$L_x V \equiv \tfrac{1}{2}\eta^2 \frac{\partial^2 V}{\partial x^2} + (-Kx + y)\frac{\partial V}{\partial x} - rV$$

$$L_y V \equiv (\eta^2 - 2Ky)\frac{\partial V}{\partial y} \tag{23.25}$$

we can then write the PDE (23.24) in the form:

$$\frac{\partial V}{\partial t} + L_x V + L_y V = 0 \tag{23.26}$$

Andreasen takes an ADI scheme to solve (23.26). This scheme is an adaption of the standard ADI scheme that does not perform well due to spurious oscillations. Andreasen employs an ADI scheme (with five points in the discretisation) that is solved using tridiagonal and band martrix solvers at each time level. An alternative to this approach is to employ a splitting method based on the formal splitting:

$$\frac{\partial V}{\partial t} + L_x V = 0$$

$$\frac{\partial V}{\partial t} + L_y V = 0 \tag{23.27}$$

Stable and second-order accurate schemes can now be produced for this problem without resorting to the somewhat more difficult five-point schemes as discussed in Andreasen (2001).

23.6   NEW DEVELOPMENTS

Both ADI and splitting are very popular methods that we can use to partition a PDE into simpler PDEs. They are called dimension-splitting methods. In this section we discuss another method that we call the corrected operator splitting (COS) method. The basic assumption is that we separate the convection/advection and the diffusion/reaction terms in the Black–Scholes equations. The method can be applied to both one-factor and multi-factor problems and we give a short summary here (see Karlsen, 2003). The authors model nonlinear problems whose solutions have sharp fronts.

Let us start with the one-factor model (23.6). Conceptually, the COS is defined by:

$$L_1 H \equiv -\frac{\partial H}{\partial t} + b\frac{\partial H}{\partial R} = 0 \quad \text{(convection)} \tag{23.28a}$$

$$L_2 H \equiv -\frac{\partial H}{\partial t} + a\frac{\partial^2 H}{\partial R^2} = 0 \quad \text{(diffusion)} \tag{23.28b}$$

In short, we approximate (23.28) by marching from n to $n + 1$ by the introduction of an intermediate step

$$L_1 H = 0, \quad H(x, 0) = H^n(x) \tag{23.29a}$$

$$L_2 H = 0, \quad H(x, 0) = H^{n+\frac{1}{3}}(x) \tag{23.29b}$$

where $H^{n+\frac{1}{3}}$ is the solution of (22.28a)).

The method can be applied to problems involving several factors. Again, we refer to Karlsen (2003). This topic could be pursued as a project in the future.

23.7 SUMMARY AND CONCLUSIONS

We have given a short introduction to modelling Asian options using a PDE formulation. These two-factor problems present their own numerical challenges because the diffusion term is missing in one of the dimensions. This leads to a first-order hyperbolic PDE which can be approximated using upwinding or downwinding correctly if we wish to get accurate results. We discuss operator splitting and ADI methods that solve the initial boundary value problems for continuously monitored Asian options.

24

Multi-Asset Options

24.1 INTRODUCTION AND OBJECTIVES

In this chapter we give an introduction to option problems with two or more correlated under-lyings. These are the so-called correlated options or multi-asset options. This chapter focuses on producing finite difference schemes for these problems, not using ADI or splitting (where an n-dimensional problem is partitioned into a sequence of one-dimensional problems) but instead solving a system of equations 'in all space variables' simultaneously. Splitting meth-ods, for example, are ideally suited to these problems but we have discussed these already. In general, matrix iterative schemes are needed because of the size of the matrices involved. For large systems, direct methods such as *LU* decomposition are inefficient and in this chapter we show how iterative methods work by explaining the point Jacobian and line Jacobian methods, although it is a good idea to investigate the Gauss–Seidel and successive over-relaxation (SOR) methods (see Thomas, 1999).

One of the goals of this chapter is to provide a setting so that financial models for correla-tion options can be posed and then mapped to a PDE formulation. We then approximate the corresponding initial boundary value problem using finite differences. Finally, we solve the discrete sets of equations using matrix iterative methods.

We note that we can easily apply the techniques of Chapters 19 and 20 (ADI and operator splitting methods) to finding approximations to the solution of correlation options problems, but this is outside the scope of this chapter. We reiterate that splitting methods are good at approximating the mixed derivative terms.

The application of finite difference schemes to n-factor option problems is in its infancy, especially with $n \geq 3$.

24.2 A TAXONOMY OF MULTI-ASSET OPTIONS

In this section we give an overview of some kinds of options that depend on two or more underlying assets. These are called correlation options in general (see Zhang, 1998, for a comprehensive introduction). Our interest in these options is to cast them in PDE form. In particular, we must define the payoff function, boundary conditions and the coefficients of the PDE. We focus on the following specific types:

- Exchange options
- Rainbow options
- Basket options
- Best/worst options
- Quotient options
- Foreign exchange options
- Quanto options
- Spread options

- Dual-strike options
- Out-performance options.

Even though many of these option problems have analytical solutions (as discussed in Zhang, 1998) we wish to approximate them using the finite difference method.

FDM is more flexible because it allows a wider range of parameters than the examples in Zhang (1998). Secondly, FDM is easier to implement than closed form solutions.

We give a basic review of statistics. First, the mean or mathematical expectation of a continuous random variable X is defined as:

$$E(X) = \int_{-\infty}^{\infty} x f(x) \, dx \qquad (24.1)$$

where $f(x)$ is the density function of the random variable. The variance of the random variable is defined as:

$$\text{Var}(X) = E\left\{ [X - E(X)]^2 \right\} = \int_{-\infty}^{\infty} [x - E(X)]^2 f(x) \, dx \qquad (24.2)$$

The variance is always non-negative; in particular, for a deterministic variable it is zero. The standard deviation is defined as the square root of the variance:

$$\sigma = \sqrt{\text{Var}(X)} \qquad (24.3)$$

The covariance between two random variables X and Y is defined as:

$$\text{Cov}(X, Y) = E\left[X - E(X) \right] \left[Y - E(Y) \right]$$

$$= \int_{-\infty}^{\infty} \int_{-\infty}^{\infty} [x - E(X)] [y - E(Y)] \, g(x, y) \, dx \, dy \qquad (24.4)$$

where $g(x, y)$ is the so-called joint density function of the variables X and Y. In general, variance is a special case of covariance, in particular $\text{Var}(X) = \text{Cov}(X, X)$. Another way to express the covariance is:

$$\text{Cov}(X, Y) = E[XY] - [E(X)][E(Y)] \qquad (24.5)$$

In general, covariance Cov can be negative, zero or positive.

We define the correlation coefficient ρ between X and Y by;

$$\rho = \frac{\text{Cov}(X, Y)}{\sqrt{\text{Var}(X)} \sqrt{\text{Var}(Y)}} = \frac{\text{Cov}(X, Y)}{\sigma_x \sigma_y} \qquad (24.6)$$

This factor can be negative, zero or positive.

If ρ is zero we say that X and Y are uncorrelated, while if it is positive or negative they are said to be positively or negatively correlated, respectively.

We now look at the stochastic differential equations for correlation options. For convenience we examine an option with two underlying assets (Zhang, 1998). The SDE for the underlying price uses the standard geometric Brownian motion and is given by:

$$dI_j = (\mu_j - g_j) I_j \, dt + \sigma_j I_j \, dW_j(t), \quad j = 1, 2 \qquad (24.7)$$

where W_j = standard Gauss–Wiener process, $j = 1, 2$

μ_j = instantaneous mean of asset j

σ_j = standard deviation of asset j or of index j

g_j = payout rate of asset j.

We can show that the solution of this SDE is given by (Karatzas and Shreve, 1991):

$$I_j(\tau) = I_j \exp\left[(\mu_j - g_j - \tfrac{1}{2}\sigma_j^2)\tau + \sigma_j W_j(\tau)\right], \quad j = 1, 2 \tag{24.8}$$

where I_j = current price of asset, $j = 1, 2$.

We now carry out some change of variables as follows:

$$x = \ln[I_1(\tau)/I_1]$$

$$y = \ln[I_2(\tau)/I_2]$$

$$\mu_x = -g_1 - \sigma_1^2/2$$

$$\mu_y = -g_2 - \sigma_2^2/2$$

$$\sigma_x^2 = \sigma_1^2 \tau$$

$$\sigma_y^2 = \sigma_2^2 \tau$$

Here $\tau = T - t$, where T is the maturity date of the option and t is the current time. Furthermore, I_1 and I_2 are the current prices of the assets.

Now we define the joint density function by:

$$f(x, y) = \frac{1}{2\pi \sigma_x \sigma_y \sqrt{1 - \rho^2}} \exp\left(-\frac{u^2 - 2\rho u v + v^2}{2(1 - \rho^2)}\right) \tag{24.9}$$

where

$$u = \frac{x - \mu_x}{\sigma_x} \quad \text{and} \quad v = \frac{y - \mu_y}{\sigma_y}$$

Finally, this can be written in either the form:

$$f(x, y) = f(y)f(x|y) \tag{24.10}$$

where

$$f(y) = \frac{1}{\sigma_y \sqrt{2\pi}} \exp\left(-\frac{v^2}{2}\right)$$

and

$$f(x|y) = \frac{1}{\sigma_x \sqrt{2\pi}\sqrt{1 - \rho^2}} \exp\left(\frac{-(u - \rho v)^2}{2(1 - \rho^2)}\right)$$

or in the form:

$$f(x, y) = f(x)f(y|x) \tag{24.11}$$

where

$$f(x) = \frac{1}{\sigma_x \sqrt{2\pi}} \exp\left(-\frac{u^2}{2}\right)$$

and

$$f(y|x) = \frac{1}{\sigma_y \sqrt{2\pi}\sqrt{1-\rho^2}} \exp\left(\frac{-(v-\rho u)^2}{2(1-\rho^2)}\right)$$

The added value of the bivariate density functions in (24.10) and (24.11) is that they are used to derive pricing formulae for many correlation options. In particular, it is possible to derive closed form solutions for European options, but American options are more problematic. We shall have mixed derivatives in the Black–Scholes partial differential equation, for example in the case of a two-factor model:

$$\rho_{ij}\sigma_i\sigma_j I_i I_j \frac{\partial^2 C}{\partial I_i \partial I_j} \tag{24.12}$$

where ρ_{ij} is a correlation coefficient between asset i and asset j.

As always, we must approximate these terms using finite differences. This problem has been discussed in detail in Chapters 19 and 20, and as we have already seen, we know that ADI schemes are less suitable than operator splitting schemes, especially in the presence of these mixed derivatives.

In the following discussion we assume that all options are European and that the maturity date is given by the symbol T. Furthermore, we assume that the underlying assets satisfy the SDEs in equation (24.7). In many of the examples, we shall assume that $n = 2$, that is some kind of two-factor systems that can be modelled effectively by finite difference schemes.

In the following sub-sections we concentrate on the following issues:

- The financial relevance
- The payoff function
- The domain of integration (i.e. the ranges that the underlying assets take).

In general, the integration domain is a source of complexity when pricing correlation options, both analytically and numerically. We shall need this information later when we map the financial model to the corresponding partial differential formulation. It is then a straightforward process.

24.2.1 Exchange options

An exchange option is one that gives the holder the right to exchange one asset for another. This implies a two-factor problem, of course. At maturity, the holder is entitled to receive one underlying asset in return for paying for the other underlying asset. An exchange option is a correlation option. The underlying assets can be in the same or different asset classes. An asset class is a specific category of assets or investments. Assets in the same class exhibit similar characteristics, for example the same business sector. The payoff function is given by:

$$\text{payoff} = \max[I_1(T) - I_2(T), 0] \tag{24.13}$$

This payoff allows us to exchange the second asset for the first asset. It is equivalent to a vanilla option if we use the strike price K instead of the second asset; we can thus view it as

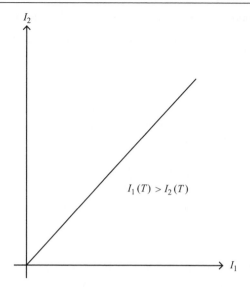

$$I_1(T) > I_2(T)$$

Figure 24.1   Integration domain for exchange option

a call option written in the first asset where the strike price is the future price of the second asset. Alternatively, we can view the exchange option as a put option where the strike price K is the same as the future price of the first option.

Expression (24.13) can be written in the following 'more readable' version:

$$\max(I_1(T) - I_2(T), 0) = \max[I_1(T), I_2(T)] - I_2(T)$$

$$\max(I_1(T) - I_2(T), 0) = I_1(T) - \min[I_1(T), I_2(T)]$$

The reader can check that these are indeed equivalent; the last two expressions are used to price the better or worse of two underlying risky assets. In general, exchange options are the simplest kind of correlation option because their integration domain is simple. This is shown in Figure 24.1. In this case the domain is where the exchange option has a positive value. In finite difference terms, we must solve the problem on a triangle.

24.2.2   Rainbow options

A good example of a rainbow option is one that is written on the maximum or minimum of two assets or indices. The payoff function on the maximum is given by:

$$\text{payoff} = \max \{w \max[I_1(T), I_2(T)] - wK, 0\} \tag{24.14}$$

where $w = +1$ for a call or -1 for a put.

Similarly, the payoff for a two-colour rainbow option on the minimum of two assets is given by:

$$\text{payoff} = \max \{w \min[I_1(T), I_2(T)] - wK, 0\} \tag{24.15}$$

The payoff for an option on the maximum of $n \geq 2$ underlying assets is:

$$\text{payoff} = \max \{w \max[I_1(T), \ldots, I_n(T)] - wK, 0\}$$

24.2.3 Basket options

Options written on baskets of risky assets can be used by portfolio managers to hedge the risks of their portfolios (Zhang, 1998). The most popular basket options are based on currencies and commodities. A basket option is defined as:

$$I(\tau) = \sum_{j=1}^{n} w_j I_j(\tau) \qquad (24.16)$$

where $w_j = $ total investment in asset j (as a percentage)

$I_j(\tau) = $ price of jth asset

and $\sum_{j=1}^{n} w_j = 1$.

An example would be a portfolio of value-weighted indices; in this case the baskets consist of assets with weights proportional to their market values. The payoff of a basket based on formula (24.16) is given by:

$$\text{payoff} = \max\{w[I(T) - K], 0\} \qquad (24.17)$$

where K is the exercise price of the option and w is as in equation (24.14). We now take an example of a two-basket option. In this case we have two weights denoted by:

$$a = w_1 > 0 \quad \text{and} \quad b = w_2 > 0$$

The domain of integration for this kind of two-asset option is shown in Figure 24.2. In general, the sign of the weights will determine the slope of the domain of integration.

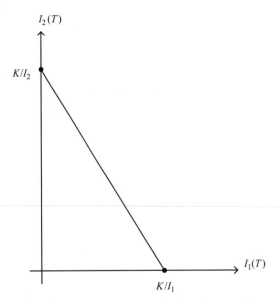

Figure 24.2   Integration domain for two-asset basket option

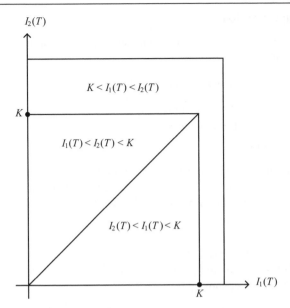

Figure 24.3 Integration domain for an option paying best of two assets

24.2.4 The best and worst

An option that pays the best (or worst) of two asset entities grants the holder the right to receive the maximum (or minimum) of the two underlying assets at maturity (Stulz, 1982). The payoff of an option paying the best and cash or the worst and cash are given by the following formulae:

$$\text{payoff} = \max c(T) = \max[I_1(T), I_2(T), K]$$
$$\text{payoff} = \min c(T) = \min[I_1(T), I_2(T), K]$$
(24.18)

where the constant K is a pre-specified amount of cash. The integration domain for an option on two assets without any cash payment is shown in Figure 24.3.

24.2.5 Quotient options

A quotient option (also called a ratio option) is one that is written on the ratio of two underlying asset prices, indices or other quantities. They take advantage of the relative performance of two assets, markets or portfolios. They are used to compare the relative performance of two assets.

The payoff function is given by:

$$\text{payoff} = \max\left[w\frac{I_1(T)}{I_2(T)} - wK, 0\right]$$
(24.19)

or equivalently as:

$$\text{payoff} = \max\left[w\frac{I_2(T)}{I_1(T)} - wK, 0\right]$$
(24.20)

where K is the strike price of the option. The integration domain is the area under the line starting from the origin with slope K.

24.2.6   Foreign equity options

These are options written on foreign equity with strike price in foreign currency. The payoff is given by the formula:

$$\text{payoff} = \max\left[wI_1(T) - wK_f, 0\right] \tag{24.21}$$

where $I_1(T) =$ foreign equity price at maturity

$K_f =$ strike price in foreign currency

$w =$ as in equation (24.14).

In general, we are interested in converting the foreign currency into domestic currency for domestic investors. To this end, let $I_2(T)$ be the exchange rate in domestic currency per unit of foreign currency; it has an SDE of the form (24.7) with

$$g_2 = r_f,$$

where r_f is the foreign interest rate.

Then the payoff of a foreign equity option in domestic currency is given as the product of (24.21) and the exchange rate, namely:

$$\text{payoff} = I_2(T)\max\left[wI_1(T) - wK_f, 0\right] \tag{24.22a}$$

or

$$\text{payoff} = \max[wI_1(T)I_2(T) - wK_fI_2(T), 0] \tag{24.22b}$$

System (24.22) is similar to a product option with a floating strike price, in fact a kind of Asian option.

24.2.7   Quanto options

A quanto option is a fixed exchange-rate foreign-equity option and its added value is to mitigate foreign exchange risks. They are used mostly in currency-related markets with the price of one underlying asset converted to another one at a fixed guaranteed rate.

The payoff for a quanto option in domestic currency is given by:

$$\text{payoff} = \bar{I}_2 \max\left[wI_1(T) - wK_f, 0\right] \tag{24.23}$$

where K_f is the strike price in the foreign currency and $\bar{I}_2$ is a fixed exchange rate.

24.2.8   Spread options

A spread option is one that is written on the difference between two indices, prices or rates. The payoff of a European option on the spread of two instruments is given by:

$$\text{payoff} = \max\left[awI_1(T) + bwI_2(T) - wK, 0\right], \quad a > 0, \quad b < 0 \tag{24.24}$$

For a standard spread option we set $a = 1$, $b = -1$ and $K = 0$. In this case the payoff is exactly the same as an exchange option. We can then view exchange options as being a specialisation of spread options. Thus, there is no point in modelling exchange options explicitly because they are subsumed in the current model.

In general we can view the spread as one imaginary asset price and this is called the one-factor model. No distinction is made between the two assets. The spread has some limitations:

- The correlation coefficient between the two assets does not appear explicitly in the pricing formula (Black–Scholes is used).
- The sensitivities of the spread option price cannot be found.
- There is an implicit assumption that the spread cannot be negative because the underlying asset price must be non-negative in a Black–Scholes formulation.

The solution to these problems is to propose a two-factor model in which the two assets are modelled explicitly. We realise this by a two-factor Black–Scholes PDE.

24.2.9   Dual-strike options

These are options with two strike prices written on two underlying assets. This category includes options on the maximum or minimum when the two strike prices have the same value. The payoff of a European-style dual-strike option on two assets is given by:

$$\text{payoff} = \max\left\{w_1\left[I_1(T) - K_1\right], w_2\left[I_2(T) - K_2\right], 0\right\} \tag{24.25}$$

where $w_j = \pm 1$, for call or put, respectively, $j = 1, 2$
and K_j = strike price of option j, $j = 1, 2$

We see that there are four combinations on equation (24.25), namely:

$$\text{Call–Call/Call–Put/Put–Call/Put–Put}$$

The first combination is discussed in detail in Zhang (1998).

24.2.10   Out-perfomance options

This is a special kind of call option that allows investors to take advantage of the expected difference in the relative performance of two underlying assets or indices. The payoff function is given by:

$$\text{payoff} = \max\left\{w\left[\frac{1_i(T)}{I_1} - \frac{I_2(T)}{I_2}\right] - wk, 0\right\} \tag{24.26}$$

where I_j = current value of underlying, $j = 1,2$

$I_j(T)$ = values at maturity, $j = 1, 2$

k = strike rate of the option

$w = \pm 1$, for call and put, respectively.

24.3   COMMON FRAMEWORK FOR MULTI-ASSET OPTIONS

In the previous section we gave a short overview of the different multi-asset option types and their applications in financial engineering. Furthermore, we gave the formulae for the payoff function for each type. This function corresponds to the initial condition in the corresponding PDE formulation. Finally, we discussed the domain of integration for a number of the types as this will be important when we set up the finite difference schemes for the two-factor Black–Scholes PDE for these option types.

There are many kind of multi-asset options in the marketplace but we shall attempt to define one general model for all of them. In particular, we shall set up the initial boundary value problem (IBVP) for the multi-factor Black–Scholes equation for them. Recall that the main attention points are:

- Define the PDE for the problem (include the mixed derivative terms)
- Define the initial condition (the payoff functions)
- Define the boundary conditions.

In general, the main difference between the various kinds of assets lies in the payoff function. The PDE term remains the same. We can formulate the IBVP in a generic context. After that we can then apply finite difference methods. Of course, the devil is in the details and we must examine each candidate solution on its merits, namely performance and accuracy. In general, the basic PDE for multi-asset options is given by:

$$\frac{\partial u}{\partial t} + Lu = 0 \qquad (24.27)$$

where

$$Lu \equiv \frac{1}{2} \sum_{i,j=1}^{n} \sigma_i \sigma_j \rho_{ij} S_i S_j \frac{\partial^2 u}{\partial S_i \, \partial S_j} + r \sum_{i=1}^{n} S_i \frac{\partial u}{\partial S_i} - ru$$

in which ρ_{ij} = asset correlations

r = risk-free interest rate

σ_j = volatility of asset j.

Each underlying asset variable has non-negative values. We need to specify boundary conditions for this PDE. One strategy is to let the PDE be applicable at $S = 0$ while we could take Dirichlet or Neumann boundary conditions at infinity, for example:

$$\left. \begin{array}{l} -\dfrac{\partial u}{\partial t} - ru = 0 \text{ as } S_j \to 0, \quad j = 1, \ldots, n \\[2mm] \text{Dirichlet boundary conditions as } S_j \to \infty, \quad j = 1, \ldots, n \end{array} \right\}. \qquad (24.28)$$

We thus conclude that the full problem specification is given by equations (24.27), (24.28) and one of the pay-off functions in section 24.2 of this chapter. We then can map this system to some kind of numerical scheme.

24.4   AN OVERVIEW OF FINITE DIFFERENCE SCHEMES FOR MULTI-ASSET PROBLEMS

There are many kinds of numerical schemes that produce an approximate solution to the initial boundary value problem defined by equations (24.27), (24.28) and a given payoff function from section 24.2. We concentrate on the finite difference method. In particular, we have already discussed alternating direction implicit (ADI) and operator splitting methods in Chapters 19 and 20, respectively. These schemes can be applied to correlation option pricing problems. We prefer splitting to ADI in general because, first, it is easier to understand and to program than ADI and, second, it is superior to ADI when it comes to approximating the cross (mixed) derivative terms. We do not examine these kinds of schemes here because we feel that we have done them enough justice in Chapters 19 and 20 and the results in those chapters are easily transferrable to the current situation. Chapter 18 discussed direct finite difference schemes for multi-dimensional time-dependent problems. In particular, we examined explicit finite difference schemes that allow us to compute a solution at time level $n + 1$ in terms of a solution at time level n. However, such schemes are only conditionally stable and we must choose a sufficiently small time step. Another approach to approximating multi-asset options by finite differences is given in Bhansali (1998).

In this chapter we approximate the solution of the multi-asset initial boundary value problem (IBVP) by a completely different approach to those we have already seen. The general approach can be paraphrased as follows: '*We discretise the IBVP in time using Rothe's method. The resulting set of equations is of elliptic type. We solve these equations using well-known iterative methods at each time level*'. Rothe's method has considerable theoretical and practical value in numerical analysis and its applications. We shall give an example in a nutshell: consider the two-dimensional heat equation:

$$\frac{\partial u}{\partial t} = \Delta u = \frac{\partial^2 u}{\partial x^2} + \frac{\partial^2 u}{\partial y^2} \tag{24.29}$$

which is defined in the continuous space (x, y, t). If we discretise in t using the implicit Euler scheme in the usual way, we get the elliptic equation:

$$\frac{V^{n+1} - V^n}{k} = \Delta V^{n+1}, \quad n \geq 0 \tag{24.30a}$$

or

$$-k\Delta V^{n+1} + V^{n+1} = V^n \tag{24.30b}$$

These are now reaction diffusion equations that we must solve at each time level. For example, we can discretise in the space variables using centred difference operators as follows:

$$-k\left(\Delta_x^2 V_{ij}^{n+1} + \Delta_y^2 V_{ij}^{n+1}\right) + V_{ij}^{n+1} = V_{ij}^n \tag{24.31}$$

where

$$\Delta_x^2 V_{ij}^n \equiv h_x^{-2}\left(V_{i+1,j}^n - 2V_{i,j}^n + V_{i-1,j}^n\right)$$

$$\Delta_y^2 V_{ij}^n = h_y^{-2}\left(V_{i,j+1}^n - 2V_{i,j}^n + V_{i,j-1}^n\right)$$

We have now a fully-discrete elliptic scheme. We now show how to solve this set of equations using matrix iterative techniques. To this end, we start with some background material on these methods. Incidentally, Rothe's method can be applied to the Black–Scholes equation but a full treatment is not discussed here.

24.5   NUMERICAL SOLUTION OF ELLIPTIC EQUATIONS

In order to motivate the theory we first start with a specific example. To this end, let us consider the Poisson equation and its associated boundary value problem on the unit square and determined by the BVP:

$$\Delta^2 u \equiv \Delta u = \frac{\partial^2 u}{\partial x^2} + \frac{\partial^2 u}{\partial y^2} = f(x, y) \text{ in } Q = (0, 1) \times (0, 1) \left.\vphantom{\frac{\partial^2 u}{\partial x^2}}\right\}$$

$$u(x, y) = g(x, y), (x, y) \in \Gamma$$

(24.32)

where $\Gamma = \left[(x, 0) \cup (x, 1) \cup (0, y) \cup (1, y), (x, y) \in \overline{Q} \right]$

The finite difference scheme is given by:

$$\Delta_x^2 U_{ij} + \Delta_y^2 U_{ij} = f_{ij}, \quad i = 1, \ldots, I-1, \quad j = 1, \ldots, J-1 \qquad (24.33)$$

and the discrete boundary conditions are given by:

$$U_{0j} = g_{0j}, \quad j = 0, \ldots, J$$

$$U_{Ij} = g_{Ij}, \quad j = 0, \ldots, J$$

$$U_{i0} = g_{i0}, \quad i = 1, \ldots, I-1$$

$$U_{iJ} = g_{iJ}, \quad i = 1, \ldots, I-1$$

(24.34)

We rewrite equation (24.33) in the equivalent form (East–West–North–South notation):

$$E_{ij}U_{i+1,j} + W_{ij}U_{i-1,j} + N_{ij}U_{i,j+1} + S_{ij}U_{i,j-1} + \alpha_{ij}U_{i,j} = f_{ij} \qquad (24.35)$$

where E, W, N, S and α are coefficients that can easily be evalutated from equation (24.33)
Rearranging this equation we get:

$$U_{i,j} = \alpha_{ij}^{-1}(f_{ij} - E_{ij}U_{i+1,j} - W_{ij}U_{i-1,j} - N_{ij}U_{i,j+1} - S_{ij}U_{i,j-1}) \qquad (24.36)$$

We use iterative schemes to solve this equation and to this end we construct a sequence of approximate solutions. In particular, the point Jacobi method (also called the method of simultaneous displacements) is defined by the iterative scheme:

$$U_{ij}^{(k+1)} = \alpha_{ij}^{-1}\left(f_{ij} - E_{ij}U_{i+1,j}^{(k)} - W_{ij}U_{i-1,j}^{(k)} - N_{ij}U_{i,j+1}^{(k)} - S_{ij}U_{i,j-1}^{(k)}\right), \quad k \geq 0 \quad (24.37)$$

In other words, we start with some arbitrary initial approximation corresponding to $k = 0$ and we calculate future values using the recurrence relation (24.37) (Peaceman, 1977). The following theorem states the conditions under which the iterative scheme (24.37) converges (see Thomas, 1999, for a good introduction to this and other related topics).

Theorem 24.1. *Let the solution of problem (24.33), (24.34) be expressed in the form:*

$$A\mathbf{x} = \mathbf{F}$$

$$x = {}^t(U_{1,1,\ldots}U_{I-1,1}, U_{1,2,\ldots}U_{I-1,J-1})$$

and A is a matrix. If A is irreducible and diagonally dominant and, for at least one j, we have

$$|a_{jj}| > \rho_j = \sum_{\substack{k=1 \\ k \neq j}}^{L} |a_{jk}|$$

then the Jacobi iteration scheme converges for any start vector.

We now consider the so-called line Jacobi method. Let us review equation (24.37). In this case the new value at a point (i, j) is calculated in terms of the old values of its neighbours. Now, instead of doing this, let us move only the values at points $(i, j - 1)$ and $(i, j + 1)$ to the right-hand side. In this case we tie the values in the x direction tightly together as the following equation shows:

For $j = 1, \ldots, J - 1$

Solve

$$E_{ij}U_{i+1,j} + \alpha_{ij}U_{ij} + W_{ij}U_{i-1,j} = f_{ij} - N_{ij}U_{i,j+1} - S_{ij}U_{i,j-1} \quad i = 1, \ldots, I - 1 \tag{24.38}$$

Next j

We solve the 'j loop' equations using a standard tridiagonal matrix solver (see Keller, 1992 and Thomas, 1998 for the theory, and Duffy, 2004 for the implementation in C++). The line Jacobi method is also applicable to general difference schemes in two and three dimensions.

There are other important iterative schemes:

- Gauss–Seidel relaxation scheme
- Successive over-relaxation (SOR) scheme
- Symmetric successive over-relaxation (SSOR) scheme.

These schemes are more efficient than the Jacobi schemes and we would advise the reader to investigate them for his or her own specific applications. More details can be found in Thomas (1999) and Peacemen (1977), for example. We are unable to include them here because of the scope. Finally, the transition to two-factor PDEs for the asset problems in this chapter will be a variation of the scheme (24.38). We omit the details, but they are not too difficult at this stage.

24.6   SOLVING MULTI-ASSET BLACK–SCHOLES EQUATIONS

We have now developed enough theory to develop suites of finite difference schemes for correlation options. As already stated, this chapter focuses on discretising the corresponding PDE in time (using a known time-marching scheme) that results in an elliptic equation. We then discretise this equation by using standard centred divided differences. The fully discrete system of equations is solved using an iterative scheme such as Jacobi, Gauss–Seidel or SOR.

Let us first examine a put basket option f with two underlyings (Topper, 1998 and 2005, and section 24.2.3 of this book). The partial differential equation is given by:

$$\tfrac{1}{2}\sigma_1^2 S_1^2 \frac{\partial^2 f}{\partial S_1^2} + \tfrac{1}{2}\sigma_2^2 S_2^2 \frac{\partial^2 f}{\partial S_2^2} + \rho\sigma_1\sigma_2 S_1 S_2 \frac{\partial^2 f}{\partial S_1 \partial S_2} +$$

$$+ (r - q_1)S_1 \frac{\partial f}{\partial S_1} + (r - q_2)S_2 \frac{\partial f}{\partial S_2} = rf - \frac{\partial f}{\partial t} \tag{24.39}$$

where D is the two-dimensional region $(0, 100) \times (0, 100)$.

The payoff for the basket put is given by:

$$f(S_1, S_2, T) = \max[0, K - (w_1 S_1 + w_2 S_2)] \text{ in } D \tag{24.40}$$

We now discuss the boundary conditions. When $S_1 = 0$ and $S_2 = 0$ we solve the basic Black–Scholes equation of a normal put with given strikes:

$$f(S_1, 0, t) = g\left(S_1, \frac{K}{w_2}, t\right) \tag{24.41a}$$

$$f(0, S_2, t) = g\left(S_2, \frac{K}{w_1}, t\right) \tag{24.41b}$$

where   First strike $= K/w_2$

Second strike $= K/w_1$

For the second boundary condition we suggest using Dirichlet boundary conditions with the value of the option equal to zero at the far field (that was chosen to be equal to 100 in Topper, 1998):

$$f(100, S_2, t) = 0 \quad \text{and} \quad f(S_1, 100, t) = 0 \tag{24.42}$$

This problem can now be solved using the iterative methods in this chapter. We give a summary of the steps in assembling the finite difference scheme for this problem:

- Discretise equation (24.39) using Rothe's method
- Discretise the resulting elliptic equation (to give a system of the form (24.35))
- Solve the schemes at each time level using Gauss–Seidel's method, for example.

Of course, we have to take boundary conditions into account as we march from time level n to time level $n + 1$. This process is well known by now.

24.7   SPECIAL GUIDELINES AND CAVEATS

Numerical analysis is as much an art as a science and it takes time and energy to come up with good schemes for a given problem. There is always a trade-off between accuracy, performance and robustness. We give some guidelines to help the reader to decide which scheme is most appropriate for his or her problem.

- Iterative FDM schemes (as discussed in this chapter) may be preferable to ADI or splitting methods because the latter methods produce inherent splitting errors. On the other hand, ADI and splitting methods are efficient whereas the direct methods use iterative schemes (these may converge slowly) to compute a discrete solution.
- For convection-dominated problems we may have difficulty with Crank–Nicolson (time-averaging), in particular we experience spurious oscillations and spikes in the solution and the 'Greeks' as well as near barriers (Tavella *et al.*, 2000). A remedy is to use the exponentially fitted schemes in each 'underlying direction' (see Dennis and Hudson, 1980 or Duffy, 1980).
- The payoff functions in section 24.2 of this chapter have discontinuous first derivatives in general, especially near the strike price and just as in the one-factor case we can expect similar problems in the two-factor case (Duffy, 2004A).
- The finite difference and finite element methods are suitable for n-factor problems with $n = 1, 2$ and 3. After that, life becomes more difficult, and in these cases we must resort to other methods, for example Monte Carlo or the meshless (meshfree) method (see Boztosun *et al.*, 2002).

- For some (most?) kinds of correlation options the integration domain is non-rectangular. For example, the domain could be a triangle. It is possible to apply FDM in these cases (see Greenspan, 1966) and, while not impossible, and we might prefer to use finite elements (Topper, 2005).
- The classic references on matrix analysis are Varga (1962) and Golub and Van Loan (1996).
- Modern schemes, such as multi-grid methods, are discussed in Thomas (1999) and Roache (1998).

24.8 SUMMARY AND CONCLUSIONS

We have given an overview of the financial background to the class of correlation options, their essential properties, payoff functions and integration domains. We then map these 'financial entities' to a multi-factor initial boundary value problem involving the Black–Scholes PDE (with correlation terms), initial condition and boundary conditions. We approximate this continuous problem by first discretising in the t direction using Rothe's method and then solving in the 'underlying asset' directions using standard elliptic solvers such as point and line Jacobi methods. We have implemented the payoff functions from this chapter as C++ classes and have included the code on the accompanying CD.

25

Finite Difference Methods
for Fixed-Income Problems

25.1 INTRODUCTION AND OBJECTIVES

In this chapter we give an introduction to fixed-income products and how to model them using partial differential equations (PDEs) and finite difference methods. In particular, we concentrate on one-factor and two-factor interest rate models and show how to formulate such problems as parabolic initial boundary value problems. To this end, we give an inventory of some of the major stochastic models that describe the behaviour of the short-term interest rate and the corresponding PDE using Ito's lemma. In this way we can describe the behaviour of interest rate related contingent claims, such as zero-coupon bonds, swaps, caplets, floorlets and plain vanilla bond options. We then move on to more complicated theory where the term structure of interest rates is determined by two factors: in general one of the factors is the short-term rate while the other term can describe the instantaneous inflation rate, the long-term rate or the spread (the difference between the long and short rates).

Our main goal in this chapter is to accentuate the PDE issues involved in interest rate modelling.

25.2 AN INTRODUCTION TO INTEREST RATE MODELLING

Our main objective is to define the partial differential equations and the corresponding initial boundary value problems that model contingent claims involving interest rates. However, we do need to give a general introduction. For a more detailed account, see Hull (2000), Wilmott (1998) and Gibson *et al.* (2001). The theory is well known and you may wish to skip this section.

A discount bound $B(t, T)$ is a zero-coupon bond that pays one current unit at time T and nothing else at any other time up to T. We see that B is a function of both t and T and in particular we have $B(T, T) = 1$. By definition, the yield to maturity $R(t, T)$ of the discount bond $B(t, T)$ is the continuously compounded rate of return that causes the bound to rise to a value 1 at time $t = T$. Then we have:

$$B(t, T) e^{(T-t)R(t,T)} = 1 \qquad (25.1)$$

By rearranging this equation we can see that the yield to maturity is:

$$R(t, T) = -\frac{\ln B(t, T)}{T - t} \qquad (25.2)$$

For a fixed t the shape of $R(t, T)$ as T increases determines the term structure of interest rates.

We now define the instantaneous risk-free interest (also called the short-term interest rate) as the following limit:

$$r(t) = \lim_{T \to t} R(t, T) \tag{25.3}$$

The forward rate $f(t, T_1, T_2)$ is a function of three parameters and it is the rate that can be agreed upon at time t for a risk-free loan starting at time T_1 and finishing at time T_2; it is given by the formula:

$$f(t, T_1, T_2) = \frac{\ln B(t, T_1) - \ln B(t, T_2)}{T_2 - T_1} \tag{25.4}$$

The instantaneous forward rate has a limit in (25.4) and is defined by:

$$f(t, T) \equiv f(t, T, T) \tag{25.5}$$

By going to the limit in equation (25.4) and using the definition in (25.5) we see that:

$$f(t, T) = -\frac{\partial \ln B(t, \tau)}{\partial \tau}\bigg|_{\tau = T} = -\frac{1}{B(t, T)} \frac{\partial B(t, T)}{\partial T} \tag{25.6}$$

After some integration we write the last expression in the equivalent form for the bond price:

$$B(t, T) = \exp\left[-\int_t^T f(t, s)\, ds \right] \tag{25.7}$$

We now turn our attention to the study of stochastic models for one-factor interest rate models.

25.3 SINGLE-FACTOR MODELS

A single-factor model for a contingent claim assumes that all information about the term structure at any point in time can be summarised by a single factor, for example the short-term interest rate $r(t)$. In this case only $r(t)$ and the expiry time T will affect the price of any interest rate contingent claim. We then write the zero-coupon price as follows:

$$B(t, T) \equiv B[t, T, r(t)] \tag{25.8}$$

We consider the short-term interest rate as the only factor driving the entire term structure. Its dynamics are given by the stochastic differential equation (SDE):

$$dr(t) = \mu_r(\,)\, dt + \sigma_r(\,)\, dW(t) \tag{25.9}$$

where we use the shorthand notation for the real-valued functions

$$\mu_r \equiv \mu_r[t, r(t)] \quad \text{and} \quad \sigma_r \equiv \sigma_r(t, r(t))$$

Now let

$$V(t) \equiv V[t, T, r(t)]$$

be any contingent claim based on $r(t)$. It can be shown that V satisfies the Feynman–Kac equation (Gibson *et al.*, 2001):

$$\frac{\partial V}{\partial t} + [\mu_r() - \lambda(t, r(t))\sigma_r()]\frac{\partial V}{\partial r} + \frac{\sigma_r^2()}{2}\frac{\partial^2 V}{\partial r^2} - r(t)V = 0 \qquad (25.10)$$

where $\lambda(t, r(t))$ is the market risk premium and it is independent of T.

We now give some examples of contingent claims V but we must first introduce some notation. Define the differential operator L by:

$$Lu \equiv \frac{\sigma_r^2()}{2}\frac{\partial^2 u}{\partial r^2} + [\mu_r() - \lambda()\sigma_r()]\frac{\partial u}{\partial r}$$

Then we can define the following kinds of interest rate products.

They all satisfy a Black–Scholes PDE with a special inhomogeneous term in each specific case. Furthermore, each type will also have its own payoff function.

- Zero-coupon bond $B(t, T)$ with maturity date T:

$$\begin{cases} \dfrac{\partial B}{\partial t} + LB - r(t)B = 0 \\ B(T, T) = 1 \end{cases} \qquad (25.11)$$

- Swap of fixed rate r^* against a floating rate r with maturity date T:

$$\begin{cases} \dfrac{\partial V}{\partial t} + LV - r(t)V + (r - r^*) = 0 \\ V(T) = 0 \end{cases} \qquad (25.12)$$

An interest rate swap is an agreement between two parties to exchange interest payments for a predefined period of time. One party (called A) agrees to pay the other party B cash flows equal to a fixed amount r^* on a notional principal for a predefined period of time. On the other hand, A receives payments from B at a floating rate r on the same notional principal for the same period. As can be seen in equations (25.12) we have a PDE as with a zero-coupon bond with an additional inhomogeneous term $(r - r^*)$ that represents the so-called coupon payment term. We note that the price of an interest rate swap can be positive or negative.

- Closely related to the swap is the swaption. This is an option on a swap and it provides the holder with the right but not the obligation to enter a swap agreement at some time in the future.

Let T and T_S be the expiry dates of the swaption and the swap, respectively (with $T < T_S$). The PDE for the swaption is the same as for the zero-coupon bond (see (25.11)). However, the payoff function is different:

$$V(r, T) = \max\{\alpha[W(r, T) - K], \ 0\}$$

where V = price of swaption

W = price of swap

K = strike price of swaption

$\alpha = -1$ for a put, $\alpha = 1$ for call.

Computationally speaking, we solve for the swap $W(r, T)$ first (using FDM or analytically, for example) and then we solve for the swaption $V(r, T)$.

- A European call option on a zero-coupon bond $B(t, T)$ with maturity $T_C < T$:

$$\frac{\partial V}{\partial t} + LV - r(t)V = 0$$

$$V(T_C) = \max [B(t, T_C) - K, 0] \tag{25.13}$$

A bond is a debt capital market instrument issued by a borrower who is then required to repay the lender/investor the amount borrowed plus interest, over a specified period of time. A zero-coupon bond is a special kind of bond. A zero-coupon bond pays a known fixed amount, called the principal at some given date in the future, the so-called maturity date T.

- A caplet at rate r^*:

$$\frac{\partial V}{\partial t} + LV - r(t)V + \min (r, r^*) = 0$$

$$V(T) = \max [r(T) - r^*, 0] \tag{25.14}$$

A caplet guarantees that the interest rate charged on a floating rate loan at any given time will be the minimum of the prevailing rate r and the ceiling rate r^*. This can be seen as insurance on the maximum interest rate level for a floating rate loan.

A caplet is similar to a call option.

- A floorlet at rate r^*:

$$\frac{\partial V}{\partial t} + LV - r(t)V + \max (r, r^*) = 0$$

$$V(T) = \max [r^* - r(T), 0] \tag{25.15}$$

A floorlet is the opposite of a caplet. It guarantees the holder to receive the maximum of the prevailing rate r and floor rate r^* on a floating rate deposit. It is a put on the spot rate.

The PDEs in all these cases are similar in structure; in fact they can be cast in a generic form, and we can approximate such equations using finite difference schemes. Some preliminary attention points are:

- We need to examine the boundary conditions when $r = 0$ and when r is large. There are several possibilities and the discovery of the correct boundary conditions is sometimes a bit fuzzy; there are severe possibilities.
- The inhomogeneous term (for example, $\min(r, r^*)$) in the above PDEs can have discontinuous first derivatives but this is not a major problem in general because it is a low-order term.
- We shall also need to model PDEs in two underlyings.

25.4 SOME SPECIFIC STOCHASTIC MODELS

There are many one-factor processes that model the short-term interest rate. We give an overview of some of these models. We are interested in the PDE formulation that is, in a sense, independent of which model we use.

We now give a list of some special cases of the general SDE (25.9). Most of them are named after the people who invented them. The partial differential equations that model the derivatives based on the models below are consequently special cases of the partial differential equations in equations (25.11)–(25.15).

25.4.1   The Merton model

Merton (1973) was one of the first to propose a stochastic model for the short rate:

$$dr(t) = \mu_r \, dt + \sigma_r \, dW(t) \tag{25.16}$$

where μ_r and σ_r are constant and $W(t)$ is the standard Brownian motion.

Furthermore, Merton assumed that the risk market premiun λ was constant.

25.4.2   The Vasicek model

In this case the short rate is modelled as an Ornstein–Uhlenbeck process:

$$dr(t) = K(\theta - r(t)) \, dt + \sigma \, dW(t) \tag{25.17}$$

where K, θ and σ are positive constants.

This process defines an elastic random walk around some trend with a so-called mean-reverting characteristic. Furthermore, this model assumes that the market risk premium λ is constant.

25.4.3   Cox, Ingersoll and Ross (CIR)

In this case interest rates are determined by the supply and demand of individuals having a logarithmic utility function. The equilibrium model is given by:

$$dr(t) = K(\theta - r(t)) \, dt + \sigma \sqrt{r(t)} \, dW(t) \tag{25.18}$$

where K, θ and σ are positive constants.

The market risk premium at equilibrium is given by:

$$\lambda(r, t) = \lambda \sqrt{r(t)}$$

The disadvantage of the above three models is that they cannot be calibrated with yield curves. To this end, a number of researchers have introduced a new class of models that do not have these problems and are consistent with existing models.

25.4.4   The Hull–White model

The general specification is (Hull and White, 1993):

$$dr(t) = ((\theta(t) - K(t))r(t)) \, dt + \sigma(t)r^\beta(t) \, dW(t) \tag{25.19}$$

and the risk premium is given by:

$$\lambda(r, t) = \lambda r^\gamma, \quad \text{with } \lambda \geq 0 \text{ and } \gamma \geq 0$$

In general, the coefficients in equation (25.19) are functions of time and can be used to calibrate exactly the model to current market prices. The down side is that the bond option price can no longer be found analytically but there again we can use numerical techniques such as the finite difference method.

25.4.5 Lognormal models

In the previous examples we modelled the short rate or the forward rate as Gaussian processes. The disadvantage is that there is a positive probability of producing negative interest rates and this implies arbitrage opportunities. To circumvent this problem we discuss a number of models that do not produce negative rates. We summarise them here for completeness. These are called lognormal models.

Black, Derman and Toy (1987):

$$\mathrm{d}\log[r(t)] = (\theta(t) - K \log(r(t))) \, \mathrm{d}t + \sigma_r \, \mathrm{d}W(t) \tag{25.20}$$

This incorporates the mean reversion feature of interest rates. This model is used by practitioners for a number of reasons as discussed in Gibson *et al.* (2001).

Numeric solutions of one-factor SDEs are given in Kloeden *et al.* (1995) and implementation details in C++ are given in Duffy (2004).

25.5   AN INTRODUCTION TO MULTIDIMENSIONAL MODELS

We now discuss interest rate models in which the short rate $r(t)$ and one or more other state variables drive the process. Single-factor models have a number of drawbacks and for this reason other models have to be found.

In Richard (1978) a model is proposed in which the term structure of interest rates is determined by the real short-term rate and the instantaneous inflation rate. These factors have independent diffusion processes:

$$\begin{aligned} \mathrm{d}q(t) &= \mu_q(t) \, \mathrm{d}t + \sigma_q(t) \, \mathrm{d}W_q(t) \\ \mathrm{d}\pi(t) &= \mu_\pi(t) \, \mathrm{d}t + \sigma_\pi(t) \, \mathrm{d}W_\pi(t) \end{aligned} \tag{25.21}$$

where W_q and W_π are independent Brownian motions.

Then, by Ito's lemma the price of a zero-coupon bond is given by the PDE:

$$\frac{\partial B}{\partial t} + L_q B + L_\pi B - rB = 0 \tag{25.22}$$

where

$$L_q B = \frac{\sigma_q^2}{2} \frac{\partial^2 B}{\partial q^2} + (\mu_q - \lambda_q \sigma_q) \frac{\partial B}{\partial q}$$

$$L_\pi B = \frac{\sigma_\pi^2}{2} \frac{\partial^2 B}{\partial \pi^2} + (\mu_\pi - \lambda_\pi \sigma_\pi) \frac{\partial B}{\partial \pi}$$

and λ_q, λ_π are risk premiums.

At face value (no pun intended), this is a well-known two-factor PDE. We notice that there is no mixed (cross-derivative) term in this equation. This is because the processes in (25.21) are independent.

We now discuss some specific models.

Brennan and Schwartz (1979) proposed a two-factor model where the term structure of interest rates depends on the short-term rate $r(t)$ and the long-term rate $l(t)$. This latter concept is defined as:

$$l(t) = \lim_{T \to \infty} R(t, T) \tag{25.23}$$

where $R(t, T)$ is the yield to maturity as defined in equation (25.2). In this case we have a joint diffusion process given by:

$$\begin{aligned} dr(t) &= \mu_r()dt + \sigma_r()dW_r(t) \\ dl(t) &= \mu_l()dt + \sigma_l()dW_l(t) \end{aligned} \tag{25.24}$$

where $W_r(t)$ and $W_l(t)$ are two correlated standard Brownian motions with

$$E(W_r(t), W_l(t)) = \rho t, \quad t \in [0, T]$$

This specification allows the model to reflect the fact that the long-term rate contains some information about the future value of the short rate, hence the correlation term.

The zero-coupon bond is defined as $B(t, T) = B(t, T, r(t), l(t))$ and satisfies the following PDE (notice the presence of the cross or mixed derivative):

$$\frac{\partial B}{\partial t} + L_r B + L_l B + \rho \sigma_r \sigma_l \frac{\partial^2 B}{\partial r \partial l} - rB = 0 \tag{25.25}$$

where

$$L_r B \equiv \frac{\sigma_r^2}{2} \frac{\partial^2 B}{\partial r^2} + (\mu_r - \lambda_r \sigma_r) \frac{\partial B}{\partial r}$$

$$L_l B \equiv \frac{\sigma_l^2}{2} \frac{\partial^2 B}{\partial l^2} + (\mu_l - \lambda_l \sigma_l) \frac{\partial B}{\partial l}$$

and $B(T, T) = 1$.

This type of PDE has already been discussed in previous chapters, in particular on how to approximate its solution using FDM by using splitting methods.

Another example is given in Hull and White (1994b) in order to resolve some of the limitations of the one-factor model:

$$\begin{aligned} dr(t) &= (\theta(t) + u - r(t)) \, dt + \sigma_1 \, dW_1(t) \\ du(t) &= -bu(t) \, dt + \sigma_2 \, dW_2(t) \end{aligned} \tag{25.26}$$

where

$$E(dW_1(t), dW_2(t)) = \rho \, dt, \quad \text{with } u(0) = 0$$

In this case the short-term rate is mean-reverting but we now have a stochastic drift u which is itself mean-reverting to 0 at the rate b. The resulting PDE is then given by:

$$\frac{\partial B}{\partial t} + L_r B + L_u B + \rho \sigma_1 \sigma_2 \frac{\partial^2 B}{\partial r \partial u} - rB = 0 \tag{25.27}$$

where

$$L_r B \equiv \frac{1}{2}\sigma_1^2 \frac{\partial^2 B}{\partial r^2} + (\theta(t) + u - ar)\frac{\partial B}{\partial r}$$

$$L_u B \equiv \frac{1}{2}\sigma_2^2 \frac{\partial^2 B}{\partial u^2} - bu\frac{\partial B}{\partial u}$$

Again, this is a PDE that can be solved using splitting methods, for example. We must take care of the mixed derivative term, of course.

25.6 THE THORNY ISSUE OF BOUNDARY CONDITIONS

In general, when solving initial boundary value problems associated with one-factor partial differential equations we must specify the boundary (auxiliary) conditions as well as the payoff conditions. Here we distinguish between one-factor and two-factor problems. In the former case we have a PDE with the short rate as one variable, while in the latter case the variables represent the short rate, for example, and some other quantity. Since the values are defined on the semi-infinite positive axis we have two points to attend to:

- Far-field condition: Truncating the semi-infinite domain to a finite domain. Another option is to find a transformation that maps the semi-infinte interval to a bounded interval.
- Defining the boundary conditions themselves.

Much of the literature is very Spartan in the author's opinion when it comes to defining boundary conditions, their numerical approximation and their assembly into the discrete system of equations. In general, a combination of mathematical, financial and heuristic reasoning allows us to find consistent and acceptable boundary conditions for a problem.

25.6.1 One-factor models

In this case the independent variable is r, the short-term interest rate. In principle it is non-negative and hence takes values in the range zero to infinity. We first truncate the semi-infinite interval to a finite interval and then we must specify conditions on the new boundary:

- For very high values of r the value of a contingent claim is zero; thus the boundary condition $V(r, t) \to 0$ as $r \to \infty$ becomes

$$V(r_{\max}, t) = 0 \tag{25.28}$$

Another common boundary condition is the Neumann boundary condition:

$$\frac{\partial V}{\partial r}(r, t) \to 0 \quad \text{as } r \to \infty \quad \text{or}$$

$$\frac{\partial V}{\partial r}(r_{\max}, 0) = 0 \tag{25.29}$$

We already know how to approximate these conditions numerically; for example, we can approximate (25.29) by one-sided (first-order accurate) divided differences or by two-sided (second-order accurate) divided differences in combination with ghost or fictitious points.

When r approaches zero (or is zero) the situation is a little more complicated. We cannot prescribe an explicit boundary condition as such (because the Black–Scholes equation is degenerate) but we allow the Black–Scholes equation to hold when $r = 0$. The resulting PDE will then be a first-order hyperbolic equation! Let us take an example. Consider first the Cox–Ingersoll–Ross (CIR) interest-rate model (Hull, 2000):

$$dr = u(r, t) \, dt + w(r, t) \, dW \tag{25.30}$$

where $u(r, t) = a - br$ and $w(r, t) = \sigma \sqrt{r}$.

The pricing equation for a zero-coupon bond in this case is given by (Tavella *et al.*, 2000):

$$\frac{\partial B}{\partial t} + \tfrac{1}{2}\sigma^2 r \frac{\partial^2 B}{\partial r^2} + (a - br)\frac{\partial B}{\partial r} - rB = 0 \tag{25.31}$$

In this model the boundary conditions at $r = 0$ is given by:

$$\frac{\partial B}{\partial t} + a\frac{\partial B}{\partial r} = 0 \quad \text{if } \sigma < \sqrt{2a} \tag{25.32}$$

This is a first-order hyperbolic equation and it must be augmented with an initial condition and boundary conditions in order to define a valid initial boundary value problem. In this case (beware characteristic direction!) we define them as follows:

$$\begin{aligned} B(r_{\max}, t) &= 0 \\ B(r, T) &= 1 \end{aligned} \tag{25.33}$$

25.6.2 Multi-factor models

In this case we have two (or more) independent variables, one for the short rate and the other for another variable such as the underlying share price S (in the case of a convertible bond, for example), the long rate or spread. We take an example of a PDE that models a convertible bond:

$$\frac{\partial V}{\partial t} + \tfrac{1}{2}\sigma^2 S^2 \frac{\partial^2 V}{\partial S^2} + \rho\sigma Sw \frac{\partial^2 V}{\partial S \, \partial r} + \tfrac{1}{2}w^2 \frac{\partial^2 V}{\partial r^2} +$$
$$+ rS\frac{\partial V}{\partial S} + (u - \lambda w)\frac{\partial V}{\partial r} - rV = 0 \tag{25.34}$$

The problem cases are at $r = 0$ and $S = 0$. For example, when $S = 0$ the PDE (25.34) reduces to the one-factor PDE on the boundary:

$$\frac{\partial V}{\partial t} + \tfrac{1}{2}w^2 \frac{\partial^2 V}{\partial r^2} + (u - \lambda w)\frac{\partial V}{\partial r} - rV = 0 \tag{25.35}$$

We see that no derivatives with respect to S appear in equation (25.35). We may be able to find an exact solution to this problem; otherwise we approximate it using the techniques in this book. On the other hand, when $r = 0$ we get the PDE (Sun, 1999):

$$\frac{\partial V}{\partial t} + \tfrac{1}{2}\sigma^2 S^2 \frac{\partial^2 V}{\partial S^2} + u\frac{\partial V}{\partial r} = 0 \tag{25.36}$$

where $w(0, t) = 0$.

We thus see that we must solve a PDE on the boundary. It is second order in S and first order in r and is similar in structure to the Asian option PDEs in Chapter 23. Ideally, an exact solution would be most advantageous, but this may not always be possible. An interesting model is the Heath–Jarrow–Morton (HJM) (Heath *et al.*, 1992) but such a discussion is outside the scope of this book.

25.7   INTRODUCTION TO APPROXIMATE METHODS FOR INTEREST RATE MODELS

Finite difference schemes can be applied to constructing schemes for one-factor and multi-factor interest rate models. The main points of attention are:

- Approximating the PDE terms by divided differences
- How to handle cross-derivatives
- Choosing between ADI and splitting methods
- Truncating semi-infinite intervals (far-field condition)
- Approximation the boundary conditions
- Assembling the discrete system of equations.

We have already discussed each of these issues in detail in previous chapters. Of particular importance in this case is the numerical approximation of the continuous boundary conditions and the presence of cross-derivatives in multi-factor models.

25.7.1   One-factor models

We take the example of a one-factor zero-coupon bond (see Tavella *et al.*, 2000). The 'forward' initial boundary value problem is given by:

$$-\frac{\partial B}{\partial t} + \frac{1}{2}\sigma^2 r\frac{\partial^2 B}{\partial r^2} + (a - br)\frac{\partial B}{\partial r} - rB = 0, \quad 0 < r < r_{\max}, \quad t > 0 \tag{25.37a}$$

$$B(r_{\max}, t) = 0, \quad t > 0$$

$$-\frac{\partial B}{\partial t}(0, t) + a\frac{\partial B}{\partial r}(0, t) = 0, \quad t > 0, \quad a > 0 \tag{25.37b}$$

$$B(r, 0) = H(r) \text{ (payoff)}, \quad 0 < r < r_{\max}$$

Please note that we are using the engineer's time. The tricky part is the boundary condition at $r = 0$, which is a first-order hyperbolic equation. We thus conclude that the bond price B is not known at $r = 0$ and for this reason we must discretise all the PDEs in problem (25.37) simultaneously. To this end, the implicit Euler scheme for the Black–Scholes equation is:

$$-\frac{B_j^{n+1} - B_j^n}{k} + \sigma_j^{n+1}D_+D_-B_j^{n+1} + \mu_j^{n+1}D_0B_j^{n+1} - r_jB_j^{n+1} = 0, \quad 1 \le j \le J - 1 \tag{25.38}$$

where $\sigma \equiv \frac{1}{2}\sigma^2 r$ (slight misuse of notation)

$$\mu \equiv a - br$$

while the scheme at $r = 0$ is given by:

$$-\frac{B_j^{n+1} - B_j^n}{k} + a\frac{B_{j+1}^{n+1} - B_j^{n+1}}{h} = 0, \quad \text{when} \quad (j = 0) \tag{25.39a}$$

or

$$B_o^{n+1}(1 + \lambda) = B_0^n + \lambda B_1^{n+1} \quad \left(\lambda \equiv \frac{ak}{h} \right) \tag{25.39b}$$

(Another possibility is to use the exact solution of the first-order PDE at $r = 0$.)

We now assemble these equations. Define the unknown vector B by:

$$B^{n+1} = {}^t(B_0^{n+1}, \dots, B_{J-1}^{n+1})$$

Then the system of equations is:

$$A^{n+1} B^{n+1} = F^n \tag{25.40}$$

where

$$A^n = \begin{pmatrix} 1 + \lambda & \lambda & & & \\ a_2^n & b_1^n & c_1^n & & \\ & \ddots & \ddots & \ddots & 0 \\ 0 & & \ddots & \ddots & c_{J-1}^n \\ & & & a_J^n & b_{J-1}^n \end{pmatrix}$$

and

$$F^n = {}^t(B_0^n, 0, \dots, 0)$$

The matrix A is an M-matrix and hence has a positive inverse. We thus conclude that our finite difference scheme is monotone. The accuracy of the scheme (25.39) is first order in time and space.

25.7.2 Many-factor models

For two-factor models we can apply ADI or splitting, although much of the literature tends to employ ADI. Furthermore, we have worked on a default risk model using ADI and Crank–Nicolson where we were not successful in obtaining good approximations, whereas application of the splitting method gave good results (Levin, 1999, private communication; Levin and Duffy, 2000). We can apply the splitting methods to the systems (25.25) or (25.27). See Chapter 19 for a full discussion.

25.8 SUMMARY AND CONCLUSIONS

We have given an introduction to the partial differential equations and corresponding initial boundary value problems that model one-factor and two-factor interest rate models. The PDEs are standard and tractable and these can be approximated by the finite difference schemes that we have already discussed in this book. Complicating factors lie in determining how to formulate and approximate the corresponding boundary conditions on the one hand and coping with mixed derivatives on the other.

Our standpoint is that splitting methods are suitable for two-factor interest rate models. They perform better than ADI methods, especially when there are mixed derivative terms in the models.

Part VI

Free and Moving Boundary Value Problems

26
Background to Free and Moving Boundary Value Problems

26.1 INTRODUCTION AND OBJECTIVES

In this chapter we examine free and moving boundary values problems from a theoretical viewpoint. Furthermore, we discuss their application to financial engineering. In particular, we discuss the early exercise feature of one-factor and multi-factor option modelling problems. This is called the American exercise feature. In short, this chapter paves the way for future chapters.

Part VI consists of four chapters. The main goal is to cover enough material to enable the reader to apply finite difference schemes to the Black–Scholes equation with a free or moving boundary.

We have written the material on free boundaries for two major reader groups. First, those readers who may have had some exposure to free boundary value problems and who wish to apply their existing knowledge to financial engineering applications. The second reason is to introduce the theory and application of free and moving boundary value problems to a wider audience – in particular to those practitioners who have not necessarily studied such problems before. To this end, we introduce the material in a step-by-step fashion, culminating with the formulation of an option pricing problem with the early exercise feature as a free boundary value problem. Having done that, we are then able to solve the problem using robust numerical methods. This is a relatively new area of research.

The range of applications of free boundary value problems in engineering and mathematical physics is quite extensive. The set of problems in financial engineering is a proper subset of these problems that we encounter in the physical sciences. There are many analogies between heat flow problems and the Black–Scholes model and numerical techniques that are used with success to solve the former problems. These can be applied to the latter group as well, as the chapters in this part will show.

26.2 NOTATION AND DEFINITIONS

Free and moving boundary value problems have their origins in the physical sciences. Problems in which the solution of differential equations must satisfy certain conditions on the boundary of a prescribed domain are called boundary value problems. In many cases the boundary of the domain is not known *a priori* but it must be determined as part of the problem. We partition such problems into two groups: first, the term 'free boundary problem' is used when the boundary is stationary and a steady-state solution exists (for example, the solution of an elliptic problem). We then have the class of moving boundary value problems that are associated with time-dependent problems (for example, defined by a parabolic partial differential equation). The unknown boundaries in the latter case are a function of both space and time. In all cases we must specify two conditions on the free or moving boundary. Of course, the usual boundary conditions are specified on the fixed boundary as well as some appropriate initial conditions, as already discussed in this book.

In general, we can classify free and moving boundary value problems into different categories depending on the types of problem that they model. For example, a one-phase problem is one where we model a PDE in a single domain with an unknown boundary. The solution on the other side of the unknown boundary is known. With two-phase problems we model different PDEs, that is, defined in two domains that are separated by a free or moving boundary. Most problems in financial engineering at the moment of writing are described as one-phase problems. In this case the solution is zero on one side of the moving boundary and it satisfies the Black–Scholes equation on the other side of the boundary, for example.

Moving boundary value problems are sometimes called Stefan problems in honour of the Austrian mathematician, J. Stefan, who in 1890 studied the melting of the polar ice cap.

26.3   SOME PRELIMINARY EXAMPLES

We discuss a number of problems in order to motivate the theory. An excellent source of these problems is Crank (1984). These problems originate in many application areas, such as:

- Soil mechanics
- Engineering
- Physical and biological sciences
- Metallurgy
- Decision and control theory.

We shall see that the techniques for these problems can be applied to pricing applications with an early exercise feature.

26.3.1   Single-phase melting ice

Consider a semi-infinite sheet of ice. The initial point is at $x = 0$ and we assume that the sheet is initially at the melting temperature, that is zero degrees. We now raise the temperature of the sheet surface at time $t = 0$ and we maintain the temperature. What we get is the following phenomenon: a boundary surface or interface is born at which melting occurs. This boundary moves from the surface into the sheet and separates a region of water from one of ice at zero temperature. Let us denote the moving boundary by the function $B(t)$. Let $u(x, t)$ be the temperature at time t and at some point x in the water phase. (The temperature on the other side of the moving boundary is zero.) Then the heat equation is valid in the liquid region and is defined by:

$$c\rho \frac{\partial u}{\partial t} = K \frac{\partial^2 u}{\partial x^2}, \quad 0 < x < B(t), \quad t > 0 \tag{26.1}$$

where c = specific heat

ρ = density

K = heat conductivity.

We augment this equation, first by a fixed boundary condition

$$u(0, t) = A, \quad t > 0 \tag{26.2}$$

where the value A is the constant surface temperature, and second by an initial condition

$$u(x, 0) = 0, \quad 0 < x < \infty, \quad t > 0$$
$$B(0) = 0 \tag{26.3}$$

Continuing, we need two further conditions on the moving boundary $x = B(t)$ namely:

$$\left. \begin{array}{c} u = 0 \\ -K\dfrac{\partial u}{\partial x} = L\rho\dfrac{d B}{d t} \end{array} \right\} t > 0 \tag{26.4}$$

where L = latent heat required to melt ice, and K and ρ are defined in (26.1).

Equation (26.4), called the 'Stefan condition', expresses the heat balance on the moving boundary. It is similar to the 'smooth pasting condition' for the pricing of American options.

The name 'one-phase' should be clear at this stage: we are modelling the temperature in the liquid region by the heat equation while in the solid region the temperature is identically zero. Thus, we do not need to model the solid region by a PDE.

26.3.2   One-factor option modelling: American exercise style

We already know that a European option can be exercised only at the expiry date. American options, on the other hand, can be exercised at any time before, or up to, the expiry date. In this section we concentrate on a put option with an early exercise feature. Let $P = P(S, t)$ be the put option price. Then P satisfies the PDE:

$$\frac{\partial P}{\partial t} + \tfrac{1}{2}\sigma^2 S^2 \frac{\partial^2 P}{\partial S^2} + rS\frac{\partial P}{\partial S} - rP = 0, \quad S > B(t), \quad 0 \le t \le T \tag{26.5}$$

Here $B(t)$ is the moving boundary. We are assuming that no dividends are paid throughout the life of the option. The terminal condition is given by:

$$P(S, T) = \max(K - S, 0), \quad S \ge 0, \quad 0 \le t \le T \tag{26.6}$$

where K is the strike price.

We now need to prescribe boundary conditions. Since the problem is defined on a region containing both fixed and free boundaries, we define the first 'fixed' boundary condition as:

$$\lim_{S \to \infty} P(S, t) = 0 \tag{26.7}$$

and the so-called pasting conditions at the free boundary as:

$$\frac{\partial P}{\partial S}(B(t), t) = -1$$
$$P(B(t), t) = K - B(t) \tag{26.8}$$

Furthermore, we define the terminal value for the free boundary as follows:

$$B(T) = K \tag{26.9}$$

Finally, 'in front' of the free boundary the option price is given by:

$$P(S, t) = \max(K - S, 0), \quad 0 \le S < B(t) \tag{26.10}$$

The problem (26.5)–(26.10) is similar to the Stefan problem that we studied in section 26.3.1. It is an example of a one-phase problem.

Since early exercise is permitted, the option price P must satisfy the constraint:

$$P(S, t) \ge \max(K - S, 0), \quad S \ge 0, \quad 0 \le t \le T \tag{26.11}$$

As in the previous section we see that there are two unknowns, namely the option price $P(S, t)$ and the free boundary $B(t)$. The curve $B(t)$ is called the optimal exercise boundary. When $S > B(t)$ we see from equation (26.5) that P satisfies the Black–Scholes equation, while if $S \le B(t)$ it is optimal to exercise the put.

26.3.3 Two-phase melting ice

This section can be skipped on a first reading without loss of continuity. We now revisit the melting-ice problem of section 26.3.1. In particular, we assume that the ice is initially at a temperature below the melting point and we assume that heat flows in both the water and ice phases. Then we must model a PDE in each phase (that is, ice and water). The problem is to find a triple:

$$u_1(x, t), \quad u_2(x, t), \quad B(t)$$

where $u_1 = $ tenperature in the water phase

$\quad\quad\quad u_2 = $ temperature in the ice phase

and $B(t) = $ the free boundary between the two phases.

The heat equation in the two phases in a bounded interval $(0, A)$ is given by:

$$c_j \rho_j \frac{\partial u_j}{\partial t} = K_j \frac{\partial^2 u_j}{\partial x^2}, \quad j = 1, 2, \quad x \in (0, A) \tag{26.12}$$

Where $c_j = $ specific heat in phase j

$\quad\quad\quad \rho_j = $ density in phase j

$\quad\quad\quad K_j = $ thermal conductivity in phase j.

In the interior of the interval $(0, A)$ there is an unknown moving boundary $B(t)$ where the following so-called Stefan condition is satisfied:

$$\left.\begin{aligned} u_1 &= u_2 = 0 \\[2mm] K_2 \frac{\partial u_2}{\partial x} - K_1 \frac{\partial u_1}{\partial x} &= L\rho \frac{dB}{dt} \end{aligned}\right\} x = B(t) \tag{26.13}$$

We must thus solve two PDEs, one in each domain. The domains are separated by a common, free boundary.

26.3.4 The inverse Stefan problem

An interesting problem is when the interface between water and ice is known. Why would we want this situation? One reason would be to let the melting interface move in a prescribed way. This is the so-called inverse Stefan problem and since the moving boundary is known we must compensate this by prescribing other conditions, for example:

- The boundary condition $g(t)$ at $x = 0$
- By prescribing a heat input $q(t)$.

The corresponding problem is now:

$$\frac{\partial u}{\partial t} = \frac{\partial^2 u}{\partial x^2}, \quad 0 < x < B(t)$$

$$u = g_0(t), \quad \frac{\partial u}{\partial x} = \lambda \frac{dB}{dt} + q(t), \quad x = B(t)$$

$$u = \varphi(x) < 0, \quad 0 < x < L, \quad t = 0 \tag{26.14}$$

$$u = g(t) < 0, \quad x = 0, \quad t > 0$$

$$B(0) = L$$

where $\lambda =$ dimensionless latent heat

$1/\lambda =$ the 'Stefan number'.

Physically, the boundary condition at $x = 0$ has to be determined such that the melting interface moves in a prescribed way. Another inverse problem is to determine the heat source $q(t)$ on the surface $B(t)$, given both $g(t)$ and $B(t)$

26.3.5 Two and three space dimensions

We can formulate the Stefan problem in n dimensions. Let us consider the situation as shown in Figure 26.1 in which two regions are separated by an unknown boundary $B(\mathbf{x}, t)$. The diffusion equation with inhomogeneous term Q is defined in each region:

$$c\rho \frac{\partial u}{\partial t} = \nabla(K\nabla) + Q, \quad \mathbf{x} \in \Omega_j, \quad j = 1, 2, \quad 0 < t < T \tag{26.15}$$

where

$$\nabla(K \nabla u) = \sum_{j=1}^{n} \frac{\partial}{\partial x_j}\left(K \frac{\partial u}{\partial x_j}\right)$$

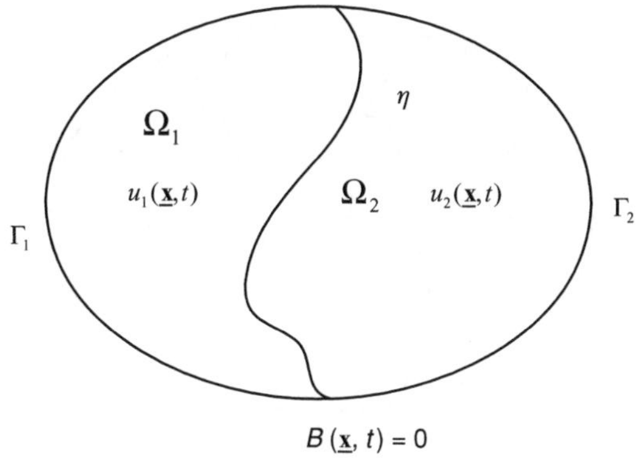

$$B(\underline{x}, t) = 0$$

Figure 26.1   Two-phase flow with moving boundary $B(\mathbf{x}, t)$

and the boundary conditions on the fixed boundaries are given by:

$$\frac{\partial u}{\partial \eta} - hu = g_j(\mathbf{x}\,t), \quad \mathbf{x} \epsilon \Gamma_j, \quad 0 < t < T \tag{26.16}$$

when η = outward normal to boundary Γ_j and where $v_\eta \equiv (\partial v / \partial \eta)$ and g_j are known, $j = 1, \dots, n$, while the conditions on the unknown boundary are given by:

$$\left. \begin{array}{l} u_1(\mathbf{x}, t) = u_2(\mathbf{x}, t) = u_m \\[2mm] \left[K \frac{\partial u}{\partial \eta} \right]_1^2 \equiv K_2 \frac{\partial u_2}{\partial \eta} - K_1 \frac{\partial u_1}{\partial \eta} = -\rho L v_\eta + g \end{array} \right\} \quad \text{on } B(\mathbf{x}\,t) = 0, \quad 0 < t < T \tag{26.17}$$

where u_m is the phase-change temperature and v_η is the velocity on the free boundary.

Finally, the initial conditions are given by:

$$\left. \begin{array}{l} u(\mathbf{x}, 0) = u_0(\mathbf{x}) \\[2mm] B(\mathbf{x}, 0) = B_0(\mathbf{x}) \end{array} \right\} \, t = 0 \tag{26.18}$$

where u_0 and B_0 are given functions.

Problem (26.15)–(26.18) is the n-dimensional equivalent of the problem (26.1)–(26.4). We shall need to understand these higher-dimensional problems when we discuss multi-factor contingent claims containing an American early exercise feature.

An interesting special case is when the free boundary is not 'well defined'. For example, between the solid and liquid phase we experience a 'mushy' phase (part ice, part water). The situation is depicted in Figure 26.2. For example, in one dimension on the interval $[-1, 1]$ we define the different regions as follows:

$$\Omega_T^- = [(x, t): -1 < x < B^-(t), \quad 0 < t < T] \, (\text{solid})$$

$$\Omega_T^+ = [(x, t): B^+(t) < x < 1, \quad 0 < t < T] \, (\text{liquid}) \tag{26.19}$$

$$\Omega_T^* = [(x, t): B^-(t) < x < B^+(t), \quad 0 < t < T] \, (\text{mushy})$$

It is obvious that this problem is more difficult to solve numerically than one-phase or two-phase time-dependent problems. Incidentally, we do not know if there is an analogy with quantitative finance applications.

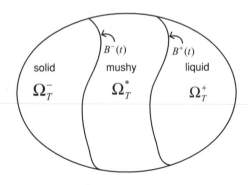

Figure 26.2   Solid, liquid and 'mushy' regions

26.3.6   Oxygen diffusion

Our last example concerns oxygen diffusing into a medium that absorbs and immobilises the oxygen at a constant rate (Crank, 1984). The concentration of the oxygen at the surface of the medium is kept constant. Then a moving boundary marks the innermost limit of oxygen penetration. The surface is then sealed so that no more oxygen penetration takes place. This problem is special because there is a discontinuity in the derivative boundary condition due to the abrupt sealing of the surface. If $u(x, t)$ denotes the concentration of oxygen free to diffuse at a distance x from the surface at time t, then the partial differential equation (in non-dimensional form) is given by:

$$\frac{\partial u}{\partial t} = \frac{\partial^2 u}{\partial x^2}, \quad (x, t) \in \Omega_T^+ \tag{26.20}$$

where

$$\Omega_T^+ = [(x, t) : 0 < x < B(t), \quad 0 < t < T]$$

and $B(t)$ is the moving boundary; the fixed boundary condition is given by:

$$u = g_0(t) \quad \text{or} \quad \frac{\partial u}{\partial x} + b(t)u = g_1(t) \tag{26.21}$$

while the free boundary condition is given by:

$$\left. \begin{aligned} u &= 0 \\ \frac{dB}{dt} &= -\frac{\partial u}{\partial x} \end{aligned} \right\} x = B(t), \quad 0 < t < T \tag{26.22}$$

When $t = 0$ the initial condition is given by:

$$\left. \begin{aligned} u(x, 0) &= u_0(x) \\ B(0) &= x_0 \end{aligned} \right\} x \in \Omega^+(0) \tag{26.23}$$

26.4   SOLUTIONS IN FINANCIAL ENGINEERING: A PREVIEW

In principle, all the examples and test cases that we have discussed in previous chapters for the European exercise case can and do have their American counterparts. We need to formulate the mathematical problem (there may be more than one formulation) and then determine how to approximate this problem using numerical methods.

26.4.1   What kinds of early exercise features?

As already mentioned, for every European option we can think of a corresponding American one. Some possibilities are:

- A one-factor model with constant volatility and no dividends. We can model this problem by the binomial method and checking for early exercise at each time level (Wilmott, 1993). Accuracy is first order, however.
- Problems with stochastic volatility: this corresponds to the Heston model with early exercise features (Oosterloo, 2003).

- Option models that use Levy processes; in this case we can formulate the problem (wait for it) as a parabolic integro differential variational inequality (PIVI).
- Asian American options.
- American passport options.
- Multi-factor options with early exercise feature.
- Problems with jumps, thus introducing integral terms as in the Merton jump model.

We shall discuss a number of these problems in the following chapters. As far as a mathematical formulation is concerned, there are several possibilities:

- We can transform the initial boundary value problem with free boundary to a nonlinear problem on a fixed domain. The free boundary is modelled as part of a nonlinear partial differential equation. This process is called 'front fixing'.
- We can add a so-called penalty term to the option PDE, thus allowing us to find the option price without having to worry about the free boundary. This is called the 'regularisaton process'.
- We can adopt a variational formulation; this results in some kind of parabolic variational inequality (PVI) or even parabolic integro-differential variational inequality (PIVI).

26.4.2   What kinds of numerical techniques?

Depending on the mathematical model, we have a number of numerical techniques at our disposal. The two main categories are those based on finite differences or approximations that rely on a variational formulation. The latter category uses many ideas from the finite element method (FEM). Again, we study the various numerical methods in more detail in the coming chapters.

26.5   SUMMARY AND CONCLUSIONS

We have given an introduction to free and moving boundary value problems by looking at some examples from heat transfer applications. The mathematical theory for such problems is well-developed and much numerical work has been done. We also discuss the initial boundary value problem (with moving boundary) that describes an option with the American exercise feature. There are many similarities between this problem and problems from the physical sciences. Thus, understanding the background to free boundary problems will be of benefit when modelling American option problems in the coming chapters.

27

Numerical Methods for Free Boundary Value Problems: Front-Fixing Methods

27.1 INTRODUCTION AND OBJECTIVES

In this chapter we introduce a class of finite difference schemes to approximate the solution of a parabolic initial boundary value problem (IBVP) with a free boundary. Not only do we wish to find the solution of the IBVP but we also need to find the position of the free boundary. To this end, we define a new variable that allows us to transform the original IBVP to one in which the free boundary is absent. The method is called front-fixing because all boundaries are known or fixed.

As an application, we apply the method to finding schemes for a one-factor put option with American exercise feature. We examine implicit, explicit and predictor–corrector schemes. Furthermore, we discuss the use of the front-fixing methods to two-factor convertible bond modelling.

27.2 AN INTRODUCTION TO FRONT-FIXING METHODS

Free boundary value problems are special because we have to find the solution of a partial differential equation that satisfies auxiliary initial conditions and boundary conditions on a fixed boundary as well as on a free boundary. The first technique that we discuss is called front fixing and in this case we track the free surface by a suitable change of variables. We then use partial differentiation to produce a nonlinear partial differential equation on a fixed domain. In the examples in this chapter we have a free boundary somewhere in the interior of the domain of interest. In this case we look specifically at the transformation that was suggested in Landau (1950)

$$x = \frac{S}{B(t)} \tag{27.1}$$

where, for the Black–Scholes equation, S is the underlying and $B(t)$ is the early exercise boundary. Now, we transform the (linear) Black–Scholes equation in the independent variables (S, t) to a nonlinear PDE in the new independent variables (x, t). In order to effect the transformation we must use partial derivatives and, to this end, we give a quick review of them. Then we look at some examples, including applications to one-factor American option pricing.

27.3 A CRASH COURSE ON PARTIAL DERIVATIVES

You can skip this sub-section if you can do partial derivatives blind-folded. In general, we are interested in functions of two variables and we consider a function of the form:

$$z = f(x, y)$$

The variables x and y can take values in a given bounded or unbounded interval. First, we say that $f(x, y)$ is continuous at (a, b) if the limit

$$\lim_{\substack{x \to a \\ y \to b}} f(x, y)$$

exists and is equal to $f(a, b)$. We now need definitions for the derivatives of f in the x and y directions.

In general, we calculate the partial derivatives by keeping one variable fixed and differentiating with respect to the other variable, for example:

$$z = f(x, y) = e^{kx} \cos ly$$

$$\frac{\partial z}{\partial x} = k \, e^{kx} \cos ly$$

$$\frac{\partial z}{\partial y} = -l \, e^{kx} \sin ly$$

We now discuss the situation when we introduce a change of variables into some problem and then wish to calculate the new partial derivatives. To this end, we start with the variables (x, y) and we define new variables (u, v). We can think of these as 'original' and 'transformed' coordinate axes, respectively. Now define the functions $z(u, v)$ as follows:

$$z = z(u, v), \qquad u = u(x, y), \qquad v = v(x, y)$$

This can be seen as 'a function of a function'. We are interested in the following result: if z is a differentiable function of (u, v) and u, v are continuous functions of x, y, with partial derivatives, then the following rule holds:

$$\begin{aligned}
\frac{\partial z}{\partial x} &= \frac{\partial z}{\partial u} \frac{\partial u}{\partial x} + \frac{\partial z}{\partial v} \frac{\partial v}{\partial x} \\[2mm]
\frac{\partial z}{\partial y} &= \frac{\partial z}{\partial u} \frac{\partial u}{\partial y} + \frac{\partial z}{\partial v} \frac{\partial v}{\partial y}
\end{aligned} \tag{27.2}$$

This is a fundamental result that we shall apply in this chapter. We take a simple example of equation (27.2) to show how things work. To this end, consider the Laplace equation in Cartesian geometry:

$$\frac{\partial^2 u}{\partial x^2} + \frac{\partial^2 u}{\partial y^2} = 0$$

We now wish to transform this equation into an equation in a circular region defined by the polar coordinates:

$$x = r \cos \theta, \qquad y = r \sin \theta$$

The derivative in r is given by:

$$\frac{\partial u}{\partial r} = \frac{\partial u}{\partial x} \frac{\partial x}{\partial r} + \frac{\partial u}{\partial y} \frac{\partial y}{\partial r} = \cos \theta \frac{\partial u}{\partial x} + \sin \theta \frac{\partial u}{\partial y}$$

and you can check that the derivative in θ is:

$$\frac{\partial u}{\partial \theta} = -r \sin \theta \frac{\partial u}{\partial x} + r \cos \theta \frac{\partial u}{\partial y}$$

hence

$$\frac{\partial u}{\partial x} = \cos \theta \frac{\partial u}{\partial r} - \frac{1}{r} \sin \theta \frac{\partial u}{\partial \theta}$$

$$\frac{\partial u}{\partial y} = \sin \theta \frac{\partial u}{\partial r} + \frac{1}{r} \cos \theta \frac{\partial u}{\partial \theta}$$

and

$$\frac{\partial^2 u}{\partial x^2} = \cos \theta \frac{\partial}{\partial r} \left(\frac{\partial u}{\partial x} \right) - \frac{1}{r} \sin \theta \frac{\partial}{\partial \theta} \left(\frac{\partial u}{\partial x} \right)$$

$$\frac{\partial^2 u}{\partial y^2} = \sin \theta \frac{\partial}{\partial r} \left(\frac{\partial u}{\partial y} \right) + \frac{1}{r} \cos \theta \frac{\partial}{\partial \theta} \left(\frac{\partial u}{\partial y} \right)$$

Combining these results allows us finally to write Laplace's equation in polar coordinates as follows:

$$\frac{\partial^2 u}{\partial r^2} + \frac{1}{r} \frac{\partial u}{\partial r} + \frac{1}{r^2} \frac{\partial^2 u}{\partial \theta^2} = 0, \quad u(l, \theta) = f(\theta)$$

Thus, the original heat equation in Cartesian coordinates is transformed to a singular initial boundary value problem of convection–diffusion type. We can find a solution to this problem using the separation of variables method, for example.

27.4   FUNCTIONS AND IMPLICIT FORMS

Some problems use functions of two variables that are written in the implicit form:

$$f(x, y) = 0$$

In this case we have an implicit relationship between the variables x and y. We assume that y is a function of x. The basic result for the differentiation of this implicit function is:

$$df \equiv \frac{\partial f}{\partial x} dx + \frac{\partial f}{\partial y} dy = 0 \tag{27.3a}$$

or

$$\frac{dy}{dx} = -\frac{\partial f / \partial x}{\partial f / \partial y} \tag{27.3b}$$

We now use this result by posing the following problem; consider the transformation:

$$\left. \begin{array}{l} u = u(x, y) \\ v = v(x, y) \end{array} \right\} \text{original equations}$$

and suppose we wish to 'transform back':

$$\left. \begin{array}{l} x = x(u, v) \\ y = y(u, v) \end{array} \right\} \text{find } x, y \text{ (inverse functions)}$$

To this end, we examine the following differentials

$$du = \frac{\partial u}{\partial x} dx + \frac{\partial u}{\partial y} dy$$

$$dv = \frac{\partial v}{\partial x} dx + \frac{\partial v}{\partial y} dy$$

(27.4)

Let us assume that we wish to find dx and dy given that all other quantities are known. Some arithmetic applied to (27.4) (two equations in two unknowns!) results in:

$$dx = \left(\frac{\partial v}{\partial y} du - \frac{\partial u}{\partial y} dv \right) / J$$

$$dy = \left(-\frac{\partial v}{\partial x} du + \frac{\partial u}{\partial x} dv \right) / J$$

(27.5)

where J is the Jacobian determinant defined by:

$$J = \begin{vmatrix} \dfrac{\partial u}{\partial x} & \dfrac{\partial u}{\partial y} \\ \dfrac{\partial v}{\partial x} & \dfrac{\partial v}{\partial y} \end{vmatrix} = \frac{\partial(u, v)}{\partial(x, y)}$$

(27.6)

We can thus conclude the following result.

Theorem 27.1. *The functions $x = F(u, v)$ and $y = G(u, v)$ exist if*

$$\frac{\partial u}{\partial x}, \quad \frac{\partial u}{\partial y}, \quad \frac{\partial v}{\partial x}, \quad \frac{\partial v}{\partial y}$$

are continuous at (a, b) and if the Jacobian determinant is non-zero at (a, b).

Let us take the example:

$$u = \frac{x^2}{y}, \quad v = \frac{y^2}{x}$$

You can check that the Jacobian is given by

$$\frac{\partial(u, v)}{\partial(x, y)} = \begin{vmatrix} \dfrac{2x}{y} & \dfrac{-x^2}{y^2} \\ \dfrac{-y^2}{x^2} & \dfrac{2y}{x} \end{vmatrix} = 3 \neq 0$$

Solving for x and y gives

$$x = u^{1/3} v^{2/3}, \quad y = u^{2/3} v^{1/3}$$

You need to be comfortable with partial derivatives and the basic results in this section are a prerequisite for what is to come. A good reference is Widder (1989).

27.5   FRONT FIXING FOR THE HEAT EQUATION

As a first example, we examine the one-dimensional Stefan problem (Crank, 1984):

$$\frac{\partial u}{\partial t} = \frac{\partial^2 u}{\partial x^2}, \quad 0 < x < s(t), \quad t > 0$$

$$u = 1, \quad x = 0, \quad t > 0 \tag{27.7}$$

$$u = 0, \quad x > 0, \quad t = 0$$

where $s(0) = 0$

$$u = 0$$

$$-\frac{\partial u}{\partial x} = \lambda \frac{ds}{dt}, \quad x = s(t), \quad t > 0$$

and $\lambda = $ latent heat.

Applying the Landau transformation where $s = s(t)$ is the moving boundary

$$\xi = \frac{x}{s(t)} \tag{27.8}$$

Using the rules for partial differentiation we can calculate the derivatives in the new variables (set $\tau \equiv t$ identically just to be complete):

$$\frac{\partial u}{\partial x} = \frac{\partial u}{\partial \xi}\frac{\partial \xi}{\partial x} + \frac{\partial u}{\partial \tau}\frac{\partial \tau}{\partial x} = \frac{1}{s(t)}\frac{\partial u}{\partial \xi} + 0 \tag{27.9a}$$

$$\frac{\partial u}{\partial t} = \frac{\partial u}{\partial \xi}\frac{\partial \xi}{\partial t} + \frac{\partial u}{\partial \tau}\frac{\partial \tau}{\partial t} = \frac{\partial u}{\partial \xi}\frac{\partial \xi}{\partial s}\frac{ds}{dt} + \frac{\partial u}{\partial \tau} = \frac{\partial u}{\partial \xi}\frac{\partial \xi}{\partial s}\frac{ds}{dt} + \frac{\partial u}{\partial t} \tag{27.9b}$$

or

$$\frac{\partial u}{\partial x} = \frac{1}{s(t)}\frac{\partial u}{\partial \xi}, \quad \frac{\partial^2 u}{\partial x^2} = \frac{1}{s(t)^2}\frac{\partial^2 u}{\partial \xi^2} \tag{27.9.c}$$

$$\left(\frac{\partial u}{\partial t}\right)_x = \frac{\partial u}{\partial \xi}\frac{\partial \xi}{\partial t} + \left(\frac{\partial u}{\partial t}\right)_\xi = \frac{-x}{s(t)^2}\frac{ds}{dt}\frac{\partial u}{\partial \xi} + \left(\frac{\partial u}{\partial t}\right)_\xi \tag{27.9.d}$$

We now get a convection–diffusion equation in the new coordinate system:

$$\frac{\partial^2 u}{\partial \xi^2} = s^2\frac{\partial u}{\partial t} - s\xi\frac{ds}{dt}\frac{\partial u}{\partial \xi}, \quad 0 < \xi < 1, \quad t > 0 \tag{27.10}$$

We have thus transformed a linear diffusion equation with a moving boundary into a nonlinear convection–diffusion equation on a fixed domain $(0, 1)$.

Furthermore, the conditions on the free boundary are given by:

$$-\frac{1}{s}\frac{\partial u}{\partial \xi} = \lambda\frac{ds}{dt}, \quad \xi = 1, \quad t > 0 \tag{27.11}$$

Looking at this equation we conclude that we now have a PDE on a fixed interval (no free boundary) but now there are two unknowns, namely the temperature u and the free surface $s = s(t)$. Thus, we have simplified the problem in one direction but it has become more complex in the other direction!

We shall discuss later how to approximate the transformed problem by finite difference schemes when we discuss one-factor American option models.

27.6   FRONT FIXING FOR GENERAL PROBLEMS

The front-fixing method can be applied to more general two-phase problems involving convection–diffusion equations (see Crank, 1984). To this end, let us examine the situation in equation (27.12). In each of the regions ($j = 1$ and $j = 2$) we have the following PDE:

$$-c_j \frac{\partial u_j}{\partial t} + \sigma_j \frac{\partial^2 u}{\partial x^2} + \mu_j \frac{\partial u_j}{\partial x} + b_j u_j = f_j(x, t), \quad 0 < t < T \quad (j = 1, 2) \qquad (27.12)$$

Phase 1 is defined by the region I ($j = 1$) and phase 2 is defined by region II ($j = 2$). Again, let $s(t)$ be the moving boundary.

The initial conditions are given by:

$$\begin{aligned}
u_1(x, 0) &= u_{10}(x), \quad l_1 \le x \le s(0) \\
u_2(x, 0) &= u_{20}(x), \quad s(0) \le x \le l_2 \quad (s(0) \text{ given})
\end{aligned} \qquad (27.13)$$

The fixed boundary conditions are of the Robin type:

$$\alpha_{1j}(t)u_j + \alpha_{2j}(t)\frac{\partial u_j}{\partial x} = \alpha_j(t), \quad j = 1, 2 \quad \text{for } x = l_j, \quad 0 < t < T \qquad (27.14)$$

The conditions on the free boundary take the following general form:

$$\left. \begin{aligned}
u_1 = u_2 &= G\left(s, \frac{ds}{dt}, t\right) \\
F\left(u, \frac{\partial u_1}{\partial x}, \frac{\partial u_2}{\partial x}, \frac{\partial u}{\partial t}, s, \frac{ds}{dt}, t\right) &= 0
\end{aligned} \right\} \begin{aligned} x &= s(t) \\ 0 &< t < T \end{aligned} \qquad (27.15)$$

We transform the PDE in each phase by the change of variables:

$$\xi_j = \frac{x - l_j}{s(t) - l_j}, \quad j = 1, 2 \qquad (27.16)$$

We show what the transformed PDE is in region I (we drop the subscript for convenience):

$$\sigma \frac{\partial^2 u}{\partial \xi^2} + (s - l_1)\left(\mu + c\xi \frac{ds}{dt}\right)\frac{\partial u}{\partial \xi} + (s - l_1)^2 bu - (s - l_1)^2 c \frac{\partial u}{\partial t}$$

$$= (s - l_1)^2 f(x, t), \quad 0 < \xi < 1, \quad 0 < t < T \qquad (27.17)$$

A similar equation holds for region II. Again, we have a nonlinear convection–diffusion equation on a fixed domain. The reader has enough information to check that (27.17) is indeed true. We shall apply this knowledge to the Black–Scholes equation.

27.7   MULTIDIMENSIONAL PROBLEMS

The one-dimensional Landau coordinate transformation (27.1) is a special case of a more general transformation of curved-shaped regions in two or more dimension to straight-edged rectangular or cubed regions (Crank, 1984; Hughes, 2000). A discussion of this problem is beyond the scope of this book; however, we do mention that such transformations may be needed in financial engineering applications, for example convertible bond modelling with an American exercise feature (Sun, 1999). We describe the basic financial problem and we show how this two-factor problem with a free boundary reduces to a problem on a fixed boundary.

A convertible bond is a bond issued by a corporation offering investors the right to convert the bond to a specified number of shares of stock from the issuing firm. The conversion option of the bond is exercisable when and if the investor wishes to do so. The holder, on the other hand, has the right but not the obligation to exchange the convertible bond for common stock of the issuing firm. In general the bond price $V = V(S, r, t)$ is a function of three variables:

- S, the stock price
- r, the spot interest rate
- t, time

The stock price S is modelled using the stochastic differential equation (SDE):

$$dS = \mu(S, t)S \, dt + \sigma(S, t) \, dX_1 \tag{27.18}$$

where dX_1 = normally, distributed random variable (mean 0 and variance dt)

$$\mu = \text{drift}$$

$$\sigma = \text{volatility}$$

The SDE for the interest rate r is given by:

$$dr = u(r, t) \, dt + w(r, t) \, dX_2 \tag{27.19}$$

where dX_2 is the normally distributed random variable (mean 0 and variable dt) and $u(r, t)$ and $w(r, t)$ are (as of now) unspecified functions.

The stock market and the fixed income market are related to each other and the correlation is given by the relationship:

$$E(dX_1, \, dX_2) = \rho(S, r, t) \, dt \tag{27.20}$$

Furthermore, we assume continuous dividends and that the bond pays a coupon at an annual rate k and that at expiry the convertible returns Z unless it has been converted into n shares in the meantime. Finally, we assume that there are no transaction costs. Then the PDE for the convertible bond V becomes (Wilmott, 1998; Sun, 1999):

$$\frac{\partial V}{\partial t} + \tfrac{1}{2}\sigma^2 S^2 \frac{\partial^2 V}{\partial S^2} + \rho\sigma Sw \frac{\partial^2 V}{\partial S \, \partial r} + \tfrac{1}{2}w^2 \frac{\partial^2 V}{\partial r^2} +$$

$$+ (r - D_0)S \frac{\partial V}{\partial S} + (u - \lambda w)\frac{\partial v}{\partial r} - rV + kZ = 0 \tag{27.21}$$

where $\lambda = \lambda(S, r, t)$ is the market price of risk.

The payoff function is given by:

$$V(S, r, T) = \max(nS, Z) \tag{27.22}$$

Since the bond can be converted into n shares of the underlying stock at any time before expiry, the price V must satisfy the so-called conversion constraint:

$$V(S, r, t) \geq nS \tag{27.23}$$

We now commence with a formulation of the problem. First, we define the PDE (27.21) that is defined in the domain $[0, B(r, t)]$, where t is in the closed range $[0, T]$. The terminal conditions are given by:

$$B(r, T) = \max\left(\frac{Z}{n}, \frac{kZ}{D_0 n}\right), \quad r_l \leq r \leq r_u \tag{27.24}$$

$$V(S, r, T) = \max(nS, Z), \quad 0 \leq S \leq B(r, T), \quad r_l \leq r \leq r_u$$

The conditions on the free boundary are given by:

$$V(B(r, t), r, t) = nB(r, t), \quad r_l \leq r \leq r_u, \quad 0 \leq t \leq T$$

$$\frac{\partial V}{\partial S}(B(r, t), r, t) = n, \quad r_l \leq r \leq r_u, \quad 0 \leq t \leq T \tag{27.25}$$

Here we are saying that the bond price and its derivative are continuous at the free boundary. We now must specify the fixed boundary condition when $S = 0$:

$$\frac{\partial V}{\partial t} + \frac{1}{2}w^2\frac{\partial^2 V}{\partial r^2} + (u - \lambda w)\frac{\partial V}{\partial r} - rV + kZ = 0 \tag{27.26}$$

In this case we are saying that the PDE is satisfied at $S = 0$; it is not allowed to specify boundary conditions because the PDE is singular at that point. We now define either of the following boundary conditions for large values of r:

$$V(r_u, t) = 0 \quad \text{or} \quad \frac{\partial V}{\partial r}(r_u, t) = 0 \tag{27.27}$$

In Sun (1999) the author takes the following change of variables in order to reduce the problem to dimensionless form:

$$s = \frac{nS}{Z}$$

$$U(s, r, t) = \frac{V(S, r, t)}{Z} = \frac{V(ZS/r, r, t)}{Z}$$

$$b(r, t) = \frac{nB(r, t)}{Z}$$

Using the Landau transformation we define new coordinate system as follows:

$$\xi = s/B(r, t)$$
$$r = r$$
$$\tau = T - t$$

Then the new variable $W(\xi, r, t)$ satisfies the nonlinear initial boundary value problem on a fixed interval:

$$\frac{\partial W}{\partial \tau} = \frac{\partial W}{\partial \xi}\frac{\xi}{b}\frac{\partial \bar{b}}{\partial \tau} + a_1\xi^2\frac{\partial^2 W}{\partial \xi^2} + a_2\xi\frac{\partial^2 W}{\partial \xi \partial r} + a_3\frac{\partial^2 W}{\partial r^2} + a_4\xi\frac{\partial W}{\partial \xi} +$$

$$+ a_5\frac{\partial W}{\partial r} + a_6 W + a_7, \quad 0 \leq \xi \leq 1, \quad r_l \leq r \leq r_u \tag{27.28a}$$

$$W(\xi, r, 0) = \max(\xi \overline{B}(r, 0), 1), \quad 0 \le \xi \le 1, \quad r_l \le r \le r_u \tag{27.28b}$$

$$W(1, r, \tau) = \overline{B}(r, \tau), \quad r_l \le r \le r_u, \quad 0 \le \tau \le T \tag{27.28c}$$

$$\frac{\partial W}{\partial \xi}(1, r, \tau) = \overline{b}(r, \tau), \quad r_l \le r \le r_u, \quad 0 \le \tau \le T \tag{27.28d}$$

$$\overline{B}(r, 0) = \max\left(1, \frac{k}{D_0}\right), \quad r_l \le r \le r_u \tag{27.28e}$$

where

$$\overline{B}(r, \tau) = B(r, T - t)$$

and

$$a_j = a_j\left(u, \lambda, w, \rho\sigma, r, k, D_0, \overline{b}, \frac{\partial \overline{b}}{\partial r}, \frac{\partial^2 \overline{b}}{\partial r^2}\right)$$

Thus, we have transformed the original convertible bond problem to a problem on a fixed boundary using the front-fixing method as introduced in this chapter. We then must solve problem (27.28) in some way. For example, Sun (1999) uses ADI methods.

27.8   FRONT-FIXING AND AMERICAN OPTIONS

In this section we discuss the details of a finite difference schemes for a one-factor American put option problem using the front-fixing method. The basic technique is discussed in Crank (1984) and has been applied to option pricing in Nielson *et al.* (2002). We recall the basic option pricing problem from Chapter 26. Applying the Landau transformation the reader may like to check that the transformed system is given by:

$$\frac{\partial P}{\partial t} + \frac{1}{2}\sigma^2 x^2 \frac{\partial^2 P}{\partial x^2} + x\left[r - \frac{B'(t)}{B(t)}\right]\frac{\partial P}{\partial x} - rP = 0, \quad x > 1, \quad 1 < x < \infty, \quad 0 \le t \le T \tag{27.29}$$

$$P(x, T) = 0, \quad x \ge 1$$

$$\lim_{x \to \infty} P(x, t) = 0$$

$$\frac{\partial P}{\partial x}(1, t) = -B(t)$$

$$P(1, t) = K - B(t)$$

$$B(T) = K$$

We now approximate this problem using finite difference schemes. There are a number of issues that we must address:

- Approximating the nonlinear differential equation: we have two unknowns, namely the put price P and free boundary B. We need to choose between explicit and implicit schemes.

- Far field condition: we truncate the semi-infinite interval and apply Dirichlet boundary conditions at the new boundary; another possibility is to define the new variable $y = x/(x + K)$. Then we get a PDE on a bounded interval.
- How to approximate the Neumann boundary condition at the boundary $x = 1$, (one-sided or two-sided schemes).

In the following we apply the scheme that is discussed in Nielsen *et al.* (2002). We first discuss the approximation of the PDE. The implicit scheme is given by:

$$\frac{P_j^{n+1} - P_j^n}{k} + \tfrac{1}{2}\sigma^2 x_j^2 D_+ D_- P_j^n + x_j \left(r - \frac{B^{n+1} - B^n}{k B^n} \right)$$

$$\times D_0 P_j^n - r P_j^n = 0 \quad (j = 1 \ldots J, \quad n = N, N - 1, \ldots, 0) \qquad (27.30)$$

Here we see that the free boundary $B(t)$ is evaluated at the time level n, thus it is unknown. We shall need a non-linear solver (for example, the Newton–Raphson method) for this problem as we shall presently see. The explicit method, on the other hand is given by:

$$\frac{P_j^{n+1} - P_j^n}{k} + \tfrac{1}{2}\sigma^2 x_j^2 D_+ D_- P_j^{n+1} + x_j \left(r - \frac{B^{n+1} - B^n}{k B^{n+1}} \right)$$

$$\times D_0 P_j^{n+1} - r P_j^{n+1} = 0 \quad (j = 1 \ldots J, \quad n = N, N - 1, \ldots, 0) \qquad (27.31)$$

Here we see that there are two 'uncoupled' unknowns at time level n, namely the put price P and the free boundary B. The corresponding system is linear. In both cases (27.30) and (27.31) we are assuming that the x interval is partitioned into $J + 1$ sub-intervals and the t interval is partitioned into $N + 1$ sub-intervals. The final conditions are given by:

$$P_j^{N+1} = 0, \quad j = 0, \ldots, J + 1$$

$$B^{N+1} = K \qquad (27.32)$$

The boundary conditions are given by:

$$P_0^n = K - B^n,$$

$$P_{J+1}^n = 0, \quad n = N, \ldots, 0 \qquad (27.33)$$

while the first-order approximation to the Neumann boundary condition is given by:

$$\frac{P_1^n - P_0^n}{h} = -B^n, \quad n = N, \ldots, 0 \qquad (27.34)$$

We are now ready to write this scheme in a more compact form that is suitable for Newton's method in the implicit case (27.30). As in Nielsen *et al.* (2002), the nonlinear system can be written in the form:

$$F(\mathbf{P}^n, B^n) \equiv A(B^n)\mathbf{P}^n - f(B^n) = 0, \quad n = N, \ldots, 0$$

$$\mathbf{P}^n = {}^t(P_2^n, \ldots, P_J) \qquad (27.35)$$

where A is a tridiagonal matrix and

$$f(\cdot) = {}^t \left(f_2(B^n), f_3(B^n), \ldots, f_J(B^n) \right)$$

Then Newton's method becomes an iterative scheme. Let $y = {}^t(P_1^n, \ldots, P_J^n, B^n)$ and define the iterative scheme:

$$y_{k+1} = y_k - J^{-1}(y_k)F(y_k), \quad k \geq 0$$

$$J = \left(\frac{\partial Fi}{\partial x_j}\right), \quad 1 \leq i, j \leq J \tag{27.36}$$

where J is the Jacobian of F (for more information on Newton's method, see Press *et al.*, 2002 or Dahlquist, 1974, for example). The algorithm for the explicit scheme (27.31) is given in Nielsen (2002). We note that the schemes in this section can be applied to approximating call options with dividends with an early exercise feature:

$$\frac{\partial C}{\partial t} + \frac{1}{2}\sigma^2 S^2 \frac{\partial^2 C}{\partial S^2} + (r - D_0)S\frac{\partial C}{\partial S} - rC = 0 \tag{27.37}$$

and

$$C(S, T) = \max(S - K, 0)$$

$$\lim_{S \to \infty} C(S, t) = S$$

$$\frac{\partial C}{\partial S}(B(t), t) = 1$$

$$C(B(t), t) = B(t) - K$$

$$B(T) = K$$

$$C(S, t) = S - K, \quad 0 \leq S < B(t)$$

27.9 OTHER FINITE DIFFERENCE SCHEMES

In this section we give some pointers to other finite difference methods that explicitly model the free boundary as part of the problem. Not all methods are equally popular. An analysis of the different methods could be the subject of an MSc of PhD thesis.

27.9.1 The method of lines and predictor–corrector

Looking at the transformed PDE (27.29) again, we decide to carry out a semi-discretisation in the x direction only while keeping t continuous. The resulting system of ordinary differential equations becomes:

$$\frac{dP_j}{dt} + \frac{1}{2}\sigma^2 x_j^2 D_+ D_- P_j + x_j \left[r - \frac{B'(t)}{B(t)}\right] D_0 P_j - r P_j = 0, \quad 1 \leq j \leq J \tag{27.38}$$

This problem can now be posed (after incorporating boundary conditions of course) as a nonlinear initial value problem (IVP):

$$U'(t) + F[t, U(t)] = 0 \quad (U(0) \text{ given}) \tag{27.39}$$

where $U = {}^t(P_2, \ldots, P_J, B)$

We can now solve this problem by a predictor–corrector method as already discussed in this book (see Conte and de Boor, 1980). The advantages of using the predictor–corrector method when compared to the finite difference schemes in Nielsen *et al.* (2002) are:

- It is a robust method and performs well under many conditions
- No need to solve a nonlinear system of equations at each time level
- Setting up the semi-discrete system of equations is easy
- It has good accuracy properties.

27.10   SUMMARY AND CONCLUSIONS

We have introduced the front-fixing method for one-factor American options. The idea is to define new variables so that the original problem with a free boundary is replaced by one containing fixed boundaries. We then must decide how to approximate this new problem using finite differences.

We discussed a number of approaches. The front-fixing method is certainly applicable to one-factor problems but it may be difficult to apply to higher-dimensional problems. For these problems, we have discussed some other techniques, such as:

- Implicit finite difference scheme
- Explicit difference scheme
- Predictor–corrector method.

Viscosity Solutions and Penalty Methods for American Option Problems

28.1 INTRODUCTION AND OBJECTIVES

In this chapter we introduce a class of finite difference schemes without having to model the free boundary explicitly. Instead, a so-called nonlinear penalty term is added to the Black–Scholes equation and a solution is produced that satisfies the constraint:

$$P(S, t) \geq \max(K - S, 0)$$

at all times. Thus, we do not have to worry about the free boundary. The penalty term is non linear and we must think about what kinds of finite difference schemes to use. However, the nonlinearity appears in the reaction (zero-order) term and hence is not too severe, at least from a computational point of view. To this end, we propose explicit, implicit and semi-implicit schemes for one-factor problems. We discuss the stability of these schemes and their applicability to multi-factor problems.

The mathematical theory in this chapter is quite advanced. You may go directly to section 28.3 if you are interested in the numerical methods.

28.2 DEFINITIONS AND MAIN RESULTS FOR PARABOLIC PROBLEMS

In this section we introduce a number of mathematical results that are related to the work in this chapter. In particular, we use some of the fundamental results from Crandall *et al.* (1992).

28.2.1 Semi-continuity

We introduce some definitions. We first introduce the concept of a metric space (Haaser and Sullivan, 1991). Let X be an arbitrary set. Then a metric or distance function d on X is a real-valued function defined on the product space $X \times X$ satisfying the following properties:

$$d(x, y) \geq 0; \qquad d(x, y) = 0 \Leftrightarrow x = y \tag{28.1a}$$

$$d(x, y) = d(y, x) \tag{28.1b}$$

$$d(x, y) \leq d(x, z) + d(z, y) \tag{28.1c}$$

Then we define X to be a metric space if it is non-empty and equipped with a metric d. In this case we use the notation (X, d).

As an example of a metric space, let X be the n-dimensional real space whose metric is the Euclidean distance function:

$$x, y \in \mathbb{R}^n, \qquad x = (x_1, \ldots, x_n), \qquad y = (y_1, \ldots, y_n)$$

$$d(x, y) = \left[\sum_{j=1}^{n} (x_j - y_j)^2 \right]^{\frac{1}{2}}$$

The reader can check that this is indeed a metric space by verifying the axioms in (28.1) Now, let (X, d) be a metric space and let f be a real-valued function defined on a subset E of X. Then f is continuous at a point $a \in E$ if for each $\varepsilon > 0$ there exists a $\delta > 0$ such that

$$f(a) - \epsilon < f(x) < f(a) + \epsilon \quad \forall x \in B(a; \delta) \cap E \tag{28.2}$$

where B $(a; \delta)$ is the open ball in X with centre a and radius δ, that is

$$B(a; \delta) = \{x \in E : d(x, a) < \delta\}, \quad \text{where } d(., .) \text{ is a metric.}$$

The function f is said to be semi-continuous if one of the inequalities in (28.2) holds. Suppose now for each $\varepsilon > 0$ there exists a $\delta > 0$ such that

$$f(x) < f(a) + \epsilon \quad \forall x \in B(a; \delta) \cap E \tag{28.3}$$

Then f is said to be upper semi-continuous at a. Similarly, f is said to be lower semi-continuous at a if for each $\varepsilon > 0$ there exists a $\delta > 0$ such that

$$f(a) - \varepsilon < f(x) \quad \forall x \in B(a; \delta) \cap E \tag{28.4}$$

Semi-continuity is a more general concept than continuity. In fact, we can prove that a real-valued function is continuous if and only if it is both upper semi-continuous and lower semi-continuous (see Rudin, 1970).

Let us take an example. Let E be a subset of a metric space X. Define the characteristic function:

$$\chi_E(x) = \begin{cases} 1, & x \in E \\ 0, & x \notin E \end{cases}$$

If E is closed then the characteristic function is upper semi-continuous; if E is open then the characteristic function is lower semi-continuous. The set E can be closed or open.

We define the following notations. Let X be a metric space. Then define the sets

$$\text{USC}(X) = \{\text{upper semi-continous functions } f : X \to \mathbb{R}^1\}$$

$$\text{LSC}(X) = \{\text{lower semi-continuous functions } f : X \to \mathbb{R}^1\} \tag{28.5}$$

These function spaces will play an important role in the following sections.

28.2.2 Viscosity solutions of nonlinear parabolic problems

The results in this section are based on the article by Crandall, Ishi and Lions (1992). Incidentally, one of the authors (P.L. Lions) received the Fields Medal (the equivalent of the Nobel Prize for mathematics) for his work on nonlinear differential equations.

We consider second-order parabolic initial boundary value problems in m dimensions. The results in Crandall *et al.* (1992) are valid for a wider class of equation than just the linear Black–Scholes equation. To this end, consider the nonlinear parabolic differential equation:

$$\frac{\partial u}{\partial t} + F(t, x, Du, D^2 u) = 0 \tag{28.6}$$

where u is a real-valued function defined on some open subset E in m-dimensional real space. Furthermore, we use the notation:

$$Du = \text{gradient of } u$$
$$D^2 u = \text{matrix of second derivatives of } u$$

These quantities are not necessarily differentiable in the classical sense and hence equation (28.6) may not have solutions in the classical sense. In this section we relax the idea of a classical solution of (28.6) by defining so-called sub- and super-solutions. There are many special cases of equation (28.6), one of which is the linear Black–Scholes equation in m dimensions:

$$F \equiv \frac{1}{2} \sum_{i=1}^{m} \sum_{j=1}^{m} \rho_{ij} \sigma_i \sigma_j S_i S_j \frac{\partial^2 P}{\partial S_i \partial S_j} +$$

$$+ \sum_{j=1}^{m} (r - D_j) S_j \frac{\partial P}{\partial S_j} - rP = 0 \tag{28.7}$$

We now need to discuss the concept of sub-solution and super-solution of equation (28.6). To this end, let Q be a locally compact subset of $\mathbb{R}^n$ and let $T > 0$. Define $Q_T = (0, T) \times Q$.

We now define one more, somewhat tricky, concept.

First, let $S(m)$ be the set of symmetric $m \times m$ matrices. If $u : Q_T \to \mathbb{R}^1$ then $P_Q^{2,+} u$ is defined by the set $(a, p, X) \in \mathbb{R}^1 \times \mathbb{R}^m \times S(m)$ and lies in $P_0^{2,+} u(s, z)$ if $(s, z) \in Q_T$ and

$$u(t, x) \leq u(s, z) + a(t - s) + \langle p, x - z \rangle + \frac{1}{2} \langle X(x - z), x - z \rangle$$

$$+ O(|t - s| + |x - z|^2) \quad \text{as } Q_T \ni (t, x) \to (s, z)$$

Here $\langle ., . \rangle$ represents the inner product in R^m. Similarly, we define $P_Q^{2,-} u = -P_Q^{2,+}(-u)$.

Definition 28.1. (Sub-solution of (28.6)) A sub-solution u of equation (28.6) satisfies $u \in \text{USC}(Q_T)$ such that

$$a + F(t, x, u(t, x), p, X) \leq 0 \quad \text{for } (t, x) \in Q_T \tag{28.8}$$

and $\qquad (a, p, X) \in P_Q^{2,+} u(t, x)$

Definition 28.2. (Super-solution of (28.6)) A super-solution v of equation (28.6) satisfies $v \in \text{LSC}(Q_T)$ such that

$$a + F(t, x, v(t, x), p, X) \geq 0 \text{ for } (t, x) \in Q_T \tag{28.9}$$

and $\qquad (a, p, X) \in P_Q^{2,-} v(t, x)$

Let us define an initial boundary value problem based on equation (28.6). For convenience we take Dirichlet boundary conditions:

$$\frac{\partial u}{\partial t} + F(t, x, u, Du, D^2u) = 0 \text{ on } Q_T \qquad (28.10a)$$

$$u(t, x) = 0, \quad 0 \le t < T, \quad x \epsilon \partial Q \qquad (28.10b)$$

$$u(0, x) = \Psi(x), \quad x \epsilon \overline{Q} \qquad (28.10c)$$

where ∂Q is the lateral boundary of Q and $\overline{Q}$ is the closure of Q.

Furthermore, let us assume that F satisfies the following: There is a function $w : [0, \infty] \to [0, \infty]$ that satisfies $w(0+) = 0$ and

$$(F(y, r, \alpha(x - y), Y) - F(x, r, \alpha(x - y), X) \le w(\alpha|x - y|^2 + |x - y|) \qquad (28.11)$$

where $x, y \in Q, r \in \mathbb{R}^1, X, Y \in S(m)$ and the following condition holds:

$$-3\alpha \begin{pmatrix} I & 0 \\ 0 & I \end{pmatrix} \le \begin{pmatrix} X & 0 \\ 0 & -Y \end{pmatrix} \le 3\alpha \begin{pmatrix} I & -I \\ -I & I \end{pmatrix} \qquad (28.12)$$

We now have the following:

Theorem 28.1. *Let $Q \subset R^m$ be open and bounded. Let $F \in C([0, T] \times \overline{Q} \times \mathbb{R}^1 \times \mathbb{R}^m \times S(m))$ and satisfy (28.11) for each fixed $t \epsilon [0, T]$ with the same function w. If u is a sub-solution of (28.10) and v is a super-solution of (28.10) then $u \le v$ on $[0, T] \times Q$.*

This result is the nonlinear and more general version of the maximum principle for linear parabolic problems (Il'in *et al.*, 1962; Duffy, 1980).

A number of articles have appeared that employ viscosity solutions in quantitative engineering (Cont and Voltchkova, 2003).

28.3 AN INTRODUCTION TO SEMI-LINEAR EQUATIONS AND PENALTY METHOD

We are interested in approximating the Black–Scholes equation (28.7) by adding a penalty term to it, thus allowing us to solve the problem without actually having to take the free boundary into account. The approach taken is an application of the viscosity solution approach. In general, the free boundary is removed by adding a small, continuous penalty term to the Black–Scholes equation (28.7) as follows:

$$\frac{\partial P_\varepsilon}{\partial t} + F + f_\epsilon(P_\epsilon) = 0 \qquad (28.13)$$

where f_ϵ is some nonlinear function of P_ϵ. We use a subscript to denote dependence on the parameter ε.

This equation is called semi-linear because it is linear in the high-order terms and nonlinear only in the zero-order term. There are various choices for the penalty term and we shall discuss them presently. There are two pressing issues:

- Does the 'perturbed' problem (28.13) have a solution?
- How do we find good finite difference schemes for the perturbed problem?

We begin our discussion with a particular case of the penalty term. For convenience, we examine the one-factor problem. First, let us assume that the payoff function for the non-perturbed Black–Scholes equation is given by:

$$P(T, S) = g(S) \tag{28.14}$$

where $g(S) = (K - S)^+ = \max(K - S, 0)$ for a put option.

We now define the penalty function as follows:

$$f_\varepsilon(P_\varepsilon) \equiv \frac{1}{\varepsilon}[g(S) - P_\varepsilon]^+ \tag{28.15}$$

where the perturbed solution P_ε satisfies:

$$\frac{\partial P_\varepsilon}{\partial t} + F + f_\varepsilon(P_\varepsilon) = 0 \tag{28.16}$$

Theorem 28.2. *Let P be the unique viscosity solution of the unperturbed Black–Scholes equation. Then, for each $\varepsilon > 0$, let P_ε be the unique viscosity solution of (28.16). Then $P_\varepsilon \to P$ in $L^\infty_{\text{loc}}(\overline{Q}_T)$ as $\varepsilon \searrow 0$.*

Another example of the penalty function is:

$$f_\epsilon(P_\epsilon) = \frac{\epsilon C}{P_\epsilon + \epsilon - q(S)} \tag{28.17}$$

where $q(S) = K - S$ and $C \geq rK$ is a positive constant.

28.4 IMPLICIT, EXPLICIT AND SEMI-IMPLICIT SCHEMES

For ease of presentation we examine the one-factor model (Nielsen *et al.*, 2002):

$$\frac{\partial P_\varepsilon}{\partial t} + LP_\epsilon + f_\epsilon(P_\epsilon) = 0, \quad S \geq 0, \quad t \in [0, T] \tag{28.18}$$

where

$$LP_\epsilon \equiv \tfrac{1}{2}\sigma^2 S^2 \frac{\partial^2 P_\epsilon}{\partial S^2} + rS \frac{\partial P_\epsilon}{\partial S} - rP_\epsilon$$

and the nonlinear term f_ϵ is given by equation (28.17).

The terminal condition is given by:

$$P_\epsilon(S, T) = \max(K - S, 0) \tag{28.19}$$

and the boundary conditions are given by:

$$P_\epsilon(0, t) = K$$
$$P_\epsilon(S, t) = 0 \text{ as } S \to \infty \text{ (far-field condition)} \tag{28.20}$$

Let us define the usual standard centred difference mesh operator in the S direction as follows:

$$L^h P_j^n \equiv \tfrac{1}{2}\sigma^2 S_j^2 D_+ D_- P_j^n + rS_j D_0 P_j^n - rP_j^n \tag{28.21}$$

Since there is a nonlinear term in equation (28.18) we must be careful about how we discretise the equation as far as time is concerned. We march from $t = T$ to $t = 0$. Three basic options spring to mind:

- *Explicit method:* We employ explicit Euler and we march from time level n (known) to time level $n - 1$ (unknown):

$$\frac{P_j^n - P_j^{n-1}}{k} + L^h P_j^n + f_j^n(P_j^n) = 0 \quad n = N+1, \ldots, 1 \tag{28.22}$$

This equation is then easily solved for the solution at time level $n - 1$. However, the scheme is only conditionally stable and the mesh size k must satisfy the inequality (Nielsen *et al.*, 2002):

$$k \leq \frac{h^2}{\sigma^2 S_{\max}^2 + r S_{\max} h + r h^2 + \frac{Ch^2}{\varepsilon}} \tag{28.23}$$

where $S_{\max}$ is the truncated value corresponding to the far-field condition.

- *Implicit method:* Here we use implicit Euler for the terms:

$$\frac{P_j^{n+1} - P_j^n}{k} + L^h P_j^n + f_j^n(P_j^n) = 0 \tag{28.24}$$

In this case we get a nonlinear equation to solve at each time step. The implicit scheme is stable.

- *Semi-implicit methods:* In this case we use explicit Euler in the nonlinear term and implicit Euler in the linear terms:

$$\frac{P_j^{n+1} - P_j^n}{k} + L^h P_j^n + f_j^{n+1}(P_j^{n+1}) = 0 \tag{28.25}$$

This is an attractive scheme: we can solve this problem at each time level by solving a tridiagonal system of equations. However, the stability criterion is given by:

$$k \leq \frac{\epsilon}{rK} \tag{28.26}$$

This is a less restrictive constraint then that in equation (28.23).

Summarising, we have discussed three schemes that approximate the Black–Scholes equation with a free boundary. We still have to be sure that the discrete equations satisfy the usual constraints:

$$P_j^n \geq \max(K - S_j, 0) \quad \forall j \tag{28.27}$$

The implicit solution (28.24) always satisfies this condition while the semi-implicit method also satisfies the constraint if the stability condition (28.26) holds.

28.5   MULTI-ASSET AMERICAN OPTIONS

The penalty method can be applied to multi-asset American option pricing problems. By adding a penalty term to the n-factor Black–Scholes PDE, we extend the solution to a fixed domain. The penalty function forces the solution to stay above the payoff function at expiry. In the case of barrier options, the penalty term is small and the solution satisfies the Black–Scholes equation approximately far away from the boundary. As before we can define semi-implicit schemes, thus avoiding the need to solving nonlinear algebraic equations. We discuss some results on the application of the penalty method to the solution of the multidimensional Black–Scholes equation (28.7). Let us take the case $m = 2$ (that is, two underlying assets) and consider the perturbed equation in conjunction with boundary and initial conditions. We write the PDE in a generic form:

$$\frac{\partial P}{\partial t} + L_x P + L_y P - rP + f_\varepsilon(P) = 0, \quad x, y > 0, \quad t \in [0, T] \tag{28.28}$$

where

$$L_x P = \tfrac{1}{2}\sigma_1^2 x^2 \frac{\partial^2 P}{\partial x^2} + (r - D_1)x \frac{\partial P}{\partial x}$$

$$L_y P = \tfrac{1}{2}\sigma_2^2 y^2 \frac{\partial^2 P}{\partial y^2} + (r - D_2)y \frac{\partial P}{\partial y}$$

$$f_\varepsilon(P) = \frac{\varepsilon C}{P + \varepsilon - q}$$

We have assumed in this case that the underlying assets are independent and thus the cross-derivative term is zero for convenience. The terminal condition is a function of the state variables x and y and is given by:

$$P(x, y, T) = \varphi(x, y), \quad x, y \geq 0 \tag{28.29}$$

The boundary conditions at $x = 0$ and $y = 0$ are:

$$P(x, 0, t) = g_1(x, t), \quad x \geq 0, \quad t \in [0, T]$$
$$P(0, y, t) = g_2(y, t), \quad y \geq 0, \quad t \in [0, T] \tag{28.30}$$

Based on financial arguments the g functions in equation (28.30) will the solution of single-asset American put problems as already discussed in earlier chapters. This is because the PDE (28.28) reduces to a single-asset PDE on the boundaries. Of course, this must be augmented by an initial condition, boundary conditions and the smooth pasting conditions. Thus, we must solve two one-dimensional American option problems to find the necessary boundary conditions in equation (28.30). The far-field boundary conditions are given by:

$$\lim_{x \to \infty} P(x, y, t) = G_1(y, t), \quad y \geq 0, \quad t \in [0, T]$$
$$\lim_{y \to \infty} P(x, y, t) = G_2(x, t), \quad x \geq 0, \quad t \in [0, T] \tag{28.31}$$

In the case of put options, for example, the contract is worthless as the price of either asset approaches infinity and hence the boundary conditions in equations (28.31) will be zero. Here the barrier function q appearing in the nonlinear term $f_\varepsilon(P)$ is defined in general as:

$$q(S_1, \ldots, S_N) = K - \sum_{j=1}^{m} \alpha_j S_j \tag{28.32}$$

This is the m-dimension generalization of the representation in (28.17). It is a payoff as discussed for multi-asset options in Chapter 24.

In the current case (two-asset model) we have the expression for a put option:

$$q(x, y) = K - (\alpha_1 x + \alpha_2 y)$$
$$\phi(x, y) = \max[q(x, y), 0]$$

(28.33)

where α_1 and α_2 are weights.

The two-dimensional equivalents of the schemes in the previous section can be created. For example, the semi-implicit scheme is given by the discrete variant of (28.28):

$$\frac{P_{ij}^{n+1} - P_{ij}^n}{k} + L_x^h P_{ij}^n + L_y^h P_{ij}^n + f_{ij}^{n+1}(P_{ij}^{n+1}) = 0$$

(28.34)

where L_x^h and L_y^h are finite difference approximations to L_x and L_y, respectively.

We have the following result.

Theorem 28.3. *For every $C \geq rK$ the approximate option prices $\{P_{ij}^n\}$ defined by the scheme (28.34) satisfies*

$$P_{ij}^n \geq \max[q(x_i y_j), 0], i = 0, \ldots, I + 1, j = 0, \ldots, J + 1, n = N + 1, N, \ldots, 0$$

if the following condition holds:

$$k \leq \frac{\varepsilon}{rK}$$

We conclude that the explicit, semi-implicit and fully implicit schemes (in the x and y directions) can be applied to the system (28.28) to (28.33). Of course, a concern is that a given scheme must not violate the early exercise constraints.

28.6   SUMMARY AND CONCLUSIONS

We have proposed several schemes that approximate the solution of one-factor and two-factor American option problems. This is a relatively new area of research. We concentrate on explicit, implicit and semi-implicit schemes. An interesting alternative would be to apply the predictor–corrector scheme to such problems. We have also given an example to show the applicability of the penalty method to multi-factor problems.

Variational Formulation of American Option Problems

29.1 INTRODUCTION AND OBJECTIVES

In this chapter we introduce a technique to approximate the solution of free and moving boundary value problems. It is related to the finite difference method as we shall presently see, but an entire book would need to be devoted to a full discussion of the technique.

Variational methods fall under the category of fixed domain methods. In general, it can be difficult to track the moving boundary directly if it does not move smoothly or monotonically in time (Crank, 1984). The moving boundary may disappear, have sharp peaks or even double back. To resolve these potential problems we reformulate the original problem whereby the Stefan condition (in finance, the smooth pasting conditions of American options) is implicitly defined as a set of equations that are defined on a fixed domain. In this case, the moving boundary appears *a posteriori*, namely as one feature of the solution.

The methods in this chapter are quite advanced, both from a mathematical and numerical point of view. The mathematical formulation uses theorems, results and concepts from a branch of mathematics called functional analysis (see Haaser and Sullivan, 1991; Adams, 1975). In particular, we seek solutions of free boundary value problems in Hilbert, Banach or Sobolev spaces. In this respect these is some common ground between what we need to know here and the mathematical basis of the finite element method (see Strang *et al.*, 1973; Aziz, 1972). The schemes reduce to a set of matrix inequalities that we must solve. The goal is to map a free or moving boundary problem to a discrete form. To this end, we propose the following activities:

A1: Financial model (partial differential inequality)
A2: Continuous variational formulation
A3: Semi-discrete approximate variational formulation
A4: Fully discrete approximate variational formulation
A5: Assembly and solution of the discrete system.

We now describe each of these activities. Activity A1 is formulated as a partial differential inequality that models the problem at hand, for example an American option valuation problem. We execute activity A2 by mapping the formulation from A1 into one in integral or variational form. In activity A3 we replace the space of functions in which the solution of A2 is sought by some finite-dimensional approximation, usually locally compact polynomial spaces (as with FEM) or by approximating the derivatives in space by divided differences (as with FDM). In activity A4 we discretise the remaining variable in the problem, namely time, using for example Crank–Nicolson or some other time-marching scheme. Finally, in activity A5 we assemble the discrete set of equations and inequalities and prepare them for standard solvers.

Before reading this chapter, we think it is necessary that you have mastered the basics of FEM given in Appendix 2.

29.2   A SHORT HISTORY OF VARIATIONAL INEQUALITIES

The origins of variational inequalities can be traced back to the late 1960s. An early reference is Lions (1971). Other researchers around this time were Enrico Magenes, Claudio Baiocchi and colleagues in Pavia (see Baiocchi and Capelo, 1984), and a classic reference on optimal control theory is Bensoussan and Lions (1978). The work that was done in those early years is now making its way into financial engineering applications.

29.3   A FIRST PARABOLIC VARIATIONAL INEQUALITY

In order to motivate variational inequalities we take a one-dimensional heat equation problem and discretise it using finite difference schemes. This model is useful because we can apply the results to American options and we can also show how the activities A1 to A5, as discussed in section 29.1, are realised. Let us reconsider the oxygen diffusion problem (Crank, 1984), and recall that this is the problem of oxygen that diffuses into some medium which absorbs and immobilises the oxygen at a constant rate. The concentration of the oxygen at the moving surface remains constant and we thus conclude that this boundary represents the limit of oxygen penetration. Let us denote this sealed surface by $s(t)$. Then the initial boundary value problem in non-dimensional form is given by:

$$\frac{\partial c}{\partial t} = \frac{\partial^2 c}{\partial x^2} - 1, \quad 0 \le x \le s(t) \tag{29.1}$$

where $\dfrac{\partial c}{\partial x} = 0, \quad x = 0, \quad t \ge 0$ (fixed boundary condition)

$c = \dfrac{\partial c}{\partial x} = 0, \quad x = s(t), \quad t \ge 0$ (free boundary condition)

$c = \frac{1}{2}(1 - x)^2, \quad 0 \le x \le 1, \quad t = 0$ (initial condition)

This problem is amenable to a variational approach. In this case we get the differential inequality:

$$\frac{\partial c}{\partial t} - \frac{\partial^2 c}{\partial x^2} + 1 \ge 0, \quad c \ge 0 \tag{29.2}$$

in conjunction with the equality:

$$\left(\frac{\partial c}{\partial t} - \frac{\partial^2 c}{\partial x^2} + 1 \right) c = 0, \quad 0 \le x \le 1 \tag{29.3}$$

This is always zero because the first inequality in (29.2) is zero in $0 < x < s(t)$ and $c \equiv 0$ in the interval $s(t) \le x \le 1$.

We now discretise this problem in space and time. In particular, we use centred differencing in space and implicit Euler in time. For the inequality (29.2) we have:

$$\frac{c_j^{n+1} - c_j^n}{k} - \frac{c_{j+1}^{n+1} - 2c_j^{n+1} + c_{j-1}^{n+1}}{h^2} + 1 \ge 0, \quad j = 1, \ldots, J - 1 \tag{29.4}$$

The Neumann boundary condition at $x = 0$ can be approximated by centred differences with ghost points:

$$\frac{c_{-1}^n - c_1^n}{2h} = 0 \tag{29.5}$$

We can put these discrete equations in the form:

$$\text{Find } \mathbf{c} \text{ where } \mathbf{c} = {}^t(c_1, \ldots, c_{J-1})$$

$$A\mathbf{c} + \mathbf{b} \geq 0; \quad \mathbf{c} \geq 0; \quad (A\mathbf{c} + \mathbf{b})\mathbf{c}^T = 0 \tag{29.6}$$

where A is a tridiagonal matrix and $\mathbf{b}$ is a known vector. This is now a problem in quadratic programming.

In Wilmott (1993) the Black–Scholes equation is transformed to the heat equation and then posed in a general linear complementarity LCP form, as follows:

$$\frac{\partial u}{\partial t} - \frac{\partial^2 u}{\partial x^2} \geq 0, \quad u - g \geq 0$$

$$\left(\frac{\partial u}{\partial t} - \frac{\partial^2 u}{\partial x^2} \right)(u - g) = 0 \tag{29.7}$$

where $g = g(x, t)$ is the transformed payoff constraint function. As in the oxygen diffusion case we can reduce this problem to the form:

$$A\mathbf{U}^{n+1} - \mathbf{b}^n \geq 0, \quad \mathbf{U}^{n+1} - \mathbf{g}^{n+1} \geq 0$$

$$\left(A(\mathbf{U})^{n+1} - \mathbf{b}^n \right)(\mathbf{U}^{n+1} - \mathbf{g}^{n+1})^T = 0 \tag{29.8}$$

Here the index n refers to discrete time levels, as in the usual sense in this book.

The next question is to determine how to solve the system (29.6), or equivalently system (29.8). There are several techniques; one of the original and famous ones is the Cryer projected SOR (PSOR) method (Cryer, 1979). We define a new notation as follows:

$$\mathbf{z} = A\mathbf{c} + \mathbf{b}$$

then

$$A\mathbf{c} = \mathbf{z} - \mathbf{b}, \quad \mathbf{c}^T\mathbf{z} = 0, \quad \mathbf{c} \geq 0, \quad \mathbf{z} \geq 0 \tag{29.9}$$

and then this problem is equivalent to the minimisation problem:

$$\text{minimize } \mathbf{b}^T\mathbf{c} + \tfrac{1}{2}\mathbf{c}^T A\mathbf{c} \text{ for } \mathbf{c} \geq 0 \tag{29.10}$$

The Cryer algorithm produces sequences of vectors as follows:

$$z_j^{(k+1)} = b_j + \sum_{i=1}^{j-1} A_{ji}c_i^{(k+1)} - \sum_{i=j}^{J} A_{ji}c_i^{(k)}$$

$$c_j^{(k+1)} = \max\left\{ 0, \ c_j^{(k)} + \omega z_j^{(k+1)}/A_{jj} \right\} \tag{29.11}$$

where J is the size of the matrix A and ω is the so-called relaxation parameter.

Theorem 29.1. *(Cryer, 1979) Let A be positive definite. Then the PSOR scheme (29.11) converges for all initial guessed $\mathbf{c}^{(0)}$ if and only if $0 < \omega < 2$.*
Caveat: The positive-definiteness of the matrix A is crucial.

The PSOR scheme can be used for schemes that result from a finite element/variational formulation of moving boundary value problems. There are many other schemes, for example the conjugate gradient method (Press *et al.*, 2002, p. 424) and Lagrange method with penalty terms (Scales, 1985), but a discussion of these issues is outside the scope of this book.

- Equations (29.1) to (29.3) correspond to the activities A1 and A2. In this case we have two equivalent formulations of the moving boundary value problem.
- Equations (29.4) and (29.5) correspond to activities A3 and A4. In this case we carry out a full discretisation in one sweep.
- System (29.6) corresponds to activity A5.

    Generalizing the problem (29.1) to convection–diffusion equations is not too difficult.

29.4   FUNCTIONAL ANALYSIS BACKGROUND

In the previous section we approximated the solution of parabolic variational inequalities by replacing derivatives by divided differences. In the following sections, however, we approximate variational inequalities using certain classes of functions. To this end, we introduce a number of function spaces and other concepts from a powerful branch of mathematics called *functional analysis*.

Let Ω be a domain in $\mathbb{R}^n$ and let p be a positive real number. We denote by $L^p(\Omega)$ the space of functions u, defined on Ω such that

$$\int_\Omega |u(x)|^p \, dx < \infty$$

We define the functional $\| \cdot \|_p$ by

$$\|u\|_p = \left\{ \int_\Omega |u(x)|^p \, dx \right\}^{1/p} \tag{29.12}$$

and we note that this is a norm in $L^P(\Omega)$, $1 \le p < \infty$. When $p = \infty$, the functional $\| \cdot \|_\infty$ defined by

$$\|u\|_\infty = \operatorname*{ess\,sup}_{x \in \Omega} |u(x)|$$

is a norm on $L^\infty(\Omega)$.

This space of functions is very important in functional analysis and its applications. Some important inequalities are:

Theorem 29.2. *(Hölder's inequality.) If $1 < p < \infty$ and $u \in L^p(\Omega)$ and $v \in L^q(\Omega)$ (where $1/p + 1/q = 1$) then $uv \in L^1(\Omega)$ and*

$$\int_\Omega |u(x)v(x)| \, dx \le \|u\|_p \|v\|_q \tag{29.13}$$

Theorem 29.3. *(Minkowski's inequality.) If $1 \le p < \infty$ then*

$$\|u + v\|_p \le \|u\|_p + \|v\|_p \tag{29.14}$$

We now turn our attention to a class of functions whose derivatives up to a certain order are in $L^P(\Omega)$. These are the so-called Sobolev spaces of integer order. To this end, we define a functional $\| \cdot \|_{m,p}$ where m is a non-negative integer and $1 \leq p \leq \infty$, as follows:

$$\|u\|_{m,p} = \left(\sum_{0 \leq |\alpha| \leq m} \|D^\alpha u\|_p^p \right)^{1/p} \quad 1 \leq p < \infty$$

$$\|u\|_{m,0} = \max_{0 \leq |\alpha| \leq m} \|D^\alpha u\|_\infty$$

where $D^\alpha u$ is the α derivative in u.

A special and common case of the above Sobolev spaces is when $p = 2$.

29.5   KINDS OF VARIATIONAL INEQUALITIES

We now introduce the reader to the subject of variational inequalities. We try to build knowledge incrementally as the subject is mathematically very sophisticated (it uses a lot of functional analysis and finite element theory).

29.5.1   Diffusion with semi-permeable membrane

Let Ω be a domain in $\mathbb{R}^n$ that is also an open bounded set with smooth boundary Γ, and let the final time $T < \infty$ be given.

Consider the problem of finding $u(x, t)$ such that

$$\frac{\partial u}{\partial t} - \Delta u = f(x, t) \in \Omega \times (0, T) \tag{29.15}$$

$$u(x, 0) = u_0(x), \quad x \in \Omega \tag{29.16}$$

$$u \geq 0, \quad \frac{\partial u}{\partial \eta} \geq 0, \quad u \frac{\partial u}{\partial \eta} = 0 \text{ for } (x, t) \in \Gamma \times (0, T) \tag{29.17}$$

where

$$\Delta u \equiv \sum_{j=1}^n \frac{\partial^2 u}{\partial x_j^2}$$

Defining $V = H^1(\Omega)$ we seek a solution $u \in V = L^2(0, T; V)$. Assume further that $f(t) \in V^*$ and $u_0 \in H = L^2(\Omega)$.

$$K \subset V, \quad K = \{v \in V : v(x) \geq 0, \quad x \in \Gamma\}$$

for any $v \in V$, with $v(t) \in K$.

We multiply equation (29.15) by $v(t) - u(t)$, and integration over Ω gives the trivial equality:

$$\int_\Omega \left[\frac{\partial u(t)}{\partial t} - f(t) \right] [v(t) - u(t)] \, dx$$

$$= \int_\Omega \Delta u(t)[v(t) - u(t)] \, dx, \quad v \in V, \quad v(t) \in K \tag{29.18}$$

We now use the divergence theorem (n-dimensional integration by parts) and using boundary conditions (29.17) we formulate (29.18) in the equivalent form by the application of the

Green's formula:

$$\int_{\Omega} \Delta u(t) \, [v(t) - u(t)] \, dt = \int_{\Gamma} \frac{\partial u(t)}{\partial \eta} [v(t) - u(t)] \, dt$$

$$- \int_{\Omega} \nabla u(t) \cdot \nabla (v(t) - u(t)) \, dt \qquad (29.19a)$$

or

$$\int_{\Omega} \{ \Delta u(t)[v(t) - u(t)] + \nabla u(t) \cdot \nabla [v(t) - u(t)] \} \, dx$$

$$= \int_{\Gamma} \frac{\partial u(t)}{\partial \eta} [v(t) - u(t)] \, dx \geq 0 \qquad (29.19b)$$

From this we deduce the inequality:

$$\int_{\Omega} \Delta u(t)[v(t) - u(t)] \, dt \; \geq \; - \int_{\Omega} \nabla u(t) \cdot \nabla [v(t) - u(t)] \, dt \qquad (29.20)$$

Finally, combining (29.18) and (29.20) produces the parabolic variational inequality:

$$\int_{\Omega} \left\{ \frac{\partial u(t)}{\partial t} [v(t) - u(t)] + \nabla u(t) \cdot \nabla [v(t) - u(t)] \right\} \, dx$$

$$\geq \int_{\Omega} f(t)[v(t) - u(t)] \, dx \quad \forall v \in K \qquad (29.21)$$

where $K = \{ v \in V; \quad v(t) \in K \text{ for a.a. } t \in (0, T) \}$ where a.a. t denotes 'for almost all t' in the Lebesgue sense.

This is the so-called continuous formulation of the free boundary problem. Of course, this problem must be approximated. For motivational purposes we return to a one-dimensional case of system (29.21), namely the oxygen absorption problem. This is a good example to use as a model.

29.5.2   A one-dimensional finite element approximation

We now discuss the variational formulation of the oxygen absorption problem (taken from the classic reference Crank, 1984). In this case we start with the system (29.1). This problem is then formulated as the one-dimensional equivalent of (29.21).

The steps that we execute in this section are:

- Formulate the continuous variational inequality
- Semi-discretisation in x using linear 'hat' functions (finite elements) piecewise polynomials
- Full-discretisation using implicit Euler or Crank–Nicolson schemes
- Assembling the set of discrete inequalities.

We multiply both sides of scheme (29.1) by $(v - c)$, where v belongs to the space of test functions

$$V = \{ v : v \in H^1(0, 1), \quad v(1) = 0 \}$$

Then using the equality:

$$\int_0^1 \left(\frac{\partial c}{\partial t} - \frac{\partial^2 c}{\partial x^2} + 1 \right)(v - c)\,dx = \int_0^1 \frac{\partial c}{\partial t}(v - c)\,dx$$

$$- \left[(v - c)\frac{\partial c}{\partial x} \right]_0^1 + \int_0^1 \frac{\partial c}{\partial x}\frac{\partial}{\partial x}(v - c)\,dx + \int_0^1 (v - c)\,dx \qquad (29.22)$$

and the fact that

$$v = c = 0 \quad \text{on } x = 1$$

$$\frac{\partial c}{\partial x} = 0 \quad \text{on } x = 0$$

we then get the rearranged form of equation (29.22), namely:

$$\int_0^1 \frac{\partial c}{\partial t}(v - c)\,dx + \int_0^1 \frac{\partial c}{\partial x}\frac{\partial}{\partial x}(v - c)\,dx$$

$$= -\int_0^1 (v - c)\,dx + \int_0^1 \left(\frac{\partial c}{\partial t} - \frac{\partial^2 c}{\partial x^2} + 1 \right)dx \qquad (29.23)$$

The final term on the right-hand-side in (29.23) is non-negative because of inequality (29.2), hence we get the variational inequality:

$$\int_0^1 \frac{\partial c}{\partial t}(v - c)\,dx + \int_0^1 \frac{\partial c}{\partial x}\frac{\partial}{\partial x}(v - c)\,dx$$

$$= -\int_0^1 (v - c)\,dx + \int_0^1 \left(\frac{\partial c}{\partial t} - \frac{\partial^2 c}{\partial x^2} + 1 \right)dx$$

$$\geq -\int_0^1 (v - c)\,dx \qquad (29.24)$$

or in more compact and general form as:

$$\left(\frac{\partial c}{\partial t}, v - c \right) + a(c, v - c) \geq (-1, v - c) \qquad (29.25)$$

where

$$(f, g) \equiv \int_0^1 fg\,dx \quad \text{(inner product)}$$

$$a(u, v) \equiv \int_0^1 \frac{\partial u}{\partial x}\frac{\partial v}{\partial x}\,dx \quad \text{(bilinear form)}$$

We now find an approximate solution to a slightly more generalised form of (29.25), namely:

$$\left(\frac{\partial u}{\partial t}, v - c \right) + a(u, v - c) \geq (f, v - c) \qquad (29.26)$$

As is common in finite element theory, we seek an approximate solution of (29.26) using combinations of linear polynomials with compact support on the interval (0, 1), namely:

$$u = \sum_{j=1}^{n} u_j \varphi_j, \qquad v = \sum_{j=1}^{n} v_j \varphi_j$$

where the support functions are defined by the formula:

$$\varphi_j = \begin{cases} [x - (j-1)h]/h, & (j-1)h \leq x \leq jh \\ [(j+1)h - x]/h, & jh \leq x \leq (j+1)h \end{cases}$$

If we now insert the above expressions for u and v into inequality (29.26) we get the following expression:

$$\int_0^1 \left[\sum_{i=1}^{n} \frac{\partial u_i}{\partial t} \varphi_i \right] \left[\sum_{j=1}^{n} (v_j - u_j)\varphi_j \right] dx$$

$$+ \int_0^1 \left[\sum_{i=1}^{n} u_i \frac{\partial \varphi_i}{\partial x} \right] \left[\sum_{j=1}^{n} (v_j - u_j)\frac{\partial \varphi_j}{\partial x} \right] dx$$

$$- \int_0^1 f \left[\sum_{j=1}^{n} (v_j - u_j)\varphi_j \right] dx \geq 0 \tag{29.27}$$

We now wish to formulate this problem in matrix form, and to this end we define the so-called mass matrix M, stiffness matrix K and inhomogeneous terms as follows:

$$M_{ij} \equiv (\varphi_i, \varphi_j)$$

$$K_{ij} = a(\varphi_i, \varphi_j), \qquad f_j = (f, \varphi_j)$$

Some arithmetic shows that:

$$\sum_{i=1}^{n} \frac{\partial u_i}{\partial t} \sum_{j=1}^{n} (v_j - u_j) \int_0^1 \varphi_i \varphi_j \, dx$$

$$+ \sum_{i=1}^{n} u_i \sum_{j=1}^{n} (v_j - u_j) \int_0^1 \frac{\partial \varphi_i}{\partial x} \frac{\partial \varphi_j}{\partial x} \, dx$$

$$- \sum_{j=1}^{n} (v_j - u_j) \int_0^1 f\varphi_j dx \geq 0 \tag{29.28}$$

or, in shorthand notation (neglecting summation signs), we get:

$$M_{ji} \frac{\partial u_i}{\partial t}(v_j - u_j) + K_{ji} u_i (v_j - u_j) - f_j (v_j - u_j) \geq 0 \tag{29.29}$$

This is a semi-discrete scheme; in other words, the x variable has been discretised while the t variable is continuous. In order to carry out the last step, namely full discretisation, we replace the t-derivative in (29.29) by a divided difference. In this case we employ an implicit Euler scheme as follows:

$$M_{ji} \frac{u_i^{n+1} - u_i^n}{k}(v_j - u_j^{n+1}) + K_{ji} u_i^{n+1}(v_j - u_j^{n+1}) - f_j(v_j - u_j^{n+1}) \geq 0 \tag{29.30}$$

or

$$\left(\frac{M_{ji}}{k} + K_{ji}\right) u_i^{n+1}(v_j - u_j^{n+1}) \geq \left(f + \frac{M_{ji}}{k}\right)(v_j - u_j^{n+1}) \tag{29.31}$$

This inequality is in the same form as (29.8) and can be solved by the Cryer algorithm, for example. We can carry out the same analysis for the convection–diffusion problem, but the mathematics become more tedious. We remark that it takes time to learn how to apply the above schemes to practical problems.

29.6 VARIATIONAL INEQUALITIES USING ROTHE'S METHOD

In the previous section we found an approximate solution to a variational inequality by first discretising in space and then in time. In this section we first discretise the PVI in time using Rothe's method. To this end, we look again at PVI (29.26) with $f = 0$ and $u = c$:

$$\left(\frac{\partial u}{\partial t}, v - u\right) + a(u, v - u) \geq 0 \tag{29.32}$$

where

$$(u, v) = \int_\Omega u(x)v(x)\,dx$$

$$a(u, v) = \int_\Omega \nabla u \cdot \nabla v\,dx$$

The first step in Rothe's method is to discretise in time; in this case we use implicit Euler method (we take $f = 0$ for convenience):

$$\left(\frac{U^{n+1} - U^n}{k}, v - U^{n+1}\right) + a\left(U^{n+1}, v - U^{n+1}\right) \geq 0, \quad \forall v \in K \tag{29.33}$$

with $U^0 = u_0(x)$, $x \in \Omega$ (given initial condition).

Rearranging terms in (29.33) gives us the elliptic variational inequality (EVI):

$$k^{-1}(U^{n+1}, v - U^{n+1}) + a(U^{n+1}, v - U^{n+1}) \geq k^{-1}(U^n, v - U^{n+1}), \quad \forall v \in K, \quad n \geq 0 \tag{29.34}$$

where U^n is known and the new bilinear form is:

$$a(u, v) = k^{-1} \int_\Omega uv\,dx + \int_\Omega \nabla u \cdot \nabla v\,dx$$

Thus, we have reduced the PVI to a sequence of EVIs at each time level. We know that the EVI problem (29.34) has a unique solution (see, for example, Rudd and Schmidt, 2002 or Glowinski et al., 1981). We thus see how useful Rothe's method is, both theoretically and numerically.

We note that the problem (29.34) can be solved at every time level using linear polynomial hat functions (see Glowinski et al., 1981). Unfortunately, any treatment is outside the scope of the current book.

29.7 AMERICAN OPTIONS AND VARIATIONAL INEQUALITIES

We have now gained enough experience of the material to tackle variational problems for American options. In fact, the problem is not much more difficult than the heat equation except that it involves an extra convection term in the bilinear form. In general, the steps are:

- Formulate the continuous variational system: we should prove existence, uniqueness and regularity results. The domain is infinite.
- Define the variational inequality on a truncated, bounded domain in n-dimensional space.
- Formulate the finite-dimensional variational inequality using finite elements or finite difference approximations to the derivatives.
- Solve the system.

29.8 SUMMARY AND CONCLUSIONS

We have given an introduction to an important branch of applied functional analysis that we call variational inequalities. A vast literature has been written on this subject but our interest lies in its applications to free boundary value problems in general and American options in particular. We discussed the following issues:

- Formulation of the continuous problem
- Formulation of the discrete problem (using finite elements or finite differences)
- Assembling the discrete set of inequalities
- Solving the discrete set of inequalities.

We have given a number of relevant and practical examples to help the reader to explore more of the literature in this field, but much more research needs to be done.

Part VII

Design and Implementation in C++

30

Finding the Appropriate Finite Difference Schemes for your Financial Engineering Problem

30.1 INTRODUCTION AND OBJECTIVES

This is the first chapter of Part VII and it is here that we summarise the finite difference schemes of the previous 29 chapters. First, we examine the problem of choosing the most appropriate scheme for a given financial problem while at the same time taking customer requirements (such as performance and accuracy issues, for example) into account. To take a specific case, we might be interested in determining what the most efficient and accurate finite difference schemes are for two-factor models containing jump terms. The answer in general to this kind of question is difficult to give unless we partition the problem into a number of more focused and simpler sub-problems. The problem is easy enough to state:

Given a precise description of a pricing problem, find the most appropriate approximate method(s) (for example, a finite difference scheme) that satisfies given functional and non-functional requirements.

We shall see in a later section how to realise this goal by implementing the problem as three main activities. Before we start, however, we must agree on what we want, namely an unambiguous description of the finite difference scheme that best fits the current problem. The input is an unambiguous description of the financial problem. The activities that glue output (the FDM product) to input (the 'raw materials' or financial product) are:

A1: Produce a continuous PDE, PIDE or PVI model from the QF model.
A2: Produce discrete FDM, FEM or Meshless models from the continuous model.
A3: Produce an optimised discrete model based on the given functional and non-functional requirements.

In general, we must make a series of decisions whose outcome will hopefully lead to the discovery of a good and workable scheme that solves the problem at hand. We try to incorporate as much know-how into the process as possible. It would be an interesting project to automate the process of mapping financial models to finite differences by encapsulating the knowledge in an adaptive database system. This topic is outside the scope of the current book. We do, however give tips and guidelines in this chapter on how to choose appropriate schemes.

The second major topic of concern in this part of the book is that, once we have short-listed a finite difference scheme we must design and implement it in some object-oriented language, for example C++ or C#. In this book we concentrate on C++ because of its wide acceptance in the financial engineering community. In particular, we pay attention to actually defining and utilising the C++ data structures (such as vectors, matrices and lattices) to help us to realise the finite difference schemes for one-factor and multi-factor pricing models. We define the 'C++ skeletons' that can be used and customised by the reader to suit his or her own models.

Furthermore, we provide C++ code for several pricing models that can be compiled and run to give real output values. In summary, this chapter is a high-level analysis of the problem of mapping the financial world to the world of finite difference schemes.

30.2   THE FINANCIAL MODEL

This book is concerned with finding robust and accurate finite difference schemes for certain kinds of derivatives products. We wish to group these products into certain categories, but there is no unique or 'best' way of doing this. In general, most models have to do with one-factor and many-factor option problems but we also discuss a number of other derivatives problems such as real options and interest rate problems. For this reason we propose the following three broad categories:

C1: One-factor models
C2: Two-factor models
C3: Many-factor models (more than two factors).

We examined several specific instances of derivative products in each category, for example:

- **C1**
  Plain vanilla options (original Black–Scholes model)
  One-factor barrier option (single barrier, double barrier)
  One-factor bond models.
- **C2**
  Basket/rainbow option on two assets
  Models with an asset and a stochastic volatility (Heston)
  Two-factor interest-rate models
  Asian options
  Merton model (asset with jumps), PIDE.
- **C3**
  Multi-asset options
  Options with early exercise feature.

Of course, the behaviour of the underlyings in these problems is described as either stochastic or deterministic processes, but our main interest lies in the unambiguous description of the initial boundary value problem that describes the derivative quantity based on those underlying quantities. This is the subject of the next section.

30.3   THE VIEWPOINTS IN THE CONTINUOUS MODEL

Since we are taking a PDE approach in this book we must address a number of 'dimensions', viewpoints and attention areas whose resolution will enable us to specify the categories C1, C2 and C3 more precisely. Again, we propose a list that we hope subsumes the most important attention points:

VC1: Payoff function and exercise style
VC2: The PDE domain and boundary conditions
VC3: Transformation variables and simplifications.

We now discuss each of these topics in more detail. We pay particular attention to nitty-gritty and 'nasty' aspects of the problem that compromise the robustness of the eventual schemes and we decide on a course of action to help to mitigate these potential risks.

30.3.1 Payoff functions

In general, the payoff function is usually defined at the expiry date $t = T$ while in general we prefer to convert this to an initial condition for the corresponding IBVP. Payoff is one of the most important pieces of the FDM jigsaw because it contains much financial information about the contingent claim. It is a function that expresses the value of the contingent claim as a function of the underlying asset price at expiry. It also needs other parameters to define it uniquely. For example, it may contain information about strike price(s) and whether the corresponding option is a call or a put. In this book we have examined both one-factor and multi-factor problems (in the latter case we examine multi-asset correlation options as well as multi-factor interest models). In general, we must write the payoff function in the following form:

```
double payoff (NPoint S)
{ // NPoint is n-dimension 'underlying' space
  // code here
}
```

We have created a hierarchy of C++ classes in which each class models a specific payoff function. In the constructor we give the parameters that are needed to allow us to define the body of the above `payoff()` function. Each concrete class is derived from an abstract base class that defines a pure virtual `payoff()` function. We note in the above pseudo-code that NPoint is an abstraction of an n-dimensional point in 'asset' space. We realise it as a template class in C++. We provide the C++ code for this hierarchy on the accompanying CD.

In general, the payoff function is a well-behaved function with the exception of certain points or hyperplanes in the region of integration. For many problems, it is either zero or a linear function of the underlying asset variable(s). Discontinuities in the payoff function or its derivatives appear at these so-called transition regions. In mathematical terms the solution of the corresponding IBVP will experience sharp spikes or oscillatory behaviour in the neighbourhood of these regions for small values of time t but the solution quickly becomes smooth. We must be aware of both of these facts when we approximate the IBVP by second-order schemes near $t = 0$. We may get inaccurate approximations to the solution of the IBVP.

Some general remarks are:

- Many multi-asset problems have similar PDE structure (and even similar boundary conditions); it is the particular form of the payoff function that distinguishes the different instances.
- It is possible to smooth or regularise the payoff function before embarking on a finite difference approximation, but we do not discuss this topic here.
- Some payoff functions may be nonlinear functions of the underlying, for example one-factor power options. This class of functions is easily incorporated into our formulations.

In this section we assume that the IBVP is defined on a bounded interval or domain. For the sake of simplicity, we examine a one-factor model on the bounded interval $(0, B)$ where the value B is the so-called 'far-field' boundary. The main boundary value types are:

B1: Dirichlet boundary conditions
B2: Neumann boundary conditions
B3: Linearity ('convexity') boundary conditions
B4: The PDE is 'continued' to the boundary (resulting in an ODE or a PDE).

We have examined these boundary conditions in detail in this book. Condition B4 refers to the fact that we allow the Black–Scholes PDE to be satisfied at $S = 0$. The resulting degenerate equation can often be solved exactly or, failing that, it will be possible to solve it using some suitable finite difference scheme. In this sense it is sometimes possible to solve the equation corresponding to B4 and thus allow us to cast it in the form B1, whether it be in continuous or discrete form.

The above discussion is easily extended to multi-factor models on n-dimensional cubes ('hypercubes').

30.3.2 Boundary conditions

One of the most difficult aspects of producing robust and accurate finite difference schemes is the imposition of appropriate boundary conditions for a given IVBP. In particular, we have a number of hurdles to overcome:

- Many problems are defined on infinite or semi-infinite intervals and domains. We must devise a means of transforming these domains to bounded domains.
- Having succeeded in transforming the original problem to a bounded domain, we must then determine the kind of boundary condition that is appropriate for the transformed problem.

We shall discuss the first problem in the next section but we shall now assume that the IBVP is such that it is defined in a bounded region. It now remains to define the boundary conditions. The easiest ones from a computational point of view are Dirichlet boundary conditions because the value of the solution is known on the boundary and this fact allows us to avoid many complications when compared with Neumann and linearity (convexity) boundary conditions that involve derivatives of the solutions on the boundary.

A special 'degenerate' boundary condition is defined when the underlying asset value is zero. In this case the Black–Scholes PDE is satisfied exactly on the boundary. In general the resulting differential equation will be of lower order than the PDE in the interior of the domain of interest. Some examples in this book are:

- The one-factor Black–Scholes PDE reduces to an ordinary differential equation (ODE) in the boundary $S = 0$. This equation has an exact solution. We thus have a Dirichlet boundary condition at $S = 0$.
- For one-factor bond models (where the underlying is the interest rate r) the second-order parabolic PDE reduces to a first-order hyperbolic PDE. In fact, this is an initial value problem whose solution can be found exactly. In more complicated cases an exact solution may not be forthcoming and we then resort to finite difference approximations or the Method of Characteristics (MOC). In the first case we have two major choices. First, we can take explicit finite difference schemes, in which case we can find an approximate solution on the boundary and are then back to Dirichlet boundary conditions. Of course, the scheme is conditionally stable. Second, we can construct unconditionally stable implicit schemes, but

we no longer have Dirichlet boundary conditions, we have in essence Neumann boundary conditions. The value on the boundary is unknown and thus must be incorporated into the full system of equations in the interior of the domain.

- For n-factor models the full PDE reduces to a first-order hyperbolic PDE. In general, we must solve these problems using numerical techniques. For example, we have mentioned how to do this in the case $n = 2$ when we discussed the Heston stochastic volatility model.
- The most tractable problems in the author's opinion are barrier option models because we define Dirichlet boundary conditions on the whole boundary.

30.3.3 Transformations

We now discuss the PDE, PIDE or PVI that describes a derivative quantity and the domain in which it is defined. In general, a given problem is defined in a domain in 'asset space' having fixed boundaries and possibly free or moving boundaries as well.

For option problems without an early exercise feature we define a PDE on a semi-infinite domain. There are no free or moving boundaries. Because we cannot fit a semi-infinite problem on a computer we must replace it by a problem on some kind of transformed domain. Popular choices are:

- Transformation to a 'symmetrical' infinite domain
- Transformation to a bounded domain
- Truncation of the semi-infinite domain.

The first two transformations are realised by a change of independent variables. For example, in one-factor models the transformation $x = \log(S)$ transforms the Black–Scholes PDE to a PDE on an infinite interval (Wilmott, 1998) while the transformation $x = S/(S + K)$ transforms it to the interval $(0, 1)$. In the latter case imposition of boundary conditions is not necessary because the coefficients of the transformed PDE are zero at the end-points. The third transformation is also popular; choose some multiple of the strike price K and use this as the so-called far-field value. Of course, we must impose boundary conditions at this point as already described.

The use of new independent variables is certainly useful for one-factor models but it lacks generality in the author's opinion. It is not clear how one would apply it to n-factor models and equations containing nonlinear terms. We prefer to tackle problems head-on by numerical methods with as little 'massaging' of the continuous problem as possible.

For option problems with early exercise feature we have an added complication. In this case we model an unknown free or moving boundary as part of the problem. In financial terms, the derivative quantity satisfies the smooth pasting conditions on this unknown boundary. Having done this we must decide how to model this free boundary. To this end, there are two main approaches:

- Model the free boundary *a priori* as part of the model
- Model the free boundary *a posteriori*.

We have given some examples of each of these approaches in this book. An example of the first approach is the front-fixing method in which we transform a linear PDE containing a free boundary to a PDE that is defined on a fixed boundary. However, the transformed PDE has a nonlinear term as the coefficient of the first derivative with respect to the underlying variable. Of course this PDE is more difficult to solve numerically than a linear PDE, but that is the price we must pay; in general, we say that the problem has become simpler in one direction but more complex in another. The second approach to solving problems with early exercise feature can be realised in a number of ways:

- Variational techniques and parabolic variational inequalities
- Regularisation techniques and penalty methods.

The first case is based on posing the original problem in integral or variational form, thus allowing us to treat the free boundary implicitly. The second approach adds a nonlinear zero-order term to the original Black–Scholes PDE thereby ensuring that the solution of the transformed PDE will automatically satisfy the well-known 'financial constraints'. Thus, we no longer need to worry about the free boundary but we will have to approximate a semi-linear PDE.

30.4   THE VIEWPOINTS IN THE DISCRETE MODEL

In general, we are pessimists (or realists?) in the sense that we assume that most, if not all, interesting and challenging problems cannot be solved exactly but we must employ numerical methods to approximate the solution of the PDE model. We now describe the most important attention points to be addressed:

- Approximating the partial derivatives appearing in the PDE (in both space and time)
- Approximating the payoff function
- Approximating boundary conditions.

We shall describe these in detail in the coming sections, but we must first determine how 'good' our finite difference schemes need to be.

30.4.1   Functional and non-functional requirements

'All schemes are equal but some schemes are more equal than others.' By this statement we mean that some schemes are better than others for a given problem. Of course, determining which scheme is best is not easy but we can provide some general guidelines. There is no best solution as such in general.

We think that quantitative analysts place great emphasis on the following properties of a numerical method:

- *Suitability*: This means that the finite difference scheme can be used to approximate the financial problem at hand. In other words, the scheme is general enough to accommodate variations in the financial problem, such as:
  ○ non-constant and nonlinear coefficients
  ○ ability to handle various kinds of payoff functions
  ○ ability to handle various kinds of boundary conditions
  ○ and more.

Finite difference methods are very flexible and can be applied to a wide range of problems, in contrast to lattice (binomial, trinomial) methods that must be 'tweaked' to make them suitable for problems that have non-constant coefficients, for example.

- *Accuracy*: The solution to the FDM scheme should be close (in some norm) to the solution of the IBVP that it approximates. In general, we are interested in point error estimates and for this reason we usually examine the L^∞ norm.

In general, there are several sources of error when we discretise an IBVP using FDM:

- Error due to space discretisation
- Error due to time discretisation
- Error due to approximation of the boundary and initial conditions
- Splitting errors with ADI and Soviet splitting methods
- Round-off errors.

Whew! With a list like this we may be wondering if we should use numerical methods in the first place. Fortunately, we can choose appropriate values for the mesh sizes in the space and time directions to give us a certain level of accuracy, as desired.

- *Performance/efficiency*: This viewpoint has two aspects. First, time efficiency refers to the amount of CPU time needed to calculate option price at time level $n + 1$ given the price at level n. In this context we speak of response time and this may vary between a few milliseconds to a couple of seconds, depending on the requirements of the trader or quantitative analyst. Some rules of thumb are:
  - explicit methods are faster than implicit methods
  - iterative methods (e.g. those in which we compare successive values of a candidate solution) tend to be slower than direct methods.

In some cases, it might be more advantageous to use explicit methods (which we know are conditionally stable) with a small mesh size in the time direction than an implicit method that must be solved using *LU* decomposition, for example, at each time level. The second aspect is that of resource efficiency. This refers to the amount of memory that we need to hold data structures such as vectors, matrices, lattices and hashtables. Since we tend to allocate memory on the heap (free store) we usually do not have to worry about memory problems. Having said that, we should avoid 'memory thrashing', that is allocating and deallocating memory on the fly because this fragments contiguous memory.

- *Ease of use/ease of implementation*: It is obvious that it is preferable to use and apply a scheme that is easy to comprehend. On the other hand, it takes a finite amount of time to learn the subject of this book and to become comfortable with it. For example, in the author's opinion the finite difference schemes in this book are easier to understand than the variational schemes and the schemes that employ the finite element method (FEM). The reader can have both short-term and medium-term goals; in the short term you can employ simpler schemes and you can advance to the more sophisticated schemes when you gain more experience.

30.4.2 Approximating the spatial derivatives in the PDE

In most cases we use three-point difference schemes to approximate the second and first-order derivatives appearing in the Black–Scholes PDE. In general we use second-order parabolic PDEs by approximating their partial derivatives by appropriate divided differences.

The Black–Scholes equation is a special case of a convection–diffusion equation (Morton, 1996). This type of equation is well known and has been studied in the context of computational fluid dynamics (CFD), and many schemes have been devised for it. A particular situation arises in so-called convective-dominated flow, whereby the convective terms are larger than the diffusion terms. In this case we may need to use special schemes, for example, finite volume methods (FVM) or exponentially splitting methods (Duffy, 1980).

A number of multi-factor PDEs in quantitative finance have components that are not of convection–diffusion type. Instead, the PDE is a first-order hyperbolic equation because the diffusion term is absent; this corresponds to a deterministic term in the PDE. Care must be taken when approximating first-order hyperbolic equations because we can only give one boundary condition, in contrast to second-order diffusion equations.

30.4.3   Time discretisation in the PDE

Most of the approximations to the time derivative are first-order or second-order accurate. The most popular schemes are implicit and explicit Euler and Crank–Nicolson. The Euler schemes are first-order accurate and, in particular for the implicit Euler scheme, we can apply Richardson extrapolation to achieve second-order accuracy. The Crank–Nicolson scheme is second-order accurate and is very popular in the quantitative finance literature, but it can produce oscillations or spikes in the solution near the strike price and barriers, for example. A good workaround is to employ implicit Euler scheme for the first few time steps (no oscillations or spikes) and Crank–Nicolson thereafterwards.

A particularly powerful scheme (that incidentally, is easy to program) is the predictor–corrector method. The method is iterative, has fast convergence properties and is second-order accurate. An important property is that, for linear PDE problems, it is not necessary to solve a tridiagonal matrix system at each time level and this has implications for the performance of schemes for both one-factor and n-factor models.

Finally, the predictor–corrector method is well suited to nonlinear problems because both the predictor and corrector steps are explicit and linear. This ideal situation is lost if we employ Crank–Nicolson or implicit Euler. In these cases we need to solve a nonlinear system of equations at each time level, something that is not to everyone's taste. This may also reduce the performance of the algorithm.

Finally, we note that the small set of schemes for solving initial value problems that we use in this book is only the tip of the iceberg. There is a huge literature on all kinds of schemes for solving IVPs – for example, Runge–Kutta methods – but a discussion of these methods is outside the scope of this book.

30.4.4   Payoff functions

We approximate the continuous payoff function by discretising the underlying asset space in some way. In many cases we create a uniform mesh but this is not mandatory. For example, we can choose more mesh points near transition regions. The accuracy and stability of various finite difference schemes in neighbourhoods of transition regions will, in part, be determined by the type of time discretisation used. For example, it is now well known that the Crank–Nicolson scheme produces oscillations when the asset price is at the money, for example. The reason for this problem is that the derivatives of the solution to the continuous IBVP become large and discontinuous, whereas lower-order Euler schemes do not have this problem. However, these latter schemes are only first-order accurate and in order to achieve second-order accuracy we can choose from a number of options:

* Implicit Euler schemes with Richardson extrapolation
* Rannacher method: using implicit Euler for the first few time steps and Crank–Nicolson thereafter
* Predictor–corrector methods.

Finally, we model the discrete payoff function as a vector/array in C++. A very important point to remember is that the discrete mesh points are defined in the interior of the domain of integration. In other words, the discrete payoff does not 'touch' the asset boundaries. The values on the boundaries will be taken care of by another vector that contains discrete boundary values. If you 'extend' the discrete payoff function to the boundaries you will get erroneous values for the discrete solution. We shall show how to define the discrete payoff function in C++ correctly in the following chapters.

30.4.5   Boundary conditions

In general, the boundary conditions corresponding to the initial boundary value problem must be discretised in some way. There are some issues to be addressed:

1. The discretised boundary conditions must be stable and accurate.
2. It must be easy to incorporate the discretised values in a neighbourhood of the boundary into the finite difference scheme throughout the full discretised domain.

In this book we tend to concentrate on first-order accurate and second-order accurate difference schemes and this position is reflected in the way we define discrete boundary conditions. First, we define first-order approximations to the derivative of the continuous solution by taking one-sided divided differences. The advantage is that this approach is easy to implement; the disadvantage is that it is only first-order accurate and this affects accuracy in the interior of the domain. Second, it is possible to get second-order accuracy by taking centred differences to approximate the first-order derivatives. However, this comes at a cost and we must introduce temporary ghost (fictitious) points that we can eliminate from the system of equations.

30.5   AUXILIARY NUMERICAL METHODS

This book focuses primarily on partial differential equations and their approximation by finite difference schemes. However, we need some other supporting numerical techniques that are needed when solving such problems. We have touched on some of them in this book but we have hardly done them justice:

- Numerical linear algebra and the solution of linear systems of equations (Golub and Van Loan, 1996)
- Numerical integration
- The foundations of numerical analysis (Dahlquist, 1974).

Furthermore, we have excluded a number of important numerical techniques for the main reason that there was not enough space!

- Solution of nonlinear systems of equations
- Interpolation and extrapolation
- Adaptive mesh methods; multi-grid methods.

Information on these subjects can be found in the numerical analysis literature.

30.6   NEW DEVELOPMENTS

Although the application of finite difference schemes to option pricing models is still in its infancy, in the author's humble opinion there is a growing interest in the method as a competitor to well-known lattice methods. This book has introduced a number of schemes that are used to solve pricing problems. We have excluded some new methods but we review them here for completeness. We summarise some new developments that are in the embryonic stages or have not yet been documented and tested by the author (we mention, however, that they are being used by a number of practitioners):

- The Meshless method
- The combination of FDM and FEM for PIDE problems
- The alternating direction explicit (ADE) method (Saul'yev, 1964; Roache, 1998).

Most of the results are anecdotal at the moment of writing but they are encouraging and the above methods could challenge the FDM 'establishment' in the future because of their ease of implementation, speed of execution and ability to model multidimensional problems. For example, ADE methods are both explicit and unconditionally stable while the Meshless method is 'dimension-blind', that is, it can handle multi-asset option models with almost as much ease as it can approximate one-factor models. Finally, for PIDE problems, it is possible to model the PDE part using finite differences while the Galerkin method (in fact, this is FEM) is suitable for the integral part.

30.7   SUMMARY AND CONCLUSIONS

In this chapter we have given a summary of the main issues involved when defining initial boundary value problems (IBVP) that describe the behaviour of derivatives (such as options) as well as the essential activities to be executed when approximating the IBVP by finite difference techniques.

This chapter serves a number of purposes. First, it is a high-level summary of the PDE and FDM techniques of the earlier part of this book. Second, it discusses a number of alternative schemes to use when approximating the solution of PDE-based pricing models. Finally, the results in this chapter will be mapped in the chapters that follow to a form that is suitable for design and implementation in C++. This chapter can be read on a regular basis to refresh your memory on PDE and FDM techniques.

31

Design and Implementation
of First-Order Problems

'Get it working, then get it right, then get it optimised.'

31.1 INTRODUCTION AND OBJECTIVES

In this chapter we start 'closing to C++ code' as it were. In particular, we commence mapping the PDE and FDM 'products' that we summarised in Chapter 30 to a working C++ program. The main challenge of course is to program FDM algorithms in C++. There are many ways of achieving this end and in this chapter we examine simple first-order hyperbolic partial differential equations (both one-factor and two-factor models) and we approximate them by using implicit in time and upwinding or downwinding schemes in space. There are three main reasons for taking this approach. First, hyperbolic equations – taken on their own – tend to be somewhat neglected in the quantitative finance literature. In fact, they crop up as boundary conditions when the Black–Scholes PDE is continued to a boundary, for example in one-factor bond-modelling problems and the Heston stochastic volatility model. Second, the schemes that we use for these problems are easy to understand because they are defined in a box or cube. We also are able to define unconditionally first-order convergent schemes without actually having to use matrix inversion techniques. The subsequent mapping of the FDM schemes to C++ will hopefully be easier than taking a full-blown two-factor Black–Scholes as a first example. Finally, we lay the foundations in this chapter for a transition to more complex problems and models. The only difference between this and subsequent chapters is the level of detail needed in mapping the finite difference schemes to C++. The code works (it is not pseudo code) and of course it can be considerably refined but our objective is to get a working system, however simple, up and running.

An important and sometimes forgotten issue is that we must start thinking about the data structures (such as vectors and matrices) that we design, implement and integrate with the finite difference schemes. This is a recurring theme in general.

31.2 SOFTWARE REQUIREMENTS

When commencing on a software project we must determine what the level of flexibility of the final software product will be. By 'flexibility' we mean the ease with which our code can be modified to suit new requirements. In general, we define three levels of software flexibility:

- Level 1 (hard-coded). The code has been developed for a specific problem. If you wish to use the code for another problem the source code must be recompiled for this new problem.
- Level 2 (using design patterns – GOF, 1995; Duffy, 2004). We decompose a software system into loosely coupled subsystems and flexibility is achieved using design patterns. The focus is on the flexibility of the numerical algorithms and less on input and output mechanisms.

- Level 3 (full-scale software systems). In general, this level is achieved by integrating the Level 2 design patterns with input and output mechanisms. For example, we use GUI controls to enter data while output data could be presented in Excel.

In this book we concentrate mainly on Level 1 aspects.

31.3   MODULAR DECOMPOSITION

The idea of breaking a problem into loosely coupled and independent software modules is not new. In fact, when the programming language Fortran was top of the heap it was standard practice to write generic software modules and reuse them without having to modify them in applications. The love affair with the object-oriented paradigm has relegated modular programming to the second division. In this chapter we redress the situation somewhat by combining the two paradigms: each independent module will be implemented as a C++ class or structure.

In this chapter we examine one-factor and two-factor first-order hyperbolic initial boundary value problems, their numerical approximation using FDM and their implementation in C++. To this end, we cluster similar functionality into classes or structures. The general system topology is shown in Figure 31.1 and displays the main concepts in the current problem as well as the relationships between them:

- HIBVP: This models the hyperbolic initial boundary value problem, including the domain space (in (x, t) coordinates) in which its PDE is defined, the coefficients appearing in the PDE as well as the initial and boundary conditions.
- HFDM: This models the finite difference scheme that approximates HIBVP. It needs a discrete mesh and this is created by Mesher code while, for both the one-factor and two-factor problems, we employ an implicit scheme in time and upwinding scheme in space.

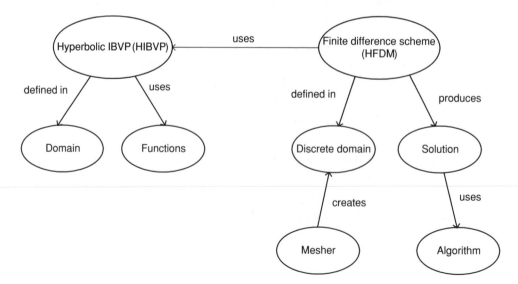

Figure 31.1   Structure of C++ design

In this chapter only the concepts HIBVP and HFDM appearing in Figure 31.1 will be implemented as C++ classes. In fact, we implement them as structs. A struct can be likened to a lightweight class because it is easier to program and has less overhead than a C++ class.

31.4   USEFUL C++ DATA STRUCTURES

In the past (and up to the present time), Fortran programmers developed scientific and engineering applications. They used ready-made modules and algorithms and integrated them within their applications. There are many Fortran libraries in the marketplace and an important subset are libraries for arrays and matrices. We have constructed similar structures in C++ (see Duffy, 2004) and can use them directly in our finite difference schemes. For those readers who are not familiar with these structures we have included an appendix (see section 31.9) describing the main functionality. The full source code can be found on the accompanying CD.

31.5   ONE-FACTOR MODELS

We examine the initial boundary value problem:

$$\frac{\partial u}{\partial t} + a(x, t)\frac{\partial u}{\partial x} = F(x, t), \quad t \epsilon (0, T)$$

$$u(0, t) = g(t), \quad t \epsilon (0, T) \tag{31.1}$$

$$u(x, 0) = f(x), \quad x \epsilon (0, 1)$$

where $a(x, t) > 0$, $x \epsilon [0, 1]$, $t \epsilon [0, T]$.

In this case we see that the characteristic direction is positive from $x = 0$ and hence the boundary condition must be defined there. This constrains the kind of finite difference scheme that we can use because it must be consistent with this. In other words, information is travelling from the inlet/downstream end-point $x = 0$ into the interior of the region.

We approximate the solution of the IBVP (31.1) using implicit Euler in time and upwinding in x. We also must approximate the initial and boundary conditions appearing in (31.1). To this end, we partition the interval $(0, 1)$ into J equal sub-intervals and the interval $(0, T)$ into N equal sub-intervals. Then the resulting finite difference scheme is given by:

$$\frac{u_j^{n+1} - u_j^n}{k} + a_j^{n+1}\frac{u_j^{n+1} - u_{j-1}^{n+1}}{h} = F_j^{n+1}, \quad 1 \le j \le J, \quad 0 \le n \le N - 1 \tag{31.2a}$$

$$u_0^n = g(t_n), \quad 0 \le n \le N \tag{31.2b}$$

$$u_j^0 = f(x_j), \quad 1 \le j \le J \tag{31.2c}$$

where
$$\left.\begin{array}{l} h = 1/J \\ k = T/N \\ a_j^{n+1} = a(jh, (n+1)k) \\ F_j^{n+1} = F(jh, (n+1)k) \end{array}\right\} \quad \begin{array}{l} 0 \le j \le J \\ 0 \le n \le N - 1 \end{array}$$

Rearranging (31.2a) by placing all known quantities on the right-hand side and all unknown quantities on the left-hand side we get the following equivalent expression:

$$u^{n+1}(1 + \lambda_j^{n+1}) = u_j^n + \lambda_j^n u_{j-1}^{n+1} + kF_j^{n+1}, \quad 1 \le j \le J, \quad 0 \le n \le N - 1 \tag{31.3}$$

where $\lambda_j^{n+1} = ka_j^{n+1}/h$ (the CFL condition).

We thus see from this equation that the solution at time level $n + 1$ and mesh-point jh is given in terms of the inhomogeneous term F, an initial condition at time level n and a boundary condition from mesh-point $(j - 1)h$.

In order to keep things concrete we examine (31.1) for the test case whose solution is $u(x, t) = x + t$. This is purely for pedagogical reasons. We encapsulate knowledge of (31.1) in a C++ struct as follows:

```cpp
struct HIBVP
{ // Assemble the defining properties of the initial
  // boundary value problem in one place.

      double T; // 'End' time
      // Coefficients in PDE
      double a(double x, double t)
      {
            return 1.0;
      }
      double F(double x, double t)
      {
            return 2.0;
      }
      // Boundary condition
      double g(double t)
      {
            return t;
      }
      // Initial condition
      double f(double x)
      {
            return x;
      }

};
```

We implicitly assume that the extent of the domain in the x direction is the interval $(0, 1)$ and that the extent in the t direction is $(0, T)$.

We now design the C++ struct that encapsulates the code for the implicit finite difference scheme (31.2). First, we discuss its member data. It consists of both mesh data and vector data that holds the solution vectors at time levels n and $n + 1$. To this end, the following code should be reasonably self-explanatory:

```cpp
      HIBVP* m_h;
      // Discrete parameters
      double h, k;              // Mesh sizes
      double J, N;              // Number of sub-divisions

      double T;                 // (Redundant)
      double t;                 // Current time level
```

```
// Vectors (work arrays)
Vector<double, int> XArr;
Vector<double, int> VOld;    // Time level n
Vector<double, int> VNew;    // Time level n+1
```

We now turn our attention to the corresponding member functions in this class. There are just three of them:

- Constructor
- Producing the result at time level $n + 1$
- Determining if the time-marching scheme has reached time T.

The constructor has two main uses; first, it constructs the mesh array and, second, it initialises the solution vectors. Please note that it has a pointer to its 'parent' HIBVP:

```
HFDM(int NX, int NT, HIBVP* myIBVP)
  { // Use this constructor
        J = NX;
        N = NT;

        m_h = myIBVP;
        T = m_h->T;
        t = 0.0;
        h = 1.0 / double (J); // Assume x-interval (0,1)
        k = T / double (N);

        XArr = Vector<double, int> (J+1, 1);
        XArr[XArr.MinIndex()] = 0.0;

        double x = h;
        for (int j = XArr.MinIndex() + 1;j <= XArr.MaxIndex(); j++)
        {
          XArr[j] = x;
          x += h;
        }

        // Work with vector at time levels n and n+1
        VOld = Vector<double, int> (J+1, 1);
        VOld[VOld.MinIndex()] = m_h -> g(t);
        for (j = VOld.MinIndex() + 1; j <= VOld.MaxIndex(); j++)
        {
          VOld[j] = m_h -> f(XArr[j]);
        }

        VNew = Vector<double, int> (VOld);

        }
```

The member function that actually calculates the solution at time level $n+1$ is based on the algorithm in equation (31.3) and is given by:

```
Vector<double, int>& result()
{ // The value of the solution at level n + 1
```

```
t + = k;
VNew[VNew.MinIndex()] = m_h → g(t);
double tmp;

for (int j = VNew.MinIndex() + 1; j <= VNew.MaxIndex(); j++)
{ // Implicit Euler
        tmp = (k * m_h ->a(XArr[j], t)) / h; // Lambda factor

        VNew[j] = (VOld[j] + (tmp * VNew[j-1])+(k * m_h ->F(t,j)) )
                              / (1.0 + tmp);

}
VOld = VNew; // Update solution at time level n
return VNew;
}
```

Finally, we have defined the following simple function to tell us if we are finished marching in time:

```
bool isDone() const
{
    if (t < T)
    {
      return false;
    }
      return true;
}
```

31.5.1   Main program and output

We have completed the discussion of the C++ code that implements system (31.3). We now give some code to show how to test the finite difference scheme. We march from $t = 0$ to $t = T$ and we print the solution (as a vector) at each time level. To this end, we have created a simple function to print a vector:

```
template <class V, class I> void print(const Vector<V,I>& v)
{
    cout << "\nARR:[";
    for (I j = v.MinIndex(); j <= v.MaxIndex(); j++)
    {
        cout << v[j] << ", ";
    }
    cout << "]";
}
```

The main program for getting the job done is as follows:

```
int main()
{
    // Define Continuous Problem
```

```
HIBVP myIBVP;
myIBVP.T = 1.0;

// Define Discrete Problem
int NX = 10;
int NT = 5;
HFDM myFDM(NX, NT, &myIBVP);
```

L1:

```
Vector<double, int> answer = myFDM.result();
print(answer);cout << " Time Level: " << myFDM.t << endl;

if (myFDM.isDone() == false)
{
        goto L1;
}

return 0;
}
```

The output from this program is:

```
ARR:[0.2, 0.3, 0.4, 0.5, 0.6, 0.7, 0.8, 0.9, 1, 1.1, 1.2] Time Level: 0.2
ARR:[0.4, 0.5, 0.6, 0.7, 0.8, 0.9, 1, 1.1, 1.2, 1.3, 1.4] Time Level: 0.4
ARR:[0.6, 0.7, 0.8, 0.9, 1, 1.1, 1.2, 1.3, 1.4, 1.5, 1.6] Time Level: 0.6
ARR:[0.8, 0.9, 1, 1.1, 1.2, 1.3, 1.4, 1.5, 1.6, 1.7, 1.8] Time Level: 0.8
ARR:[1, 1.1, 1.2, 1.3, 1.4, 1.5, 1.6, 1.7, 1.8, 1.9, 2] Time Level: 1
```

31.6   MULTI-FACTOR MODELS

We now turn our attention to a two-factor generalisation of system (31.1). This is a first-order hyperbolic initial boundary value problem in the space dimensions x and y and in the time dimension t. We define the problem on a unit square in (x, y) space and we assume that information is coming from the boundaries $x = 0$ and $y = 0$. The specification is given by the system:

$$\frac{\partial u}{\partial t} + a\frac{\partial u}{\partial x} + b\frac{\partial u}{\partial y} + cu = F, \quad x\epsilon(0, 1), \quad y\epsilon(0, 1), \quad t\epsilon(0, T)$$

$$u(0, y, t) = g_1(y, t), \quad y\epsilon(0, 1), \quad t\epsilon(0, T)$$

$$u(x, 0, t) = g_2(x, t), \quad x\epsilon(0, 1), \quad t\epsilon(0, T) \tag{31.4}$$

$$u(x, y, 0) = f(x, y), \quad x, y\epsilon(0, 1)$$

where

$$a(x, y, t) \geq \alpha > 0 \quad \text{and} \quad b(x, y, t) \geq \beta > 0 \tag{31.5}$$

From the inequalities in (31.5) we know that information is coming from the lower boundaries $x = 0$ and $y = 0$ and hence the boundary conditions in (31.4) are the correct ones.

We propose the following finite difference scheme to approximate the solution of system (31.4): in the space dimensions we use the appropriate first-order upwinding schemes while in the time dimension we use the implicit Euler scheme:

$$\frac{u_{i,j}^{n+1} - u_{i,j}^{n}}{k} + a_{i,j}^{n+1} \frac{u_{i,j}^{n+1} - u_{i-1,j}^{n+1}}{h_1} + b_{i,j}^{n+1} \frac{u_{i,j}^{n+1} - u_{i,j-1}^{n+1}}{h_2}$$

$$+ c_{i,j}^{n+1} u_{i,j}^{n+1} = F_{i,j}^{n+1}, \quad 1 \le i \le I, \quad 1 \le j \le J, \quad 0 \le n \le N-1 \qquad (31.6a)$$

$$u_{0,j}^{n} = g_1(jh_2, nk), \quad 1 \le j \le J, \quad u_{i,0}^{n} = g_2(ih_1, nk), \quad 1 \le i \le I \qquad (31.6b)$$

$$u_{i,j}^{0} = f(ih_1, jh_2), \quad 1 \le i \le I, \quad 1 \le j \le J \qquad (31.6c)$$

Rearranging the terms in equation (31.6a) allows us to write the discrete solution at any point in terms of known quantities:

$$u_{i,j}^{n+1}(1 + A_{i,j}^{n+1} + B_{i,j}^{n+1} + kc_{i,j}^{n+1}) = u_{i,j}^{n} + A_{i,j}^{n+1} u_{i-1,j}^{n+1} + B_{i,j-1}^{n+1} u_{i,j-1}^{n+1} + kF_{i,j}^{n+1} \quad (31.7)$$

where

$$A \equiv \frac{ka}{h_1} \quad \text{and} \quad B \equiv \frac{kb}{h_2} \qquad (31.8)$$

Remark. We note that schemes (31.3) and (31.7) are both positive in the sense that positive initial condition, boundary conditions and forcing terms lead to a positive/monotone scheme.

We now discuss how to implement scheme (31.6) in C++. In fact, we copied the source code from the one-factor solution. Of course, we had to modify the code but the basic structure is the same as before. In fact, we implement the concept map in Figure 31.1 in the current case as well. In short, we have everything 'doubled' with respect to the one-factor case, for example:

- Mesh arrays in both the x and y dimensions
- The solution at each time level n is a two-dimensional matrix instead of a one-dimensional vector
- Instead of single 'for' loops we now have two 'for' loops.

The member data for the class that implements the two-factor finite difference scheme is given by:

```
HIBVP* m_h;                    // Pointer to PDE object
// Discrete parameters
double h1, h2, k;              // Mesh sizes
double J1, J2, N;              // Number of sub-divisions

double T;                      //(Redundant)
double t;                      // Current time level

// NumericMatrix (work arrays)
Vector<double, int> XArr;
Vector<double, int> YArr;

NumericMatrix<double, int> MOld;    // Time level n
NumericMatrix<double, int> MNew;    // Time level n+1
```

As with the one-factor case we now turn our attention to the corresponding member functions in this class. There are only three of them:

- Constructor
- Producing the result at time level $n + 1$
- Determining if the time-marching scheme has reached time T.

The code for the constructor is responsible for creating the mesh arrays XArr and YArr as well as defining the discrete initial condition, that is the solution at time level $n = 0$ (expressed as a matrix):

```
HFDM(int NX, int NY, int NT, HIBVP* myIBVP)
{ // Use this constructor

    J1 = NX; J2 = NY; N = NT;
    m_h = myIBVP;
    T = m_h->T; t =  0.0;
    h1 = 1.0 / double (J1)      // Assume x-interval (0,1)
    h2 = 1.0 / double (J2);     // Assume y-interval (0,1)
    k = T / double (N);

    XArr = Vector<double, int> (J1+1, 1);
    XArr[XArr.MinIndex()] = 0.0;

    double x = h1;
    for (int j = XArr.MinIndex() + 1; j <= XArr.MaxIndex(); j++)
    {
        XArr[j] = x;
        x += h1;
    }

    YArr = Vector<double, int> (J2+1, 1);
    YArr[YArr.MinIndex()] = 0.0;

    double y = h2;
    for (j = YArr.MinIndex() + 1; j <= YArr.MaxIndex(); j++)
    {
        YArr[j] = y;
        y += h2;
    }
    // Work with NumericMatrix at time levels n and n+1
    MOld = NumericMatrix<double, int> (J1+1,J2+1,1,1);

    // Initialise boundary conditions x = 0 and y = 0
    for (int ii = MOld.MinColumnIndex();
            ii <= MOld.MaxColumnIndex(); ii++)
        { // x == 0
          MOld(MOld.MinRowIndex(), ii) =
                m_h->g(XArr[XArr.MinIndex()], YArr[ii], t);
    }
    for (int jj = MOld.MinRowIndex(); jj <= MOld.MaxRowIndex(); jj++)
    { // y == 0

        MOld(jj, MOld.MinColumnIndex()) =
                m_h ->g(XArr[jj], YArr[YArr.MinIndex()], t);
        }
```

```
    // Now the initial conditions 'off' the characteristic boundaries
    for (int kk = MOld.MinColumnIndex()+1;
            kk <= MOld.MaxColumnIndex(); kk++)
    {
        for (j = MOld.MinRowIndex()+1;
          j <= MOld.MaxRowIndex(); j++)
        {
          MOld(j, kk) = m_h -> f(XArr[j], YArr[kk]);
        }
    }
    MNew = NumericMatrix<double, int> (MOld);
}
```

The function to actually calculate the solution at time level $n + 1$ in the form of a matrix is given by the following code (it is based on the algorithm (31.7)):

```
double tmp1, tmp2, factor;
for (int kk = MNew.MinColumnIndex() + 1;
            kk <= MNew.MaxColumnIndex(); kk++)
{ // Implicit Euler
    for (int j = MNew.MinRowIndex() + 1;
            j <= MNew.MaxRowIndex(); j++)
    {

        tmp1 = (m_h->a(XArr[j], YArr[kk], t) * k) / h1;
        tmp2 = (m_h->a(XArr[j], YArr[kk], t) * k) / h2;
        factor = 1.0 + tmp1 + tmp2
            + (k*m_h->c(XArr[j], YArr[k], t+k));

        MNew(j, kk) = MOld(j,kk) + (tmp1 * MNew(j-1, kk))
        + (tmp2 * MNew(j,kk-1))+(k * m_h->F(XArr[j],YArr[kk],t));
        MNew(j, kk) = MNew(j,kk) / factor;
    }
}
```

The full source code can be found on the accompanying CD.

31.7 GENERALISATIONS AND APPLICATIONS TO QUANTITATIVE FINANCE

In this chapter we have deliberately made things as concrete and as hard-coded as possible. We have avoided clever C++ tricks and design patterns (for the moment, at least) in order to help the reader to understand the essentials of the C++ code that implements the finite difference schemes. We now give a list of the features in the current version of the software as well as some guidelines on how to make the software more flexible.

- *Input* (All input is hard-coded into the program at the moment). Input the functions defining the initial boundary value problem (systems (31.1) and (31.4)). It is possible to extend the set of IBVPs that can be modelled in the software by defining standard interfaces and then loading components that implement these interfaces by using dynamic link libraries or assemblies, for example. In this way, we create software that works with any IBVP and that does not have to be modified for each new set of parameters.

In general, we should enter all discrete data (for example, the number of mesh points) using dialog boxes and other graphic user interface (GUI) controls. In this chapter we use the C++ iostream library for input (and output).

- *Calculation and number crunching:* The code implements a specific finite difference scheme. If we wish to implement another scheme, such as explicit Euler or Crank–Nicolson, we must insert the code and recompile. If we wish to have a more flexible regime, we could define various so-called strategy objects (GOF, 1995; Duffy, 2004) with each strategy implementing a specific finite difference scheme. We can dynamically load each strategy by implementing it as a dynamic link library or assembly.

- *Output:* The solution at each time level in all cases is either a one-dimensional or two-dimensional structure. In the current version the values in these arrays are printed using the iostream library. This is a basic techniques and is a good way to test and debug the algorithms. For example, the simple procedure to print a matrix is given by:

```
void printNumericMatrix (const NumericMatrix<double, int>& mat)
{  // Print every vector in the NumericMatrix
   for (int i = mat.MinRowIndex(); i <= mat.MaxRowIndex(); i++)
   {
       cout << "\n" << i << ": ";
       for (int j=mat.MinColumnIndex();j<=mat.MaxColumnIndex(); j++)
       {
           cout << mat(i,j) << ", ";
       }
   }
   cout << endl;
}
```

In later versions we could display the solution in other media, such as Excel.

- *Reusability and maintainability:* The class HFDM contains a lot a functionality (as seen by the large number of member data). In fact, it contains functionality for both mesh generation and the details of the algorithm that implements the finite difference scheme. It is a good idea to create dedicated classes for mesh generation and algorithms. To this end, we should partition HFDM into more loosely coupled parts. The advantages are that HFDM becomes less monolithic and it promotes reusability. For example, mesher functionality can be used in many other finite difference schemes and not just the schemes in this chapter. We shall show how to achieve this end in a future chapter.

31.8   SUMMARY AND CONCLUSIONS

We have shown how to map FDM algorithms to C++ code by taking a hyperbolic initial boundary value problem as test case. The problem uses a one-step method in time and an upwinding scheme in space. This ensures that we do not get bogged down (at least, not yet) in solving a matrix system at each time level and this approach allows us to concentrate on the essential algorithmic and coding issues. Furthermore, we have avoided sophisticated design patterns and clever tricks because their introduction would confuse the understandability of the code.

We hope that this chapter will have helped the reader to appreciate the link between FDM and C++.

31.9   APPENDIX: USEFUL DATA STRUCTURES IN C++

We concentrate on one-dimensional and two-dimensional data structures. To this end, we introduce basic *foundation* classes, namely:

- `Array`: sequential, indexible container containing arbitrary data types
- `Vector`: array class that contains numeric data
- `Matrix`: sequential, indexible container containing arbitrary data types
- `NumericMatrix`: matrix class that contains numeric data.

The code for these classes is on the accompanying CD. The classes `Array` and `Vector` are one-dimensional containers whose elements we access using a single index while `Matrix` and `NumericMatrix` are two-dimensional containers whose elements we access using two indices.

We now discuss each of these classes in more detail.

We start with the class `Array`. This is the most fundamental class in the library and it represents a sequential collection of values. This template class that we denote by `Array <V, I, S>` has three generic parameters:

- `V`: the data type of the underlying values in the array
- `I`: the data type used for indexing the values in the array
- `S`: the so-called storage class for the array.

The storage class is in fact an encapsulation of the STL `vector` class and it is here that the data in the array is actually initialised. At the moment there are specific storage classes, namely `FullArray<V>` and `BandArray<V>` that store a full array and a banded array of values, respectively.

Please note that it is not possible to change the size of an `Array` instance once it has been constructed. This is in contrast to the STL `vector` class in which it is possible to let it grow.

The declaration of the class `Array` is given by:

```
template <class V, class I=int, class S=FullArray<V>  >
class Array
{
private:
      S m_structure;        // The array structure
      I m_start;            // The start index

};
```

We see that `Array` has an embedded storage object of type `S` and a start index. The default storage is `FullArray<V>` and the default index type is `int`. This means that if we work with these types on a regular basis we do not have to include them in the template declaration. Thus, the following three declarations are the same:

```
Array<double, int, FullArray<double> > arr1;
Array<double, int> arr1;
Array<double> arr1;
```

You may choose whichever data types that are most suitable for your needs. The constructors in `Array` allow us to create instances based on size of the array, start index and so on.

The constructors are:

```
Array();                          // Default constructor
Array(size_t size);               // Give length start index ==1
Array(size_t size, I start);      // Length and start index
Array(size_t size, I start,
      const V& value);            // Size, start, value
Array(const Array<V, I, S>& source);  // Copy constructor
```

Once we have created an array, we may wish to navigate in the array, access the elements in the array and to modify these elements. The member functions to help you in this case are:

```
// Selectors
I MinIndex() const;               // Return the minimum index
I MaxIndex() const;               // Return the maximum index
size_t Size() const;              // The size of the array
const V& Element(I index) const;  // Element at position

// Modifiers
void Element(I index, const V& val);  // Change element at position
void StartIndex(I index);             // Change the start index

// Operators
virtual V& operator [] (I index);     // Subscripting operator
virtual const V& operator [] (I index) const;
```

This completes the description of the Array class. We do not describe the class that actually stores the data in the array. The reader can find the source code on the accompanying media kit.

We now discuss the Vector and NumericMatrix classes in detail. These classes are derived from Array and Matrix, respectively. Thus all the functionality that we have described in previous sections remains valid for these new classes. Furthermore, we have created constructors for Vector and NumericMatrix classes as well. So what do these classes have that their base classes do not have? The general answer is that Vector and NumericMatrix assume that their underlying types are numeric. We thus model these classes as implementations of the corresponding mathematical structures.

We have implemented Vector and NumericMatrix as approximations to a vector space. In some cases we have added functionality to suit our needs. However, we have simplified things a little because we assume that the data types in a vector space are of the same types as that of the underlying field. This is for convenience only and it satisfies our needs for most applications in financial engineering. Class Vector is derived from Array. Its definition in C++ is:

```
template <class V, class I=int, class S=FullArray<V> >
class Vector: public Array<V, I, S>
{
private:

    // No member data
};
```

We give the prototypes for some of the mathematical operations in `Vector`. The first group is a straight implementation of a vector space; notice that we have applied operator overloading in C++:

```
Vector<V, I, S> operator - () const;
Vector<V, I, S> operator + (const Vector<V, I, S>& v) const;
Vector<V, I, S> operator - (const Vector<V, I, S>& v) const;
```

The second group of functions is useful because it provides functionality for offsetting the values in a vector:

```
Vector<V, I, S> operator + (const V& v) const;
Vector<V, I, S> operator - (const V& v) const;
Vector<V, I, S> operator * (const V& v) const;
```

The first function adds an element to each element in the vector and returns a new vector. The second and third functions are similar except that we apply subtraction and multiplication operators, respectively. Class `NumericMatrix` is derived from `Matrix`. Its definition in C++ is:

```
template <class V, class I=int, class S=FullMatrix<V> >
class NumericMatrix: public Matrix<V, I, S>
{
private:

    // No member data
};
```

The constructors in `NumericMatrix` are the same as for `Matrix`. We may also wish to manipulate the rows and columns of matrices and we provide 'set/get' functionality. Notice that we return vectors for selectors but that modifiers accept `Array` instances (and instances of any derived class!):

```
// Selectors
Vector<V, I> Row(I row) const;
Vector<V, I> Column(I column) const;

// Modifiers
void Row(I row, const Array<V, I>& val);
void Column(I column, const Array<V, I>& val);
```

Since we shall be solving linear systems of equations in later chapters we must provide functionality for multiplying matrices with vectors and with other matrices:

- Multiply a matrix and a vector
- Multiply a (transpose of a) vector and a matrix
- Multiply two matrices.

We give some simple examples showing how to create vectors and how to perform some mathematical operations on the vectors.

```
// Create some vectors
Vector<double, int> vec1(10, 1, 2.0); // Start = 1, value 2.0
Vector<double, int> vec2(10, 1, 3.0); // Start = 1, value 3.0
```

```
Vector<double, int> vec3 = vec1 + vec2;
Vector<double, int> vec4 = vec1 - vec2;

Vector<double, int> vec5 = vec1 - 3.14;
```

We give an example to show how to use numeric matrices. The code is:

```
int rowstart = 1;
int colstart = 1;
NumericMatrix<double, int> m3(3, 3, rowstart, colstart);
for (int i = m3.MinRowIndex(); i <= m3.MaxRowIndex(); i++)
{
    for (int j = m3.MinColumnIndex(); j <= m3.MaxColumnIndex(); j++)
    {
        m3(i, j) = 1.0 /(i + j -1.0);
    }
}
print (m3);
```

The output from this code is:

```
MinRowIndex: 1 , MaxRowIndex: 3
MinColumnIndex: 1 , MaxColumnIndex: 3

MAT:[
Row 1 (1,0.5,0.333333,)
Row 2 (0.5,0.333333,0.25,)
Row 3 (0.333333,0.25,0.2,)]
```

For more information on the above classes, see the code on the accompanying CD and Duffy (2004) for some applications.

32

Moving to Black–Scholes

We may consider ourselves lucky when, trying to solve a problem, we succeed in discovering a simpler analogous problem.

George Polya

32.1 INTRODUCTION AND OBJECTIVES

In this chapter we continue with our discussion of finite difference schemes and their implementation in C++. Whereas we considered first-order hyperbolic equations (convection equations) in Chapter 31, we now examine the two-dimensional heat equation. In particular, we wish to show how to map the FDM schemes for the equation to C++. This is a diffusion equation and an important component of the Black–Scholes equation. Understanding how to program the heat equation will allow us to generalise our code to handle two-factor option pricing problems. As before, we use an explicit scheme to avoid making things more complicated than necessary.

In general we must determine how we are going to solve a problem using finite difference schemes and also determine the resources we need. Summarising, the major attention points are:

A1: An unambiguous specification of the PDE model
A2: Determining which FDM model to use
A3: Implementing the model in C++.

These are the major issues we must resolve. They are not the only ones because we shall also need to addresses issues such as design patterns and integration of the C++ code in production environments.

In general, the so-called lifecycle of a financial derivatives product is given by the following activities:

- *Financial model:* The activity in which the quantitative engineer defines stochastic equations, parameters, constraints and historical/calibrated data for the problem at hand.
- *PDE model*: We map the financial model to an initial boundary value problem that unambiguously describes the derivative product. We produce the following products:

  – The coefficients of the PDE
  – The boundary conditions
  – The initial condition (the payoff function).

- *FDM model:* We must choose which finite difference scheme is most suitable for the current PDE model. There are many choices at this stage and the final one will be determined by a number of factors, some of which we discuss in the next section. In general, we do not wish to 'over-engineer' our schemes while at the same time we must satisfy customer requirements such as accuracy and performance.

- *Design model:* We decide how flexible the eventual software product should be. That is, before we implement the algorithms in C++ we determine the level to which the software product will need to be customised in the future. To this end, we apply the design pattern technique as originally discussed in GOF (1995) and elaborated in Duffy (2004).
- *C++ model:* We now implement the design model using C++. To this end, we need to create new functionality as well as reusing existing code and libraries. For example, we use the Standard Template Library (STL) and the C++ datastructures in Duffy (2004).
- *Production model*: Here we integrate the C++ code from the previous model into a real-life development environment. For example, we could choose for a Microsoft Windows environment, in which case we can integrate the C++ software with a number of software environments:

  – Graphical User Interfaces (Windows Forms, MFC)
  – Relational database systems (Oracle, SQL Server)
  – Visualisation Software (Excel, GDI+, OpenGL)
  – Real-time data feeds.

In this chapter we focus mainly on activities A2, A3 and, to a certain extent, activity A1.

32.2   THE PDE MODEL

In general, we model derivatives product by a generalised Black–Scholes PDE or PIDE (in the latter case there is an integral term that models jumps). In this book we concentrate on one-, two- and three-factor models. Of course, one-factor models are the easiest to formulate and to solve, both from a numerical and a computational point of view. In general, the underlyings for one-factor models are typically:

- The asset price S (or a future, commodity or stock)
- The interest rate r.

The two-factor models in this book had to do with the following kinds of problems:

- Multi-asset models (for example, the maximum of two assets)
- Two-factor interest-rate models
- Real options (for example, wood harvesting).

The coefficients of the Black–Scholes equation must be determined in each case.

We now complete the description of the PDE model by specifying the initial or payoff condition and the corresponding boundary conditions. The payoff function depends on the underlying prices and on a set of other parameters, usually strike prices. It is well-behaved in general; however, it (or its derivatives) may be discontinuous at certain points.

Specifying boundary conditions seems to be a black hole at the moment of writing. In general, the Black–Scholes equation is defined on a semi-infinite interval and in many cases we must modify the equation so that it becomes a PDE on some bounded domain. There are two main approaches:

- Truncate the infinite domain, thus getting a bounded domain
- Use a change of variables to transform the semi-infinite domain to a bounded domain.

The first approach is very popular and authors use the term 'far-field' condition to denote the fact that they are working on a truncated interval and that 'new' boundary conditions need to be specified there. The most popular types of boundary condition are:

- Dirichlet (value of solution known on boundary)
- Neumann (first derivative of solution known on boundary)
- Linearity (second derivative of solution known on boundary).

The linearity boundary condition is sometimes known as the convexity boundary condition. Finally, must we specify a boundary condition when the underyings are zero? The answer is 'no' because the Black–Scholes equation degenerates at this point and no boundary conditions are allowed! Instead, the PDE is satisfied at this point. The equation can be:

- An ordinary differential equation
- A first-order hyperbolic equation
- A lower-order Black–Scholes equation.

A closed solution may or may not be possible in this case.

32.3 THE FDM MODEL

The FDM model is concerned with the setting up of the discrete set of equations that approximate the initial boundary value problem. To this end, we must produce discretisations for:

- The derivatives in the PDE
- The coefficients in the PDE
- The initial condition
- The boundary conditions.

In general, we employ centred difference schemes to approximate the space derivatives while we use one-step methods to approximate the time derivatives (in the future it might be worth while investigating multi-step methods). On the boundary, we can employ one-sided, first-order methods or second-order methods using 'ghost' (fictitious) points.

In general, boundaries and boundary conditions complicate the finite difference schemes. For example, problems on semi-infinite space domains must be truncated to bounded domains and then we must specify appropriate boundary conditions at this new 'far-field' boundary. Finally, if we are modelling American option problems we must model the unknown moving 'optimal exercise' boundary. We have already discussed a number of ways of doing this:

- The Landau transformation (change of variables)
- Penalty methods
- Variational methods.

The first two methods lead to nonlinear and semi-linear PDEs, respectively. We can approximate them using implicit, semi-implicit or explicit schemes. The end product from the FDM model is an unambiguous set of equations that we can now design and implement in a programming language.

32.4 ALGORITHMS AND DATA STRUCTURES

Having set up the discrete system of equations that allows us to march from one time level to the next, we need some kind of language and a set of data structures that we use to bridge the gap between the finite difference schemes and the implementation (in C++, for example). In general, the description of the marching process is procedural in nature, reminiscent of the way Fortran programs are written. The process uses a combination of object-oriented data structures and generic functions. The data structures hold the results of calculations as well as input data while the generic functions transform continuous functions into their discrete equivalents, for example. A high-level description of the process that maps the finite difference scheme to a more computable form is as follows:

1. Read input from the continuous problem (coefficients, initial and boundary conditions, domain).
2. Create a two-dimensional mesh (this is not time-dependent, so it can be initialised just once).
3. Choose type of scheme; (in this chapter we take centred differences in space and explicit Euler in time).
4. Create the discrete initial condition (the solution at time level $n = 0$).
5. 'Start of Main Loop'; increment time level (from n to $n + 1$).
6. Calculate discrete boundary conditions.
7. Calculate discrete solution at level $n + 1$ in terms of discrete solution at previous level n and discrete boundary conditions.
8. Postprocessing; store newly computed values in repository.
9. If we have reached the expiry time then stop; else go to step 5.

In fact, these steps are quite general and can be applied to many problems. Of course, the devil is in the details, as the saying goes. We shall show how these steps are realised for the specific case of the two-dimensional heat equation.

32.5   THE C++ MODEL

In this phase we implement the FDM model and the corresponding algorithms in C++. In general, we can use a combination of procedural and object-oriented programming techniques. In this chapter we concentrate on using object-oriented building blocks (for examples, vectors, matrices and tensors) and then using these in procedures to calculate the solution.

The reusable classes are:

- `Vector`: A class that models fixed-sized arrays with the corresponding mathematical structure
- `NumericMatrix`: a matrix class that is endowed with mathematical properties
- `Tensor`: A container that holds an array of matrices. We need this class because it will hold the calculated data from the finite difference schemes at each time level.

Furthermore, we have defined a number of generic functions that are of use in this context, for example:

- Transforming continuous functions to discrete equivalents
- Properties of vectors and matrices, for example norms.

We shall give concrete examples of C++ code when we discuss finite difference schemes for the two-dimensional heat equation.

32.6 TEST CASE: THE TWO-DIMENSIONAL HEAT EQUATION

In this section we discuss the problem of the flow of heat in a thin rectangular plate R of length L and width M that is situated in the xy plane (Kreider *et al.*, 1966). We assume that heat is neither gained nor lost across the faces of the plate. This means that we can prescribe Dirichlet boundary conditions on the boundary of R. Furthermore, we assume that the initial temperature distribution $f(x, y)$ is known. The initial boundary value problem now becomes:

$$\frac{\partial u}{\partial t} = \frac{\partial^2 u}{\partial x^2} + \frac{\partial^2 u}{\partial y^2} \text{ in } R \tag{32.1a}$$

$$u = 0 \text{ on } \partial R \text{ (boundary of } R) \tag{32.1b}$$

$$u(x, y, 0) = f(x, y) \text{ in } R \tag{32.1c}$$

We now describe how to approximate the solution of problem (32.1) using finite difference schemes, and we then map the FDM algorithms to C++ code.

32.7 FINITE DIFFERENCE SOLUTION

We now discuss a particular finite difference scheme that approximates the solution of the initial boundary value problem (32.1). We use centred differencing in space and explicit Euler in time:

$$\frac{U_{ij}^{n+1} - U_{ij}^n}{k} = \Delta_x^2 U_{ij}^n + \Delta_y^2 U_{ij}^n, \quad 1 \le i \le N_x - 1, \quad 1 \le j \le N_y - 1 \tag{32.2}$$

Since this scheme is explicit in time we can rearrange the terms in equation (32.2) to produce a solution at the time level $n + 1$:

$$U_{ij}^{n+1} = \lambda_1 \left(U_{i+1,j}^n + U_{i-1,j}^n \right) + \lambda_2 \left(U_{i,j+1}^n + U_{i,j-1}^n \right)$$
$$+ (1 - 2\lambda_1 - 2\lambda_2)U_{i,j}^n, \quad 1 \le i \le N_x - 1, \quad 1 \le j \le N_y - 1 \tag{32.3}$$

where $\lambda_1 = k/h_x^2$ and $\lambda_2 = k/h_y^2$.

The initial condition and boundary conditions are defined by:

$$U_{ij}^0 = f(x_i, y_j), \quad 1 \le i \le N_{x-1}, \quad 1 \le j \le N_{y-1} \tag{32.4}$$

$$U_{0j}^n = 0, \quad 0 \le j \le N_y; \qquad U_{Ij}^n = 0, \quad 0 \le j \le N_y$$

$$U_{i0}^n = 0, \quad 0 \le i \le N_x; \qquad U_{iJ}^n = 0, \quad 0 \le i \le N_x \tag{32.5}$$

$$(Ih_x = N_x, \quad Jh_y = N_y)$$

We have chosen the boundary conditions as zero in this case but it is easy to adapt the scheme to non-zero boundary conditions.

We note that the scheme (32.3) is conditionally stable. It is possible to show, using von Neumann analysis or by the maximum principle, that the mesh size k in the time direction must satisfy the constraint:

$$1 - 2(\lambda_1 + \lambda_2) \ge 0$$

$$k \le \frac{1}{2\left(1/h_x^2 + 1/h_y^2\right)} \tag{32.6}$$

32.8   MOVING TO SOFTWARE AND METHOD IMPLEMENTATION

Having defined the continuous problem (32.1) and its discrete approximation (32.2)–(32.5) we must now decide on how to 'get this stuff into the computer'. In general, we create code that realises these two models. We must take all parameters (in the broadest sense of the word) into account.

In this section we give a step-by-step account of how we have implemented the C++ solution to the current problem. You can apply these steps to more general problems.

32.8.1   Defining the continuous problem

Since we are working with system (32.1) at the moment we see that there are three main parameters:

- The region R in which the heat equation is defined
- The initial condition
- The boundary condition (of Dirichlet type).

We assume that the region is a rectangle $(0, L) \times (0, M)$ and that the time interval is $(0, T)$. We define the parameters as follows:

```
double L = 1.0; double M = 1.0;
double T = 1.0;
```

We now define the initial and boundary conditions (you can change the bodies for other test cases) as follows:

```
double IC(double x, double y)
{
    if (x > y)
        return x;

    return 0.0;
}
double BC(double x, double y, double t)
{
    return 1.0;
}
```

We have now completed the specification of the continuous problem.

32.8.2   Creating a mesh

We now need to discretise the region $(0, L) \times (0, M) \times (0, T)$. In this case we use constant mesh sizes for ease of discussion. In the current example we partition each interval into a number of subintervals:

```
int NX = 10; int NY = 10; int NT = 40;

// Calculated values
double hx = L / double(NX);
double hy = L / double(NY);
double k = T / double(NT);
```

We now need to code the parameters as defined in equation (32.3) as well as discrete mesh points in the *x* and *y* directions:

```
double a = hx*hx;
double b = hy*hy;
double lambda1 = k / a;
double lambda2 = k / b;
double factor = 1.0 - 2.0*(lambda1 + lambda2);

// Create mesh points in x and y directions
Range<double> rx(0.0, L);
Range<double> ry(0.0, M);
Vector<double, int> xMesh = rx.mesh(NX);
Vector<double, int> yMesh = ry.mesh(NY);
```

We note that the variable factor must be positive, otherwise this explicit finite difference scheme will not be stable.

We now create discrete versions of the initial and boundary conditions. To this end, we use a utility function (see code on CD) that allows us to do this:

```
NumericMatrix<double, int> V_IC
    = createDiscreteFunction(IC,rx, ry, NX, NY);
```

Basically, this generic function creates a matrix of discrete values at the mesh points in the finite difference scheme.

Defining the discrete boundary conditions requires a bit more work. First, we have to define the function at the four boundaries of the rectangle *R* and then use it in the current example. We define the discrete boundary condition by traversing the straight-line segments that enclose the region *R*.

```
void DiscreteBC(
const Vector<double, int>& xMesh, const Vector<double, int>& yMesh,
        double t,double (*Boundary NumericMatrix<double, int>& Solution)
{
    // Initialise the 'extremities' of the solution, that is along
    // the sides of the domain

    int i, j; // Index for looping

    // Bottom
    int index = Solution.MinColumnIndex();
    for (i = Solution.MinRowIndex();
    i <= Solution.MaxRowIndex(); i++)
    {
        Solution(i, index) = BoundaryCondition(xMesh[i], 0.0, t);
    }
    // Top
        // code removed
    // Left
        // code removed
    // Right
```

```
index = Solution.MaxRowIndex();

for (j = Solution.MinColumnIndex();
    j <= Solution.MaxColumnIndex(); j++)
    {
    Solution(index, j) = BoundaryCondition(yMesh[yMesh.MaxIndex()],
        yMesh[j], t);
    }
}
```

This function uses a function pointer as input and we apply it in the current context as follows (in this case we augment the discrete initial condition with its values on the boundary):

```
double current = 0.0; // Time counter
DiscreteBC(xMesh, yMesh, current, BC, V_IC);
```

Summarising, we can now define the discrete boundary condition at any time level as well as defining the discrete initial condition (that is, at $t = 0$).

32.8.3 Choosing a scheme

In this chapter we have given one choice of scheme, namely explicit Euler (32.2). To program this scheme all we need are two matrices, one for level n (the initial condition) and the other for level $n + 1$ (the current value). The code for this algorithm is:

```
DiscreteBC(xMesh, yMesh, current, BC, V_NEXT);
for (int j = V_IC.MinColumnIndex()+1;
j < V_IC.MaxColumnIndex(); j++)
{
    for (int i = V_IC.MinRowIndex()+1;
i < V_IC.MaxRowIndex(); i++)
    {
        V_NEXT(i, j)=lambda1*(V_IC(i+1, j)+V_IC(i-1, j))
            + lambda2 * (V_IC(i, j+1) + V_IC(i, j-1))
            + factor * V_IC(i, j);
    }
}
```

Notice that we must first update the boundary conditions first for the solution at time level $n + 1$. Having calculated this value we place it in a tensor (array of matrices):

```
// Now the data structure to hold all values, all start indices
// start at 1.
Tensor<double, int>
repository(V_IC.Rows(), V_IC.Columns(), NT+1);

// Postprocessing ...
index++; repository[index] = V_NEXT; // Add matrix to tensor
```

32.8.4   Termination criterion

Since we are time marching as it were from $t = 0$ and $t = T$ we need to test when the scheme has finished. In this case we prefer to use the following loop (by the way, this is the only place we use this construction):

```
L1: // Calculate the next level

        // Go to next time level
        current += k;

if (current < T)
{
        V_IC = V_NEXT;
        goto L1;
}
```

Notice that the time is incremented as well as the solution being updated from time level n to $n + 1$.

32.9   GENERALISATIONS

Once you understand everything about the solution to a given problem (no matter how trivial it might appear) you can then start thinking how to generalise it to more complicated problems. In other words, we subsume current solutions in larger, more embrasive solutions.

32.9.1   More general PDEs

In this chapter we have discussed the two-dimensional heat equation with Dirichlet boundary conditions. We can modify the schemes and code to handle convection terms, reaction terms and even nonlinear terms in the PDE. Furthermore, we may have Neumann or convexity boundary conditions. Finally, we need to create finite difference schemes for one-factor models on the one hand and three-factor models on the other.

The contents of this chapter can be generalised to solve the two-factor Black–Scholes PDE, for example.

32.9.2   Other finite difference schemes

We can adapt the scheme in this chapter to suit various requirements:

- Convection–diffusion and Black–Scholes equations
- Various kinds of boundary conditions.

In particular, we can adapt the code to allow us to approximate the solution of the two-factor Black–Scholes model.

32.9.3   Flexible software solutions

In general, it is a good tactic to solve a simpler analogous problem first in order to get the structure right. Then we could progressively modify the software to suit new customer requirements.

Let us take an example. Suppose that we wish to adapt the code in this chapter to the case of the PDE that models multi-asset options that we discussed in Chapter 24. There is a large gap in functionality between what we have and what we want. How do we proceed? There are different strategies, one of which we now discuss. First, we must now model a convection–diffusion equation and to this end we modify scheme (32.2) for the new PDE. Furthermore, the code that implements the new scheme will need to be written. Second, and in contrast to the hard-coded initial condition in this chapter, we can model the C++ payoff class hierarchy (as introduced in Chapter 24 and coded in Chapter 33) and use it in our code. Finally, we have to take new kinds of boundary conditions into account and this is always the most demanding part of the exercise.

We now test the software to see if it works and if it produces accurate results. Once that has been done we can then support new kinds of difference schemes, such as implicit Euler. We then must enter a new round of extensions to the software. It is an incremental process.

32.10 SUMMARY AND CONCLUSIONS

We have implemented the explicit Euler difference scheme for the two-dimensional heat equation using C++. We have partitioned the problem in such a way that it becomes clear how to map the concepts in the PDE and FDM formulations to C++ code. Furthermore, knowing how the software product has been designed will help the reader to apply the same techniques to more complex problems in quantitative finance.

C++ Class Hierarchies for One-Factor and Two-Factor Payoffs

33.1 INTRODUCTION AND OBJECTIVES

In this chapter we discuss a number of topics that have to do with the numerical and computational aspects of payoff functions for one-factor and multi-factor option pricing problems. These are important topics because modelling payoff functions is a vital activity in all phases of the software lifecycle:

A1: (Continuous) payoff function in the Black–Scholes PDE
A2: (Discrete) payoff function in the FDM schemes
A3: Implementing continuous and discrete payoff functions in C++.

We have already discussed what is needed to realise activities A1 and A2. In particular, we have discussed payoff functions for call and put one-factor models as well as payoff functions for multi-asset options (the latter group was discussed in Chapter 24). Furthermore, the discrete payoff functions were modelled in the corresponding finite difference schemes. In general, these discrete functions are defined at mesh-points but difficulties arise at certain points, in principle those points where the payoff (or its derivatives) is discontinuous, for example:

- Points in time where stock price is monitored
- Interesting regions where we would like to have more data points (for example, near the strike price)
- Other points of discontinuity of the continuous payoff function.

The problem with non-smooth payoff functions is that approximating them using 'bad' schemes will lower the global accuracy of the difference scheme. Worse still, the discrete option price will have spurious oscillations or spikes, thus rendering the values useless for hedging purposes. We discuss these problems and suggest some remedies.

Topic A3 is next, and in particular we discuss how to model one-factor and two-factor continuous payoff functions in C++. We concentrate most of our attention on the one-factor case while we give a short overview of how we developed the corresponding two-factor models. As a practical example, we create a class hierarchy of option payoff functions in the single-factor case. The ideas can be generalised to multi-factor option models. We have three design techniques in C++ for modelling payoff functions. First, we create an abstract payoff class and derive each specific payoff class from it; for example, we have defined classes for calls, bull spreads and other single-factor options. The second approach uses composition by defining a generic payoff class that contains a link to the algorithm that actually implements the payoff function. The last design is to implement a payoff class that contains a function pointer as member data. This function pointer implements the specific payoff functionality. In short, we can choose the most appropriate design to suit our needs. In this sense we can offer 'heavyweight', 'lightweight' and 'super-lightweight' functionality for modelling payoff functions.

Finally, we show how to integrate the payoff classes in other classes that model the PDEs and FDM methods in this book. More information, including code and extra documentation, can be found on the accompanying CD.

33.2   ABSTRACT AND CONCRETE PAYOFF CLASSES

By definition, an abstract class is one that cannot have any instances – that is, one from which no objects can be created. We can produce abstract classes by defining at least one function to be pure virtual. A concrete class, on the other hand, is one that is not abstract. In other words, we can create instances of concrete classes.

What is the relationship between concrete and abstract classes? Usually an abstract class will be a base class for many other derived classes (which may themselves be abstract or concrete). The nice feature of this setup is that derived classes (if they wish to be concrete, that is) *must* implement the pure virtual member functions, otherwise they will also be abstract.

An example of an abstract class is one that models one-factor option payoffs. In fact, we create an abstract base class called Payoff that implements a pure virtual member function to calculate the payoff value for a given stock price. The header file is given by:

```
class Payoff
{
public:

        // Constructors and destructor
        Payoff();                           // Default constructor
        Payoff(const Payoff& source);       // Copy constructor
        virtual ~Payoff();                  // Destructor

        // Operator overloading
        Payoff& operator = (const Payoff& source);

        // Pure virtual payoff function
        virtual double payoff(double S) const = 0;    // Spot price S
};
```

We notice that this class has no member data and this is advantageous because derived classes will not inherit unwanted members. Specific payoff classes can be defined by deriving them from Payoff and implementing the payoff() function. We look at call options in detail. The header file is given by:

```
class CallPayoff: public Payoff
{
private:
        double K;                   // Strike price
public:

        // Constructors and destructor
        CallPayoff();
        CallPayoff(double strike);
        CallPayoff(const CallPayoff& source);
        virtual ~CallPayoff();
```

```
// Selectors
double Strike() const;              // Return strike price

// Modifiers
void Strike(double NewStrike);      // Set strike price

CallPayoff& operator = (const CallPayoff& source);

// Implement the pure virtual payoff function from base class
double payoff(double S) const;      // For a given spot price
};
```

We see that this class has private member data representing the strike price of the call option as well as public set/get member functions for this data. Furthermore, we have coded all essential functions in this class:

- Default constructor
- Copy constructor
- Virtual destructor
- Assignment operator.

Finally, we must implement the payoff() function, otherwise CallPayoff will itself be an abstract class.

We now look at the bodies of the member functions of CallPayoff. In general, a constructor in a derived class must initialise its local data and the data in the class that it is derived from. For the former case we use normal assignment but we use the so-called colon syntax to initialise the data in a base class. For example, the copy constructor in CallPayoff is given by:

```
CallPayoff::CallPayoff(const CallPayoff& source): Payoff(source)
{ // Copy constructor

    K = source.K;
}
```

In this case we initialise the data in Payoff by using the colon syntax (of course there is no data in the base class at the moment, but this is irrelevant). There is something subtle happening here, namely the fact that the compiler knows what Payoff(source) is. The reason that the code is acceptable is due to the Principle of Substitutability; this means that a function that accepts a reference to a base class (in this case the copy constructor in Payoff) can be called by giving an instance of a derived class. This is of course related to the fact that an instance of a derived class is also an instance of its base class.

We now discuss how to implement the assignment operator in the derived class. In general, the steps are:

1. Check that we are not assigning an object to itself
2. Assign the base class data
3. Assign the local data in the derived class
4. Return the 'current' object.

The code that performs these steps is given by:

```
CallPayoff& CallPayoff::operator = (const CallPayoff &source)
{ // Assignment operator
```

```
    // Exit if same object
    if (this==&source) return *this;

    // Call base class assignment
    Payoff::operator = (source);

    // Copy state
    K = source.K;

    return *this;
}
```

In derived classes we may have private member data and it is usual to provide public member functions to access it:

```
double CallPayoff::Strike() const
{// Return K

    return K;
}
void CallPayoff::Strike(double NewStrike)
{// Set K

    K = NewStrike;
}
```

Finally, each derived class must implement the payoff function and in the case of a call option this is given by the following code:

```
double CallPayoff::payoff(double S) const
{ // For a given spot price
    if (S > K)
            return (S - K);

    return 0.0;

    // remark; possible to say max (S - K, 0) if you prefer
}
```

We can define other kinds of payoff classes as derived classes of Payoff; see Figure 33.1. We can define payoff functions for trading strategies involving options (see, for example, Hull, 2000), such as:

- *Spreads:* We take a position on two options of the same kind. A bull spread entails we buy a call option on a stock with strike K_1 and sell a call on the same stock at a higher price K_2. A bear spread is similar to a bull spread except that $K_1 > K_2$. A butterfly spread involves positions in options with three different strike prices.
- *Straddles:* We buy a call option and a put option with the same strike price and expiry date.
- *Strangles:* We buy a put and a call with the same expiration dates and different strike prices.

We implement each of these strategies by a separate derived class of Payoff called BullSpreadPayoff and then by implementing the payoff function. For example, for a bull spread the payoff function is:

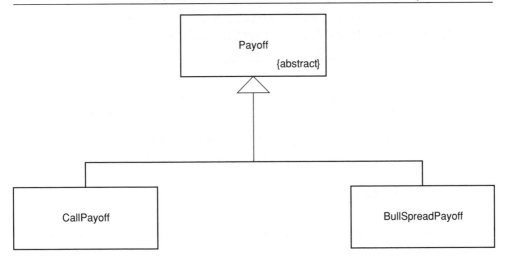

Figure 33.1 Payoff hierarchy: Version 1

```
double BullSpreadPayoff::payoff(double S) const
{ // Based on Hull's book
        if (S >= K2)
                return K2 - K1;
        if (S <= K1)
                return 0.0;
        // In the interval [K1, K2]
        return S - K1;
}
```

33.3   USING PAYOFF CLASSES

We now give some examples of using payoff classes. We first consider payoffs for a call option. To this end, we create a call payoff with strike $K = 20$ and we can query for a given stock value and compute the payoff function:

```
CallPayoff call(20.0);

cout << "Give a stock price (plain Call): ";
double S;
cin >> S;

cout << "Call Payoff is: " << call.payoff(S) << endl;
```

We now create a bull spread payoff and we note that it has four member data, namely two strike prices and the cost to buy a call as well as the sell price for the second call. The code is:

```
double K1 = 30.0;          // Strike price of bought call
double K2 = 35.0;          // Strike price of sell call
double costBuy = 3.0;      // Cost to buy a call
```

```
double sellPrice = 1.0;     // Sell price for call
BullSpreadPayoff bs(K1, K2, costBuy, sellPrice);

cout << "Give a stock price (BullSpread): ";
cin >> S;

cout << "Bull Spread Payoff is: " << bs.payoff(S) << endl;
cout << "Bull Spread Profit is: " << bs.profit(S) << endl;
```

Incidentally, the C++ code for the profit() function is given by:

```
double BullSpreadPayoff::profit(double S) const
{ // Profit
     return payoff(S) - (buyValue - sellValue);
}
```

The techniques developed in this section can be used in other applications in which we need to create derived classes in C++.

33.4   LIGHTWEIGHT PAYOFF CLASSES

In this section we discuss another design in order to implement payoff functions. In section 33.3 we created a 'heavyweight' derived class for each kind of new payoff function. Once we create an instance of a payoff class in Figure 33.1 it is then not possible to change it to an instance of another class. For example, this approach might be difficult when we model chooser options in C++ (recall that a chooser is one where the holder can choose whether to receive a call or a put).

In order to resolve these and possible future problems, we adopt another approach. The UML class diagram for this solution is shown in Figure 33.2. In this case we create a single payoff class that has a pointer to what is essentially an encapsulation of a payoff function. The pattern in Figure 33.2 is called the *strategy* pattern (GOF, 1995). This pattern allows us to define interchangeable algorithms that can be used by many clients, as we can see in Figure 33.2;

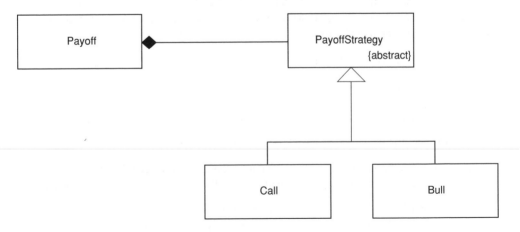

Figure 33.2   Payoff hierarchy: Version 2 (using Strategy pattern)

each instance of `Payoff` has a pointer to a payoff strategy and this pointer can be changed at run-time. The header file for the concrete class `Payoff` is:

```
class Payoff
{
private:
        PayoffStrategy* ps;
public:
        // Constructors and destructor
        Payoff(PayoffStrategy& pstrat);

        // Other member functions
};
```

We see that we must give a reference to a payoff strategy. We have programmed the strategy classes in Figure 33.2 in one file as follows:

```
class PayoffStrategy
{
public:
        virtual double payoff(double S) const = 0;
};

class CallStrategy : public PayoffStrategy
{
private:
        double K;
public:
        CallStrategy(double strike) { K = strike;}
        double payoff(double S) const
        {
                if (S > K)
                        return (S - K);
                return 0.0;
        }
};
```

We have also created a simple strategy for a bull spread. An example of using the new configuration is now given, where we create a payoff and can choose its strategy type:

```
// Create a strategy and couple it with a payoff
    CallStrategy call(20.0);
    Payoff pay1(call);
```

This approach allows our software to be more efficient and flexible than the use of class inheritance.

33.5   SUPER-LIGHTWEIGHT PAYOFF FUNCTIONS

We now discuss the last design technique for creating payoff functions and classes. It is less object-oriented than the first two approaches (by the way, this does not necessarily make it bad) because we create a class with a function pointer as member data. This function pointer will be assigned to a 'real' function representing some payoff function. For convenience we look at special one-factor payoffs and in fact we create a class as follows:

```
class OneFactorPayoff
{
private:
     double K;
     double (*payoffFN)(double K, double S);

public:
     // Constructors and destructor
     OneFactorPayoff(double strike,
     double(*payoff)(double K,double S));

     // More

     double payoff(double S) const;      // For a given spot price
};
```

The bodies of these member functions are given by:

```
OneFactorPayoff::OneFactorPayoff(double strike,
double (*pay)(double K, double S))
{
     K = strike;
     payoffFN = pay;
}


double OneFactorPayoff::payoff(double S) const
{ // For a given spot price

     return payoffFN(K, S); // Call function
}
```

How do we use this class? Well, we carry out the followings steps:

1. Write the payoff functions you would like to use.
2. Create an instance of OneFactorPayoff with the payoff function of your choice.
3. Test and use the payoff class.

An example of specific payoff functions is:

```
double CallPayoffFN(double K, double S)
{
          if (S > K)
                  return (S - K);
          return 0.0;
}
```

```
double PutPayoffFN(double K, double S)
{
        // max (K-S, 0)
        if (K > S)
                return (K - S);
        return 0.0;
}
```

An example of the code is:

```
int main()
{
    OneFactorPayoff pay1(20.0, CallPayoffFN);

    cout << "Give a stock price (plain Call): ";
    double S;
    cin >> S;

    cout << "Call Payoff is: " << pay1.payoff(S) << endl;

    OneFactorPayoff pay2(20.0, PutPayoffFN);
    cout << "Give a stock price (plain Put): ";
    cin >> S;

    cout << "Put Payoff is: " << pay2.payoff(S) << endl;

    return 0;
}
```

This option can be quite effective; you do not have to create classes, just 'flat' C functions that you use as function pointers in existing classes.

33.6 PAYOFF FUNCTIONS FOR MULTI-ASSET OPTION PROBLEMS

We have created a C++ class hierarchy for two-dimensional payoff functions. The functionality is based on the theory in Chapter 24. The base class is:

```
class MultiAssetPayoffStrategy
{
public:
    virtual double payoff(double S1, double S2) const = 0;
};
```

Here we see that there is no member data and only one pure virtual member function that takes two input arguments. Specific payoff functionality is encapsulated in derived classes. We have implemented most of the payoff functions from Chapter 24 in this way. We give the code for exchange options, basket options and spread options:

```
class ExchangeStrategy : public MultiAssetPayoffStrategy
{
private:
                // No member data
```

```cpp
public:
        ExchangeStrategy() { }
        double payoff(double S1, double S2) const
        {
                return max(S1-S2, 0.0);
        }
};

class BasketStrategy : public MultiAssetPayoffStrategy
{ // 2-asset basket option payoff

private:
        double K;                // Strike
        double w;                // +1 call, -1 put
        double w1, w2;           // w1 + w2 = 1

public:

        BasketStrategy(double strike, double cp,
        double weight1, double weight2)
        {

        K = strike; w = cp; w1 = weight1; w2 = weight2;
        }
        double payoff(double S1, double S2) const
        {
                double sum = w1*S1 + w2*S2;
                return max(w* (sum - K), 0.0);
        }
};

class SpreadStrategy : public MultiAssetPayoffStrategy
{
private:
        double K;                    // Strike
        double w;                    // +1 call, -1 put
        double a, b;                 // a > 0, b < 0

public:
        SpreadStrategy(double cp, double strike = 0.0,
        double A = 1.0, double B = -1.0)
        { K = strike; w = cp; a = A; b = B;}
        double payoff(double S1, double S2) const
        {
                double sum = a*S1 + b*S2;
                return max(w* (sum - K), 0.0);
        }
};
```

Please see the code on the accompanying CD on how to integrate these functions with FDM schemes.

33.7   CAVEAT: NON-SMOOTH PAYOFF AND CONVERGENCE DEGRADATION

The fact that the payoff function is not smooth at certain points has major consequences for the accuracy of finite difference schemes that are not able to handle discontinuities. We give some remarks on some popular schemes:

- Explicit schemes are easily to implement, do not suffer from oscillation problems but are only conditionally stable.
- Implicit schemes are also oscillation-free, unconditionally stable but only first-order accurate.
- The Crank–Nicolson scheme is (theoretically) second-order accurate but it is well known that it produce spurious oscillations and spikes near the strike price, barriers and monitoring points.

What we would ideally like is an unconditionally stable, second-order scheme that is able to produce good results even when the payoff function or its derivatives are discontinuous at certain points. There are three main ploys for achieving this end. First, we can define 'hybrid' schemes that combine the best of the above schemes. The second approach is to modify the payoff function in some way so that it becomes smooth. The third option is to combine the first two options. We discuss each of these options in turn.

A popular hybrid method is discussed in Rannacher (1984). This scheme uses fully implicit Euler for the first few time steps and Crank–Nicolson after that. The scheme is stable, first-order accurate and is oscillation-free. Another, less-well known but powerful scheme is to use Richardson extrapolation in combination with implicit Euler (Gourlay, 1980). The resulting scheme is stable, second-order accurate and again oscillation free.

We now discuss function smoothing. Some techniques are:

- Averaging the initial condition
- Projecting the initial condition onto a set of basis functions (Rannacher, 1984).

Let $f = f(S)$ be the one-factor payoff function. Then the discrete averaging function is defined as:

$$f_j = \frac{1}{S_{j+\frac{1}{2}} - S_{j-\frac{1}{2}}} \int_{S_{j-\frac{1}{2}}}^{S_{j+\frac{1}{2}}} f(S_j - y)\, dy \qquad (33.1)$$

where $S_{j+\frac{1}{2}} = (S_j + S_{j+1})/2$.

The validity of this method was proved in Kreiss (1970) and Thomée (1974). We mention that this method has also been applied to the binomial method in Heston (2000).

The projection method, on the other hand, uses some of the techniques that we introduce in Appendix 2. We attempt to find an approximation F to the payoff f by describing it in terms of piecewise polynomial hat functions:

$$F(x) = \sum_{j=1}^{N} c_j \varphi_j(x) \qquad (33.2)$$

where $c_j =$ unknown coefficients
        $\varphi_j =$ linear hat functions

and we calculate the unknown function by minimising the functional

$$\int_\Omega (F - f)^2 \mathrm{d}x \qquad\qquad (33.3)$$

where Ω is the computational domain.

The objective is to calculate the unknown coefficients in (33.2) and they can be found as the solution of the linear system:

$$AU = b \qquad\qquad (33.4)$$

where $\quad U = {}^t(c_1, \ldots, c_N)$
$\qquad\quad A = (a_{ij})_{1 \le i, j \le N}, \quad a_{ij} \equiv (\varphi_i, \varphi_j)$
$\qquad\quad b = (b_j)_{1 \le j \le N}, \quad b_j \equiv (\varphi_j, f)$

and $(., .)$ denotes the inner product as defined by $\quad (f, g) = \int_\Omega f(x)g(x)\,\mathrm{d}x$.

In general, it is possible to calculate the integrals analytically, but for more complex payoff functions we can use some kind of numerical integration scheme (as discussed in Appendix 1), for example, Simpson's rule applied to the right-hand side of (33.4) in the case of complex payoff functions.

Finally, we can combine smoothing and the Rannacher method to get a stable, second-order accurate and oscillation-free finite difference scheme (Rannacher, 1984). It gives good results for supershare binary call options (which behave as a discrete delta function near the strike price) whose payoff is defined as follows:

$$V(t = T) = \begin{cases} 0, & S < K \\ 1/d, & K \le S \le K + d \\ 0, & S > K + d \end{cases} \qquad\qquad (33.5)$$

We see in this case that there are discontinuities at the point $S = K$ and $S = K + d$. In general, we advise the use of Rannacher schemes instead of Crank–Nicolson.

33.8   SUMMARY AND CONCLUSIONS

We have constructed C++ class hierarchies for one-factor and two-factor payoff functions based on the other chapters in this book. In particular, we have coded the payoff functions for the multi-asset problems in Chapter 24.

A less well-documented problem is that standard and much-loved schemes (like Crank–Nicolson) give low accuracy when the payoff function or its derivatives is discontinuous. To this end, we discussed a number of schemes that do not have spurious oscillations or spikes. For example, one good method is due to Rannacher (1984).

Appendix 1
An Introduction to Integral and Partial Integro-Differential Equations

A1.1 INTRODUCTION AND OBJECTIVES

This appendix is a self-contained introduction to a number of mathematical and numerical techniques that we shall need when modelling certain kinds of derivative products. It provides background information relating to the contents of Chapter 17. Although numerical integration techniques are not used very much in conjunction with FDM we think it is important to give a concise introduction to this topic.

In particular, we introduce the so-called partial integro-differential equations (PIDEs) that arise in option pricing theory where the underlying asset is driven by a Levy process or by some general time-inhomogeneous jump–diffusion process (Øksendal and Sulem, 2005). In this case we recall the PIDE :

$$\frac{\partial V}{\partial t} = \tfrac{1}{2}\sigma^2 S^2 \frac{\partial^2 V}{\partial S^2} + (r - \lambda K)S\frac{\partial V}{\partial S} - rV + \left(\lambda \int_0^\infty V(S\eta)g(\eta)\,\mathrm{d}\eta - \lambda V\right) \quad \text{(A1.1)}$$

where $T - t$ = time to expiry

r = continously compounded risk free interest rate

$g(\eta)$ = probability density function of the jump amplitude η

σ = constant volatility

K = expected relative jump size given by $K = E(\eta - 1)$

This equation is a modification of the original Black–Scholes equation and we see that it contains an integral on the semi-infinite positive real line. This PIDE is found by application of the generalised Ito formula to the following stochastic differential equation:

$$\frac{\mathrm{d}S}{S} = \mu\,\mathrm{d}t + \sigma\,\mathrm{d}z + (\eta - 1)\,\mathrm{d}q \quad\quad\quad \text{(A1.2)}$$

where μ = drift rate

σ = volatility

$\mathrm{d}z$ = increment of a Gauss–Wiener process

$\mathrm{d}q$ = Poission process.

In general, we cannot hope to get a closed solution to the equation (A1.1) and we must then resort to numerical methods. Equation (A1.1) is a combination of a convection–diffusion PDE and an integral term. It will be fairly obvious that solving (A1.1) numerically will be somewhat more difficult than solving one-factor Black–Scholes PDEs because we must approximate a PDE and an integral equation simultaneously. Some of the challenges that spring to mind are:

- We must come up with a scheme that models both the PDE term and integral term in (A1.1).
- The integral is defined on a semi-infinite interval and we must thus truncate it.

- The solution might be discontinuous at some points, at worst, or have large gradients, at best. The solution may not exist in the classical, pointwise sense.
- How can we construct economical and accurate schemes that approximate the solution of (A1.1)?

Before we can embark on this problem we need to discuss a number of techniques that will help us to find finite difference schemes that approximate the solution of equation (A1.1). To this end, we introduce a number of topics:

- A short history of integration and quadrature schemes for finding approximations to integrals. This is standard numerical analysis and the information can be found in good numerical analysis books (for example, Dahlquist, 1974; Conte and de Boor, 1980). We include a discussion for completeness.
- An introduction to integral equations in one dimension.
- Numerically solving integral equations. We discuss a number of methods, including the Galerkin method, numerical integration techniques and others.
- A discussion of PIDEs in financial engineering, in particular for problems that are based on exponential Levy and Variance Gamma processes. This is a new area of research.

In general, an understanding of integration theory is an asset because it is used in many areas of quantative finance. We expect to find generalisation of (A1.1) in future applications, for example two-dimensional cases (La Chioma, 2003; Carr, 2004, personal communication; Øksendal, 2004).

A1.2   A SHORT INTRODUCTION TO INTEGRATION THEORY

Integrals and integration theory are used in many financial applications. To this end, we must realise that there are different ways of defining the integral of a function. When integrating in one dimension, for example, we partition an interval into smaller sub-intervals and then approximate the function on each sub-interval in some way. Finally, by taking limits (for example, letting the number of sub-intervals tend to infinity) we arrive at an approximation to the integral. There are a number of approaches:

- Riemann integral (Spiegel, 1969)
- Riemann–Stieljtes integral (Rudin, 1964; Haaser and Sullivan, 1991)
- Lebesgue integral (for a readable account see Spiegel, 1969; for a more advanced treatment see Rudin, 1970)
- Ito integral (Kloeden et al., 1995).

We now examine each of these approaches. We restrict our attention to real-valued functions of a single real variable in this chapter:

$$y = f(x), \quad x, y \in \mathbb{R}^1$$

Many of the results carry over to real-valued and complex-valued functions of several variables, but a discussion of these topics is outside the scope of this book.

A1.2.1   Riemann integration

This is the integral that is taught in introductory courses in calculus. Let $y = f(x)$ be defined and bounded on the closed interval $[a, b]$. We define a so-called partition of $[a, b]$. In order to motivate the theory we need two definitions.

Definition A1.1. A real number u is called an upper bound of a set S of real numbers if for all x in S we have $x \leq u$. If an upper bound p can be found such that for all upper bounds u we have $p \leq u$, we say that p is the least upper bound (l.u.b.) or supremum (sup) of S. We write this quantity as sup S.

Definition A1.2. A real number l is called a lower bound of a set S of real numbers if for all x in S we have $x \geq l$. If a lower bound p can be found such that for all lower bounds l we have $p \geq l$, we say that p is the greatest lower bound (g.l.b.) or infimum (inf) of S. We write this quantity as inf S.

We now define the quantities:

$$M_j = \text{l.u.b. } f(x) \text{ in } [x_{j-1}, x_j]$$
$$m_j = \text{g.l.b. } f(x) \text{ in } [x_{j-1}, x_j] \tag{A1.3}$$

and then we form the sums:

$$S = \sum_{j=1}^{n} M_j \Delta x_j \quad \text{("upper sum")}$$

$$s = \sum_{j=1}^{n} m_j \Delta x_j \quad \text{("lower sum")} \quad \Delta x_j = x_j - x_{j-1} \tag{A1.4}$$

By varying the partition we can obtain sets of values for S and s. We now define:

$$I = \text{g.l.b. of values of } S \text{ for all partitions}$$
$$J = \text{l.u.b. of values of } s \text{ for all partitions} \tag{A1.5}$$

These values always exist and are called the upper and lower Riemann integrals of $f(x)$, respectively. If $I = J$ we say that $f(x)$ is Riemann integrable on $[a, b]$ and we denote this common value by:

$$\int_a^b f(x)\, dx$$

If these two values are different, we say that $f(x)$ is not Riemann integrable in $[a, b]$. For example, the function

$$f(x) = \begin{cases} 1, & x \text{ rational} \\ 0, & x \text{ irrational} \end{cases} x \in [a, b]$$

is not Riemann integrable (see Spiegel, 1969). Another example of a function that is not Riemann integrable is

$$\int_0^\infty \left| \frac{\sin x}{x} \right| dx$$

For a somewhat more intuitive approach to Riemann integration, it is possible to define the Riemann integral as the limit of a sum. In this case we partition $[a, b]$ as before but now we define certain points in the interior of each sub-interval

$$x_{j-1} \leq \xi_j \leq x_j, \quad j = 1, 2, \ldots, n$$

and based on these points we form the sum

$$\sum_{j=1}^{n} f(\xi_j) \Delta x_j, \quad \Delta x_j = x_j - x_{j-1} \tag{A1.6}$$

Let $\delta = \max \Delta x_j, \quad j = 1, \ldots, n$, then the Riemann integral is defined by the limit

$$\int_a^b f(x) \, dx = \lim_{\substack{n \to \infty \\ \delta \to 0}} \sum_{j=1}^{n} f(\xi_j) \Delta x_j \tag{A1.7}$$

provided that the limit exists independently of the way that we choose the points of the subdivision.

Formula (A1.7) will be the basis for a number of numerical integration schemes. In many cases we assume the mesh size is a constant that we usually denote by h. We give some examples of common schemes:

Rectangle rule: $\xi_j = \frac{x_{j-1}+x_j}{2}$

Trapezoidal rule: $\xi_j = x_j$

Furthermore, the idea can be used to motivate stochastic integrals.

A1.2.2 Riemann–Stieltjes integration

We are now interested in an integration theory that can be used to treat both continuous and discrete random variables. This is the Riemann–Stieltjes integral and it is particularly useful in probability theory. It is a generalisation of the Riemann integral. In particular, we are interested in defining the integral

$$\int_a^b f(x) \, d\alpha(x) \tag{A1.8}$$

where α is a monotonically increasing function on the interval $[a, b]$. We assume that $\alpha(a)$ and $\alpha(b)$ are finite. As before, we create a partition P of $[a, b]$ and define the quantity

$$\Delta \alpha_j = \alpha(x_j) - \alpha(x_{j-1})$$

We generalise equations (A1.4) by defining the following quantities:

$$U(P, f, \alpha) = \sum_{j=1}^{n} M_j \Delta \alpha_j \quad \text{('upper sum')}$$

$$L(P, f, \alpha) = \sum_{j=1}^{n} m_j \Delta \alpha_j \quad \text{('lower sum')} \tag{A1.9}$$

where M_j and m_j have been defined in (A1.3).

We now define

$$I \equiv \text{g.l.b. } U(P, f, \alpha)$$
$$J \equiv \text{l.u.b. } L(P, f, \alpha)$$

(A1.10)

If $I = J$ then we denote their common value by the term in expression (A1.8) and this is then called the Riemann–Stieltjes integral of f with respect to α over the interval $[a, b]$.

The Riemann–Stieltjes integral is used in probability theory, for example, when defining expectations of random variables (Mikosch, 1998).

A1.2.3 Lebesgue integration

The Riemann integral has a number of shortcomings that we remedy by using the Lebesgue integration technique. As we have already seen, the former method uses intervals and their lengths while the Lebesgue method uses more general point sets and their measures.

In order to define what Lebesgue integration is, we must introduce a number of concepts:

- Measurable sets
- Measurable functions
- The Lebesgue integral for bounded and unbounded measurable functions.

In rough terms we define measure as a generalisation of the concept of length. We extend the concept to arbitrary sets on the real line and in this case we speak of the measure of a set. We denote the measure of a set E by $m(E)$ and we endow it with the following properties:

A1: $m(E)$ is defined for each set E

A2: $m(E) \geq 0$

A3: (*Finite additivity.*) If $E = \cup_{j=1}^{n} E_j$, where the E_j are mutually disjoint, then $m(E) = \sum_{j=1}^{n} m(E_j)$

A4: (*Denumerable additivity.*) if $E = \cup_{j=1}^{\infty} E_j$, where the E_j are mutually disjoint, then $m(E) = \sum_{j=1}^{\infty} m(E_j)$.

A5: (*Monotonicity.*) If $E_1 \subset E_2$, then $m(E_1) < m(E_2)$

A6: (*Translation invariance.*) If each $x \in E$ is translated by equal distances in the same direction on the real line, then the measure of the translated set is the same as that of $m(E)$

A7: If E is an interval, then $m(E) = L(E)$, the length of E.

The exterior or outer measure m_e of a set E has the following properties

B1: $m_e(E)$ is defined for each set E

B2: $m_e(E) \geq 0$

B3: $m_e(\cup_{j=1}^{\infty} E_j) \leq \sum_{j=1}^{\infty} m_e(E_j)$ whether the E_j are disjoint or not

B4: Exterior measures are translation invariant (as in Axiom A6).

Definition A1.3. A set E is said to be measurable with respect to the outer measure $m_e(E)$ if for all sets T (the so-called test sets)

$$m_e(T) = m_e(T \cap E) + m_e(T \cap \tilde{E})$$

where $\tilde{E}$ is the complement set of E

Another equivalent definition of set measurability is

Definition A1.4. A set E is measurable if for all test sets T

$$m_e(T) \geq m_e(T \cap E) + m_e(T \cap \tilde{E})$$

This inequality is often used to test if a set is measurable.

Definition A1.5. The Lebesgue exterior (outer) measure of a set E is

$$m_e(E) = \text{g.l.b.} \quad L(K) \text{ for all open sets } K \supset E$$

Here we state that the open set K is expressed as a countable union of mutually disjoint open intervals.

In other words, this measure is the greatest lower bound of the lengths of all open sets K that contain E. In general, if a set is measurable in the sense of Definition A1.5 we then say that it is Lebesgue measurable and we denote its measure as $m(E)$, which is the same as its outer measure.

We now introduce measurable functions. Let E be a measurable set and let $f(x)$ be a real valued function defined on E. We say that $f(x)$ is Lebesgue measurable if for each real number k the set of values x in E for which $f(x) > k$ is measurable. If $f(x)$ is measurable we then call it a measurable function. Now, let $f(x)$ be bounded and measurable on the interval $[a, b]$. Suppose that α and β are any two real numbers such that $\alpha < f(x) < \beta$. We divide the range $[\alpha, \beta]$ into n sub-intervals

$$\alpha = y_0 < y_1 < \cdots < y_{n-1} < y_n = \beta$$

Let us define the following sets:

$$E_j = \{x : y_{j-1} < f(x) < y_j\}, \quad j = 1, 2, \ldots, n$$

Since $f(x)$ is measurable we know that these sets are not only measurable but also disjoint. Define

$$S = \sum_{j=1}^{n} y_j m(E_j)$$

$$s = \sum_{j=1}^{n} y_{j-1} m(E_j)$$

and define the quantities I and J as in equation (A1.5) applied to the current quantities S and s. Then if $I = J$ we say that $f(x)$ is Lebesgue measurable on $[a, b]$ and we denote the integral as

$$\int_a^b f(x)\, dx \tag{A1.11}$$

and we call this the Lebesgue definite integral of $f(x)$ on the interval $[a, b]$. If this integral exists, we write

$$\int_a^b f(x)\, dx < \infty \tag{A1.12}$$

We now discuss the meaning of the Lebesgue integral for unbounded functions. Suppose for the moment that $f(x)$ is always non-negative, unbounded and measurable. Define the function

$$[f(x)]_p = \begin{cases} f(x), & \forall x \in E \text{ such that } f(x) \leq p \\ p, & \forall x \in E \text{ such that } f(x) > p \end{cases}$$

where p is a natural number.

For each fixed p, $[f(x)]_p$ is bounded and measurable and hence Lebesgue integrable. Now we define the Lebesgue integral of $f(x)$ in E as

$$\int_E f(x)\,dx = \lim_{p \to \infty} \int_E [f(x)]_p\,dx \qquad (A1.13)$$

By definition, this limit is either bounded or infinite. In the former case we say that the Lebesgue integral of $f(x)$ exists, otherwise we say that it does not exist or is infinite.

Finally, we note that the Lebesgue integral can be applied to measurable functions on unbounded sets or intervals, for example

$$\int_a^\infty f(x)\,dx = \lim_{b \to \infty} \int_a^b f(x)\,dx \qquad (A1.14)$$

for either non-negative or non-positive functions.

For an arbitrary function f we now define the meaning of the integral

$$\lim_{b \to \infty} \int_a^b f(x)\,dx$$

To this end, we define the integral of this function in terms of the Lebesque integral of its positive 'parts' namely:

$$\int_a^\infty f(x)\,dx = \int_a^\infty f^+(x)\,dx - \int_a^\infty f^-(x)\,dx, \quad f \equiv f^+ - f^- \qquad (A1.15)$$

where

$$f^+(x) = \sup[0, f(x)] = \begin{cases} f(x), & f(x) \geq 0 \\ 0, & \text{otherwise} \end{cases}$$

$$f^-(x) = \sup[0, -f(x)] = \begin{cases} 0, & f(x) \geq 0 \\ -f(x), & f(x) < 0 \end{cases}$$

Thus, the integral is expressed in terms of two simpler integrals.

An excellent introduction to integration theory is Spiegel (1969).

A1.3   NUMERICAL INTEGRATION

This section is a crash course in numerical integration. In general we cannot hope to evaluate a given integral in closed form and we must resort to approximate methods. We do not discuss all possibilities here but we develop just enough techniques to enable us to move on to the numerical approximation of integral equations and partial integro-differential equations. For more detailed discussion of numerical integration we refer the reader to Dahlquist (1974) and Conte and de Boor (1980).

Many of the techniques and methods for numerical integration can be derived from the results in section A1.2. In general, a given numerical integration technique is similar to the discrete sum in equation (A1.7). Let us take some examples based on this idea. Using the usual notation for the partition of the interval $[a, b]$ as before, we propose a numerical integration scheme namely the Rectangle rule is given by:

$$\int_a^b f(x)\,dx \approx h \sum_{j=1}^n f_{j-\frac{1}{2}}, \quad h \equiv \frac{b-a}{n}$$

$$f_{j-\frac{1}{2}} \equiv f(\frac{x_{j-1}+x_j}{2}), \quad j = 1, \ldots, n$$

(A1.16)

This is a so-called composite rule because we apply a certain formula on each sub-interval of $[a, b]$. We can see that this formula is a special case of equation (A1.7) with a constant mesh size h and the meshpoints ξ_j chosen appropriately, in this case by setting

$$h = \Delta x_j \quad \forall j = 1, \ldots, n \quad \text{and} \quad \xi_j = \tfrac{1}{2}(x_{j-1} + x_j)$$

Another option is to take the values of the function at the mesh points and then take the average. This is the so-called Trapezoidal rule. In its 'basic' or non-composite form it is given by

$$\int_a^b f(x)\,dx \approx \frac{h}{2}(f(a) + f(b))$$

(A1.17)

and in composite form as

$$\int_a^b f(x)\,dx \approx \frac{h}{2} f_0 + h \sum_{j=1}^{n-1} f_j + \frac{h}{2} f_n,$$

(A1.18)

$$f_j \equiv f(x_j), \quad j = 0, \ldots, n, \quad h = (b-a)/n$$

A popular method is Simpson's rule:

$$\int_a^b f(x)\,dx \approx \frac{h}{6}\left[f(a) + 4f\left(\frac{a+b}{2}\right) + f(b)\right]$$

(A1.19)

and its composite form is

$$\int_a^b f(x)\,dx \approx \frac{h}{6}\left[f_0 + f_n + 2\sum_{j=1}^{n-1} f_j + 4\sum_{j=1}^n f_{j-\frac{1}{2}}\right]$$

(A1.20)

Having introduced a number of numerical integration rules, we must ask ourselves the following questions:

- For which classes of functions are these methods suitable?
- Given a mesh size h, what is the accuracy of the approximation?
- Can we devise adaptive numerical integration schemes? That is, given a desired tolerance or accuracy, can we devise a scheme that approximates the integral to within that tolerance?

We discuss the first two topics now. In general, accuracy is proved by using Taylor expansions and using the concept of truncation or discretisation errors. Define

$I(f)$ =exact integral of f on $[a, b]$
$I^h(f)$ = some numerical integral rule that approximates $I(f)$
$E^h(f) = I(f) - I^h(f)$, the so-called trunction error when $h = b - a$.

Then we wish to find bounds on the truncation error. We give some estimates for some of the above schemes, for example

$$\text{Rectangle rule:} \quad E^h(f) = \frac{f'(\eta)(b-a)^2}{2}, \quad \eta \in (a, b)$$

(A1.21)

$$\text{Trapezoidal rule:} \quad E^h(f) = -f''(\eta)\frac{(b-a)^3}{12}, \quad \eta \in (a, b)$$

These are known as local truncation errors. In general, the interval $[a, b]$ will be a small sub-interval of length $h = b - a$. Then the global truncation error is one power of h less than the local truncation error. For example, the Trapezoidal rule is locally third-order accurate but globally second-order accurate.

The above rules assume that the mesh size h is known. In some cases we may wish to automatically select the mesh size. To this end, we can apply Richardson extrapolation to the Trapezoidal rule (for example). We begin with a fairly large mesh size and then we halve the mesh size and use extrapolation until two values agree to within a certain tolerance. This process is called Romberg integration and it can be implemented as a binomial tree, a data structure that is used in option pricing. For more information, see Dahlquist (1974) and Stoer and Bulirsch (1980).

A1.3.1 Integrating badly behaved functions

In the previous section we implicitly assumed that the function to be integrated was smooth. In fact, the truncation error in (A1.21) is expressed in terms of the derivatives of f at certain points. This may give problems if f or its derivatives are discontinuous (or don't even exist in the classical sense) at certain points in $[a, b]$. We then speak of an improper integral, in particular the integrand f can possess a number of properties that compromise the effectiveness of standard numerical integration routines (see Press *et al.*, 2002, p. 146). These problems are:

1. The integrand f has an integrable singularity at a known or unknown point or points in the open interval (a, b)
2. The upper limit is $b = \infty$ and/or the lower limit $a = -\infty$
3. $f(x)$ has an integrable singularity at either $x = a$ or $x = b$ (or both)
4. $f(x)$ tends to a finite limit at $x = a$ or at $x = b$ but it cannot be evaluated right on one of these end-points (for example, $f(x) = \sin x / x$ when $x = 0$)

A thorough classification of improper integrals is given in Widder (1989), ch. 10.

Some of these scenarios occur in financial engineering applications and in particular we have to deal with them when we approximate PIDEs using finite difference schemes. The above numerical integration routines do not always work and we must resort to mesh-refinement as discussed in Press *et al.* (2002). A discussion of this topic is outside the scope of this chapter; however, we do propose a numerical integration scheme (that we call the Tanh rule) that the author discovered by chance (serendipity) when working with finite difference schemes for convection–diffusion schemes (see Duffy, 1980). We have carried out extensive numerical tests in one and two dimensions and have found the scheme to be very robust. In particular, the scheme is able to handle the above four scenarios with ease. The basic rule in one and two dimensions is given by

$$\int_a^b f(x)\,dx \approx 2\tanh\left[\frac{h}{2}f\left(\frac{a+b}{2}\right)\right] \tag{A1.22a}$$

and

$$\int_c^d \int_a^b f(x,y)\,dx\,dy \approx 4\tanh\left[\frac{hk}{4}f(m1,\ m2)\right] \tag{A1.22b}$$

with $h = b - a$
$\qquad k = d - c$

$\qquad m_1 = \tfrac{1}{2}(a+b)$

$\qquad m_2 = \tfrac{1}{2}(c+d)$

The extended version for the Tanh rule in one and two dimensions is given by

$$Q^h(f) \equiv 2\sum_{j=1}^n \tanh\left[\frac{h}{2}f(x_{j-\frac{1}{2}})\right] \tag{A1.23a}$$

and

$$Q^{h,k}(f) \equiv 4\sum_{j=1}^n \sum_{k=1}^m \tanh\left[\frac{hk}{4}f(x_{j-\frac{1}{2}},\ y_{k-\frac{1}{2}})\right] \tag{A1.23b}$$

where the intervals (a, b) and (c, d) are divided into n and m equal sub-intervals, respectively.

Scheme (A1.22) is 'singularity-insensitive' and we can use it with impunity without having to manage singularities explicitly.

There is no advantage using this method over standard integration schemes for well-behaved functions but for functions with singularities we do notice a certain robustness. The method is first-order accurate $O(h)$. Some of the 'nasty' functions on the interval $(0, 1)$ that we have tested are:

$$\frac{x}{e^x - 1}, \quad \frac{\log x}{1 - x}, \quad \frac{\log x}{1 - x^2}, \quad \frac{1}{1 + x}, \quad \frac{\log(1+x)}{x}, \quad \frac{x^b - x^a}{\log x} \tag{A1.24}$$

Some examples of the extended two-dimensional Tanh rule on the square $(-1, 1) \times (-1, 1)$ are:

$$\frac{1}{1 - xy} \quad \frac{1}{r} \tag{A1.25}$$

where $r = \sqrt{x^2 + y^2}$.

We now finish this section by discussing an adaptive form of the Tanh rule in one dimension. We know that (by numerical validation)

$$|Q^h(f) - I(f)| \le Mh \tag{A1.26}$$

where $I(f) \equiv \int_a^b f(x)\,dx$ and constant M is independent of h.

We apply the Tanh rule on meshes of size h and $h/2$, then calculate the quantity

$$R^{h/2}(f) = 2Q^{h/2}(f) - Q^h(f) \tag{A1.27}$$

In other words, we apply scheme (A1.23) on two consecutive meshes as it were.

This quantity $R^{h/2}(f)$, as defined in (A1.27), will then be a second-order approximation to the integral. This is easy to prove and we already have discussed this topic in Part I. Defining the constant that is called *the order of convergence p* by the expression

$$p = \frac{\log(e^h / e^{h/2})}{\log 2}$$

and *the error term* by

$$e^h = |Q^h(f) - I(f)|$$

we then see from experiments that $p = 1$, thus confirming the first-order property of the rule.

All this leads us to an algorithm for the adaptive Tanh rule: assume that we want our rule to be accurate to a given tolerance TOL. Then the algorithm goes as follows:

Set $h := (b - a)/4$;
Iter := 0;

Repeat:

$$\text{diff} = |Q^h(f) - Q^{h/2}(f)|$$
$$\text{iter} = \text{iter} + 1$$
$$h := h/2$$

Until (diff < TOL)

A1.3.2   Integrals on infinite intervals

Integrals on infinite and semi-infinite intervals occur in many practical problems. For example, many of the PIDEs that model contingent claims using Levy processes lead to such integrals (see Øksendal and Sulem, 2005). Thus, we need to devise accurate and robust schemes for these cases. Let us take an example

$$\int_{-\infty}^{\infty} f(x) \, dx$$

We assume that $f(x)$ is small enough outside some range $R > 0$. Then we truncate the above integral to one of the form

$$\int_{-R}^{R} f(x) \, dx$$

and then apply our favourite rule to this latter integral. A good example is the Gaussian function

$$\int_{-\infty}^{\infty} e^{-x^2} \, dx = \sqrt{\pi} = 1.772454$$

Setting $R = 4$ and using the Trapezoidal rule gives

$$\int_{-4}^{4} e^{-x^2} \, dx \approx \begin{cases} 1.772636 & (h = 1) \\ 1.772453 & (h = 0.5) \end{cases}$$

These are encouraging results. Thus, for functions that decay fast enough we can achieve economical schemes for integrals on infinite intervals.

A1.4   AN INTRODUCTION TO INTEGRAL EQUATIONS

In one sense an integral equation is the mirror image of a differential equation. Differential equations have been studied extensively for the past 200 years while integral equations have received somewhat less attention during that period. However, integral equations are interesting in their own right and are beginning to surface in the financial engineering literature (Øksendal and Sulem, 2005).

We begin by taking an example of an integral equation. Consider the initial value problem (IVP)

$$u' = f(x, u), \quad 0 < x < 1$$
$$u(0) = A$$

(A1.28)

By integrating (A1.28) between 0 and some specific value t we get the integral equation

$$u(t) = \int_0^t f(x, u(x)) \, dx + A$$

This equation is a simple example of a nonlinear Volterra equation of the second kind. In general, the function $u = u(x)$ is unknown. A more general form is given by

$$u(t) = \lambda \int_0^t f(t, x, u(x)) \, dx + g(t)$$

where λ is some parameter that may or may not be known.

It can be shown that this latter problem has a unique solution under certain conditions, the main ones being that some terms in the above equation satisfy a Lipschitz condition, namely

$$|g(t_1) - g(t_2)| \leq L_1 |t_1 - t_2|$$

and

$$|f(t, x, v_1) - f(t, x, v_2)| \leq L_2 |v_1 - v_2|$$

where L_1 and L_2 are two constants and in this case we see the close relationship between integral equations and two-point boundary value problems. Another example of an integral equation is taken from Keller (1992). To this end, let us examine the two-point boundary value problem in self-adjoint form

$$Lu(x) \equiv [p(x)u'(x)]' - q(x)u(x) = f(x), \quad a < x < b$$
$$u(a) = u(b) = 0$$

(A1.29)

where

$$p(x) > 0, \quad q(x) \geq 0$$

The Green's function is determined by the differential operator L and the boundary conditions in problem (A1.29). Then the solution of (A1.29) is given by

$$u(x) = - \int_a^b g(x, \xi) f(\xi) \, d\xi$$

(A1.30)

where $g(x, \xi)$ is the Green's function, as already discussed in Chapter 3.

Let us take a specific example of (A1.30). To this end, consider the nonlinear problem:

$$L_0 u \equiv u'' = f(x, u), \qquad u(a) = u(b) = 0 \tag{A1.31}$$

where

$$g_0(x, \xi) = \begin{cases} x(1 - \xi), & x < \xi \\ (1 - x)\xi, & x > \xi \end{cases}$$

Then the solution of (A1.31) is given by

$$u(x) = -\int_0^1 g_0(x, \xi) f(\xi, u(\xi)) \, d\xi \tag{A1.32}$$

This is of course a nonlinear equation in u and we must resort to numerical methods to solve it. What you gain on the swings, you lose on the roundabouts! Finally, the nonlinear problem

$$Lu = f(x, u, u'), \quad a < x < b$$
$$u(a) = u(b) = 0 \tag{A1.33}$$

has the solution

$$u(x) = -\int_a^b g(x, \xi) f(\xi, u(\xi), u'(\xi)) \, d\xi \tag{A1.34}$$

and we thus see that this is also a nonlinear equation. We discuss nonlinear integral equations shortly. Equations similar to (A1.34) occur in financial engineering applications, for example option models containing jumps.

For a good introduction to the numerical solution of integral equations, see Keller (1992).

A1.4.1 Categories of linear integral equation

We now categorise linear and nonlinear equations. We first discuss linear equations. The two main categories are named after Volterra and Fredholm, the mathematicians who studied these equations. Here follow the main categories (see Golberg, 1979)

$$\text{Fredholm (second kind):} \quad u(t) = g(t) + \int_a^b K(t, s) u(s) \, ds \tag{A1.35a}$$

$$\text{Fredholm (first kind):} \quad \int_a^b K(t, s) u(s) \, ds = g(t) \tag{A1.35b}$$

$$\text{Wiener–Hopf:} \quad u(t) = g(t) + \int_0^\infty K(t - s) u(s) \, ds \tag{A1.35c}$$

$$\text{Volterra (second kind):} \quad u(t) = g(t) + \int_a^t K(t, s) u(s) \, ds \tag{A1.35d}$$

$$\text{Volterra (first kind):} \quad \int_0^t K(t, s) u(s) \, ds = g(t) \tag{A1.35e}$$

Integral equations are closely related to integral transforms, some of which we now summarise (see Zemanian, 1987).

Two-sided Laplace transform:

$$F(s) = \int_{-\infty}^{\infty} f(t)e^{-st}\,dt \tag{A1.36a}$$

Weierstrass transform:

$$F(s) = \frac{1}{\sqrt{4\pi}} \int_{-\infty}^{\infty} f(t)\exp\left[-\frac{(s-t)^2}{4}\right]\,dt \tag{A1.36b}$$

Convolution transform:

$$F(s) = \int_{-\infty}^{\infty} f(t)G(s-t)\,dt \tag{A1.36c}$$

where G is the kernel function

These kinds of transforms are commonly seen in the quantitative finance literature.

A1.4.2   Categories of nonlinear integral equations

We finally give some examples of nonlinear integral equations:

$$\text{Urysohn (second kind):} \quad u(t) = g(t) + \int_a^b F(t, s, u(s))\,ds \tag{A1.37a}$$

$$\text{Urysohn (first kind):} \quad \int_a^b F(t, s, u(s))\,ds = g(t) \tag{A1.37b}$$

$$\text{Urysohn Volterra:} \quad u(t) = g(t) + \int_a^t F(t, s, u(s))\,ds \tag{A1.37c}$$

In general, we must provide rigorous proofs for the existence and uniqueness of the solutions of both linear and nonlinear integral equations, but such a topic is outside the scope of this book. For more information, please consult Golberg (1979) or Tricomi (1957); the interplay between differential and integral equations is discussed in Yosida (1991) and a number of mathematical results are proved there. Existence and uniqueness theorems can be proved by the theory called functional analysis.

A1.5   NUMERICAL APPROXIMATION OF INTEGRAL EQUATIONS

We now give an introduction to the numerical approximation of integral equations and we concentrate on linear Fredholm equations of the second kind, because these are found in financial engineering applications at the moment of writing.

Let us again consider the Fredholm equation of the second kind

$$u(x) - \int_a^b K(x, y)u(y)\,dy = f(x) \tag{A1.38}$$

In this case we call the function $K(x, y)$ the kernel of the integral equation and in many cases we can assume that it is symmetric, that is $K(x, y) = K(y, x)$ (see Tricomi, 1957). We also assume that K is smooth. We can classify numerical methods for equation (A1.38) into four broad categories (Golberg, 1979):

- Analytical and semi-analytical methods
- Kernel approximation methods
- Projection methods (for example, Galerkin methods)
- Quadrature methods.

We give a short overview of each of these techniques but our main interest will centre on quadrature methods because of their ease of implementation.

Each of these methods is used in quantitative finance.

A1.5.1 Analytical and semi-analytical methods

In general, we cannot expect to find an analytical solution to an integral equation. We might get lucky sometimes. For example, the Abel equation

$$\int_0^x \frac{u(y)}{\sqrt{x-y}} \, dy = f(x) \tag{A1.39}$$

has the amazingly simple solution (Tricomi, 1957; Cochran, 1972)

$$u(x) = \frac{1}{\pi} \frac{d}{dx} \int_0^x \frac{f(y)}{\sqrt{x-y}} \, dy \tag{A1.40}$$

Failing to find an analytical solution, the next best thing is possibly to find a semi-analytical solution. There are a number of possibilities such as iteration, numerical inversion of transforms and Wiener–Hopf factorisation.

A1.5.2 Kernel approximation methods

In this case we construct a sequence of kernels that converge to the given kernel $K(x, y)$ in some topology. To this end, we define a variant of equation (A1.38) as follows:

$$u_n(x) - \int_a^b K_n(x, y) u_n(y) \, dy = f(x), \quad n \geq 1 \tag{A1.41}$$

where K_n = approximating kernel, $n = 1, 2, \ldots$

u_n = approximation to u.

In general, we usually only discuss degenerate kernels – that is, those that are cross-products of terms in a single variable:

$$K_n(x, y) = \sum_{j=1}^n a_{n,j}(x) b_{n,j}(y) \tag{A1.42}$$

In this case it is then possible to write equation (A1.41) as a linear systems of equations (see Golberg, 1979).

A1.5.3   Projection methods (Galerkin methods)

These methods include collocation, the method of moments, the Galerkin method and the method of least squares. They can all be posed in a functional analytic form. This demands some knowledge of functional analysis, in particular Banach spaces and linear mappings between Banach spaces (see Adams, 1975; Haaser and Sullivan, 1991). Let X be a Banach space and define the operator $A : X' \to X$ (where X' is the dual space of X). In general we assume that the kernel K is integrable. Then, we can write equation (A1.38) in operator form as

$$(I - A)U = F \tag{A1.43}$$

where

$$Au = \int_a^b K(x, y)u(y)\,dy \tag{A1.44}$$

Having done this we can now approximate X by a sequence of finite-dimensional subpaces (for example, polynomials or piecewise polynomials). A definitive discussion of this approach can be found in Ikebe (1972).

A1.5.4   Quadrature methods

This is probably the most well-known numerical technique (Press $et\ al.$, 2002) and it seems to be the approach taken in most articles on pricing applications with jumps (Cont and Voltchkova, 2003). In short, we apply some quadrature rule to the integral in equation (A1.38). For example, in Cont and Voltchkova the authors apply the Trapezoidal rule while in this section we use Simpson's rule. The resulting method in this context is then usually called the Nyström method, and is as follows:

- Define the following mesh points and values for even values of n

$$t_{j,n} \equiv a + jh, \quad j = 0, \ldots, n$$

$$\omega_{0,n} = \omega_{n,n} = \frac{h}{3}$$

$$\omega_{2j-1,n} = \frac{4h}{3}, \qquad \omega_{2j,n} = \frac{2h}{3},$$

where $h = (b - n)/n$.

- Apply Simpson's rule to the integral term for any point x in the interval (a, b):

$$u_n(x) - \sum_{j=0}^{n} \omega_{j,n} K(x, t_{j,n}) u_n(y_{j,n}) = f(x), \quad a \le x \le b$$

This is a kind of semi-discrete scheme because the integral term in (A1.38) has been replaced by a discrete equivalent but the variable x is still continuous.

- We now choose special mesh points for x, namely the mesh points. Set

$$x = t_{i,n}, \quad i = 0, \ldots, n$$

then

$$u_n(t_{i,n}) - \sum_{j=0}^{n} \omega_{j,n} K(t_{i,n}, t_{j,n}) u_n(t_{j,n}) = f(t_{i,n})$$

This last set of equations is equivalent to the matrix system

$$(I - A)U = F \tag{A1.45}$$

where

$$A = (\omega_{j,n} K(t_{i,n}, t_{j,n})), \quad 1 \le i, j \le n$$

and

$$U = {}^t(u_0(t_{0,n}), \ldots, u_n(t_{n,n}))$$

- The next step is to solve (A1.45) by a matrix solver. The matrix A is a full matrix in general and this can be a disadvantage for time-dependent financial engineering applications, and in these cases we may need to resort to iterative methods.

There is a wealth of information pertaining to existence and uniqueness results for the solution of system (A1.45). See, for example, Cochran (1972) and Golub and Van Loan (1996).

A1.5.5 Integral equations with singular kernels

We have now discussed quadrature rules but it is known that accuracy problems arise when the kernel $K(x, y)$ has singularities. In Press *et al.* (2002) the authors have a number of suggestions for coping with these singularities:

- Remove the singularity by a change of variable.
- Factoring: set $K(x, y) = w(x)L(x, y)$, where $w(x)$ is a singular function and $L(x, y)$ is smooth. We then use a Gaussian quadrature formula based on $w(x)$ as a weight. However, the actual process can be quite cumbersome.
- Use 'special' quadrature formulae, for example using polynomials or splines.
- A special case of a singularity is when the interval of integration is infinite or semi-infinite. In this case we truncate the interval (the authors claim that this should be done only as a last resort, but no evidence is given as to why this approach is not acceptable). In many cases the kernel approaches zero very quickly (as in financial engineering applications).
- A nasty problem is when the kernel $K(x, y)$ is singular along the line $x = y$. Then the popular Nyström method fails and in this case we must subtract the singularity. We experience this when modelling with Levy processes.

Examples of the above-mentioned kernels can be found in the integral equation (see Yosida, 1991)

$$K(x, y) = \frac{p(x, y)}{(x - y)^\alpha}$$

where $0 < \alpha < 1$ and $p(x, y)$ is a continuous function. Thus, $K(x, y)$ is the product of a smooth and a singular function.

Another example is the Lalesco–Picard equation (Tricomi, 1957)

$$u(x) - \lambda \int_{-\infty}^{\infty} e^{-|x-y|} u(y) \, dy = f(x)$$

In this case the kernel has an infinite norm.

Another example of a singular kernel arises when we model Carr–Geman–Madon–Yor (CGMY) processes

$$K(x) = \begin{cases} C \dfrac{\exp(-G|x|)}{|x|^{1+\alpha}}, & x < 0 \\[3mm] C \dfrac{\exp(-M|x|)}{|x|^{1+\alpha}}, & x > 0 \end{cases}$$

for constant $C > 0$, $G \geq 0$, $M \geq 0$, $\alpha < 2$.

We must take singular kernels into account because they arise in financial engineering applications (see Cont and Voltchkova, 2003). In particular, we must be able to accommodate problems with infinite activity and this requirement leads to the existence of singular kernels. For example, we may get a singularity at zero of the integral kernel. In these cases standard numerical integration techniques and FFT, for example, may not always be applicable.

Finally, we could modify the Nyström method by using the Tanh rule instead of Simpson's rule to produce the following semi-discrete scheme:

$$u_n(x) - 2\sum_{j=0}^{n} \tanh\left[\frac{h}{2}K(x, t_{j+\frac{1}{2}})n\right] u_n(t_{j,n}) = f(x), \quad a \leq x \leq b \qquad (A1.46)$$

A1.6   SUMMARY AND CONCLUSIONS

We have given an introduction to integral equations, some of their applications and how to approximate their solutions using numerical quadrature rules. Furthermore, we gave a crash course on numerical integration of functions of one variable. The theory in this chapter was used in Chapter 17 where we introduced partial integro-differential equations (PIDEs) in option pricing problems in the presence of jumps.

In our opinion, this appendix should be useful to readers because it brings a number of mathematical and numerical techniques together in one place. It can be used as a quick reference guide and 'pointer' to more detailed texts.

An Introduction to the Finite
Element Method

A2.1 INTRODUCTION AND OBJECTIVES

In this appendix we give an introduction to the finite element method (FEM). Our main goal is to discuss enough material to help the reader with more advanced texts. The finite element method has its roots in papers by Richard Courant (Courant, 1943) and John Lighton Synge (see Synge, 1952 and 1957). The 1960's were the golden years of FEM. Engineers started to apply the method to a wide range of applications in structural and civil engineering and fluid dynamics (Hughes, 2000). It was in the late 1960's that mathematicians started to take an interest in the field and they developed a rigorous foundation for future study and there has since been a rapid growth in the number of mathematics books on the subject. For example, when the current author embarked on FEM very few books was available (Strang and Fix, 1973, was the only one I could find at the time), but by 1991 more than 400 books on FEM were in existence.

FEM was first applied to equilibrium and time-independent problems, and was later applied to time-dependent problems. More recently, the method is becoming popular in financial engineering applications, as witnessed by the number of articles being published on the subject and the arrival of monographs (see, for example, Topper, 2005). In particular, the success or failure of FEM for time-dependent problems will probably depend on a number of technical and organisational factors, such as:

- Is it a suitable technology for financial engineering applications?
- Does it produce accurate results?
- How much effort (human, machine) is needed to achieve a given level of accuracy?
- How long does it take to understand and to apply FEM to financial engineering problems?
- Is the code for FEM applications stable, easy to maintain and to adapt?

We discuss a number of problems and we model them using FEM:

- Using FEM for a simple scalar initial value problem in one dimension.
- One-dimensional heat equation: This problem has two independent variables (namely time t and space x). We discretise in two steps: first, in the x direction using 'hat' functions and the result is a system of ordinary differential equations in t. We subsequently approximate this system using Crank–Nicolson, Runge–Kutta or predictor–corrector methods, for example.
- Simple wave equation: This is in fact a convection (advection) equation, an essential component in the Back–Scholes equation. Again, we discretise first in x, then in t. Here we devote some attention to proving that the schemes are stable and convergent (based on Duffy, 1977).

For a treatment of the finite element method in option pricing applications, see Topper (2005), and it is our hope that this appendix will help you when embarking on more advanced FEM literature.

A2.2   AN INITIAL VALUE PROBLEM

We take a simple problem to motivate the finite element method, namely a scalar, linear first-order initial value problem (IVP) on the unit interval $I = (0, 1)$:

$$u' + au = f(x), x \in (0, T)$$

$$u(0) = 0 \tag{A2.1}$$

where $a(x) \geq \alpha > 0 \quad \forall x \in [0, T]$.

As the solution of this problem is known, it provides a good test case (note that we have also discussed this problem from the viewpoint of FDM in Duffy, 2004). We note that (A2.1) is in so-called differential form. The essence of FEM, on the other hand, is to transform this problem into one that is in variational or integral form. To this end, we multiply each side of the differential equation in (A2.1) by some unspecified function v. For the moment we accept this at face value.

Before we map the above system to variational form, we must digress to give an introduction to a certain class of functions. We shall soon return to problem (A2.1).

Central to the theory of finite elements is the idea of integrability of functions and of their derivatives. Let f be a measurable real-valued function on $I = (a, b)$, and let $0 < p < \infty$ be a real number. We define the quantity

$$\|f\|_p := \left(\int_I |f|^p \, dx \right)^{1/p} \tag{A2.2}$$

and we further denote $L^p(I)$ to be set of those functions f for which

$$\|f\|_p < \infty$$

In mathematical terms, $\|f\|_p$ is called the L^p norm of f.

Definition. A norm on a vector space X is a real-valued mapping $f : X \to \mathbb{R}$ such that

(i) $f(x) \geq 0, x \in X$ with equality if and only if $x = 0$
(ii) $f(cx) = |c| f(x)$, for all $x \in X$, for all $c \in \mathbb{R}$
(iii) $f(x + y) \leq f(x) + f(y)$, for all $x, y \in \mathbb{R}$.

A normed space is a vector-space X that is provided with a norm.

The case of interest for us in definition (A2.2) is when $p = 2$. In this case we speak of functions being 'square-integrable'. It is also possible to define a class of functions whose derivatives are also square-integrable. We define the quantity

$$\|f\|_{1,2} := \left[\|f\|_2^2 + \left\| \frac{df}{dx} \right\|_2^2 \right]^{\frac{1}{2}}$$

We define $H^1(I)$ to be set of those functions that have square-integrable first derivatives and for which $\|f\|_{1,2} < \infty$. Usually we write $\|f\| \equiv \|f\|_2$ and $\|f\|_1 = \|f\|_{1,2}$ when no confusion can occur.

We now define the inner product of two square-integrable functions f and g by

$$(f, g) = \int_0^1 f(x)\, g(x)\, \mathrm{d}x$$

We now return to problem (A2.1) and define the weak solution for it. Define the space

$$V = H^1(I) \cap \{v : v(0) = 0\}$$

If we multiply each side of equation (A2.1) by a function $v \epsilon V$, we can then define the weak approximation to (A2.1) as follows.
Find $u \epsilon V$ such that

$$\left(u' + au, v\right) = (f, v) \quad \text{for all} \quad v \epsilon V \tag{A2.3}$$

We can show that problem (A2.3) has a unique solution if the data is smooth enough, but we do no do so here. We show uniqueness. To this end, let u_1 and u_2 be two solutions to (A2.3), and set $e = u_1 - u_2$. Then, from (A2.3) we have

$$\left(e', v\right) + (ae, v) = 0, \quad v \epsilon V$$

In particular, setting $v = e$, we get

$$\tfrac{1}{2}\left[e^2(1) - e^2(0)\right] + \alpha\|e\|^2 \le (e', e) + (ae, e) = 0$$

from which we conclude that $\|e\| = 0$. Since this is a norm we conclude that $u_1 = u_2$.

Equation (A2.3) will serve as the basis for the finite element method, in which case the infinite-dimensional space V will be replaced by a finite-dimensional sub-space.

To this end, suppose that N is a positive integer and that $I = (0, 1)$ is divided into sub-intervals $I_j = \left(x_j, x_{j-1}\right)$ where the mesh δ is defined by

$$\delta : 0 = x_0 < x_1 < \cdots < x_N = 1$$

with $\quad h_j = x_j - x_{j-1}, \quad h = \max h_j, \quad j = 1, \ldots, N$

Let k be an non-negative integer. We define the space $P_k(E)$ (where E is a subset of the real line) to be the space of those functions which are polynomials of degree less than or equal to k on E. Moreover, let $C^0(I)$ be the space of continuous functions on the interval I. Finally, we define the space

$$V_k^h(\delta) = \{v \epsilon C^0(I) : v_{I_j} \epsilon P_k(I_j), \quad j = 1, \ldots, N, \; v(0) = 0\}$$

This is a finite-dimensional sub-space of the infinite-dimensional space V defined earlier, called the space of piecewise polynomials of degree k.

In this section we shall deal exclusively with the case $k = 1$, in which we call $V_1^h(\delta)$ the space of piecewise linear polynomials. For convenience, we set $V^h \equiv V_1^h$.

Suppose that $\varphi_1, \ldots, \varphi_m$ are elements of V^h, and let $\mathbf{y} = c_1\varphi_1 + \cdots + c_m\varphi_m$, where $c_j \epsilon \mathbb{R}, \; j = 1, \ldots, m$. The vector $\mathbf{y}$ is said to be a linear combination of the elements $\varphi_1, \ldots, \varphi_m$. The elements $\varphi_1, \ldots, \varphi_m$ are said to be linearly independent if the identity $c_1\varphi_1 + \cdots + c_m\varphi_m = 0$ implies that $c_1 = c_2 = \cdots = c_m = 0$.

The maximum number of linearly independent vectors in V^h is called the dimension of V^h and such vectors span V^h. Thus every element $w^h \epsilon V^h$ can be written as a combination

$$w^h = c_1\varphi_1 + \cdots + c_m\varphi_m$$

Theorem A2.1. *The maximum number of linearly independent elements for V_k^h (written as $\dim V_k^h$) is Nk. Thus,*

$$\dim V_k^h = Nk$$

Proof. We evaluate the number of free terms that need to be determined for an arbitrary $w^h \epsilon V_k^h$. Now, in each subinterval I_j, w^h can be written as

$$w^h = \sum_{j=0}^{k} c_j x^j$$

so that there are $(k+1)$ parameters to be evaluated on each sub-interval. Since $w^h \epsilon C^0(I)$, $N-1$ continuity constraints are introduced at the interior nodes of the mesh. Furthermore, $w^h(0) = 0$, which introduces one more constraint. Hence the total numer of free parameters is

$$N(k+1) - (N-1) - 1 = Nk.$$

Construction of basis functions in the case $k = 1$ (these are the piecewise linear 'hat' functions, see Strang and Fix, 1973, or Huyakorn and Pinder, 1983).

The basis functions are defined by

$$\varphi_j(x_k) = \delta_{jk} = \begin{cases} 1, & j = k \\ 0, & j \neq k \end{cases}$$

It is easily verified that $\varphi_j(x) \equiv 0$ except in case of the following sub-intervals:

$$\varphi_j(x) = \begin{cases} \dfrac{x - x_{j-1}}{h_j}, & x_{j-1} \leq x < x_j \\[2mm] \dfrac{x_{j+1} - x}{h_{j+1}}, & x_j \leq x \leq x_{j+1} \\[2mm] j = 1, \ldots, N-1 \end{cases}$$

When $j = N$ we have

$$\varphi_N(x) = \frac{x - x_{N-1}}{h_N} \text{ if } x_{N-1} \leq x \leq x_N,$$

$$\varphi_N(x) \equiv 0 \quad \text{otherwise}$$

The finite-dimensional analogue of (A2.3) is given by:

Find $u^h \epsilon V^h$ such that

$$\left(\frac{du^h}{dx}, v\right) + \left(au^h, v\right) = (f, v) \quad \forall v \epsilon V^h \tag{A2.4}$$

Theorem A2.2. *Problem (A2.4) has a unique solution.*

Proof. Since the problem is finite-dimensional, uniqueness implies existence (Kreider *et al.*, 1966). Set $v = u^h$ in (A2.4). We then get

$$\left(\frac{du^h}{dx}, u^h\right) + \left(au^h, u^h\right) = \left(f, u^h\right)$$

or

$$\tfrac{1}{2}u^{h^2}(1) + \alpha \|u^h\|^2 \leq \left(f, u^h\right) \leq \|f\|\|u^h\| \tag{A2.5}$$

where we have used Hölder's inequality (Adams, 1975) on the right-hand side of (A2.5). Hence $\|u^h\| \leq M \|f\|$, where M is some constant that is independent of h. Thus, problem (A2.4) has a unique solution.

We now construct the difference schemes using the basis functions in the following representation for u^h:

$$u^h(x) = \sum_{j=1}^{N} u_j \varphi_j(x)$$

To this end, we write (A2.4) in the equivalent form by inserting the above representation into it. (we assume that the coefficient a in equation (A2.1) is constant):

$$\left(\frac{du^h}{dx}, \varphi_k\right) + \left(au^h, \varphi_k\right) = (f, \varphi_k), \quad k = 1, \ldots, N \quad \left(\varphi'_j \equiv \frac{d\varphi_j}{dx}, \quad j = 1, \ldots, N\right)$$

Hence

$$\sum_{j=1}^{N} u_j \left(\varphi'_j, \varphi_k\right) + a \sum_{j=1}^{N} u_j \left(\varphi_j, \varphi_k\right) = (f, \varphi_k), \quad k = 1, \ldots, N \quad \text{(A2.6)}$$

Noting that $\left(\varphi_j, \varphi_k\right) = 0$ for $|j - k| \geq 2$, we get from equation (A2.6)

$$u_{k-1}(\varphi'_{k-1}, \varphi_k) + u_k(\varphi'_k, \varphi_k) + u_{k+1}(\varphi'_{k+1}, \varphi_k)$$
$$+ a[u_{k-1}(\varphi_{k-1}, \varphi_k) + u_k(\varphi_k, \varphi_k) + u_{k+1}(\varphi_{k+1}, \varphi_k)] = (f, \varphi_k), \quad k = 1, \ldots, N$$

Some basic arithmetic shows that:

$$\begin{aligned}
\left(\varphi'_{k\pm 1}, \varphi_k\right) &= \pm\tfrac{1}{2}, & \left(\varphi'_k, \varphi_k\right) &= 0 \\
(\varphi_{k-1}, \varphi_k) &= \tfrac{1}{6}h_k, & (\varphi_k, \varphi_k) &= \tfrac{1}{3}(h_k + h_{k+1}), \quad 1 \leq k \leq N-1 \\
(\varphi_{k+1}, \varphi_k) &= \tfrac{1}{6}h_{k+1} \\
\left(\varphi'_{N-1}, \varphi_N\right) &= -\tfrac{1}{2}, & (\varphi_{N-1}, \varphi_N) &= \tfrac{1}{6}h_N \\
\left(\varphi'_N, \varphi_N\right) &= \tfrac{1}{2}, & (\varphi_N, \varphi_N) &= \tfrac{1}{3}h_N
\end{aligned}$$

Finally the set of equations (A2.6) becomes

$$a_k u_{k-1} + b_k u_k + c_k u_{k+1} = (f, \varphi_k), \quad 1 \leq k \leq N-1$$

and

$$a_N u_{N-1} + b_N u_N = (f, \varphi_N)$$

where $a_k = -\tfrac{1}{2} + ah_k/6, \ 1 \leq k \leq N$
$b_k = a(h_k + h_{k+1})/3, \ 1 \leq k \leq N-1$
$c_k = \tfrac{1}{2} + [ah(k+1)]/6, \ 1 \leq k \leq N-1$
$b_N = \tfrac{1}{2} + ah_N/3$

The system can be solved using *LU* decomposition (Duffy, 2004) Having found the vector ${}^t(u_1, \ldots, u_N)$ it is now possible to find the solution of (A2.4) at any point $\hat{x} \in \overline{I} = [0, 1]$. This value is given by:

$$u^h(\hat{x}) = \sum_{j=1}^{N} u_j \varphi_j(\hat{x})$$

A2.2.1   Remarks and special cases

1. In practice the integrals (f, φ_k), $k = 1, \ldots, N$ would be approximated by some numerical integration scheme. For example, choosing the mid-point rule, we get

$$f_k \equiv (f, \varphi_k) = \int_{x_{k-1}}^{x_{k+1}} f(x)\varphi_k(x)\,dx$$

$$= \int_{x_{x-1}}^{x_k} f(x)\varphi_k(x)\,dx + \int_{x_k}^{x_{k+1}} f(x)\varphi_k(x)\,dx$$

$$\cong \tfrac{1}{2}\left[h_k f\left(x_{k-\frac{1}{2}}\right) + h_{k+1} f\left(x_{k+\frac{1}{2}}\right) \right]$$

2. It is interesting to see what the corresponding difference scheme is in the case where the mesh is uniform, i.e. $h_j = \text{constant} \equiv h$, $j = 1, \ldots, N$.

   After some rearranging, we get the scheme

$$\frac{u_{k+1} - u_{k-1}}{2h} + \frac{a}{6}(u_{k-1} + 4u_k + u_{k+1}) = f(x_k)$$

which is the discrete analogue of the equation $u' + au = f$.

Of course, this scheme is a sledge-hammer but it does show the essence of FEM.

A2.3   THE ONE-DIMENSIONAL HEAT EQUATION

There is an enormous literature on the application of the finite element method to parabolic equations in one and several space dimensions. It is not possible to deal with all the different approaches here but we shall take the simple one-dimensional heat equation (Strang and Fix, 1973). The problem and its finite element approximation should be accessible enough so that the reader can use the results to understand and learn more challenging problems, for example the Black–Scholes equation (Topper, 2005; Foufas *et al.*, 2004).

We examine the model heat equation problem:

$$\frac{\partial u}{\partial t} - \frac{\partial^2 u}{\partial x^2} = f(x, t), \quad 0 < x < \pi, \ t > 0$$

$$u(x, 0) = u_0(x), \quad 0 < x < \pi \tag{A2.7}$$

$$u(0, t) = \frac{\partial u}{\partial x}(\pi, t) = 0, \quad t > 0$$

Physically, this initial boundary value problem models the flow of heat in a finite rod. At one end $x = 0$ the temperature is kept at zero degrees while at the other end $x = \pi$ there is no flow in or out of the rod (it is insulated). There is a non-zero forcing term $f(x, t)$ that corresponds to an inhomogeneous source term. Initially (that is, $t = 0$) the temperature distribution is given along the length of the rod.

It is possible to find a closed solution to (A2.7) (using Separation of Variables technique, for example). In this section we approximate the problem using finite elements. In fact, we shall employ the linear hat polynomials that we introduced in section A2.2 for discretisation in the x direction. Eventually, we shall solve a fully discrete set of equations. The main activities in this process are:

A1: Set up the continuous semi-discrete variational formulation
A2: The approximate semi-discrete variational formulation using linear hat polynomials
A3: Set up the fully discrete scheme (discrete time levels) using Crank–Nicolson time averaging, for example.

In activities A1 and A2 the time variable t is continuous while in activity A3 it has been discretised. Furthermore, in activity A1 the x variable is continuous while in activity A2 we discretise it using the hat functions.

We now discuss activity A1. Multiplying the PDE in (A2.7) by some smooth function v that vanishes at $x = 0$ and then, integrating by parts (while using the boundary conditions for the solution u) we get the variational form of equation (A2.7), namely:

Find $u \in V$ such that

$$a(u, v) \equiv (u_t, v) + (u_x, v_x) = (f, v) \quad \forall v \in V \tag{A2.8}$$

where $V = H^1 \cap \{v : v(0) = 0\}$, $(.,.)$ is the inner product in $(0, \pi)$, and the subscripts denote derivatives of u and v with respect to the variables x and t.

We see that this variational formulation incorporates the differential equation and the boundary conditions, but we still have to define the initial condition for this new formulation. This is usually the projection of the initial condition in (A2.7) onto the space V.

We now discuss activity A2 and we use the same notation as in section A2.2. We assume that the approximate solution can be written in the form:

$$u^h(x, t) = \sum_{j=1}^{N} u_j(t)\varphi_j(x) \tag{A2.9}$$

then the approximate semi-discrete formulation is given by:

Find $u^h \in V^h$ such that

$$a(u^h, v) \equiv \left(\frac{\partial u^h}{\partial t}, v\right) + \left(\frac{\partial u^h}{\partial x}, \frac{\partial v}{\partial x}\right) = (f, v) \quad \forall v \in V^h \tag{A2.10a}$$

and

$$(u^h(\cdot, 0), v) = (u_0, v) \quad \forall v \in V^h \tag{A2.10b}$$

where V^h is the space of piecewise linear 'hat' functions already described.

By inserting the representation (A2.9) into (A2.10a)–(A2.10b) and using the integral relations from section A2.2 we can show that the system (A2.10) can be posed as a first-order initial value problem (IVP):

$$MU'(t) + KU(t) = F(t)$$
$$U(0) = U_0 \tag{A2.11}$$

where M and K are matrices, and $U(t) = {}^t(u_1(t), \ldots, u_N(t))$.

Typically, the Toeplitz matrices M and K have representations of the form (on a uniform mesh of size h):

$$M = \frac{1}{6} \begin{pmatrix} 4 & 1 & & & 0 \\ 1 & \ddots & & \ddots & \\ & & \ddots & \ddots & 1 \\ 0 & & & 1 & 4 \end{pmatrix} \tag{A2.12a}$$

$$K = h^{-2} \begin{pmatrix} 2 & -1 & & & 0 \\ -1 & \ddots & & \ddots & \\ & & \ddots & \ddots & -1 \\ 0 & & & -1 & 2 \end{pmatrix} \tag{A2.12b}$$

The final activity is A3. To this end, we discretise the time variable t in the IVP (A2.11). This is old hat by now and we have lots of choices:

- Runge–Kutta methods
- Euler schemes
- Crank–Nicolson (CN)
- Many others.

The financial engineering community seems to have homed in on CN, so we shall discuss its applicability in this case. For convenience, we take the right-hand side of (A2.11) to be zero. The fully discrete scheme then becomes:

$$M(U^{n+1} - U^n) + \frac{Kk}{2}(U^{n+1} + U^n) = 0, \quad n \geq 0 \tag{A2.13a}$$

or

$$\left(M + \frac{Kk}{2}\right) U^{n+1} = \left(M - \frac{Kk}{2}\right) U^n \tag{A2.13b}$$

$$U^{n+1} = \left(M + \frac{Kk}{2}\right)^{-1} \left(M - \frac{Kk}{2}\right) U^n \tag{A2.13c}$$

Normally, this gives a solution at time level $n + 1$:

$$U^{n+1} = \left(I + \frac{M^{-1}Kk}{2}\right)^{-1} \left(I - \frac{M^{-1}Kk}{2}\right) U^n$$

We thus have a scheme for computing the value at level $n + 1$ based on the value at level n. For example, we can use LU decomposition (see Keller, 1992 and Duffy, 2004 for details in C++.) We are now done.

The step-by-step account in this section serves as a pattern in general for solving time-dependent problems using FEM; first discretise in space, then in time. We can apply the same technique to the Black–Scholes parabolic equation.

A good exercise would be to convert the Black–Scholes equation to the heat equation using a change of variables (Wilmott, 1998) and then use FEM as described here to find an approximate solution, possibly with support for non-constant meshes. An advantage of this approach is that discontinuous initial conditions (as in digital options) are approximated by smoothed discrete equivalents using the projection in equation (A2.10b). This avoids spurious oscillation problems.

A2.4 CONVECTION EQUATION IN ONE DIMENSION

Having discussed FEM for a simple diffusion equation (the heat equation) we now move on to a discussion of its applicability to first-order hyperbolic PDEs. These equations are part of the Black–Scholes PDE and are present in Asian option PDEs. Unlike diffusion equations, where initial discontinuities become smoothed out, the solution of a convection equation remains discontinuous if the initial conditions are discontinuous. Even worse, a continuous solution at $t = 0$ can become discontinuous after some time.

We give a scheme for a scalar convection equation, based on Baker (1975), that was generalised to systems of equations in Duffy (1977).

A2.4.1 Finite element formulation

We introduce a partial differential equation in two independent variables, namely a space variable x and a time variable t. The problem now is one of finding a function $u = u(x, t)$ in the region $Q = I \times J = (0, 1) \times (0, T)$, where $0 < T < \infty$ such that

$$\frac{\partial u}{\partial t} + a \frac{\partial u}{\partial x} = f(x, t), \quad (x, t) \in Q, \quad a > 0 \text{ constant} \tag{A2.14}$$

$$u(0, t) = g(t), \quad t \in J \quad \text{(boundary condition)} \tag{A2.15}$$

$$u(x, 0) = u_0(x), \quad x \in I \quad \text{(initial condition)} \tag{A2.16}$$

We shall now propose a finite element scheme to solve this system. (It was proposed in Baker (1975) for the scalar case and generalised in Duffy (1977) for systems of equations.)

The method is based on a rather crucial step. Let u be the solution of (A2.14)–(A2.16) and let v be a smooth function. Integration by parts shows us that

$$\left(a \frac{\partial u}{\partial x}, v \right) = - \left(au, \frac{\partial v}{\partial x} \right) + a \left[u(1, t) v(1) - g(t) v(0) \right]$$

In the sequel we shall assume further that $v(1) = 0$. We define the generalised L^2 space as

$$L^2[0, T; L^2(I)] = \{ v : (0, T) \to L^2(I), \quad |||v||| < \infty \}$$

where the norm $|||.|||$ is defined by

$$|||v||| = \left(\int_0^T ||v(., t)||^2 \, dt \right)^{\frac{1}{2}}$$

and $||v(., t)||$ is the 'standard' L^2 norm, i.e.

$$||v(., t)|| = \left(\int_0^1 |v(x, t)|^2 \, dx \right)^{\frac{1}{2}}.$$

The so-called weak formulation of (A2.14) – (A2.16) is given by:

Find $u \in L^2[0, T; L^2(I)]$ with $u_t \in L^2[0, T; L^2(I)]$ such that

$$\left(\frac{\partial u}{\partial t}, v\right) - \left(au, \frac{\partial u}{\partial x}\right) = (f, v) + ag(t)v(0), \quad v \in \overset{\circ}{H}(I) \qquad (A2.17)$$

where $\overset{\circ}{H}(I) = \{v : v, v_x \in L^2(I), v(1) = 0\}$.

Using the notation developed in section A2.2 we define the spaces

$$S^h = \{v : v \in P_k(I_j), \ j = 1, 2, \ldots, N\}$$

$$V^h = \{v \in C^0(I) : v \in P_{k+1}(I_j), \ j = 1, \ldots, N, \ v(1) = 0\}$$

We note that S^h is a subspace of $L^2(I)$ (and we do not assume continuiity at the interior mesh points) and V^h is a subspace of $\overset{\circ}{H}(I)$; furthermore, you can check that:

$$\dim S^h = \dim V^h = N(k + 1)$$

The finite-dimensional semi-discrete scheme is defined as:

Find $u^h : [0, T] \to S^h$ such that

$$\left(\frac{\partial u^h}{\partial t}, v\right) - \left(au^h, \frac{\partial v}{\partial x}\right) = (f, v) + ag(t)v(0) \ \forall \ v \in V^h, \quad t > 0$$

$$(v^h(., 0), v) = (u_0, v) \quad \forall \ v \in S^h \text{ (Projection of } u_0 \text{ onto } S^h) \qquad (A2.18)$$

Theorem A2.3. *(Baker, 1975). Let u be the solution of (A2.14)–(A2.16). Then there is a constant C which is independent of h such that*

$$\sup_{0 \le t \le T} \|u - u^h\|(t) \le Ch^{k+1}$$

where u^h is the solution of system (A2.18).

Thus, we see that increasing the order k of the approximating polynomial space increases the accuracy of the scheme.

We now construct the corresponding system of ordinary differential equations for (A2.18) in the case $k = 0$. In this case S^h is the space of piecewise constant step functions. We then know from above that its dimension is $N(k + 1) = N$. Let $\{\varphi_j\}_{j=1}^N$ and $\{\psi_j\}_{j=1}^N$ be basis functions in S^h and V^h, respectively and given by

$$\varphi_j(x) = \begin{cases} 1, & \text{if } x \in (x_{j-1}, x_j) \\ 0, & \text{otherwise } j = 1, \ldots, N \end{cases}$$

and $\{\psi_j\}_{j=1}^N$ are linear hat functions. Thus, S^h is a space of constant step functions and V^h is a space of linear hat functions.

From (A2.18) we see that

$$\sum_{j=1}^N \left[\frac{du_j}{dt}(\varphi_j, \psi_k) - au_j(\varphi_j, \psi_k')\right] = (f, \psi_k) + ag(t)\psi_k(0)$$

and after having done some arithmetic, we see that

$$\frac{1}{2}\left(h_k\frac{\mathrm{d}u_k}{\mathrm{d}t} + h_{k+1}\frac{\mathrm{d}u_{k+1}}{\mathrm{d}t}\right) - a\left(u_k - u_{k+1}\right) = (f, \psi_k), \quad k = 2, \ldots, N - 1$$

$$\frac{h_1}{2}\frac{\mathrm{d}u_1}{\mathrm{d}t} + au_1 = (f, \psi_1) + ag\left(t\right), \quad k = 1$$

These equations represent a system of ordinary differential equations. In order to produce a unique solution we must specify initial conditions. These are given by the L^2 projection of u_0 onto the finite-dimensional space S^h

$$\left(u^h(., 0), \varphi_k\right) = (u_0, \varphi_k), \quad k = 1, \ldots, N$$

Since $u^h(x, 0) = \sum_{j=1}^{N} u_j(0)\varphi_j(x)$ the above projection becomes

$$u_j(0) = h_j^{-1}\int_{x_{j-1}}^{x_j} u_0(x)\,\mathrm{d}x, \quad j = 1, \ldots, N$$

In practice we calculate the integrals appearing above by some numerical integration technique. We have now constructed a system of ODEs that can be solved using standard time discretisation schemes.

A2.4.2 Stability and convergence

We now discuss the stability and convergence properties of another semi-discrete scheme from Dupont (1973). It is a traditional FEM scheme in the sense that we do not integrate by parts in the x direction. You may skip this section on a first reading.

We consider the scalar hyperbolic problem in two independent variables

$$\frac{\partial u}{\partial t} + Lu = f \tag{A2.19}$$

where L is a first-order linear operator defined by

$$Lu \equiv a\frac{\partial u}{\partial x}, \quad a > 0 \quad \text{constant}$$

We hope that the finite elements that are produced are 'close' to the true mathematical and physical interpretation of (A2.19). For example, if the mathematical problem satisfies the conservation of energy, then so will the discrete problem, and if energy is decreasing in the analytical problem, then it is also decreasing in the discrete case.

By multiplying equation (A2.19) on both sides by u and integrating, we get

$$\left(\frac{\partial u}{\partial t}, u\right) + (Lu, u) = 0$$

or

$$\frac{1}{2}\frac{\mathrm{d}}{\mathrm{d}t}\|u\|^2 + (Lu, u) = 0$$

where $\|u\|$ is the L_2 norm of u in the interval $(0, 1)$. If $(Lu, u) = 0$, then the equation is called conservative and if $(Lu, u) \leq 0$ it is called dissipative. In the latter case energy is decreasing.

Hyperbolic systems are either conservative or weakly dissipative, which means that energy leaks slowly out at the boundary.

We consider the initial boundary value problem (IBVP)(A2.14)–(A2.16) again and let us assume without loss of generality that $g(t) \equiv 0$.

We now define the space

$$S = \left\{ u : u, \frac{\partial u}{\partial x} \in L^2(I), \quad u(0) = 0 \right\}, \quad I = (0, 1)$$

Now, multiplying (A2.14) by some $v \in S$, we get

$$\left(\frac{\partial u}{\partial t}, v \right) + \left(a \frac{\partial u}{\partial x}, v \right) = (f, v) \tag{A2.20}$$

Lemma A2.1. *Let $u = u(x, t)$ be a solution of (A2.20), then*

$$\|u\| \leq C\{\|f\|_{L^2[0,T; L^2(I)]} + \|u_0\|\}$$

where

$$\|f\|_{L^2[0,T; L^2(I)]} = \left(\int_0^T \|f(., t)\|^2 \, dt \right)^{\frac{1}{2}}$$

Proof. Setting $v = u$ in (A2.20) we get

$$\left(\frac{\partial u}{\partial t}, u \right) + a \left(\frac{\partial u}{\partial x}, u \right) = (f, u)$$

or

$$\frac{1}{2} \frac{d}{dt} \|u\|^2 + au^2(1, t) = (f, u) \tag{A2.21}$$

We now use the Cauchy inequality

$$ab \leq \frac{\varepsilon}{2} a^2 + \frac{b^2}{2\varepsilon}, \quad \text{for any } \varepsilon > 0$$

applied to (A2.21) to get

$$\frac{1}{2} \frac{d}{dt} \|u^2\|(t) \leq \frac{\epsilon}{2} \|f\|^2(t) + \frac{1}{2\epsilon} \|u\|^2(t)$$

integrating this last equation from $t = 0$ to $t = \xi$, for some $\xi > 0$ gives

$$\sup_{0 < \xi \leq T} \|u\|^2(\xi) \leq \|u_0\|^2 + \epsilon \sup_{0 \leq \xi \leq T} \int_0^\xi \|f\|^2(t) \, dt + \epsilon^{-1} \sup_{0 \leq \xi \leq T} \int_0^\xi \|u\|^2(t) \, dt$$

$$= \|u_0\|^2 + \epsilon \int_0^T \|f\|^2(t) \, dt + \epsilon^{-1} \int_0^T \|u\|^2(t) \, dt$$

$$\leq \|u_0\|^2 + \epsilon \int_0^T \|f\|^2(t) \, dt + \epsilon^{-1} T \sup_{0 < \xi \leq T} \|u\|^2(\xi)$$

Choosing ϵ such that $\epsilon^{-1}T = \frac{1}{2}$ gives

$$\sup_{0 < \xi \le T} \|u\|^2(\xi) \le c_1(T)\{\|u_0\|^2 + \|f\|^2_{L^2[0,T;L^2(I)]}\}$$

$$\le C_1(T)\{\|u_0\| + \|f\|_{L^2[0,T_j L^2(I)]}\}^2$$

and the result of the lemma follows.

We now define the piecewise polynomial space

$$S^h = \{v : v \in C^o(I), \quad v|_{I_j} \in P_k(I_j), \quad j = 1, \ldots, N, \quad v(0) = 0\}$$

The Galerkin approximation (or the so-called semi-discrete finite element scheme) is defined by:

Find a function $u^h : [0, T] \rightarrow S^h$ such that

$$\left(\frac{\partial u^h}{\partial t}, v\right) + \left(a\frac{\partial u^h}{\partial x}, v\right) = (f, v) \quad \forall v \in S^h$$

$$\left(u^h(0) - u_0, v\right) = 0 \quad \forall v \in S^h$$

(A2.22)

The last equation in (A2.22) means that $u^h(0)$ is the L_2 projection of the function $u_0 = u_0(x)$ onto S^h.

Theorem A2.4. *Let u and u^h be the solutions of (A2.20) and (A2.22), respectively. Then*

$$\|u - u^h\|(t) \le Ch^{k-1}$$

where the constant C is independent of h.

For a proof of this theorem see Dupont (1973).

We now calculate the corresponding difference scheme which results from (A2.22) in the case of piecewise linear polynomials ($k = 1$) and constant mesh size. We set

$$u^h(x, t) = \sum_{j=1}^{N} u_j(t)\varphi_j(x),$$

where $\{\varphi_j\}_{j=1}^N$ are the piecewise linear 'hat' functions that form a basis for S^h. We can then write the variational formulation in (A2.22) as:

$$\sum_{j=1}^{N} \frac{du_j}{dt}(\varphi_j, \varphi_k) + a\sum_{j=1}^{N} u_j\left(\frac{d\varphi_j}{dx}, \varphi_k\right) = (f, \varphi_k), \quad k = 1, \ldots, N$$

or

$$\frac{h}{6}\left(\frac{du_{k-1}}{dt} + 4\frac{du_k}{dt} + \frac{du_{k+1}}{dt}\right) + a\left(\frac{u_{k+1} - u_{k-1}}{2}\right) = (f, \varphi_k), \quad k = 1, \ldots, N-1$$

and

$$\frac{h}{6}\left(\frac{du_{N-1}}{dt} + 2\frac{du_N}{dt}\right) + a\left(\frac{u_N - u_{N-1}}{2}\right) = (f, \varphi_N)$$

Initial conditions become

$$\sum_{j=1}^{N} u_j(0) \left(\varphi_j, \varphi_k \right) = (u_0, \varphi_k), \quad k = 1, \ldots, N \quad (L^2 \text{ projecting of } u_o)$$

We thus arrive at an IVP that we can solve using Crank–Nicolson, for example. We have already discussed this problem in section A2.3 (scheme (A2.13)).

A2.5   ONE-FACTOR BLACK–SCHOLES AND FEM

The finite element method presented in this appendix can be applied to the one-factor Black–Scholes equation.

$$-\frac{\partial u}{\partial t} + \frac{1}{2}\sigma^2 S^2 \frac{\partial^2 u}{\partial S^2} + rS\frac{\partial u}{\partial S} - ru = 0 \tag{A2.23}$$

A number of authors have applied FEM to solve this problem (Foufas *et al.*, 2004; Topper, 2005). The major challenge is to define suitable approximation spaces and to set up the continuous and approximate formulations of the problems. There are numerous solutions but we focus on one approach, taken from Wheeler (1975) for parabolic problems in a single variable. Similar schemes were used in Duffy (1977) for hyperbolic systems of equations. A short overview has already been given in section A2.4.1. The results of the following discussion include conclusions that are applicable to the Black–Scholes equation. To this end, define the invervals and the operator

$$Lu \equiv \frac{\partial}{\partial x}\left[a(x)\frac{\partial u}{\partial x}\right] - b(x)\frac{\partial u}{\partial x} + c(x)u \tag{A2.24}$$

where $I = (0, 1)$, and $J = (0, T)$.

We wish to find a function u such that

$$\frac{\partial u}{\partial t} + Lu = f \quad \text{in } Q = I \times J.$$

This model is reasonably generic and includes many special and interesting cases from real life applications. It is a model for Black–Scholes even though the elliptic operator L in (A2.24) is written differently from what we are used to in the financial literature. The reader can check that the Black–Scholes equation (A2.23) is consistent with (A2.24) if we define the coefficients a and b by:

$$a = \tfrac{1}{2}\sigma^2 S^2$$

$$b = (\sigma^2 - r)S$$

We also assume that the elliptic problem:

$$Ly = g, \quad \text{where } g \in C(I)$$

$$y(0) = y(1) = 0 \tag{A2.25}$$

has a unique solution. Here $C(I)$ is the set of continuous functions on I. Furthermore, we assume that the coefficient $a(x)$ satisfies:

$$0 < \alpha_0 \le a(x) \le \alpha_1$$

This inequality is not true in the case of Black–Scholes (A2.23) but it can be resolved by the change of variables $x = \log(S)$, and we then get a modified PDE resulting in:

$$-\frac{\partial u}{\partial t} + \frac{1}{2}\sigma^2 \frac{\partial^2 u}{\partial x^2} + \left(r - \frac{1}{2}\sigma^2\right)\frac{\partial u}{\partial x} - ru = 0 \qquad (A2.26)$$

We now get down to the business. We define the so-called H^{-1} Galerkin formulation polynomials. Using the notation as in section A2.2 we define the space:

$$S^h(-1, r, \delta) \equiv \{v | v \in P_r(I_j), \quad j = 1, \ldots, N\}$$

This is the space of functions that are piecewise polynomials of degree r on each sub-interval. They are not necessarily continuous across internal boundaries. We also define the space:

$$S^h(k, r, \delta) = \{v \in C^k(I) | v \in P_r(I_j), \quad j = 1, \ldots, N\}$$

Finally, let us define for convenience the spaces:

$$S^h = S^h(k, r, \delta) \quad \text{for } k \ge -1$$
$$V^h = S^h(k + 2, r + 2, \delta) \cap H_0^1(I)$$

where

$$H_0^1(I) = H^1(I) \cap \{v : v(0) = v(1) = 0\}$$

We are now ready to formulate the semi-discrete problem:

Find $U : [0, T] \rightarrow S^h$ such that

$$\left(\frac{\partial U}{\partial t}, v\right) = \left(U, L^*v\right) + (f, v) \quad \forall v \in V^h, \quad t \in J \qquad (A2.27)$$

with $U(\cdot, 0)$ appropriately defined, usually a projection of $u(x, 0)$ onto S^h. Here L^* is the adjoint operator of the operator L.

It can be shown that this schemes give high-order accuracy (Wheeler, 1975). It can be discretised in time to give a fully discrete scheme, for example implicit Euler:

Find $\{U^n\}_{n=0}^{N}$ such that

$$\left(\frac{U^{n+1} - U^n}{k}, v\right) = \left(U^{n+1}, L^*v\right) + \left(f^{n+1}, v\right) \quad \forall v \in V^h \qquad (A2.28)$$
$$U^0 \sim u_0$$

Building the system of equations from equation (A2.28) takes place as in previous sections.

A2.6   COMPARING AND CONTRASTING FEM AND FDM

There are many similarities between the finite element method and the finite difference method. Since they both address the same kinds of issues and problems in financial engineering the reader might be wondering which method to use in general or in a particular context. There is no black and white answer, but we shall try to give some answers.

- *Learning curve*: This is steeper with FEM than with FDM. Some people see FEM as a branch of applied functional analysis and they use concepts such as Hilbert and Sobolev spaces, variational formulations and domain triangulation in their work. FDM is easier because it just replaces derivatives by divided differences. FEM has its roots in engineering and structural analysis. It is also extremely useful for integral equations.
- *Accuracy*: In theory, higher order accuracy is possible with FEM but we must construct piecewise polynomial spaces of higher degree. We get 'polynomial snaking' effects, which means that the number of sub-intervals where the piecewise basis polynomial is non-zero increases with the degree of the polynomial.

Since FEM is an integral formulation it is better at approximating discontinuous coefficients than FDM.

- *Multi-factor problems*: FEM suffers from the same 'curse of dimensionality' as FDM does. Three dimensions is the limit (it would seem), after which things tend to become intractable. A possible cure for this problem is to use Meshless or some form of operator splitting.
- *Domain of integration*: FEM is particularly good at modelling problems with irregular domains, while FDM has difficulties with such domains. On the other hand, most problems in financial engineering are defined in boxes and cubes.

A2.7   SUMMARY AND CONCLUSIONS

We have given an introduction to the finite element method (FEM). We have included this appendix because FEM has many similarities with FDM and is needed in other applications in which variational or integral formulations are used – for example, free and moving boundary value problems, as discussed in this book.

Finally, we hope that the reader will be able to appreciate what FEM can mean for his or her applications in the years to come.

Bibliography

Abramowitz, M. and Stegun, I.A. (1972) *Handbook of Mathematical Functions*. Dover, New York.

Adams, R.A. (1975) *Sobolev Spaces*. Academic Press, New York.

de Allen, D. and Southwell, R. (1955) *Relaxation methods applied to determining the motion, in two dimensions, of a viscous fluid past a fixed cylinder. Quart. J. Mech. Appl. Math.*, 129–145.

Andersen, L. and Andreasen, J. (2000) *Jump–diffusion processes: Volatility smile fitting and numerical methods for option pricing. Rev. Operat. Res.* **4**, 231–262.

Andreasen, J. (2001) *Turbo Charging the Cheyette Model, Working paper*, Bank of America, London.

Arbib, M. (ed.) (1998) *The Handbook of Brain Theory and Neural Networks*. MIT Press, Cambridge, MA.

Ayache, E., Forsyth, P.A. and Vetzal, A.R. (2002) *Next generation models for convertible bonds with credit risk. Wilmott J.*, December.

Aziz, A.K. (ed.) (1972) *The Mathematical Foundations of the Finite Element Method with Applications to Partial Differential Equations*. Academic Press, New York.

Baiocchi, C. (1972) *Su un problema di frontiera libera a questioni di idrualica. Ann. Mat. Pura Applic.*, **92** (4), 107–127.

Baiocchi, C. and Pozzi, G.A. (1977) *Error estimates and free boundary convergence for a finite difference discretisation of a parabolic variational inequality. Rev. Franc. Autom. Info. Rech. Opt. Anal.*, **11**, 315–340.

Baiocchi, C. and Capelo, A. (1984) *Variational and Quasivariational Inequalities: Applications to Free Boundary Problems*. John Wiley & Sons, New York.

Baker, G.A. (1975) *A finite element method for first-order hyperbolic equations. Math. Comp.*, **29**, 995–1006.

Bank, R.E., Rose, D.J. and Fichtner, W. (1983) *Numerical simulation of hot-electron phenomena. SIAM J. Scient. Statist. Comp.*, 4 (3, September).

Bates, D.S. (1991) *The crash of '87: Was it expected? The evidence from options markets. J. Finance*, **XLVI** (3, July).

Bates, D.S. (1996) *Jumps and stochastic volatility: Exchange rate processes implicit Deutsche Mark options. Rev. Finan. Stud.*, **9** (1, Spring).

Bear, J. (1979) *Hydraulics of Groundwater Flow*. McGraw-Hill, New York.

Bensoussan, A. and Lions, J.L. (1978) *Applications des inéquations variationnelles en contrôle stochastique*. Dunod, Paris.

Bhansali, V. (1998) *Pricing and Managing Exotic and Hybrid Options*. McGraw-Hill Irwin Library Series, New York.

Bhar, R., Chiarella, C., El-Hassan, N. and Zheng, X. (2000) *The reduction of forward rate dependent volatility HJM models to Markovian form: Pricing European bond options. J. Comput. Finan.*, **3** (3, Spring).

Black, F. and Scholes, M. (1973) *The pricing of options and corporate liabilities. J. Polit. Econ.*, **81**, 637–659.

Black, F., Derman, E. and Toy, W. (1987) *A one-factor model of interest rates and its applications to Treasury Bond options. Finan. Anal. J.*, 33–39.

Bird, R.B., Stewart, W.E. and Lightfoot, E.N. (1980) *Transport Phenomena*. John Wiley & Sons, New York.

Bobisud, L. (1967) *Second-order linear parabolic equations with a small parameter. Arch. Ration. Mech. Anal.*, **27**.

Boyarchenko, S. and Levendorskii, S. (2002) *Barrier options and touch-and-out options under regular Levy processes of exponential type*. Working paper.

Boyle, P. (1986) *Option valuation using a three jump process. Internat. Options J.*, **3**, 7–12.

Boyle, P. and Lau, S.H. (1994) *Bumping up against the barrier with the binomial method. J. Derivatives*, **1** (4), 6–14.

Boztosun, I. and Charafi, A. (2002) *An analysis of the linear advection–diffusion equation using mesh-free and mesh-dependent methods. Engin. Anal. with Bound. Elem.*, **26**, 889–895.

Brennan, M.J. and Schwartz, E.S. (1979) *A continuous time approach to the pricing of bonds. J. Bank. Finan.*, **3**, 135–155.

Briani, M., La Chioma, C. and Natalini, R. (2004) *Convergence of numerical schemes for viscosity solutions to integro-differential degenerate parabolic problems arising in financial theory. Numer. Math.*, **98** (4), 607–646.

Broadie, M., Glasserman, P. A. and Kou, S. (1997) *Continuity correction for discrete barrier options. Math. Finan.*, **7** (4).

Bronson, R. (1989) *Theory and Problems of Matrix Operations*. Schaum's Outline Series, McGraw-Hill, New York.

Cao, L.M. and Tran-Cong, T. (2003) *Solving Time-Dependent PDEs with a Meshless IRBFN-Based Method. International Workshop on Meshfree Methods*.

Carr, P. and Chou, A. (1997) *Hedging Complex Barrier Options*. Working paper.

Carr, P. and Madan, D.B. (1999) *Option valuation using the fast Fourier transform. J. Comput. Finan.*, **2** (4, Summer).

Carrier, G.F. and Pearson, C.E. (1976) *Partial Differential Equations, Theory and Technique*. Academic Press, New York.

Carslaw, H.S. and Jaeger, J.C. (1965) *Conduction of Heat in Solids*. Clarendon Press, Oxford.

Carverhill, A.P. (1995) *A simplified exposition of the Heath–Jarrow–Morton model. Stoch. Stoch. Rep.*, **53**, 227–240.

Cheyette, O. (1992) *Markov Representation of the Heath–Jarrow–Morton Model*, Working paper, BARRA.

La Chioma, C. (2003) *Integro-differential problems arising in pricing derivatives in jump-diffusion markets*. PhD thesis, Rome University.

Clewlow, L. and Strickland, C. (1998) *Implementing Derivatives Models*. John Wiley & Sons, Chichester, UK.

Clough, R.W. (1960) *The finite element method in plane stress analysis. Proc. 2nd ASCE Conf. on Electronic Computation*. Pittsburgh, PA, September 8–9.

Cochran, J.A. (1972) *The Analysis of Linear Integral Equations*. McGraw-Hill, New York.

Constanda, C. (2002) *Solution Techniques for Elementary Partial Differential Equations*. Chapman & Hall/CRC, Boca Raton.

Cont, R. and Voltchkova, E. (2003) *A Finite Difference Scheme for Option Pricing in Jump Diffusion and Exponential Levy Models*. Internal Report CMAP, number 513, September.

Conte, R. and de Boor, C. (1980) *Elementary Numerical Analysis. An Algorithmic Approach*. McGraw-Hill, New Auckland.

Cooney, M. (1999) *Benchmarking numerical solutions of European options to the Black–Scholes partial differential equation*. MSc thesis, Trinity College, Dublin, Ireland.

Cooney, M. (2000) *Report on the accuracy and efficiency of the fitted methods for solving the Black–Scholes equation for European and American options*. Working report, Datasim Education Ltd, Dublin.

Courant, R. (1943) *Variational methods for the solution of problems of equilibrium and vibrations. Bull. Am. Math. Soc.*, **49**, 1–23.

Courant, R. and Hilbert, D. (1968) *Methoden der Mathematischen Physik II*. Springer-Verlag, Berlin.

Cox, J.C., Ingersoll, J.E. and Ross, S.A. (1985) *A theory of the term structure of interest rates. Econometrica*, **53**, 385–407.

Craddock, M., Heath, D. and Platen, E. (2000) *Numerical inversion of Laplace transforms: A survey of techniques with applications to derivative pricing. J. Comput. Finan.*, **4** (1, Fall).

Crandall, M.G., Ishi, H. and Lions, P.L. (1992) *User's guide to viscosity solutions of second order partial differential equations. Bull. Am. Math. Soc.*, **27** (1, July), 1–67.

Crank, J. (1964) *The Mathematics of Diffusion.* Clarendon Press, Oxford.

Crank, J. (1984) *Free and Moving Boundary Problems.* Clarendon Press, Oxford.

Cryer, C. (1979) *Successive overrelaxation methods for solving linear complementarity problems arising from free boundary value problems.* Presented at a seminar held in Pavia (Italy), September–October 1979, Roma 1980.

Crouzeix, M. (1975) *Sur l'approximation des equations différentielles opérationnelles linéaires par des methods de RUNGE–KUTTA. PhD thesis*, University Paris VI.

Dahlquist, G. (1974) *Numerical Methods.* Prentice-Hall, Englewood Cliffs, NJ.

Dautray, R. and Lions, J.L. (1983) *Mathematical Analysis and Numerical Methods for Science and Engineering. Volume 6, Evolution Equations III.* Springer, Berlin.

Davis, P.J. (1975) *Interpolation and Approximation.* Dover, New York.

de Bruin, M.G. and Van Rossum, H. (eds) (1980) *Padé Approximation and its Applications.* Springer-Verlag, Berlin.

Dennis, S.C.R. and Hudson, J.D. (1980) *Further accurate representations of partial differential equations by finite-difference methods. J. Inst. Maths. Applic.*, pp. 369–379.

D'Halluin, Y., Forsyth, P.A. and Vetzal, K.R. (2004) *Robust numerical methods for contingent claims under jump diffusion processes.* Working paper, University of Waterloo.

Dixit, A.K. and Pindyck, R.S. (1994) *Investment Under Uncertainty.* Princeton University Press.

Doob, J.L. (1942) *The Brownian movement and stochastic equations. Ann. Math.*, **43**, 351–369.

Douglas, J. Jr and Rachford, H.H. (1955) *On the numerical solution of heat conduction equations in two and three dimensions. Trans. Am. Math. Assoc.*, **82**, 421–439.

Duff, I., Erisman, A. and Reid, J. (1990) *Direct Methods for Sparse Matrices.* Clarendon Press, Oxford.

Du Plessis, N. (1970) *An Introduction to Potential Theory.* Oliver & Boyd, Edinburgh.

Duffy, D.J. (1977) *Finite elements for mixed initial boundary value problems for hyperbolic systems of equations.* MSc thesis, Trinity College, Dublin, Ireland.

Duffy, D.J. (1980) *Uniformly convergent difference schemes for problems with a small parameter in the leading derivative.* PhD thesis, Trinity College, Dublin, Ireland.

Duffy, D.J. (2004) *Financial Instrument Pricing in C++.* John Wiley & Sons, Chichester.

Duffy, D.J. (2004A) *A critique of the Crank–Nicolson scheme, strengths and weaknesses for financial instrument pricing. Wilmott Mag.*, July 2004.

Dupont, T. (1973) *Galerkin methods for first order hyperbolics: An example. SIAM J. Numer. Anal.*, **10**, 890–899.

Dutton, J.A. (1986) *Dynamics of Atmospheric Motion.* Dover, New York.

D'yakonov, E.G. (1962) *Difference schemes with split operators for unsteady equations* (Russian). *Dokl. Akad. Nauk. SSSR*, **144** (1), 29–32.

D'yakonov, E.G. (1963a) *Difference schemes for solving the boundary problems. USSR Comp. Math.*, **3** (1), 55–77.

D'yakonov, E.G. (1963b) *Difference Schemes with split operators for multidimensional unsteady problems USSR Comp. Math.*, **3** (4), 581–607.

D'yakonov, E.G. (1964) *Difference Schemes with split operators for general parabolic equations of second order with variable coefficients. USSR Comp. Math.*, **4** (2), 91–110.

Farrell, P. et al. (2000) *Robust Computational Techniques for Boundary Layers.* Chapman and Hall/CRC Bota Raton.

Fasshauer, G.E., Khaliq, A.Q.M. and Voss D.A. (2003) *Using meshfree approximation for multi-asset American option problems.* Working paper.

Faulhaber, O. (2002) *Analytic methods for pricing double barrier options in the presence of stochastic volatility.* PhD thesis, University of Kaiserslautern, Germany.

Foufas, G. and Larson, M.G. (2004) *Valuing European, barrier, and lookback options using the finite element method and duality techniques.* Working paper, Chalmers University.

Fraser, D.A. (1986) *The Physics of Semiconductor Devices.* Clarendon Press, Oxford.

Friedman, A. (1979) *Time dependent free boundary problems. SIAM Rev.*, **21** (2, April).

Friedman, A. (1982) *Variational Principles and Free-Boundary Problems.* John Wiley & Sons, New York.

Friedman, A. (1983) *Partial Differential Equations of Parabolic Type*. Robert E. Krieger Publishing Co., Huntington, NY.

Friedrichs, K.O. (1958) *Symmetric positive linear differential equations. Comm. Pure Appl. Math.*, **XI**, 333–418.

Fu, M.C., Madan, D.B. and Wang, T. (1998) *Pricing continuous Asian options: A comparison of Monte Carlo and Laplace transform inversion methods. J. Comp. Finan.*, **2** (2, Winter 1998/1999).

Fusai, G. (2004) *Pricing Asian options via Fourier and Laplace transforms. J. Comp. Finan.*, **7** (3, Spring).

Geman, H. and Yor, M. (1996) *Pricing and hedging double barrier options. Math. Finan.*, **6**, 365–378.

George, P.L. (1991) *Automatic Mesh Generation, Application to the Finite Element Method*. John Wiley & Sons, Chichester.

Gerschgorin, S. (1931) *Über die Abrenzung der Eigenwerte einer Matriz. Izv. Akad. Nauk SSSR Ser. Mat.*, **7**, 749–754; **16**, 22, 25.

Gibson, R., L'Habitant, F.S. and Talay, D. (2001) *Modeling the term structure of interest rates: A review of the literature*. Working paper, June 2001.

Glowinski, R., Lions, J.L. and Trémoliéres (1981) *Numerical Analysis of Variational Inequalities*. North-Holland Amsterdam.

Godounov, S. (1973) *Equations of Mathematical Physics* MIR Moscow (in French).

Godounov, S. et al. (1979) *Numerical Resolution of multidimensional Problems in Gas Dynamics*. MIR Moscow (in French).

Godunov, S. and Riabenki. V.S. (1987) *Difference Schemes, An Introduction to the underlying Theory*. North-Holland Amsterdam.

GOF: Gamma, E., Helm, R., Johnson, R., Vlissides, J. (1995) *Design Patterns, Elements of Reusable Object-Oriented Software*. Addison-Wesley, Reading, MA.

Golberg, M.A. (ed.) (1979) *Solution Methods for Integral Equations*. Plenum Press, New York.

Goldberg, S. (1966) *Unbounded Linear Operators Theory and Applications*. Dover Publications Inc., New York.

Goldberg, S. (1986) *Introduction to Difference Equations*. Dover Publications Inc., New York.

Golub, G. and Van Loan, C.F. (1996) *Matrix Computations* (3rd edition). Johns Hopkins University Press.

Gourlay, A.R. (1970) *Hopscotch: A fast second-order partial differential equation solver. J. Inst. Math. Applic.*, **6**, 375–390.

Gourlay, A.R. and Morris, J.Ll. (1980) *The extrapolation of first order methods for parabolic partial differential equations II. SIAM. J. Numer. Anal.*, **17** (5, October).

Greenspan, D. (1966) *Introductory Numerical Analysis of Elliptic Boundary Value Problems*. Harper & Row, New York.

Gushchin, V.A. and Shcennikov, V.V. (1974) *A monotone difference scheme of second-order accuracy. Zh. vychisl. Mat. Mat. Fiz.*, **14** (3), 789–792.

Gustafsson, B., Kreiss, H.O. and Sundström, A. (1972) *Stability theory of difference approximations for mixed initial boundary value problems, II. Math. Comp.*, **26** (119, July).

Haaser, N.B. and Sullivan, J.A. (1991) *Real Analysis*. Dover, New York.

Hardy, R.L. (1971) *Multiquadric equations of topography and other irregular surfaces J. Geophysics Res.*, **176**, 1905–1915.

Hardy, R.L. (1990) *Theory and applications of the multiquadric-biharmoinc method: 20 years of discovery Comp. Math. Applic.*, **19** (8/9), 163–208.

Haug, E. (1998) *The Complete Guide to Option Pricing Formulas*. McGraw-Hill, New York.

Heath, D., Jarrow, R. and Morton, A. (1992) *Bond pricing and the term structure of interest rates: A new methodology for contingent clam valuation econometrica*, **60**, 77–105.

Heston, S.L. (1993) *A closed-form solution for options with stochastic volatility with applications to bond and currency options. Rev. Financ. Stud.*, **6** (2), 327–343.

Heston, S. and Zhou, G. (2000) *On the rate of convergence of discrete-time contingent clams. Math. Finan.*, **10**, 53–75.

Hill, J.M. (1987) *One-Dimensional Stefan Problems: An Introduction*. Longman Scientific & Technical, Harlow.

Hille, E. and Philips, R.S. (1957) *Functional analysis and semi-groups. Am. Math. Soc. Colloq. Publ.*, Vol. 31, Providence, RI.

Hochstadt, H. (1964) *Differential Equations*. Dover Publications Inc., New York.

Hsu, H. (1997) *Probability, Random Variables and Random Processes*. Schaum's Outline Series. McGraw-Hill, New York.

Hughes, T.J.R. (2000) *The Finite Element Method, Linear Static and Dynamic Finite Element Analysis*. Dover, New York.

Hull, J. and White, A. (1993) *One factor interest rate models and the valuation of interest rate derivative securities*. J. Finan. Quant. Anal., **28** (2, June) 235–254.

Hull, J. and White, A. (1994) *Numerical procedures for implementing term structure models I: single factor models*. J. Derivatives, Fall, pp. 7–16.

Hull, J. and White, A. (1994b) *Numerical procedures for implementing term structure models II: two factor models*. J. Derivatives, Winter, pp. 37–49.

Hui. C.H. (1997) *Time-dependent barrier option values*. J. Futures Markets, **17** (6), 667–688.

Hull, J. (2000) *Options, Futures and other Derivative Securities*. Prentice-Hall, Englewood Cliffs, NJ.

Hundsdorfer, W. and Verwer, J.G. (2003) *Numerical Solution of Time-Dependent Advection-Diffusion-Reaction Equations*. Springer, Berlin.

Huyakorn, P.S. and Pinder, G.F. (1983) *Computational Methods in Subsurface Flow*. Academic Press, Orlando.

Ikebe, Y. (1972) *The Galerkin method for the numerical solution of Fredholm integral equations of the second kind*. SIAM Rev., **14** (2, July).

Ikeda, T. (1983) *Maximum Principle in Finite Element Models for Convection-Diffusion Phenomena*. North-Holland Publishing Co., Amsterdam.

Ikonen, S. and Toivanen, J. (2004) *Operator Splitting Methods for American Options with Stochastic Volatility*. European Congress on Computational Methods in Applied Sciences and Engineering.

Il'in, A.M. (1969) *Differencing scheme for a differential equation with a small parameter affecting the highest derivative*. Mat. Zam., **6**, 237–248.

Il'lin, A.M, Kalashnikov, A.S. and Oleinik, O.A. (1962) *Linear Equations of the Second Order of Parabolic Type* (translation). Russian Mathematical Surveys.

Ingersoll, J.E. (1987) *Theory of Financial Decision Making*. Rowman & Littlewood.

Insley, M.C. and Rollins, K. (2002) *Real options in harvesting decisions on publicly owned forest lands*. Working paper, University of Waterloo, Canada.

Isaacson, E. and Keller, H. (1966) *Analysis of Numerical Methods*. John Wiley & Sons, New York.

Jaillet, P., Lamberton, D. and Lapeyre, B. (1988) *Variational Inequalities and the Pricing of American Options*. Internal report, CERMA-ENPC, La Courtine.

Jamet, P. (1970) *On the convergence of finite-difference approximations to one-dimensional singular boundary-value problems*. Numer. Math., **14**, 355–378.

Jarrow, R. and Turnbull, S. (1996) *Derivative Securities*. South-Western College Publishing, Cincinnati, Ohio.

Kansa, E.J. and Carlson, R.E. (1995) *Radial basis functions: A class of grid-free scattered data approximations*. J. Comp. Fluid. Dynam., **3** (4), 489–496.

Kangro, R. and Nicolaides, R. (2000) *Far field conditions for Black–Scholes equations*. SIAM J. Numer. Anal., **38** (4), 1357–1368.

Karatzas, I. and Shreve, S.E. (1991) *Brownian Motion and Stochastic Calculus*. Springer, New York.

Karlsen, K.H. and Risebro, N.H. (2000) *Corrected operator splitting for nonlinear parabolic equations*. SIAM J. Numer. Anal., **37** (3), 980–1003.

Keller, H. (1968) *Numerical Methods for Two-Point Boundary-Value Problems*. Blaisdell Publishing Company, Waltham.

Keller, H. (1971) *A new difference scheme for parabolic problems*. In B. Hubbard (ed.), *Numerical Solution of Partial Differential Equations–II*. Academic Press, New York.

Keller, H. (1992) *Numerical Methods for Two-Point Boundary-Value Problems*. Dover, New York (2nd edition, additional chapters compared to first edition).

Kinsler, L.E., Frey, A.R., Coppins, A.B. and Saunders, J.V. (1982) *Fundamentals of Acoustics* (3rd edition). John Wiley & Sons, New York.

Kloeden, P., Platen, E. and Schurz, H. (1994) *Numerical Solution of SDE Through Computer Experiments*. Springer, Berlin.

Kloeden, P., Platen, E. and Schurz, H. (1995) *Numerical Solution of Stochastic Differential Equations*. Springer, Berlin.

Kluge, T. (2002) *Pricing derivatives in stochastic volatility models using the finite difference method.* Diploma thesis, Technical University, Chemnitz.

Koc, M.B., Boztosun, I. and Boztosun, D. (2003) *On the Numerical Solution of Black–Scholes Equation.* International Workshop on Meshfree Methods.

Kou, S.G. (2003) *On pricing of discrete barrier options. Statistica Sinica*, **13**, 955–964.

Kreider, D.L., Kuller, R.G., Ostberg, D.R. and Perkins, F.W. (1966) *An Introduction to Linear Analysis.* Addison-Wesley, Reading, MA.

Kreiss, H.O., Thome, V. and Widlund, O. (1970) *Smoothing of initial data and rates of convergence for parabolic difference equations. Comm. Pure Appl. Math.* **23**, 241–259.

Kress, R. (1989) *Linear Integral Equations.* Springer, Berlin.

Kunitomo, N. and Ikeda, M. (1992) *Pricing options with curved boundaries. Math. Finan.*, **2** (4), 275–298.

Landau, H.G. (1950) *Heat conduction in a melting solid. Quart. Appl. Math.*, **8**, 81–94.

Larsson, S., Thomée, V. and Wahlbin, L.B. (1998) *Numerical solution of parabolic integro-differential equations by the discontinuous Galerkin method. Math. Comp.*, **67** (221, January), 45–71.

Lawson, J.D. and Morris, J.Ll. (1978) *The extrapolation of first order methods for parabolic partial differential equations, I. SIAM. J. Numer. Anal.*, **15** (6, December).

Ladyženskaja, O.A., Solonnikov, V.A. and Ural'ceva, N.N. (1988) *Linear and Quasi-linear Equations of Parabolic Type.* American Mathematical Society.

Lax, P. (1973) *Hyperbolic Systems of Conversation Laws and the Mathematical Theory of Shock Waves.* SIAM, Philadelphia.

Leisen, D.P.J. (1999) *Valuation of barrier options in a Black–Scholes setup with jump risk. Europ. Finan. Rev.*, **3**, 319–342.

Le Roux, M.N. (1979) *Approximation d'équations paraboliques par de méthodes multipas á pas variables*, PhD thesis, University Paris VI.

Lesaint, P. and Raviart, P.A. (1974) *On a finite element method for solving the neutron transport equation.* In C. de Boor (ed.), *Mathematical aspects of finite elements in partial differential equations.* Academic Press, New York.

Levin, A. and Duffy, D.J. (2000) *Two-factor Gaussian term structure: Analytics, historical fit and stable finite-difference pricing schemes.* Paper presented at Courant Institute Financial Seminars New York University.

Lions, J.L. (1971) *Optimal Control of Systems Governed by Partial Differential Equations.* Springer, Berlin.

Lo, V.S.F. (1997) *Boundary hitting time distributions of one-dimensional diffusion processes.* PhD thesis, Statistical Laboratory, University of Cambridge.

Lotka, A.J. (1956) *Elements of Mathematical Biology.* Dover, New York.

Magenes, E. (1972) *Su alcuni problemi di frontiera libera connessi con il comportamento dei fluidi nei mezzi porosi.* Pubblicazioni N. 27, Laboratoria di Analis Numerica, Pavia, Italy.

Meirmanov, A.M. (1992) *The Stefan Problem.* Walter de Gruyter, Berlin.

Merton, R. (1973) *Theory of rational option pricing. Bell J. Econ. Manage. Sci.*, **4**, 141–183.

Merton, R. (1976) *Option pricing when underlying stock returns are discontinuous. J. Financ. Econ.*, 125–144, May.

Mikosch, T. (1998) *Elementary Stochastic Calculus.* World Scientific, Singapore.

Mirani, R. (2002) *Application of Duffy's finite difference method to barrier options.* Working paper, Datasim BV.

Mirani, R. (2002b) *Exponentially fitted schemes for Asian options*, Working paper, Datasim BV.

Mitchell, A.R. and Griffiths, D.F. (1980) *The Finite Difference Method in Partial Differential Equations.* John Wiley & Sons, Chichester, UK.

Moore, R.E. (1966) *Interval Analysis.* Prentice-Hall, Englewood Cliffs, NJ.

Moore, R.E. (1979) *Methods and Analysis of Interval Analysis.* SIAM, Philadelphia.

Morton, K.W. (1996) *Numerical Solution of Convection-Diffusion Problems.* Chapman and Hall, London.

Mun, J. (2002) *Real Options Analysis.* John Wiley & Sons, New Jersey.

Nelken, I. (1995) *Handbook of Exotic Options.* Probus, Chicago, IL.

Nielson, B.F., Skavhaug, O. and Tvelto, A. (2002) *Penalty and front-fixing methods for the numerical solution of American option problems. J. Comp. Finan.*, **5** (4, Summer).

Ockendon, J.R. and Hodgkins, W.R. (1975) *Moving Boundary Value Problems in Heat Flow and Diffusion.* Clarendon Press, Oxford.

Øksendal, B. (1998) *Stochastic Differential Equations*. Springer, Berlin.

Øksendal, B. and Sulem, A. (2005) *Applied Stochastic Control of Jump Diffusions*. Springer, Berlin.

Oosterloo, C.W. (2003) *On multigrid for linear complementarity problems with applications to American-style options. Electronic Transactions on Numerical Analysis* (Vol. 15, pp. 165–185). Kent State University.

Pao, C.V. (1992) *Nonlinear Parabolic and Elliptic Equations*. Plenum Press, New York.

Peaceman, D. (1977) *Fundamentals of Numerical Reservoir Simulation*. Elsevier, Amsterdam.

Petrovsky, I.G. (1991) *Lectures on Partial Differential Equations*. Dover Publications, New York.

Pilipović, D. (1998) *Energy Risk*. McGraw-Hill, New York.

Press, W.H., Teukolsky, S.A., Vetterling, W.T. and Flannery, B.P. (2002) *Numerical Recipes in C++*. Cambridge University Press.

Rannacher, R. (1984) *Finite element solution of diffusion problems with irregular data. Numer. Math.*, **43**, 309–327.

Rhee, H., Aris, R. and Amundsen, N.R. (1986) *First-Order Partial Differential Equations, Volume I*. Dover Publications, New York.

Rhee, H., Aris, R. and Amundsen, N.R. (1989) *First-Order Partial Differential Equations, Volume II*. Dover Publications, New York.

Rich, D.R. (1994) *The mathematical foundations of barrier option-pricing theory. Adv. Futures Options Res.*, **7**, 267–311.

Richard, S. (1978) *An arbitrage model of the term structure of interest rates. J. Finan. Econ.*, **6**, 33–57.

Richtmyer, R.D. and Morton, K.W. (1967) *Difference Methods for Initial-Value Problems*. Interscience Publishers (John Wiley), New York.

Ritchken, P. (1995) *On pricing barrier options. J. Derivatives*, Winter.

Roache, P. (1998) *Fundamentals of Computational Fluid Dynamics*. Hermosa Publishers, Alburquerque.

Roscoe, D.F. (1975) *New methods for the derivation of stable difference representations for differential equations. J. Inst. Math. Applic.*, **16**, 291–301.

Rothe, E. (1931) *Wärmeleitungsgleichung mit nichtkonstanten Koeffizienten. Math. Ann.*, **104**, 340–362.

Rubinstein, L.I. (1971) *The Stefan Problem Translations of Mathematical Monographs*, Vol. 27. Am. Math. Soc., Providence, RI.

Rudd, M. and Schmidt, K. (2002) *Variational inequalities of elliptic and parabolic type. Taiwan. J. Math.*, **6** (3), 287–322.

Rudin, W. (1964) *Principles of Mathematical Analysis*. McGraw-Hill, New York.

Rudin, W. (1970) *Real and Complex Analysis*. McGraw-Hill, New York.

Samarski, A.A. (1971) *Introduction to the Theory of Difference Schemes*. Nauka, Moscow.

Saulyev, V.K. (1964) *Integration of Equations of Parabolic Type by the Method of Nets*. Pergamon Press, Oxford.

Scales, L.E. (1985) *Introduction to Non-linear Optimization*. Macmillan, London.

Schwarz, E. (1982) *The pricing of commodity linked bonds. J. Finan.*, **37**, 525–539.

Scott, L.O. (1997) *Pricing stock options in a jump-diffusion model with stochastic volatility and interest rates: Applications of Fourier inversion methods. Math. Finan.*, **7** (4, October), 413–426.

SIAM (1983) *Proc Conf. on Numerical Simulation of VLSI Devices*, September 1983, Volume 4, Number 3.

Smith, G.D. (1978) *Numerical Solution of Partial Differential Equations: Finite Difference Methods*. Clarendon Press, Oxford.

Spiegel. M. (1969) *Theory and Problems of Real Variables, Lebesgue Measure and Integration*. Schaum's Outline Series. McGraw-Hill, London.

Spiegel, M. (1999) *Complex Variables*. Schaum's Outline Series. McGraw-Hill, London.

Steinberg, M. (2003) *Pricing of discrete barrier options*. MSc thesis, Kellogg College, Oxford.

Stoer, J. and Bulirsch, R. (1980) *Introduction to Numerical Analysis*. Springer-Verlag, New York.

Strang, G. and Fix, G. (1973) *An Analysis of the Finite Element Method*. Prentice-Hall, Englewood Cliffs, NJ.

Stulz, R.W. (1982) *Options on the minimum or the maximum of two risky assets: Analysis and application J. Finan. Econ.*, **10**, 161–185.

Sun, Y. (1999) *High order methods for evaluating convertible bonds*. PhD thesis, University of North Carolina.

Synge, J.L. (1952) *Triangulation in the hypercircle method for plane problems. Proc. R. Irish Acad.*, Vol. 54A21.

Synge, J.L. (1957) *The Hypercircle Method in Mathematical Physics*. Cambridge University Press, UK.

Tangmanee, S. (1977) *Finite element approximation to mixed initial boundary value problems for first order hyperbolic systems*. PhD thesis, Trinity College, Dublin.

Tavella, D. and Randall, C. (2000) *Pricing Financial Instruments, The Finite Difference Method*. John Wiley & Sons, New York.

Tolstov, G. (1962) *Fourier Series*. Dover, New York.

Topper, J. (1998) *Finite element modeling of exotic options*. Discussion paper, University of Hannover.

Topper, J. (2005) *Financial Engineering with Finite Elements*. John Wiley & Sons, Chichester, UK.

Thomas, J.W. (1998) *Numerical Partial Differential Equations, Volume I. Finite Difference Methods*. Springer, New York.

Thomas, J.W. (1999) *Numerical Partial Differential Equations, Volume II. Conversation Laws and Elliptic Equations*. Springer, New York.

Thomée, V. and Wahlbin, L.B. (1974) *Convergence rates of parabolic difference schemes for non-smooth data. Math. Comp.*, **28** (125), 1–13.

Tricomi, F.G. (1957) *Integral Equations*. Dover, New York.

Uhlenbeck, G.E. and Ornstein, L.S. (1930) *On the theory of Brownian motion. Phys. Rev.*, **36**, 823–841.

Vasicek, O. (1977) *An equilibrium characterization of the term structure. J. Finan. Econ.*, **6**, 177–188.

Van Deventer, D. and Imai, K. (1997) *Financial Risk Analytics*. Irwin, Chicago.

Varadhan, S.R.S. (1980) *Diffusion Problems and Partial Differential Equations*. Tata Institute of Fundamental Research, Bombay.

Varga, R.S. (1962) *Matrix Iterative Analysis*. Prentice-Hall Inc., Englewood Cliffs, NJ.

Vichnevetsky, R. and Bowles, J.B. (1982) *Fourier Analysis of Numerical Approximations of Hyperbolic Equations*. SIAM, Philadelphia.

Wang, M.C. and Uhlenbeck, G.E. (1945) *On the theory of Brownian motion, II. Rev. Modern Phys.*, **17**, 323–342.

Wheeler, M.F. (1975) *An H^{-1} Galerkin method for parabolic problems in a single space variable. SIAM J. Numer. Anal.*, **12** (5, October).

Widder, D.V. (1989) *Advanced Calculus*. Dover, New York.

Wilmott, P., Dewynne, J. and Howison, S. (1993) *Option Pricing*. Oxford Financial Press, UK.

Wilmott, P. (1998) *Derivatives*. John Wiley & Sons, Chichester, UK.

Yanenko, N.N. (1971) *The Method of Fractional Steps*. Springer-Verlag, Berlin.

Yosida, K. (1991) *Lectures on Differential and Integral Equations*. Dover, New York.

Zeidler, E. (1990) *Nonlinear Functional Analysis and its Applications: Nonlinear Monotone Operators*. Springer-Verlag, New York.

Zemanian, A.H. (1987) *Generalized Integral Transformations*. Dover, New York.

Zhang, P.G. (1998) *Exotic Options: A Guide to Second-Generation Options* (2nd edition). World Scientific, New York.

Zvan, R., Forsyth, P.A. and Vetzal, K.R. (1997) *Robust Numerical Methods for PDE Models of Asian Options. J. Comp. Finan.*, **1** (2, Winter 1997/1998).

Zvan, R., Forsyth, P.A. and Vetzal, K.R. (1998) *A penalty method for American options with stochastic volatility. J. Comp. Appl. Math.*, **91**, 199–218.

Index